PIT-MEN, PREACHERS AND POLITICS

PIT-MEN, PREACHERS & POLITICS

The effects of Methodism in a Durham mining community

ROBERT MOORE

Senior Lecturer in Sociology, University of Aberdeen

CAMBRIDGE UNIVERSITY PRESS

Published by the Syndics of the Cambridge University Press
Bentley House, 200 Euston Road, London NW1 2DB
American Branch: 32 East 57th Street, New York, N.Y.10022

© Cambridge University Press 1974

Library of Congress Catalogue Card Number: 73–88307

ISBN: 0 521 20356 2

First published 1974

Printed in Great Britain by
Western Printing Services Ltd, Bristol

CONTENTS

Acknowledgements   ix

List of abbreviations   xi

Introduction   1

1   Historical background   28

2   The Deerness Valley   64

3   The social and economic basis of paternalism: the colliery-owners in the Deerness Valley   78

4   Village Methodism – I   93

5   Village Methodism – II: the structure of the Methodist societies in the Deerness Valley   120

6   The respectable Methodists and the old Liberalism   140

7   The radicals and the Labour Movement, 1900–1926   169

8   Methodists in action: three political case studies   191

9   1970 – a postscript   214

Conclusions   222

Appendix I: research strategy and techniques   230

Appendix II: the Methodist community and objections to Anglican union   237

Appendix III: the religious statistics   240

Appendix IV: occupational status, social mobility and the structure of Methodist leadership   243

Notes   254

Bibliography   273

Glossary   279

Index   281

For my mother and father
Kathleen and Douglas Moore

ACKNOWLEDGEMENTS

An adequate list of all those who helped with the research that has provided the basis for this work would substantially lengthen the work itself, therefore I can only thank a few individuals and organisations who gave me the most assistance.

The University of Durham provided a grant from the research fund which paid research expenses for the first two years. The Social Science Research Council made a grant which enabled a full-scale project to be mounted for one year. Without help from these two sources there would have been no research.

The Methodist archivist, Dr J. C. Bowmer, helped me throughout and gave me access to both the Methodist Archives and the Library of the Wesley Historical Society. Dr Bowmer also appears anonymously in the text; he is a Cornsay Colliery man. Dr Seaman, the Durham County archivist, and his assistant, Miss Smith, not only helped me with sources but took a great interest in my work. The chairman of the Darlington district of the Methodist Church and the superintendents in the Deerness Valley, Crook and Durham gave me free access to all the records in their possession. The one exception to this Methodist helpfulness caused me to travel many hundreds of miles in search of alternative sources and delayed one part of the work for three years. Records were also consulted with the kind permission of the Durham Miners' Association, Oxfordshire County Record Office, the director of education for County Durham, the city librarians in Durham and Darlington. The National Coal Board, South Durham area, and especially Mr Graham, the last manager at Esh Winning, and his staff, gave me much help, and access to their records.

Parts of Chapter 7 draw on the very extensive collection of letters, essays, speeches and notes left by John George Harrison when he died in 1921 at the age of thirty-one. I am most grateful to his daughter, Mary Willan, for allowing me access to all these papers. I hope she will one day write her father's biography.

A major source of data was provided by the local newspapers; my thanks are due to the management and staff of the *Durham County*

Acknowledgements

Advertizer. Without the use of their invaluable records little could have been achieved.

It would be quite invidious to attempt to thank the men and women of the villages individually. Some helped me in a series of long conversations, others with a single piece of information or a comment. Many searched their houses and produced vital documents. All showed unfailing friendship and hospitality. It was good to be among the people of the Deerness Valley and I would like to thank them all for their contributions to this work, and for much else besides. This work is about them and their fathers, and I hope that in some way they will feel that I have written it *for* them.

At the University of Durham I was especially grateful to John Rex for constant intellectual stimulation and encouragement. Colleagues and post-graduates, especially in our Thursday evening seminar, gave me more help than they realised and made me rethink much of my work. John Peel of the London School of Economics gave me much help and encouragement during the later stages, and made many valuable suggestions. None of these bear responsibility for the inadequacies of the work, which they made me see. Anne Williams and Linda Garbutt did most of the typing for the research; this was a major contribution to the total enterprise, for which I would like to thank them. Hazel King typed this book, for which I am very grateful.

John Grant, my research assistant from 1968 to 1969, did much of the work on Pease and Partners and in investigating the life histories and contemporary activities of the non-Methodists in the villages. My research methods class in Durham (1969–70) helped in collecting survey and other data, and Ian Procter helped with the tabulations.

I would like to thank the ministers in Esh Winning and their wives, who have given me unfailing support and assistance, as well as their friendship and pastoral concern from 1965 to 1970. Throughout the work Tom Greener, a valley Methodist and a distinguished schoolteacher, has been my constant critic; for his constancy and his criticism I am deeply indebted to him. Neither he nor anyone else mentioned is responsible for opinions expressed or errors of fact or judgement; these will be among my unique contributions to this enterprise.

ROBERT MOORE

Aberdeen, 1972

NOTE. The people and events described in this book are real persons and real events, except where tact has dictated that names of people or places should be concealed.

ABBREVIATIONS

C.S.U.	Christian Social Union
C.W.S.	Co-operative Wholesale Society
D.C.	*Durham Chronicle*
D.C.A.	*Durham County Advertizer*
D.M.A.	Durham Miners' Association
D.M.R.A.	Durham Miners' Reform Association
E.P.C.	Employers' Parliamentary Council
I.L.P.	Independent Labour Party
L.R.C.	Labour Representation Committee
M.F.G.B.	Miners' Federation of Great Britain
M.N.C.	Methodist New Connexion
N.-P.U.	Non-Political Union
P.M.	Primitive Methodist
S.D.F.	Socialist Democratic Federation
S.S.J.	*Sunday School Journal*
T.U.C.	Trades Union Congress
W.M.	Wesleyan Methodist

Introduction

Sociologists seem to have neglected the persistent presence of Methodism, whereas historians have argued about it for as long as historians have attempted to give an account of the development of the social and political institutions of modern Britain. Lecky and Buckle, for example, were among the first who tried to take stock of the radical transformation of British society and construct an account of what had actually happened. What kind of society had been created, and by what processes? Both accepted the common nineteenth-century belief that modern society was marked by the advance of reason and the decline of religion, that the ancient superstition was being replaced by science and the culture of democracy, and would continue to be so replaced.

Buckle argued that the progress of mankind depended on the development of the spirit of free enquiry and the dissemination of knowledge. 'Intellectual' truth had to take precedence over 'moral' truth. The main hindrance to these processes was the protective attitude of church and state which did not allow men to think for themselves and develop intellectually.[1]

Lecky in his *Rationalism in Europe* selected beliefs in witchcraft, miracles and future punishment as particular examples of the whole range of religious beliefs that had been a brake upon the development of civilisation. The power of such beliefs had been very great, but it was being overcome by the rational spirit of modern, scientific man. Lecky nonetheless finished his work on rationalism with a curious note of regret at the passing of the spirit of self-sacrifice for the sake of absolute beliefs and its replacement by the idea of utility.[2]

Thus for both Buckle and Lecky religion was a feature of a past age and it embodied a spirit that was antipathetic to the spirit of modern times. Yet both had to face the awkward fact that religion had made some kind of *positive* contribution to the development of modern society. Lecky saw this contribution as being made in the religious revival at the beginning of the eighteenth century, as we shall see.

Sociologists have perhaps too readily accepted the view that religion

1

was a feature of a past age. While they accepted that religion had made some sort of contribution to modern culture and given ritual acknowledgement to the Protestant Ethic thesis, they nonetheless believed that religion was declining.

In France, Elie Halévy, naturally perhaps, asked slightly different questions about the rise of modern Britain. For him, the question was not merely one of describing the institutions and processes, but of explaining how Britain became a modern, bourgeois society without a bloody revolution. By a process of elimination he arrived at the conclusion that religion, religious institutions and traditions, played a significant part in preventing revolution. Halévy, we should note, needed (as a Frenchman) to understand why the bourgeoisie had not revolted in Britain, as much as to explain why the proletariat failed to rebel. As we shall see, these were closely related questions for Halévy.

In Germany Max Weber also applied himself to the question of how rational capitalism, and a rational secular culture, had developed out of pre-existing structures and traditions. He believed the modern proletariat to be relatively indifferent to religion, but nonetheless recognised the importance of religion, at the cultural and motivational levels, in the rise of capitalist society and the bourgeois entrepreneur. Weber's *The Protestant Ethic and the Spirit of Capitalism* alone among his extensive works on religion provides a clear indication of the importance he attached to religion in the development of the modern world.

These four scholars were, in their own ways, liberals. None of them was a full-time historian and only Weber was – from time to time – a full-time academic. A later generation of professional historians, of Left-wing persuasion, adopted a rather different perspective on the problem of Methodism. The Webbs, the Hammonds, Eric Hobsbawm and Edward Thompson started from the knowledge that we had become an industrial society, and that something was known about the social reorganisation that made up that process of becoming. They showed not a little nostalgia for a (possibly mythical) golden age of pre-industrial proletarian community life, they underlined the violence and the exploitation of the transition from traditional to modern, and they seemed to be asking questions relating to the problem of how to change capitalist society rather than how it came about.

We would be mistaken if we assumed that there was unanimity among historians on the Left in their attitude to the past and to one another. The Webbs, for example, were not concerned (like Marx) with the withering away of the state but with the creation of a state which embodied 'the nobler aspect of the medieval manor'.[3] This implied paternalism seen in the context of the social background of the Fabians earned the contempt of Eric Hobsbawm. Hobsbawm was interested in industrial proletarian groups such as gas-workers, and in his *Primitive Rebels* turned to consider the peasants and the *lumpen proletariat*. Edward Thompson, however, found his labour heroes among the skilled craftsmen of an earlier pre-industrial, industrial order. He seems to mourn the passing of the community of the stockinger and weaver, the traditional artisan and craftsman. The mystery of the craft was swept away by capitalism and it is this, rather than the creation of an urban industrial proletariat and their associations, that interests Thompson.

None of these authors is personally very sympathetic to religion, yet all had to face the incontrovertible fact that Protestant sects were training grounds for working-class leaders. Beyond recognising this they sought to emphasise the social control functions of religion and to use its persistence to explain the lack of class consciousness and sustained revolutionary fervour among the workers in the industrial revolution. Like the early historians and later sociologists they seem to share the rationalist's hope of the withering away of religion. Our main criticism of all the historians is that there has been more debate than the research findings can sustain on the problem of religion.[4]

Methodist historians of Methodism originally seem to have relied upon the conclusions of earlier historians. Indeed the 'Halévy thesis' seems to be more cited than consulted and Lecky is seldom given a footnote when named in defence of the anti-revolutionary thesis on Methodism.[5] Modern Methodist historians seem to have been writing a defence of Methodism against the modern labour historians; they have attempted to show that Methodism had a positive and 'good' role in the development of modern working-class movements.

Arnold Toynbee seems to provide a link between the rationalist, Socialist and Methodist historians. In his *Lectures on the Industrial Revolution* Toynbee, like Lecky, stressed the importance of the historical method.[6] The study of history was necessary in order to understand the present. Toynbee noted the decline of traditional society and the emergence of the cash nexus: 'Political Economy, it was said, destroyed the moral and political relations of men, and dissolved the social union.'[7] But, according to Toynbee, the use of the historical method would enable one to show that the so-called laws of political economy were not immutable, but relevant to a certain stage of civilisation only. In relativising the 'laws' of political economy, Toynbee also tried to show that intervention in the 'struggle for existence' was a major element of the whole of human history.[8]

Thus Toynbee was able to reject the necessity of 'free competition of unequal industrial units' and advocate intervention in the economy – for the good of all – in, for example, housing programmes.[9] This modest

Fabianism, derived from historical study, provides us with a direct connexion with the work of the Webbs, and through them, the Fabians.

Toynbee, a disciple of T. H. Green, was not a Socialist. He defined Socialism, very explicitly, in the same way that Wearmouth was to define it, implicitly, later: Socialism is an extension of Liberalism.[10] In this context trade unions can be viewed favourably by Liberals as well as by Fabians; 'Employers are beginning to recognise the necessity of them, and the advantages of being able to treat with a whole body of workmen through their most intelligent members.'[11] This view of the trade unions is one that will be echoed by Liberal entrepreneurs and trade-union leaders, in the earlier chapters.

If traditional social relations had broken down in the industrial revolution then they were to be replaced by voluntary associations (including the trade unions) and the development of self-help. These efforts to restore the 'social union' for the common good could be aided by the state. The state was to ensure steady and adequate wages and regulate the conditions of labour. Here, in Toynbee, we see a variety of themes including those typical of diverse traditions including Samuel Smiles, the Utilitarians and the Fabians. Toynbee's themes have set the tone of modern historical discussion on the problem of the disruption caused by the industrial revolution (a term given currency in the English language by Toynbee[12]) and the nature of the new social order that was to emerge. Such themes were also central to the origins of sociology.

Methodism has been a stubborn fact for historians, a problem for the Left and something to be defended by Methodists. It has been largely ignored by sociologists. Sociologists of religion have, of course, written on aspects of Methodism; but sociologists interested in the problems that taxed the historians mentioned above, problems of development and modernisation in Britain, problems of stratification, class consciousness and political sociology, have just not paid attention to religion. Recently, however, Crouch and Martin have raised the question of religion in the context of social stratification in trying to explain the peculiar stability of British society.[13] In seeking the basis of this stability they incorporate ideas advanced by MacIntyre and by Halévy, which will be examined below. Intelligible answers can be advanced in partly religious terms because of the nature of British dissent and the compromises surrounding the survival of the dissenting tradition and their apparent embodiment into the political style of working-class movements. Sociologists have perhaps hitherto accepted the views of historians too readily in this field. Even if sociologists see religion as marginal and a declining influence in history, they might at least have asked questions about the past role of religion in shaping present institutions and beliefs, and the implications of this for their current and future development.

In the second volume of his *History of England in the Eighteenth Century*, Lecky discussed the loosening of traditional social ties brought about by industrialisation and urbanisation, to the point at which the cash nexus was the strongest bond. This was especially the case in the relationships between employers and employed. The beginning of the eighteenth century was, for Lecky, a time at which class differences were obvious and widening and when class warfare was imminent. But instead of this war there was a religious revival which 'opened a new spring of moral and religious energy among the poor, and at the same time gave a powerful impulse to the philanthropy of the rich'.[14] On the basis of 'testimonies as to the healthful and becalming tendencies'[15] of Methodism from Lecky and others, Townsend was able to assert in his *New History of Methodism* that Methodism had 'saved the country from such a cataclysm as happened in France'.[16]

Halévy, like other French historians (including his teacher, Taine, named by Townsend in *New History*), asked 'why did England not have a revolution?' He concluded that one could not find the answer in economic or political institutions alone. The religious revival of the early eighteenth century was a vital factor.[17] The 'Halévy thesis' has been central to subsequent discussion of the political effects of Methodism.

Two sets of sociological assumptions underlying the Halévy thesis have remained relatively unexamined.[18] Firstly, Halévy believed that the English nation was (and still is) a nation of puritans and that the English character was serious, reserved and melancholic as compared to the gay, extroverted and irreligious French temperament. Thus the revival of 1739 was a revival, a reawakening, of aspects of traditional English culture: 'la vieille inspiration puritaine, qui avait triomphé un siècle plus tôt, aux temps de la République de Cromwell'.[19] Thus Halévy has a theory about English character which seems to beg some of the questions he set out to answer by suggesting that the English already had characteristics which the revival is otherwise thought to have produced.

The more substantial assumption made by Halévy concerns the way in which Methodism operated upon the English population, for in this part of the argument Halévy advances a theory about the working class and its relations to other classes. According to Halévy: 'Le prolétariat des manufactures et des usines, aggloméré autour des centres industriels, est accessible à la contagion rapide de toutes les émotions violentes. Mais c'est une foule ignorante, incapable de prévoir et de décider elle-même en quel sens se portera son enthousiasme.'[20] The working class thus failed to revolt because it lacked the necessary middle-class leadership. This pattern was to be repeated when the working class was deprived of leaders at the time of Chartism a century later, and 'the populace fell back into a state of incoherence, demoralisation and at last apathy'.[21]

Halévy seems to assume that the working class is a bovine mass without its own leadership and ideas. Secondly, he assumes that the working class are dependent on the middle classes for ideological leadership. These are assumptions that cannot be accepted without more adequate evidence to support them.

In *A History of the English People in 1815*, published in 1924, Halévy's position is slightly different, for he distinguishes between the bourgeoisie and a working-class élite:

> a system of economic production that was in fact totally without organisation of any kind would have plunged the kingdom into violent revolution had the working classes found in the middle class leaders to provide it with a definite ideal, a creed, a practical programme. But the elite of the working class, the hard-working and capable bourgeois, had been imbued by the Evangelical movement with a spirit from which the established order had nothing to fear.[22]
>
> (trans. Watkins and Barker, vol. 1, p. 371)

It is not altogether clear who now leads the working class, the middle class or a working-class élite. There can be no objection to the suggestion that both were influenced in the way suggested. But if Halévy means that, the working-class élite notwithstanding, the working class were a bovine mob led by the bourgeoisie, then there is still considerable objection to his thesis on these grounds. If, on the other hand, Halévy means that Methodism influenced the working class through the élite of the working class then we might proceed to test a reasonable and unobjectionable theory.

Halévy's thesis is more complex than his critics have suggested precisely because he was saying that the 1739 revival was a revival of something already existing in the English character: 'Le réveil évangélique de 1739 ne fut donc pas un commencement absolu, une création *ex nihilo*: il consiste dans une combinaison nouvelle d'éléments préexistants et parfaitement définis.'[23] These elements were the reserve and melancholy mentioned above. But what this analysis means is that Methodism heightened and refocused features of English culture rather than creating new ones. Thus for the upper classes the revival was 'la réaction religieuse et morale' against venality and scepticism in church and state. The old puritanism was reformulated, and religious certainty was reasserted. Hannah More and William Wilberforce, among others, sought to reform not only the working classes but the outlook and behaviour of the upper and middle classes, and not without effect, for according to Gillispie the revival 'restrained the plutocrats who had newly arisen from the masses from vulgar ostentation and debauchery'.[24]

According to Charles Gillispie, 'For Halévy the main thing about evangelicalism was not that it was true religion but that it led to individual self-restraint.'[25] This self-restraint was born (or reborn) of the dissenting tradition. This tradition was typified, for Halévy, in the rights of free association. Dissenting groups could only survive if they disciplined their own members in order to avoid confrontations with the state. Thus free associations voluntarily restricted the liberty of their individual members in order to survive, and this, according to Halévy, was as important in the eighteenth century as in the earlier part of the seventeenth century. The spirit of self-discipline and mutual restraint was thus revived with the revival of religion and morality in the eighteenth (and nineteenth) century.

In reforming the morals of both the masses and their superiors the revived puritanism provided a new basis for the lower and upper classes to collaborate. Thus even though in the nineteenth century men may have pursued goals antipathetic to one another they pursued them on the basis of a set of shared assumptions. Restraint, tolerance, a 'live and let live' attitude were available as a basis for relationships between the classes when other ties had been dissolved. 'A pragmatic approach to problems, co-operativeness, tolerance, a gift for compromise . . .', these are what Alasdair MacIntyre calls the secondary virtues.[26] They are secondary because they relate not to the ends that men pursue but to how they pursue them, and to the manner in which they handle conflicts of goals. If then the 'Halévy thesis' is that religion provided a basis for cooperation in a situation of potential or actual conflict, through the development of these secondary virtues, then his thesis forms part of the argument of this book which deals with Methodism at the end of the nineteenth century and the beginning of the twentieth.

We have dwelt upon Halévy because he is usually represented in an over-simple version and defended or attacked by assertion rather than detailed argument. Himmelfarb has put the situation well:

> A distinguished sociologist, [Lipset] aware of the dissatisfaction with the Halévy thesis, has described it as an 'area of considerable scholarly controversy' – on the assumption, presumably, that he

had been afforded a glimpse of only the tip of the iceberg. Unfortunately there is little beneath the tip. The whole of this 'area of considerable scholarly controversy' consists of a ten-page essay, several pages of a large volume, some paragraphs in a biographical article, portions of book reviews, and isolated, undocumented, but increasingly common statements to the effect that the thesis is no longer tenable.[27]

The most damaging criticism that can be made of Halévy is that he does not ask seriously whether religion can have any meaning for the individual proletarian believer, or indeed for a working-class élite. John and Barbara Hammond and Edward Thompson suggested that religion might have a personal meaning for the believer whatever his social position. The Hammonds believed that the worker needed beliefs to lift him into a significant world of meanings which transcended everyday life. The miner and the weaver wanted 'a religion that recognised that the world did not explain itself'.[28] Religion in fact gave the oppressed 'an assurance that their obscure lives had some significance and moment'. These 'functions' of religion we can acknowledge as universal functions of religion in all ages. But 'The Methodist taught that men were not so helpless as they seemed for religion could make them independent of the conditions of their lives.'[29] Such notions might have been the basis for a radical political response to social conditions. But this radical potential was reduced by Methodists accepting deprivation as a trial of faith rather than a political challenge.

The Hammonds also underlined the paradoxes of Methodism. As long as religion was part of the civil constitution of society, religious questioning was a questioning of that constitution, and thus Methodism was associated with sedition. It could be, we should note in passing, that the Weslyan propaganda denying this suggestion of sedition may have been at the root of the anti-revolutionary literature.[30] Edward Thompson noted the paradoxes also; Methodism was a religion of despair and rebellion, producing submission and political leadership among working men who lived earnest and disciplined lives while engaging in spiritual orgies.

Before moving to a more detailed discussion of Thompson we should take note of Eric Hobsbawm's 'ten page essay' in *Labouring Men*.[31] Hobsbawm remarked that Methodism and radicalism advanced together and that in modern times pious men of various faiths have led, or been active in, revolutionary movements. Thus other creeds may have been as important as Methodism. Had 'other factors' been ripe, Hobsbawm concludes, Methodism could not have averted revolution. The fact was that down to 1840 there was a good deal of revolutionary

8

feeling latent in England, but the upper classes never lost control of the situation. What Hobsbawm does not examine are the reasons for the other factors not being ripe; it may have been that there were cultural factors, to some degree derived from religious sources, which enabled the upper classes to keep control. This could have been deduced from Halévy's argument, yet Hobsbawm rejects Halévy.[32]

Thompson[33] in common with the Hammonds, saw two sides to Methodism. Firstly it served the interests of the bourgeoisie because it 'weakened the poor from within, by adding to them the active ingredient of submission; and they [the leaders of Methodism] fostered within the Methodist church those elements most suited to make up the psychic component of the work-discipline of which the manufacturers stood in most need'.[34] Thus Methodism helped provide the motivations for the new work discipline needed in industrial society. It did this in a negative sense by overcoming 'the older, half-pagan popular culture, with its fairs, its sports, its drink and its picaresque hedonism'.[35] In the positive sense noted by Thompson above, it contributed to the rationalisation of work through self-discipline whereby, ideally, 'the labourer must be turned "into his own slave-driver"'.[36] Methodism did not become a vehicle for a radical political response to the destruction of the old order and the rigours of the new because it 'brought to a point of hysterical intensity the desire for personal salvation'.[37] The Methodist sought self-mastery and self-perfection rather than striving to change the world.

Thompson makes the Weberian point that discipline was maintained mutually by sect members, and backsliding meant expulsion from the only community men knew in the industrial wilderness. The dedication required to maintain personal membership and to sustain the activities of the chapel carried over into the organisation of trade unions. Thus Methodism also served the working class by producing working-class leaders with a 'capacity for sustained organisational dedication and (at its best) a high degree of personal responsibility'.[38] The Methodist was able to carry into political activity (given that Methodism may not have actually encouraged that activity) a sense of earnestness, of dedication and of a 'calling' that was to be important for the organisations so led.

Thompson's analysis is somewhat unbalanced by his transparent dislike of Methodism. Because of this he stresses those features of Methodism which he believes inhibited the rise of working-class consciousness, and in doing this he can make easy psychological targets of selected Methodist hymns and revivalist practices. But one obvious question arising from this kind of analysis is why were 'so many working people...willing to submit to this form of psychic exploitation?'[39]

Thompson's answers to this question complicate the rest of the argument. He suggests that the evidence of Sunday school primers and the dogmas of such men as Jabez Bunting do not necessarily tell us what happened in the local community: 'What the orthodox Methodist minister intended is one thing; what actually happened in many communities may be another.'[40] But almost the whole of Thompson's argument rests upon the evidence of orthodox writers and especially upon the words of Methodist hymns. Either this is valid evidence which tells us about local Methodism, or it is not. If it is valid evidence then the question, 'Why submit?' remains; if not, then Thompson's thesis must fall because he has not produced the relevant evidence to support it. This latter situation introduces an argument that is quite unacceptable, for Thompson would be arguing that official Methodism was a form of religious terrorism, so why did men endure it? It could only be because they believed in something other than the terrorist formulation.

This problem in Thompson's argument arises from the lack of material on local Methodism and our real uncertainty about the form in which orthodox (or 'official') Methodism was expressed at the local level. In his 1968 'Postscript' to *The Making of the English Working Class* Thompson answers Himmelfarb's contention that he and Hobsbawm have avoided a confrontation by saying that the evidence is inconclusive. What he does not say is that we need not *more* evidence, but evidence of a *different kind* to validate his thesis. For a scholar who recognises the inconclusiveness of the evidence Thompson seems to argue with a remarkable degree of confidence.

A second problem arises from Thompson's idea that dogma was modified in the local community. He argues, for example, that: 'As a dogma Methodism appears as a pitiless ideology of work. In practice this dogma was in varying degrees softened, humanized, or modified by the needs, values, and patterns of social relationship of the community within which it was placed.[41] He develops this later to say that the more closely knit the community in which Methodism took root, the more the local people made Methodism 'their own'.[42]

Earlier, however, Thompson suggested that the Methodist brotherhood was the only community group which members knew in the industrial wilderness. The confusion here needs to be sorted out; it seems that Methodism can be found in two situations: firstly, in a situation of social dislocation Methodism provides a primary community to replace the institutions and relations lost in the process of change. Secondly, Methodism may be the religion of established working-class communities, which already have an elaborate work and leisure culture pre-dating the arrival of Methodism. It seems that Thompson confuses these two situations and makes it especially difficult to understand what he means by 'Methodism' and by 'community'. The two lines of criticism point to the need for a careful reformulation of Thompson's argument. Until this is done the defects of the argument do much to vitiate its tentative conclusions.

Some of the detailed data that the work of Hobsbawm and Thompson demand are provided in the histories of Methodism written by Robert Wearmouth. His work on the later period of Methodism, from the mid-nineteenth century onwards, brings us to this study.

Wearmouth believed that Methodism was essentially a revivalist religion and that its progress depended on the degree of evangelical fervour with which it was preached.[43] The apolitical nature of Methodism as a system of beliefs stands out from Wearmouth's studies. Niebuhr's comment that the leaders of the Methodist movement were 'impressed not so much by the social evils from which the poor suffered as by the vices to which they had succumbed'[44] seems to be largely borne out by Wearmouth's work. For example: [In 1883] 'Believing that religion needed to be more widely applied if radical changes were to be made, the Wesleyans redoubled their efforts to preach the gospel to the poor.'[45] The main fear of Methodists was of open conflict threatening social order. When they did recognise social evils they preached personal regeneration to the sufferers and advocated reform by the state. They did not advocate independent struggle by the workers. Thus in the 1892 Coal Dispute it was social cohesion rather than class interests that were supported by the Methodists: 'the fierce struggle between capital and labour gives us much concern. The collision of these great industrial forces in the lockout and the strike is a peril to the social fabric. On every movement and on every man that helps to bind them into harmonious action we implore the blessing of the God of peace'.[46]

By the 1890s the P.M.s were emphasising the importance of workers' organising against capitalists, but: 'It is not victory that should be sought by either party, but a basis upon which both parties could work harmoniously. Conditions imposed by sheer force on either side can not contain a settlement.'[47] The assumptions underlying such a statement are as important as the statement itself. They include the notion of the inherent harmony of interests between labour and capital. Labour is 'a party' in the language of contractual rather than class relationships. The development of social and political thought within the churches will be discussed in the next chapter.

Wearmouth develops a thesis on Methodism and the reforming spirit of Liberalism in the nineteenth century without difficulty. In his discussion of the twentieth century there is a loss of confidence apparent

11

in the argument. Much of the discussion of the political influence of Methodism refers back to the nineteenth century or to working-class leaders who survived from the nineteenth century into the twentieth century.[48] Wearmouth lists overlapping members of Methodism and political movements but gives no details of the relation between politics and Methodist ideas. The latter part of the final volume of his history thus becomes diffuse and unconvincing.

Part of Wearmouth's problem arises from the fact that there is little connexion between Socialism and Methodism, according to his own data. He obscures this by assuming that there is a strong connexion. He adjusts his definition of Socialism to mean social reform of a kind approved by Methodists. Socialism is based in the perceived need for fundamental social structural change in which class conflict plays an important and positive role. Twentieth-century Methodist reformism might have been more far-reaching than the nineteenth-century kind, but by this definition it was not Socialism. Methodists did not, for example, question the institution of private property, only the irresponsible use of private property.

Wearmouth changes the name of Methodist Liberalism to Socialism in the twentieth century, just as many Liberal Methodists changed their name to Labour. He does not enquire into the extent to which the change of name represented a change of substance, and in this sense Wearmouth is himself part of the Liberal–Methodist tradition. Methodism is not located within a systematic analytical framework in his work. He seems to want to show that Methodism was influential in the rise of the Labour Party *and* that this was beneficial.

It is generally agreed that Methodism produced working-class leaders. The merit of Wearmouth's work is that he presents copious biographical data on the character of leaders which Methodism produced. We have already noted in passing (Introduction, n. 22, p. 6) Wearmouth's comment on the acceptability of these working-class leaders to established authority. Wearmouth quotes Andrew Carnegie who said of John Wilson, a Methodist M.P. and a leader of the D.M.A. in 1915, 'We should run a man with a record like his for the Presidency.'[49] A correspondent in the *D.C.A.* had previously asked why it was that the Esh Winning Methodists accepted Carnegie's money, in the form of a grant for an organ, when it was stained with the blood of Carnegie's workers. Of William Crawford, another Durham Methodist miners' leader it was said: 'Since he has been at the head of the Union, trade disputes have been rare, and, on the whole, short-lived, and probably Mr. Crawford himself would ask for no higher reward.'[50]

There is evident agreement in the analyses of Thompson and Wearmouth that Methodism was apolitical and anti-radical. Both indicate that Methodism produced working-class leaders nonetheless, although neither spells out the connexion between the beliefs and the actions of these leaders. Wearmouth says less than Thompson about the wider cultural impact of Methodism. One point is agreed by all commentators on Methodism and the working class; however else they may have interpreted its effects they all assert that Methodism provided a training in democracy. Whatever orthodox Methodists may have preached, the chapel was a school for democrats and a source of popular leaders.

From their very different orientations Thompson and Wearmouth imply that service in a trade union might be carried out as a 'calling' and both indicate the qualities of discipline and dedication that can be carried over from religious to trade-union activities. This leaves us with the question of the way in which Methodist trade unionists pursue conflict. How far they would go in the pursuit of trade-union interests is a valid question to which neither Thompson nor Wearmouth provides an adequate answer. Wearmouth's data might be interpreted to suggest that the Methodist trade unionist believed in negotiated settlements rather than conflicts, he preferred not to strike and would certainly not threaten established order with violence. This answer would be entirely consistent with Weber's contention that the 'political apparatus of force could not possibly provide a place for religious virtue'[51] in the life of the Protestant.

The miners' leaders were generally Liberals and opponents of Socialism and ideas of class conflict. The union leadership developed trade-union consciousness but not class consciousness. They would never see themselves as miners with a class interest in a market-based society as distinct from contracting parties to a legitimate market relationship. The Socialist trade unionist experiences something of a conflict of interests: as a trade unionist he seeks the best immediate terms and the least hardship for his men, and this usually entails getting them back to work as soon as possible, or avoiding a strike altogether. As a Socialist he seeks the confrontations that will lead to the conflict which will change the basic economic and social arrangements of the whole society. This kind of tension is not described by any of the authors so far discussed, and it rarely occurs amongst the Methodists studied here.

With the exception of Wearmouth we have been considering authors who were mainly interested in a period of Methodism in which it found a relatively effervescent, evangelical expression, and, moreover, at a time when it was not altogether respectable in the eyes of the establishment. This was hardly the case in the later period, in which this study is set, but for which there is a lack of commentaries. Nevertheless, these historians advance a number of relevant ideas about the way in which

Methodism 'works' in society, especially upon the working class, which may have a more universal validity. For example, it seems as if the established order had nothing to fear from Methodist leaders of working men in either the earlier or the later period, because in both periods they acted with self-discipline and restraint. But if we were to summarise the state of the argument about Methodism among historians we would say that there is a lack of definitional clarity combined with a failure to study Methodism situationally (for example Thompson's elision of different kinds of working class 'communities'). Although Halévy, Thompson, Hobsbawm and Wearmouth all have reasonable hypotheses, the debate is grounded on very few solidly-researched data. Where there are data (Wearmouth) they are not organised around clear theoretical formulations but in accordance with an implicit and normative theory. The methodological and technical problems encountered in the research reported in this book themselves point to the difficulties and indicate the need for further comparative studies. While Himmelfarb may have misjudged the quality of the argument about the Halévy thesis, she was correct in suggesting that there is less beneath the tip of the iceberg than Lipset might have assumed.

SOCIOLOGICAL TREATMENT OF METHODISM

English sociologists have been necessarily interested in questions of social class and class consciousness. The problems of class consciousness and 'false consciousness' are derived from the continuing debate with Marx and Marxists. Religion seems to have been peripheral to these debates, bracketed as either false consciousness or a residual phenomenon that will eventually disappear with the development of science and human rationality.

One of the most influential contemporary writers on stratification is David Lockwood. Lockwood's article on 'Sources of Variation in Working Class Images of Society' provided a model for explaining different working-class views of the class structure.[52] Two of his three images of society are relevant in our historical context, the traditional proletarian and the traditional deferential. The traditional proletarian sees society divided into 'Us' and 'Them'; it is a dichotomous, conflict image of society. The traditional deferential sees society as graded, every man having his place in a status order. Plainly we should expect trade-union consciousness and class consciousness to emerge more readily among those who adhere to a proletarian image of society than among the traditional deferential.

The origins of working-class images of society are to be found in the work and community situation of the worker, according to Lockwood.

'The work and community relationships of traditional workers involve them in mutually reinforcing systems of interpersonal influence.'[53] The deferential worker comes into contact with middle-class people at work and in the community. He works in a smaller enterprise, run on a relatively personal and particularistic basis. The proletarian worker typically works in a larger enterprise, mixing only with his work-mates, and he may live in a relatively isolated working-class community. Work-mates develop their own leisure patterns and community institutions independent of the employing class – who in the community of the deferential would occupy positions of leadership in local associations.

Lockwood quotes the miners as typical of the traditional proletarian worker. This is consistent with certain traditional middle-class images of the miner, and has a *prima facie* validity given a long history of industrial disputes in the coal industry. Miners live in homogeneous communities which have articulated a very distinctive culture. They work, today, in relatively large industrial units and show marked solidarity in the bargaining and ritual activities of the trade union such as galas, and miners' picnics.

Lockwood's specific model of the miner seems to be based almost entirely on the study by Dennis, Henriques and Slaughter, *Coal Is Our Life*. This study emphasises the proletarian solidarity of the mining community. Nonetheless there are hints in the text that not all miners are beer-drinking gamblers, men pursuing short-term pleasures, innocent of long-term planning in their lives. For example:

> The pursuit of leisure in Ashton has two principal characteristics. It is vigorous and it is predominantly frivolous. Without wishing to enter into the question of which are 'better' or 'worse' ways of spending leisure time, it should be explained that the word frivolous is used in the sense of 'giving no thought for the morrow'. It is used in this way as a contrast to those forms of recreation which pursue a definite aim such as intellectual improvement by means of study in adult classes or discussion groups, or spiritual improvement through membership of a church.[54]

'Serious' leisure activities will be discussed, say the authors, 'when the place of the churches in the life of the Ashton miner is discussed'.[55] Unfortunately only one and one-third pages are devoted to this discussion which comprises a statement of the memberships and a listing of the ancillary organisations of the churches.[56]

Two discrepancies must be explained between *Coal Is Our Life* and the present study. Firstly, the historical evidence suggests that the serious-minded and the religious miners may have been disproportionately influential on the life of the community. Why do Dennis *et al.* devote so little attention to them? It may have been that in Ashton the religious miners were not or never had been significant in the community, or it could have been that the researchers were either not interested in the religious miners, or assumed them to be of marginal importance. Either way, we have no evidence from Ashton which helps to answer the question.

Secondly, the Ashton account suggests that the miners were to a great extent traditional proletarian workers. Why are they so different from the miners whom we are to encounter in this study, and the miners referred to in studies to be cited in Chapter 2? Two reasons for this may be advanced.

The economic and political history of the Ashton area may be rooted in social relations quite different from those studied elsewhere and in Durham. We can point to a number of ways in which Yorkshire differed from Durham. The Yorkshire coalfield, for example, produced for a domestic market and therefore did not experience the wide fluctuations in the price of coal that were common in exporting coalfields like Durham. In this situation the minimum wage and the eight-hour day were reasonable objectives and the Yorkshire miners were united in their pursuit of these objectives from 1889 onwards.

Unfortunately only the first volume of Machin's *The Yorkshire Miners* was ever published. This volume takes us up to 1881 only. In 1881 the defeated remnants of the three Yorkshire unions amalgamated with Ben Pickard as their secretary. The three unions had been weak and disunited through the 1870s and they were additionally weakened by the activities of the coal-owners. The Yorkshire management were aggressive in the 1870s; they had not, like the Durham owners, learnt the advantages of arbitration. They used their power instead to attack wages and the position of the checkweighman. Thus in this very early period when the Durham union was emerging as a recognised and respectable body for negotiating with ownership the Yorkshire miners were experiencing defeat.

The Yorkshire owners also seem to have been prone to use a greater degree of violence against their men than the Durham owners. Thus in 1893 troops were called to Pontefract; finding no riots they returned to barracks, but were recalled by the owners. This provoked resentment among the miners which led to the shooting of eighteen men in Featherstone (two fatally). Actions such as these pass into legends which keep alive a tradition of bitterness. Thus in the earliest days of the unions Durham and Yorkshire do seem to have had very different histories. These differences may go some way towards explaining later differences, but it is difficult to judge how influential the early periods of the 1870s and 1890s were on events occurring forty or even sixty years later.

Yorkshire had its Methodists too. Ben Pickard, the 'iron man' who led the miners in 1893 (as chairman of the M.F.G.B.) was a strict Wesleyan and a teetotaller. Pickard was also a Liberal and an opponent of Socialism. This, however, may be slightly misleading as the Yorkshire Liberals had adopted the eight-hour day and the minimum wage as policy objectives. Thus they had stolen the fire of the Socialists who used the failure to adopt these policies as the basis for their attack on the Durham leadership.

Despite the differences between the early histories of Ashton and Durham, there is also a similarity in the union leadership. As yet therefore, this is no indication of later differences, and the only distinguishing feature of the area is the difference in the market for its coal.

In the second place, the Ashton study was undertaken after the Second World War and some twenty years therefore after the end of this study. Thus the Ashton study may be different from this only because it has chosen a later development of the same society.

The Ashton miners had experienced the General Strike and the Depression. The immediate post-Second-World-War period was one of high political activity by the Labour Government and this activity included the nationalisation of the coal-mines. One would expect these experiences to be conducive to the development of a class-conscious proletarian view of the social world. The views formed in such experiences might, irrespective of the coalfield, contrast sharply with the views of men whose prime years had been spent in the relative prosperity and paternalism of the late nineteenth century. This book's study stops short of the Second World War, and the worst years of the Depression. The Ashton study itself is relatively ahistorical, so we are unable to resolve the extent to which this study and the Ashton study concern different stages of the same development, or reveal more general differences between the two districts.

As the next chapter will show, the miners were traditionally conservative and resisted traditional proletarian social imagery. Class consciousness and Socialism are forms of deviance in the period of this book. Lockwood seems to have over-simplified the question of the relation between work, community and social beliefs. The miners had a strong sense of occupational community, but class consciousness did not develop from this in any mechanical way. It is perfectly possible for miners to have developed a consciousness of market interest, and in defending this interest to have confirmed the social order rather than challenging it.

Lockwood does not consider that men need to be *converted* to a traditional proletarian image of society. According to his argument the proletarian view flows directly from the social relations of work and community. This entails a double fault in his analysis. Firstly, it leads him away from a consideration of those social situations in which traditionally proletarian workers might in fact have been deferentials. Secondly, his analysis neglects the importance of ideas as such in the formulation of images of society. Religious and economic ideas may shape men's interpretations of the social relations they experience, as was recognised by all the authors we have so far considered. Because of this Lockwood misses the important question of the role of movements and parties in actually changing men's understanding of the social world in which they live.

We are concerned with the way in which men see themselves in the world of social inequality. The United Kingdom has always been a very unequal society in terms of the distribution of wealth, income, prestige and political power. In some respects it is remarkable that the nation can be so unequal and yet so peaceful. But there are many ways in which men may perceive social inequality – in fact they may not perceive inequality at all, only social differences.

A man may, for example, see himself as part of a vertical social structure. He knows his place in society by those above and below him in a hierarchy of power, and perhaps of merit. Secondly, a man may take a more 'functional' view of social relations: this might be based on the market or the division of labour; sectors or interests might be recognised, but not classes. Thus a man may recognise his common interest with other joiners, sailors or coal-hewers or his common interest with men at his own skill level *vis-à-vis* other levels of skill in the same trade. This kind of consciousness we might call 'trade-union consciousness'. It may be that this stage of consciousness precedes class consciousness as such.

The class view of inequality over-rides sectional or trade-union interests and emphasises the horizontal integration of society. Irrespective of trade or skill level it recognises the common interests of all workers, employers and capitalists. This view may also transcend national considerations to include notions of the common interest of all working classes. This view of inequality is more likely to be part of a conflict model of society than the trade-union view – though this may entail elements of conflict.

The first two views of social inequality are very common in Britain, the third is much rarer although it sometimes features in certain kinds of rhetoric. We will see below that there was at the beginning of the twentieth century a strong possibility that the class-conscious view of the social world might have replaced trade-union consciousness as the most common and best articulated working-class view of society. We will examine the extent to which religion may have contributed to the

18

failure of the class identity to supersede the strength of the trade unions.

The three views are over-simplified in this presentation; there are many sub-types of each kind and also overlapping occurs. Class consciousness is sometimes assumed to be measurable by patterns of voting. Labour voting is often taken to equal 'socialist' or class-conscious voting. This is not assumed to be the case in the present work, for reasons which will soon be apparent. As we are not equating Labour with Socialism it is as well to add, at this point of the discussion, a brief statement of what will be understood by Socialism. A Socialist view entails a criticism of the whole system of economic and social relations of capitalism – not criticisms of its malfunctioning. Socialists believe that the capitalist mode of production and most social relations within capitalism are intrinsically exploitative and that they should be abolished. The classes living off rent and profit should also be abolished. These aims can only be realised through a fundamental, revolutionary, change in the nature of society. The necessary changes can be brought about by the direct political action of the proletariat acting as a class. Conflict (and violence according to some views) has a positive role in the pursuit of these political goals.

This story will attempt to explain the coherence of religious, economic and political beliefs and the way in which these beliefs were institutionally supported by non-conformity, the Co-operative Movement, the union leadership *and* ownership and management. In this situation a proletarian view of society and Socialist voting becomes highly deviant and something which has to be explained, rather than assumed.[57]

METHODS OF RESEARCH

The final section of this introductory chapter describes the intellectual organisation of the research that was carried out between 1966 and 1970. The initial impetus for this study came partially from a general interest in the sociology of English labour history, but more specifically from an interest in the sociology of religion, and in Max Weber's hypotheses. It is from Max Weber that the methodology of this study is also derived.

In an earlier publication I explored the complexity of the Protestant Ethic argument.[58] I was concerned to dispel simplistic interpretations of Weber's work on the Protestant Ethic by setting it in the context of his sociology of religion and historical sociology. Weber did not say that behaviour was directly and only explicable in terms of the actor's beliefs. In his discussion of the Protestant Ethic Weber showed that

Protestantism was historically effective not only because belief created new motivations (though it did this) but because it helped develop a new, rationalistic and secular culture which was conducive to the development of science, commerce and new work routines. Furthermore, Protestantism was institutionalised in sects which served to maintain the discipline of the believers and provide economic opportunities for their members. The pariah status of these sects had the consequence of forcing them to locations where they were able to take advantage of new resources and preventing them from investing their capital in land, politics or dilettante education.

It is intrinsically difficult to show that a specific action followed from a particular belief and such over-simplification will be avoided. This research rather tries to show not only how beliefs are merely conducive to certain behaviour, or make certain courses of action more likely than others, but how the spread of beliefs affects the life of the whole community, and how the creation of religious institutions have important unintended consequences for the community. For example, the Hammonds and Thompson point to the way in which Methodist chapels equipped men to lead trade unions; this was not the intention in establishing the chapels, but an unintended consequence of creating a particular kind of chapel organisation.

The original essays, *The Protestant Ethic and the Spirit of Capitalism* deal with the role of Protestantism in the emergence of an entrepreneurial bourgeoisie in the seventeenth and eighteenth centuries. Weber makes no more than passing comment on the role of Protestantism for the working class, for example: 'The power of religious asceticism provided [the bourgeois businessman] in addition with sober, conscientious, and unusually industrious workmen, who clung to their work as to a life purpose willed by God.'[59] By and large Weber was not concerned with the working classes in these essays. Nonetheless helpful material can be extracted on the effects of religion on the working class. Most notable in this respect is the concept of 'inner worldly asceticism'. This and other related ideas are developed most fully in Weber's *Economy and Society*. It is around the ideas derived from these sources that most of our analysis is organised.

In salvation religions the believer may see himself either as the instrument of God, doing His work, or as a vessel of God through whom His spirit is expressed. The first Weber calls the ascetic, the second the mystic.[60] In addition the believer's asceticism or mysticism may be oriented primarily to the next world, or to activities in this world. In Weber's terms the believer may be an other-worldly or an inner-worldly ascetic or mystic.

The ascetic may reject the world or may participate in activities within the world's institutions – while opposing them. He is 'in' the world but not 'of' the world. The world becomes, as it were, a test-bed for the ascetic temper. The world is God's world, only its present fallen state is rejected:

> the order of the world in which the ascetic is situated becomes for him a vocation which he must fulfil rationally...although the enjoyment of wealth is forbidden to the ascetic it becomes his vocation to engage in economic activity which is faithful to rationalised ethical requirements and which conforms to strict legality. If success supervenes upon such acquisitive activity, it is regarded as the manifestation of God's blessing upon the labour of the pious man and of God's pleasure with his economic pattern of life.[61]

The ascetic thus attempts to bring about a patterning of his whole life towards the goal of salvation and towards the fulfilment of his vocation in the world.

Weber's discussion is mainly in the field of economic activity; he thought that the inner-worldly ascetic could engage in business activities without too great a compromise with 'the world'. Weber is mainly concerned with artisans and small traders, not the modern corporation boss, because it could be argued that the latter is oriented to 'average human qualities, to compromises, to craft, and to the employment of other ethically suspect devices and people'.[62] This orientation, according to Weber, is typical of political activity and thus he argues that it is easier to be an ethically correct and successful businessman than a politician.

In his analysis of the relation between religion and politics Weber suggests that whilst the 'Christian religion of love' might lead to a loss of secular concern, the inner-worldly ascetic can nonetheless compromise with political power structures. This is done 'by interpreting them as instruments for the rationalised ethical transformation of the world and for the control of sin'.[63] But the compromise is limited and conditional. Political parties and the state remain ethically suspect and may act only for the 'control of sin'. Radical changes in social structure may not be sought through politics, but only through the ethical transformation of the world – by changing men rather than changing society. Thus in Halévy's words Methodists 'would never be weary of insisting that national regeneration could be achieved only by the regeneration of individuals'.

The historical material so far considered suggests that working men were able to work in a dedicated way in trade union and political organisations. It was possible for men to have a calling or vocation in this kind of activity. Nonetheless we should not expect, from Weber's analysis, to find these men interested in revolutionary politics; their political activities, for example, would consist of attempts to influence the state to adopt laws which would curb sin and encourage morally good behaviour. The validity of this contention will be tested especially in the rare situations in which Methodists do actually engage in revolutionary politics.

In his discussion of the religion of disprivileged strata Weber suggests that ethically rational congregational religion is characteristic of the artisan and craftsman strata. The proletariat in modern industrial society is largely indifferent to religion, although sometimes through the activities of religious missionaries its members might give expression to their distress in an emotional way. By artisans and craftsmen Weber seems to mean independent, skilled workers, not wage labourers. To work under a contract at negotiated piece-rates is, subjectively at least, to be in a different situation from a wage labourer. Thus the face-workers, who technically were craftsmen and who worked relatively free of immediate supervision, are for present purpose artisans rather than proletarians. Weber said: 'Wherever the attachment to purely magical or ritualistic views has been broken by prophets or reformers, there has...been a tendency for artisans, craftsmen and petty bourgeois to incline towards a (often primitively) rationalistic ethical and religious view of life.'[64] It is the rationalistic ethic that creates self-discipline among the artisans and craftsmen.

The material for this present research has been concentrated on those data concerned with religious calling and self-disciplined, rational activity. This in turn has focussed on the notion of inner-worldly asceticism in order to indicate the ways in which religion and religious activity affected men's adjustment to the world of social and economic affairs. Crucially we are concerned with expressions of the idea of calling or vocation and the ways in which these notions are expressed in activity in the mundane affairs of the mining community. These expressions voice the idea of 'stewardship' and the desire to cultivate God-given 'talents', but these words are more or less alternative formulations of the idea of calling.

This means that the more mystical aspects of Methodism have been underemphasised, those aspects of Methodism which are purely 'an expression of some distress'[65] or 'soteriological orgies'.[66] It becomes a highly ethical treatment of Methodism, perhaps underplaying the more purely spiritual or mystical aspects of the believer's life. This is a significant omission, for the miner's work situation has features congruent both with the artisan's situation and the situation of the more oppressed sections of the proletariat. One would expect to find therefore that the miner's religion had features typical of the religion of artisans and the religion of the 'lowest classes'. This is seen most clearly in the question of *conversion*. Attempts to gain converts were often conducted in what seem to have been evangelical orgies, with great emotional outbursts, confession of sin, self-abasement before God, with expressions of a desire for a new life. Some sort of personal experience of salvation was, at the beginning of the period, almost an essential requirement for becoming a Methodist. Having been converted the convert lived a new, ethically rational life, but he might engage nonetheless in further 'orgies' in renewing his own conversional experience, and in seeking new converts. Thus there were important ecstatic and mystical elements in working-class Methodism, but they are not at the centre of our interest.

There is no necessarily simple connection between believing and acting and we are not in any case attempting simple religious explanations of the courses of events here observed. The language of causal analysis is ill-suited to this enterprise. One suggestion, for example, is that the adoption of Methodism has effects upon certain individuals not only because they believe certain things but because certain patterns of behaviour are expected of them by other Methodists. One cannot simply say that Methodist *belief* caused the pattern of behaviour.

We are concerned above all with the 'elective affinity' between religious and other ideas, especially if we are to avoid 'religious' explanations. Two examples may be used to illustrate what is meant by this.

Firstly, what qualities in Liberalism or Liberal beliefs make Methodists so responsive to Liberalism? Why do Liberalism and Methodism, in other words, seem to cling together? The belief in the minimal intervention of the state for the 'rationalised ethical transformation of the world and the control of sin' is entirely compatible, Weber said, with the '*laissez-faire* doctrine of the "Manchester School" '.[67] This economic doctrine was at the heart of the Liberal Party's thinking at the end of the nineteenth century. *Laissez-faire* beliefs were also very generally held; it was an intellectual orthodoxy. It also embodied the individualism of which Protestantism was the foundation. The individual stood alone not only before the majesty of God but before the forces of the market. Liberal ideas of the market and especially the implied functional harmony of society fit readily with the view derived from Paul's teaching that all Christians are members of one body, with their functions (which are also callings) to perform.

Secondly, why did Methodists not think of the clash of class interests as explaining certain kinds of conflict? Why did the Methodist Liberal trade-union leaders find it impossible to define the conflicts in which they were engaged as class conflicts – even as late as 1926? The answer probably lies in the universalism of Methodism. Salvation is not for an elect only; all stand in need of salvation. Christ died for all men, and we are all of the same estate; 'All have sinned and fallen short of the Glory of God.'[68] The message of Methodism is not sectional but universal. If the world is viewed as being peopled by sinners all in equal need of salvation, all standing under God's judgement, it is difficult, if not irrelevant, to think in terms of sectional interests. Equality on this basis is entirely in accord with individualism nonetheless, for it is each individual who will be judged. This fits also with *laissez-faire* Liberalism and Pauline functionalism.[69] These various views are formidably coherent with one another. It is possible to discuss this coherence and to understand how one view reinforces another, but it is extremely difficult – and perhaps quite inappropriate – to attach causal primacy to one set of beliefs, or to part of the whole coherent set of beliefs. Therefore this analysis stresses the coherence, congruence, consistency and reinforcement of beliefs and activities, rather than attributing causes.

In the course of the analysis of the effects of religion in a small population of miners we also find a gratuitous illustration, or elaboration, of another Weberian observation. In Chapter VI of *Economy and Society,* in the discussion of the functions of religion for privileged and disprivileged strata, Weber suggests that religion tends to have *compensatory* functions for the disprivileged. Religion provides the disprivileged with the assurance that whilst they may be insignificant by human evaluation, they will *become* something in the future – if only in the afterlife. The privileged, however, need some assurance that they have a right to enjoy their privileges, comfort and happiness. Religion assures them that they have a right to their position, that they have earned it or are otherwise entitled to it.[70]

It seems logical to infer from this that if a disprivileged stratum becomes upwardly mobile, religion will change its function in their lives. Elements of this change can be found; in the early 'frontier' days of the village evangelical religion and conversion experiences seem to compensate for the wretched social conditions and low esteem of the miner. But later, with a Methodist leadership firmly established in the community, among both miners and tradesmen, Methodism became a mark of respectability. There is a sense in which the relative success of the Methodist can be seen as the fruit of piety, a faithful and upright life, and to this extent religion reinforces the position of prominent Methodists.

It will be seen also from the foregoing discussion that the effects of religion may be indirect. The saliency of specific religious belief may vary from society to society and situation to situation. Religious beliefs may constitute part of a shared universe of meaning – evaluations and significances – amongst the members of a society. They are the beliefs that are taken for granted, the statements that are presumed to be obvious. Religion is expressed in social relations, attitudes and ways of doing things, not in theological formulations. They may be partially articulated in proverbs or aphorisms or embodied in elaborate myths. Perhaps it is only rarely that religious beliefs are systematised and articulated by specialists in religious belief or by religious virtuosi. The relationship between the beliefs of theologians, religious functionaries, priests and popular beliefs is always problematic. The 'church' is always more or less in a state of tension with both popular religiosity of an explicit kind and the basic assumptions of the populace. The formally religious too may hold unorthodox beliefs and adhere to 'subterranean theologies'.[71] It is for this reason that we have criticised the way in which Thompson has analysed Methodism and for this reason, too, that we have concentrated our study on one small population rather than adopting a more eclectic approach.

Another implication of the indirect effect of religion is that religion may be influential beyond its immediate membership. People who were not members of the chapels were found to hold some 'religious' beliefs in common with those who were members. Many were related or married to Methodists, they shared meanings and evaluation – some of which were derived from Methodism – with their kin. Others may from time to time have participated, albeit marginally, in the life of the chapels. Thus religion has a cultural influence which extends beyond formal membership, but which it is difficult to evaluate.

In summary, the debate about the Halévy thesis has not reached any satisfactory resolution. Commentators have been unable to grapple with the problems raised by Halévy because they have interpreted 'Methodism' in a very general sense, and based their understanding of it on orthodox statements by religious functionaries. Historians have also dealt with Methodism and its effects in different social and economic circumstances and not asked precise questions about its effects in particular, specified circumstances. Thus both Hobsbawn and Thompson are able to suggest that their apparently contrary theses are not mutually exclusive – but we have no guide as to the contextual relevance of either thesis.

One of the major sociological attempts to discuss the relation between social relationships and social consciousness has produced a relatively mechanistic theory which ignores the possibility of ideas and beliefs independently affecting men's understanding of their social experience.

The material of the present study is organised around two key concepts derived from Max Weber. The notion of *inner-worldly asceticism* is used to illustrate the connexions between beliefs and activity in economic and political affairs. Religious beliefs are not seen as being exclusively influential and the Weberian notion of *elective affinity* is used implicitly in the way we try to understand the manner in which beliefs from different sources relate to one another.

In general terms the objectives of this enquiry may be summarised as follows: firstly, to find out what effect, if any, religion had on the political views and activities of miners – specifically did Methodism encourage or inhibit the development of class politics? Secondly, we want to know the mechanisms by which these beliefs were sustained in changing economic and political circumstances. Thirdly, we want to know what kind of men emerged as political leaders among the miners, what was their political *modus operandi* and how they responded to crises. The answers to these questions will be found not only in the nature of their beliefs, but in the constraints and expectations of membership of a particular kind of religious organisation. Finally we want to know the extent to which men developed new political outlooks and broke with traditional ways either within the Methodist tradition or in the act of breaking with it.

We are concerned with the effects of religion amongst people at a specific point of time and in a specific location. We are not concerned with the prime origins of Methodism, and any light that we may throw upon this is entirely incidental. By 1870 Methodism was a group of established national movements, the influence of which had been felt nationally as well as locally. In concentrating upon one small valley, one small part in the whole development of human civilisation, the aim is to clarify and elaborate the issues raised by the historians, using the conceptual tools developed by Max Weber.

The main thesis of this work is that the effect of Methodism on a working-class community was to inhibit the development of class consciousness and reduce class conflict. Plainly these assertions do not exhaust the possible effects of religion. Our discussion will, therefore, try to show the particular social and economic circumstances in which Methodism had these effects.

Three lines of argument will be developed. Firstly, that the beliefs of Methodists did not specifically entail a social outlook which included notions of class interest and conflict. This sustains the contention that 'churches do not as a rule accept the validity of the struggle between employer and employee'.[72] Methodist beliefs were more congruent with a view of society divided into the saved and the unsaved, in which ethical issues were more important than economic or political issues.

Furthermore not only did the saved/unsaved dichotomy cut across social classes based on economic definitions but groups in different class positions shared common views of the world, rooted in shared religious beliefs.

Secondly, as a corollary of the first point it will be argued that while Methodism did produce political leaders amongst working men it did not produce leaders who would articulate and pursue class interests as such. The characteristic working-class leader was sustained, and his political stance validated, by relatively favourable economic circumstances. Thus as his political activities began to succeed, his working position was reinforced.

The third theme originally played a theoretically minor part in the analysis, but at the end seemed more important: Methodism was institutionalised as part of the community, not restricted to formal religious associations. The constraints on a member of a communal organisation were rather different from the constraints of an associational type of organisation.[73] Methodism in the community became more communal and less associational as a result of, for example, intermarriage. An understanding of this gives a deeper insight into the orientations of Methodists in situations of political conflict. The conclusion of the historical account is that the Methodists were so emphasising traditional and communal values and activities that they became increasingly disconnected not only from current political issues but even from official Methodist policy discussions and liturgical changes.

This will not be a wholly 'religious' explanation of courses of events. As Liston Pope observed:

> Religious forces have not been the crucial dynamic factor in culture; neither have they been an opiate of the people or an unmitigated sanction of the *status quo*. Sweeping assertions of this sort are too uncritical and undiscriminating to represent accurately the diverse ways in which religious agencies function. Several of these general theories illumine particular aspects of inter-relationship but are false when applied to other areas; each fails adequately to allow for the multiplicity and reciprocity of relationships.[74]

The aim will be, therefore, to explore the interrelations between religious, political, economic and ideological factors. This in turn will bring a greater understanding of English labour history and, more importantly, will show the interdependence of sociology, history and social history.

1 Historical background

The four villages in which this study was conducted were, and still are, small and relatively isolated villages surrounded by hills and woods. But they were part of a national and world economy and their trade unions and political parties were part of national movements.

Coal-mining, that 'highly contentious and most political industry'[1] is an industry marked by regional variations in problems of extraction and marketing. Durham, for example, exported most of its coal, much of it to the Baltic, whereas Yorkshire produced for a home market. Thus each coalfield, whilst geographically adjacent to the other, was nonetheless operating in a different market situation. Within a coalfield, too, there are local variations, based not only on geology but on the relation of a specific product to a specific market. Thus, when the *D.C.* reports closure in times of prosperity and the opening of a new seam in a slump it is because of the specific need for a particular coal. The opening or closing of a blast furnace, or the rise and fall of a Midland iron company explain these local (and usually minor) anomalies. Parts of Durham produced gas and coking coal of high quality and supplied the northern iron and steel industry and the London and south-eastern gas companies. In 1879 the adoption of the Gilchrist Thomas steel-making process led to the development of new centres of steelmaking in the Middlesbrough area and this expansion was accelerated by the rapid growth of ship-building on the Tees, Tyne and Wear. There was also a degree of vertical integration whereby steel companies owned coal-mines and used them to supply their furnaces. But coal, especially in Durham, was subject to market forces beyond local control, so that the business of mining coal was not just a simple question of maximising output in order to maximise prosperity.

The early part of our period was a time of economic change. Profits, rents and interest were depressed by falling prices at the end of the nineteenth century. But wages and the standard of living were rising from 1850 to 1870 and then most markedly from 1876 to 1886. In Court's opinion, 'this great turn for the better freed the mid-Victorian age from social quarrels to a degree rare in history; it also bred an unguarded mood of optimism'.[2] The mood was not entirely unguarded. The Royal Commission on Industry and Trade of 1885–6 was a result of questioning accepted notions of progress and prosperity. In agriculture it was the 'Great Depression', not apparently limitless prosperity, that marked the 1870s.

The production of coal and the employment of miners rose steadily in County Durham: between 1880 and 1905 production rose from 28·1 million tons to 37·4 million tons and employment rose from 71,800 to 85,900. But by the end of the nineteenth century the proportion of the employed national population in the county had fallen. After 1900 real national income stopped growing and 'wage-earners felt the check severely as prices rose and the cost of living with it'.[3] From 1896 to 1913 retail prices rose by nearly one-third, while from 1899 to 1913 the real value of wages fell by about 13%. During the war the cost of living doubled (July 1914 to July 1918) and at the end of the war wholesale prices were 140% above pre-war. By the end of 1920 shop prices were 125% of 1914 prices.

The structure of industry itself was changing, although this may not have been immediately apparent from the villages. According to Court:

> joint stock finance. . .the amalgamation and trade association movements – these were creating between 1880 and the first world war an industrial society very different from that which classical economists had known. The direct personal relations. . . between master and servant. . .remained strong in many firms and in many industries, particularly in some parts of the country. . . but over a large part of the field they were beginning to be replaced by corporate and associate life in many forms, not only among businessmen but also among the industrial workers as trade unions grew. . .collective and sectional loyalty to shareholders or directors or the trade association or the union tended to replace personal loyalty.[4]

Court's judgement is that at the end of the nineteenth century, 'the specifically nineteenth century conditions of British industry and social life were at an end'.[5]

The large corporation was not a British innovation; cartels and trusts were growing rapidly in the very different conditions of industrialisation to be found in Germany and the U.S.A. In America, for example, Andrew Carnegie was building the largest iron and steel empire in the world. Curiously, a small part of the profits of this empire were one day to be invested in an organ for a chapel in one of the villages of this study. 'The economies of scale' and the need to improve efficiency and competitiveness became apparent to the British industrialists who faced new overseas rivals in a situation in which much

British industrial plant was becoming obsolete. In fact as early as 1886 British iron and steel were second to America's and by 1900 they had fallen behind Germany, too.[6]

One response to this was for British capital to go overseas to finance the development of certain colonies, and to America and Japan. In other words, British capital helped finance Britain's industrial rivals. British industry in turn enjoyed the temporary economic benefits of equipping its rivals with the machinery by which Britain's industry was to be overtaken. These considerations take on an added significance when we see that Britain remained heavily over-committed to traditional industries; coal, iron and steel and textiles accounted for 46% of our industrial output and 70% of all exports.[7] The competition for markets (as distinct from investment opportunities) had already led the European Powers into the 'scramble for Africa' and to the extension of the British Empire. Imperial questions were to be of utmost political importance at the turn of the century and in the debate about free trade which gathered momentum at that time. But in the situation of international economic competition it was found to be easier to switch markets than to modernise and diversify. Lancashire, for example, just changed market to India and the Far East when faced with effective competition elsewhere. By such means British industry was able to remain relatively prosperous until the change to war production created a new situation.

During the First World War there was a high demand for coal and the government took a large measure of control over the industry. Coal exports had been rising in the first part of the century, from 42 million tons in 1901 to over 73 million tons in 1913,[8] but coal brought diminishing returns as the easy seams were worked out and as new sources of power, like oil and electricity, were developed. The price of coal fell after the war and the industry was decontrolled in spite of the recommendation by the Sankey Commission that coal should be nationalised.

In the early 1920s, however, industrial disputes overseas raised the demand for British coal and wages were kept up by subsidy in order to avoid industrial conflict in the U.K. The ultimate solution to the problem of falling demand and falling profits 'took the form of an attack upon labour costs, by the simple and most direct way, the alteration of wages and hours'.[9] In other words, wages were to be reduced and the working day lengthened. The national wage agreements were not renewed in 1925 and it was proposed to reduce wages competitively between coalfields. 'Every miner, and especially every worker in the export fields, knew what his fate was to be.'[10] The discussion of these events and the miners' fate belongs to a later part of this chapter.

The Second World War renewed the demand for coal and for mining labour. The government again took extensive powers to control the industry and the post-war Labour Government nationalised the coal industry. The output of coal was raised to meet heavy demand until 1951. But from then on the demand for coal declined as it was replaced by other fuels. The history of the Durham miners, for example, is from then on a history of the planned rundown of the coal industry.[11] In this situation the function of the union was transformed from that of defending traditional economic interests to facilitating a smooth rundown of the industry.[12]

Nationalisation achieved what the private owners failed to achieve: the economies of scale, heavy capital investment in mechanisation, and the planned, systematic reduction of the labour force.

The changes in the economics and structure of the coal industry have been reflected in County Durham. The earliest pits were close to the surface, seeking easily-won coal in the drift mines in the west of the county. The late nineteenth-century boom created the pits of mid-Durham, deeper pits with shafts and more extensive haulage equipment. Pits such as these were the economic core of the villages in our study. In the 1960s the coal industry in the county was being concentrated in the very deep and highly-mechanised pits of the east coast. The coking coal of the east coast is inferior to that of the Victoria seam in mid-Durham – but it can be cut by machine in six-foot seams and larger, rather than being won by hand in a fourteen-inch seam.

Thus the period of our study is one of continuous economic change. Industry which had made Britain a world power, and 'the workshop of the world' was rapidly changing its techniques, its scale and its economic structure. We are studying the period of the change from the classic 'nineteenth century' of the textbooks to the twentieth century of the large-scale corporation and of highly-rationalised production based on modern fuels, methods and materials. These wide-ranging changes were accompanied by considerable industrial and political conflict.

THE TRADE UNIONS

During the 1870s the trade unions consolidated their position by gaining legal protection of their status. The Trade Union Act of 1871 protected union members from prosecution for being in restraint of trade, and the Conspiracy and Protection of Property Act of 1875 removed the possibility of prosecution for criminal conspiracy arising from a trade dispute. These two Acts plus the 1876 Trade Union Act Amendment Act gave the unions a security they had not enjoyed before.

The trade unionism that was thus afforded protection from the criminal law was the 'old' unionism of skilled workers. In the late 1880s, however, the 'New Unionism' began to develop amongst the less skilled workers. This form of unionism was organised on an industrial rather than a craft basis. The big, general unions of the new unionists were led by men who adopted militant policies and who quite consciously set themselves up against what they regarded as the compliant, respectable leaders of the old unions.[13] The names of Will Thorne and Annie Besant, respectively organising the gas-workers and Bryant and May's match girls, are popularly associated with the movement, and the Dock Strike of 1889 is usually taken to epitomise new unionism. Clegg *et al.* have argued that the roots of the new unionism were to be found in the new concern for poverty, aroused by, and expressed in, such works as *The Bitter Cry of Outcast London* (1883), and in Socialism.[14] The Socialists had been organising among the London unemployed in the period 1885–7 and were becoming increasingly important among the trade unions. In 1884 the Reform and the Redistribution Acts respectively gave more power to the working class by fully enfranchising them. The act of organising workers thus took on a new significance.

The new unionism did not, however, sweep on, unchecked, to power. Over a long period it met with opposition within the existing trade-union movement and in the 1890s it experienced a series of set-backs as a result of a counter-attack from the employers. Thus, for example, soon after the Hull dockers suffered a major defeat all the east coast unions were gone and the seamen's union had gone into liquidation. A year earlier, in 1893, the National Free Labour Association was formed to provide strike-breakers in industrial disputes. In 1898 the employers formed an organisation, parallel to the T.U.C., the E.P.C. The most important victory for employers was probably the defeat of the Amalgamated Society of Engineers by the Engineering Employers' Federation in 1897–8.

At the turn of the century it seemed as if the solid gains made by the unions were to be lost. The new struggle for trade-union rights centred around the Taff Vale decision. One of the functions of the E.P.C. was to advise employers on the rights and on the implications of legal and legislative decisions.[15] On the basis of the *Lyons* v. *Wilkins* decision (1900) the E.P.C. advised its members to make a legal case against picketing. This suggestion was adopted by Beasley, the general manager of the Taff Vale railway line who was in dispute with the Amalgamated Society of Railway Servants over union recognition. The society struck for recognition as a result of local, unofficial action led by James Holmes and his militant supporters. Beasley called in the

Free Labour Association and issued injunctions to restrain the union leaders, and the union itself, from unlawful picketing. As a result of mediation the men returned to work with their union unrecognised by the Taff Vale Company. The court upheld Beasley's injunction, arguing that the trade union had the essential qualities of a corporation and could therefore be sued for the wrongful conduct of its agents. As was expected, the Appeal Court rejected this contention, but contrary to expectations the House of Lords restored the original judgement, in 1901.

Beasley proceeded with an action for damages against the union. When the matter was finally settled it had cost the Railway Servants £42,000.[16] But even more important than the cost of the case was the fact that it now seemed possible to take legal action against almost anything a union might do in pursuit of an industrial dispute.[17]

While not denying the legal importance of the Taff Vale decision Bealey and Pelling have questioned its direct relevance to the rank and file membership of the trade unions. They suggest that the Taff Vale issue was not important in the two by-elections of 1901. The Anglo-Boer War and jingoism may also have diverted attention from this domestic matter. The Lords' decision nonetheless had a galvanising effect on the trade unions' leadership and it can be argued that the decision was a turning-point for the trade union and labour movements. It looked as if the wielders of power in industry and the law were virtually in an organised conspiracy against labour.[18] Even the exemplars of the old unionism, the moderate Lib.-Labs., were alarmed by developments. There seemed to be no alternative course of action but to turn to direct parliamentary action in pursuit of trade-union interests. Sociologically, this is a crucial juncture because it is the point at which trade unionists saw that they had *political* interests separable from (but related to) their traditional *economic* interests. In practical terms it meant that many more trade unionists were now willing to affiliate themselves to the L.R.C.[19] This L.R.C. was the basis of the Labour Party.

THE LABOUR PARTY

Traditionally, labour representation had been effected by the election of working men as Liberal M.P.s or through Liberal alliances with working men. The working-class Liberal M.P.s usually served on the radical wing of the Liberal Party where also were to be found some middle-class supporters of trade union and working-class aspirations.[20] The Liberal tradition was closely associated with Non-conformity and one recurring theme of this book will be the ways in which Liberalism and Non-conformity fitted together. The key political issue for many trade unionists at the end of the nineteenth century was whether working men should continue to accept representation through the Liberal Party – with all the compromise that this entailed – or whether they should seek independent Labour representation.

The L.R.C. was formed in London in February 1900 as a result of a meeting sponsored by the T.U.C. to discuss Labour representation.[21] Why the L.R.C. came to be created is not hard to understand. One important factor was the rise of the new unskilled unions with their militant leaders, another was the rise of Socialism in its various forms of Fabianism, I.L.P. and S.D.F. These movements represented and created men who were deeply dissatisfied with the existing channels of expression. According to Pelling the Liberal Party had become rigid in its structure and was locally controlled by businessmen and Non-conformist ministers.[22] The Liberals rarely chose workers as parliamentary candidates; only where working-class voting strength was overwhelming – as in the mining areas – did working men become M.P.s. Liberals also adopted patronising attitudes towards working men. Furthermore, during the 1890s, as we have seen, the trade-union movement received many setbacks and it did not look as if they would gain any redress through the Liberal Party (which was, anyhow, in opposition). Independent Labour representation thus appeared to be a necessity.

This view was not readily adopted by the more traditional trade unionists and their leaders. It took the Taff Vale decision to convince the Liberal trade unionists that they really did need independent representation in Parliament. In 1903, three years after its foundation, the L.R.C. agreed not to support Liberal or Conservative candidates and to raise a parliamentary fund for Labour candidates.[23] The former agreement was nonetheless amended somewhat to allow trade-union officials to remain Liberals. There is no need to rehearse the conflicts within the early Labour party caused by Labour's traditional affiliation with Liberalism and their earlier need to enter into electoral arrangements with the Liberal Party. Such conflicts are authoritatively recounted in the work of Pelling and others, and will be amply illustrated when we turn to the specific case of the coal-miners.

The L.R.C.'s first contribution to a General Election was £33. In the 1900 Election the L.R.C. had two successful candidates. Keir Hardie was elected at Merthyr; Hardie, an I.L.P. member, was a firm believer in an Independent Labour stance. Richard Bell, returned at Derby, was a Liberal on all but narrowly trade-union affairs. This difference symbolises the division within the Labour Party to which we have already alluded. These two M.P.s were outnumbered by eight

Lib.-Labs. and could not therefore claim to be the sole representatives of Labour.

The L.R.C. achieved some by-election successes and was able to find common ground with the Liberals and various bases for 'arrangements' with them in spite of I.L.P. pressure to make an independent stand. The L.R.C. and the radicals found common cause in opposition to the Anglo-Boer War, and the L.R.C. and the Liberals in general stood together on the 1902 Education Act, Tariff Reform and the Chinese labour question in South Africa.[24] The number of affiliated members of the L.R.C. grew, however, as the unions increasingly saw the need for their own parliamentary representatives in order to restore the legal status of the trade unions. Thus, by the end of 1902 only the miners remained outside the L.R.C.

In 1903 the L.R.C. raised funds to pay its M.P.s and became a more effective party, relatively free of its sponsors on a day-to-day basis and able to discipline its representatives through financial sanctions. In the Election of 1906 which resulted in a Liberal land-slide victory the L.R.C. gained 29 seats. This was over half of the Labour representation for there were 14 non-L.R.C. miners' M.P.s returned and another 9 Lib.-Lab. trade union M.P.s. On the assembly of the 1906 Parliament the L.R.C. became the Labour Party.[25]

It remained difficult for the Labour Party to break its connection with the Liberals. It could not actively *oppose* the social reform programme of the Liberal Government and after 1910 it could only oppose the Liberals at the cost of bringing down the government. Yet, the Liberal Government did little that was actually pro-Labour in any decisive way, except for a Trades Disputes Act in 1906 which protected union funds from the sort of action that had ensued from the Taff Vale dispute. The traditional link between the Labour Party and the Liberal Non-conformist tradition was in fact strengthened by the influx of the miners' leaders and mining M.P.s when the M.F.G.B. affiliated itself to the party – the last big union to do so. The conflict between the Socialists and the traditionalists was expressed in Victor Grayson's victory in a three-cornered electoral contest in 1907 which he won as a 'clean Socialist' without Labour Party support. The Socialists were defeated within the party during 1910–11 but one result of this was the creation of the British Socialist Party in 1911 which took the S.D.F. branches of the I.L.P. and Clarion Clubs from the Labour Party.

THE MINERS

The suggestion that the miners were in some way different from other unions has been a refrain running through this brief recital of labour history. The differences could easily be exaggerated by looking at union leaderships alone, but the facts are that the miners' leaders epitomised the Liberal Non-conformist leadership of labour, and under this leadership the mining unions were slow to accept an independent political stance and were the last to affiliate themselves to the Labour Party. Even after this affiliation, a number of miners' leaders refused to be bound by the Party constitution.

Only to say that 'the miners were different' is in itself misleading because there were significant differences between miners themselves. The Durham and Northumberland leadership, for example, maintained its extreme Liberal outlook for longer than other districts. The north-eastern miners carried their beliefs to the point of remaining outside the M.F.G.B. The M.F.G.B. was formed in 1889 largely on the initiative of the secretaries of the Yorkshire and Lancashire unions. Yorkshire was the largest constituent, and Durham and Northumberland remained outside with some unaffiliated Scottish and Lancastrian unions and the South Wales sliding-scale associations (see below).[26] Durham affiliated in 1892 after the federation had contributed to the Durham strike fund (in an attempt to win them to the M.F.G.B.) but was expelled in the following year. Durham actually lost its dispute in 1892 and the men returned to work at a reduced wage. In 1893, however, the M.F.G.B. was involved in a major lock-out when the owners sought to reduce wages, and the M.F.G.B. won.[27] The conflict was very bitter and entailed great hardship for the miners, whose suffering aroused considerable public sympathy. The outcome was that the men returned to work without a reduction and a conciliation board was set up under an independent chairman.

In accounting for the differences between Durham and the M.F.G.B. one might look at important economic factors; for example, the main M.F.G.B. strength lay in the districts producing for the home market. Durham and South Wales were exporting districts. But looking more closely at the history of the Durham miners, the first half of the nineteenth century is a history of defeat. The miners fought the owners with the strike weapon in 1832, 1844 and 1863–4 and had been beaten, forced back to work with their union broken and funds depleted.[28] The new union, the D.M.A., was formed in 1869. In 1872 the union negotiated the abolition of the bond, a hated system similar to indentured labour which tied a miner to an employer for a year with few legally enforceable obligations on the employer in return. In 1872 also, through national legislation they won some security for the check-weighman's position.

The leadership of the new D.M.A. was committed to advancing the men's cause by negotiation rather than industrial action. The situation in Durham was exactly paralleled by that in South Wales. Evans, in his *The Miners of South Wales*, says of the period after 1875:

> the employers would probably have been able to crush any unions which appeared, as they had, in fact, destroyed those of an earlier period. The inoffensive policy of the local associations led the coal owners to tolerate, and even to assist, their continuance, and their existence at least prepared the men for more effective organisation.[29]

It was this 'inoffensive' compromise position that the Durham, South Wales and Derbyshire leadership represented. It may also be true that many of their views, about liberal economics, the homogeneity and harmony of society and the local community, were ideas that developed as a means of coming to terms with relative powerlessness.

The moderate men of South Wales (Isaac Evans, David Morgan, William Brace and William Abraham – 'Mabon'), of Derbyshire (Haslam and Harvey) and County Durham (Crawford and Wilson) were all associated with religious Non-conformity and political Liberalism. They opposed industrial militancy and – eventually – the affiliation of the miners' unions to the Labour Party.[30]

What then were the policies of this leadership? The leaders advocated moral force rather than strikes as a means to promote the miners' cause.[31] Moral force could be exerted through reason, at the table, in the conciliation process. The Durham, Northumberland and South Wales miners carried this to another stage by instituting the sliding scale, whereby miners' wages were tied to the selling price of coal. With such an automatic arrangement there was virtually no need for trade unions. According to R. Page Arnot sliding-scale associations took the place of unions and 'suffocated trade unionism in South Wales'.[32] Evans also suggests that the sliding scale (which lasted until 1902 in South Wales) kept interest in trade unions low.[33] The Welsh leaders, especially Mabon, always advised against abandoning the sliding scale. The advocacy of the sliding scale entailed more than making wage levels automatic. It entailed propagating an assumption about the harmony of interest of labour and capital. The leaders accepted this assumption and believed that industrial conflict arose from misunderstanding.

In periods of relative prosperity the sliding scale provided a wage on which the miner could maintain a family. This was not the case when coal prices were low. Towards the end of the century the demand for a living wage emerged amongst miners, as coal prices fell. Arnot has said that by 1893 the men believed in a living wage rather than the laws of supply and demand.[34] It was certainly the case that the Derbyshire miners were arguing for a minimum wage in that year.[35]

The miners' leaders in Durham and South Wales resisted the demand, which they saw as a breach of economic principle that could not be supported by the operation of the market. Instead they supported restriction of output, in order to raise the price of coal. The Welsh rejected this because, according to Evans, they wanted immediately visible improvements in their wages.[36] But at least the strategy of restricting output was based upon the same economic laws as the sliding scale, and thus did not compromise the economic principles of the Durham miners. In these differences we see just some of the regional differences between miners, which made federation and common policy formulation so difficult.

The Northumberland and Durham miners also opposed the eight-hour day, which had been an object of Welsh policy since 1888.[37] The objection was rooted in both local practice, and economic principle. The Northumberland and Durham miners already worked a six-hour day. The men worked two six-hour shifts and the boys one shift of twelve hours. The eight-hour day would have reduced the boys' working day and forced the men into a three-shift system. The men were not accustomed to three shifts, much domestic and social reorganisation would have had to follow such a change, and the men's hours would probably have had to be increased to eight.

Thus the north-eastern hewers opposed the eight-hour day. Those north-eastern leaders who were also M.P.s represented the miners on the Parliamentary Committee of the T.U.C., but they were not representatives of the federated miners. They in fact prevented the parliamentary committee from carrying out the instructions of the T.U.C., even when the congress gave overwhelming support to the eight-hour day. Thus, according to Clegg: 'Together with the miners' members from the north east, a substantial group of coal-owners and other Liberal employers remained determined and vociferous opponents of the (1892) Bill.'[38] Wilson, the Durham leader, 'attacked successive bills, usually in close collaboration with Sir James Joicey, chief of the Durham coal owners'.[39] The rejection of the eight-hour day was to be crucial in the relation of the Durham miners to the miners of Britain until the early years of the twentieth century, and to the achievement of the eight-hour day as such.

Divisions on the eight-hour day influenced the development of the M.F.G.B. Scotland and Wales were in the van of the movement for the restriction of hours, but Durham and Northumberland were sufficiently opposed for them to refuse to join the federation at its foundation in 1888. The opposition of the Durham and Northumberland miners was effective in the 1902 attempt to secure legislation by the M.F.G.B. They effectively prevented the passage of eight-hour legislation until

1908. After then, according to Arnot, John Wilson's influence began to wane.[40]

The sliding scale itself also divided the Durham miners from the federation. The M.F.G.B. was striving to end 'the system by which wages were settled by the course of coal prices ... and to replace it by a legal minimum wage ... independent of the fluctuations of the coal market'.[41] This was an affront to the beliefs of the Durham leadership; they not only believed in their sliding scale but had actually agreed a negotiating procedure with the masters in 1892, thus creating one of the earliest such arrangements in the industry. Not even after 1893 did the federated areas have the kind of negotiating machinery that had been created in Durham.[42] There seemed to be no need to depart from this arrangement or from the market principles, in fixing wages. The South Wales miners left the M.F.G.B. in 1889 because they, too, favoured the sliding scale.

The cautious outlook of the north-eastern miners' leadership did not go unchallenged. Some militancy was generated in Northumberland, for example, when there was a strike against a 15% wage cut in 1887. Tom Mann was among the militants who came in to help organise.[43] A change in the Northumberland leadership in 1890 was followed by unofficial strikes in which the employers 'lamented the union's loss of control'.[44] From 1894 onwards the I.L.P. made a special effort in Durham during which time George Jacques, a local I.L.P. member, campaigned unsuccessfully for the endorsement of the eight-hour day policy.[45] From the late 1890s a dissident platform was established at the Durham Gala from which spoke Tom Mann and Prince Kropotkin among others. In 1898 two Socialists were elected to the Executive Committee of the D.M.A. By this time some of the leaders had accepted a few Socialist ideas and they were certainly alarmed by the failure of legislation to protect the unions and by the employers' counter-attacks.

The Socialists also appeared as the champions of unity amongst the miners because they supported not only federation policies (the eight-hour day and the minimum wage) but federation itself. The Rosebery Settlement of the national dispute in November 1893 had been a victory for the principles of federation; together the federated miners had resisted the owners, and the unfederated miners had paid for their lack of unity in 1892. Lessons such as this were almost bound to be learnt in Durham, sooner or later. John Wilson appreciated the point but drew from it conclusions quite contrary to the Socialists. He believed that concerted action by the miners would have a bad effect on class harmony: 'Therefore he stood ... for a kindly [local] agreement with the coal owners.'[46]

By and large the Liberal leadership resisted Socialist ideas and regarded Socialists as trouble-makers. Williams has described how in
Derbyshire Haslam blamed the I.L.P. and the Socialists for the Taff
Vale decision and how as late as 1912 Harvey and other moderates
were condemning Hardie and Lansbury. Even the M.F.G.B. preferred
the infirm Woods as their vice-president rather than the Socialist
Smillie in 1904. Arnot has argued that by 1904 the M.F.G.B. was
itself a conservative body.[47] In 1906, for example, the M.F.G.B. voted
against affiliation to the L.R.C. although the decision was reversed the
following year. Sidney Webb believed that the lack of unity amongst
the miners weakened the position of not only the D.M.A. but the miners
nationally also.[48]

It hardly needs to be said that the Socialists attempting to infiltrate
or convert men in the north-east of England found few allies amongst
the union leadership in the first decades of this century. They found
some among the rank and file of younger men. As we shall see when
we enquire into village politics there was an element of generational
conflict embodied in the Liberal–Socialist conflicts of the period. The
'leaders of Durham and Northumberland, many of them widely respected as men of outstanding capacity, really stood for a different con-
ception of trade unionism, one that had grown up in the 60s and 70s'.[49]
While the old leadership in South Wales was discredited in the Cambrian Combine Strike of 1910, their colleagues in Durham lasted until
the First World War; then, so rapid was the turnover that by 1918
only two agents had been full-time employees of the D.M.A. before
1911.

It was perhaps only with the settlement of the 'socialist' issues of the
eight-hour day and the minimum wage that the Labour Movement
as such grew in Durham because there remained no grounds on which
to resist Labour policy. The I.L.P. had consisted mainly of short-lived
branches, separate from the union lodges and lacking sustained support.[50] The D.M.A. was affiliated to the Labour Party and supported it
thereby as well as providing the organisational base for Labour
politics in the county.

INDUSTRIAL STRIFE

The end of the first decade of this century was marked by renewed
industrial conflict. The number of working days lost by strikes had
been less than 5 million per year between 1898 and 1908 but in 1911
more than 10 million days were lost and in 1912 more than 40 million.
In 1910 the Cambrian Combine dispute began, from 1909–10 the north-
east shipyards struck, in 1910 cotton struck, the shipbuilders and

London printers began disputes which carried them into 1911. In 1910 the Durham miners were out for three months. In 1911 the seamen struck, also the dockers in Hull, London and Liverpool and the Liverpool railway workers. Warships appeared in the harbours and troops on the streets, men were shot. Then in 1912, the miners had a national strike for their minimum wage. In the following year the London taxi-drivers struck and there was severe rioting during the Dublin tram strike.

What was the cause of all this activity? Technical change was certainly important; the working out of easy seams made it more difficult for the coal miner to maintain his earnings and the introduction of the petrol engine obviously changed the conditions of the cabbies' work. But there were also other factors.

In 1909 the Osborne judgement prevented unions making an automatic levy on their members for political purposes. This judgement made it look, once again, as if the Labour Party – growing in Parliament – was to be thwarted in the courts. Two elections in 1910 then depleted Labour's finances. This general situation gave greater credence to the views of the Syndicalists who were advocating policies of direct action by the trades unions in order to take control of the economy by industrial means. The direct effects of Syndicalism, especially Syndicalist theory, may have been relatively slight, but industrial unionism and the creation of alliances like the Triple Alliance of miners, railwaymen and transport workers were policies favoured and encouraged by Syndicalists. Kendal perhaps exaggerates when he says that, 'A wild, elemental, pent-up force seemed suddenly let loose, disregarding precedents and agreements...forcing conservative trade union leaders ahead of it like fallen leaves driven before an autumn wind...'[51] But it does seem as if Taff Vale and the Osborne case had had some influence in galvanising the trade unions into a level of industrial and political activity that had rarely been seen before. There was a sense in which this represented the beginning of a broad-fronted working-class movement rather than a conglomeration of individual trade-union actions. In 1910 the Industrial Workers of Great Britain, modelled on the America International Workers of the World ('The Wobblies'), was recruiting on Clydebank where it reached a peak membership of 10,000.[52] In 1912 *The Miners' Next Step* was published, making a Syndicalist plea for the taking over of the mines. The demand for 'one big union' and the public ownership of important industries plainly takes workers beyond trade-union negotiations into the realm of radical, if not revolutionary, politics.

In this period also the sympathetic strike and other sympathetic actions were deployed by workers in support of other workers. Action was sufficiently united for the Shipping Federation, for example, to be unable to use blackleg labour in 1911. Some 125,000 seamen were on strike backed by dockers and carters. The London dockers meanwhile encouraged the women of the East End to strike, and by so doing the women, too, gained wage increases.

The disputes of 1910 onwards were conducted with considerable aggression at times, showing that the government and the employers were prepared to use extra-parliamentary methods (the National Free Labour Association and physical force) to achieve their ends, while restricting the unions' ability even to take 'legitimate' parliamentary action. But alongside these new developments old conflicts continued. The old and new unionisms, for example, had clashed within mining even while the miners fought the owners. The Cambrian Combine Strike arose from local geological problems and the reduction of hours after the 1908 eight-hour legislation which together made it difficult for the men to maintain their wages. The Ely Pit failed to agree new prices and 13,000 men of the Combine came out on strike.[53] Real power went to the hands of the strike committee. Safety men were called out, and this was something which had never happened under traditional leadership. Blacklegs came in under police protection and then troops. One man was killed and 500 injured. But the men went back to work, more or less in defeat, after the M.F.G.B. withdrew financial support.

Productivity was declining in the pits and this was accentuated by the Eight-Hour Act. In 1879 hewers had drawn an average of 4·23 tons a shift; in 1900 3.48 tons, but in 1911 they were drawing only 3·30 tons. In 1908, in relative depression, wages averaged 7s. 4d. a shift and in the relative prosperity of 1911, 6s. 9½d. The minimum wage policy thus seemed more advantageous for the miners and in 1912 they struck for it. But the Welsh miners voted against the continuation of the strike; this was a blow for the militants who had replaced the old leadership after the Cambrian Combine Strike.

Industrial unrest continued until the war. Two were killed and hundreds injured in Dublin during the tram strike and Jim Larkin, the Syndicalist 'Irish agitator', was arrested (but he managed to address strikers whilst wearing a false beard!). Jacobs biscuit workers and the Dublin coal-merchants also struck and the T.U.C. sent funds and raised subscriptions to aid the Irish workers. Dangerfield went so far as to suggest that the First World War saved Britain from a Syndicalist-style General Strike.[54] It was certainly true that the Syndicalists were active in the Industrial Workers of Great Britain, the Cambrian Combine dispute and the Irish Transport and General Workers' Union, but were they converting workers to their views or only capitalising on immediate conflicts? Even these conflicts may be over-stated because between 1911 and 1914 trade was good, and on average fewer working days were lost than in 1892–8, when the working population was smaller. Also miners' wages rose after 1912 and Labour lost seats to Liberals in two Derbyshire mining constituencies in 1912 and 1914 respectively. The Liberal influence in the Party was increased in 1909 with the inflow of mining M.P.s with the affiliation of Durham. In 1910 the Syndicalists whilst carrying a resolution for 'one big union' at the T.U.C. failed to find any enthusiasm for its implementation.[55]

What was happening within the political parties during this early part of the century? We shall examine the Liberal Party below. Among organised labour the members and leaders of trade unions were developing a degree of class consciousness. Their economic and political position *vis-à-vis* the employers was very obvious in the conflicts of the period. This does not mean to say that they were developing class consciousness in the classic Socialist sense of the word.[56]

The development of the Labour Party was not, therefore, necessarily a development of Socialism. While there were Socialists within the Labour Party, the Party developed as a means of increasing the extent and effectiveness of Labour representation in Parliament, not as a means of creating a Socialist society. In 1902 a parliamentary debate on the legal position of the trade unions showed that Labour could hope to gain little from the government which adopted the E.P.C.'s position on the matter.[57] Thus even in Durham, the stronghold of Liberal–Labourism, the Miners' Council voted for increased labour representation in Parliament.[58]

In the early years of the century the Labour Movement turned away from imperial issues to domestic matters and during the period of Liberal rule from 1906 onwards the Labour Party developed policies on issues like pensions, school meals, and the right to work. These were matters which affected all the working class including the poor and unorganised workers. But they were also issues on which Labour was more or less upstaged by the Liberals because they required only a slightly more collectivist and positive role for the state, such as the Liberals were already considering, not a radical transformation of society.

Ramsay MacDonald, the secretary of the L.R.C., believed that 'the Labour Party should keep in close touch with Liberalism, and especially with the Liberal voters whose approval at the forthcoming [1905] General Election he was at great pains to secure'.[59] That the Labour Party entered into electoral 'arrangements' (some secret) with the Liberals angered the I.L.P. MacDonald, however, disavowed the Marxism of the Socialist groups because he felt that Parliament should represent all classes and not be a battleground (a nice example of the idea of 'fair-play').[60]

Needless to say, the Socialists in the Labour Movement opposed this policy which seemed to be a development or extension of traditional Liberal views. The north-east was one area in which the Socialists hoped to win the rank and file of the working class. During the 1904 Gala it was argued from the I.L.P. platform that wages were not beyond the control of man. This was in opposition to the official Liberal line of the official leadership. According to Bealey and Pelling from about 1905 the I.L.P. concentrated on Northumberland and Durham 'where circumstances seemed ripe for a speedy growth of the socialist movement in the coalfields'.[61] In Durham the advocates of joining the M.F.G.B. were often leaders of the I.L.P. and as a result of the I.L.P.'s 'strenuous proselytising exertions' the Durham union was 'soon honeycombed with disaffection'.[62] This view of the situation will be encountered in Chapter 7. The fact is that whatever the influence of the I.L.P. before the war, Durham never became a stronghold of Socialism.

It seemed that as Labour representation grew and the trade unions began to dominate the Labour Party that the Socialist influence declined. Trade-union domination was finally institutionalised when the federal structure of the Party was changed by making election to the executive by a vote of the whole conference. This reduced the power of the affiliated Socialist societies and trade councils and gave the trade unions the decisive block vote which they hold to this day. This change was made to exclude I.L.P.'ers in 1917 because they tended to resist the call-up and oppose the war. They, as will be seen later, gave the party a 'bad name' and were a nuisance.

But the Party had earlier lost a substantial number of Socialists; this happened in 1911 with the formation of the British Socialist Party. The Socialists who left were active in the promotion of Syndicalism and the Triple Alliance, and in this they were joined by the Marxists who left Ruskin Hall to found the Labour Colleges.[63]

The position of the Labour Party was consolidated by the war because it was drawn into the process of government during the coalition and because the working class itself was seen to be as important on the home front as its young men in the trenches. The 1917 Constitution of the Party included the now famous Clause Four which according to Pelling was a victory for the Socialist influence in the Party.[64] But we might argue that it was an epitaph for Socialism, perhaps included to please the minority of Socialists or to salve the consciences of the majority with residual or muddled Socialist views. The Labour Party has never actually sought the most equitable distribution of the fruits of industry by any means whatever and has not even sought it when nationalising a narrow range of industries. The Party policy document of 1918 called for a national minimum wage, subsidisation of social services, the use of the profits of economic expansion to create educational and cultural opportunities and the democratic control of industry (but not in the Syndicalist sense).

POST-WAR RELATIONS

After the war there was a greater separation of trade union and Party functions. The officials of trade unions became more engrossed with union affairs as unions became respectable bodies for government to consult and they neglected the Party. Fewer officials became M.P.s or officers of the Party. It might also be suggested that the House of Commons became more of a place to send retired or unsuccessful trade-union officials.

During the war the government had worked out generous reconstruction plans to create a society fit for heroes. But the post-war boom led to an abandonment of these plans, to the decontrol of industry and an end to plans for nationalisation, although the railways were re-organised before being decontrolled.[65] This was followed by a demand for reductions in taxation and government expenditure, leading to the 'Geddes Axe' on public spending, which fell first on the 1918 Education Act.

In 1922 Labour won 142 seats, more than the Liberals. In the 1923 Election on the issue of tariff reform the Conservatives lost seats and Labour formed a government under Ramsay MacDonald. This government could only survive with Liberal support, so once more Labour had to collaborate with the Liberals and would not have been able to implement a radical policy had they wanted to do so. In the Election of October 1924 Labour gained more votes but went out of office; it was in this election that the forged 'Zinoviev Letter' was used to create enormous hostility towards the Labour Party. The Conservative Government that was returned to office was ready to do battle with the miners.

The miners had expected the nationalisation of coal immediately after the war and would have struck for this if Lloyd George had not called an enquiry. The Sankey Commission recommended nationalisation but the government rejected this. Temporary and subsidised wage increases staved off conflict until 1921 when the export market for coal collapsed due to the competition from German reparation coal (this was ironic because one-fifth of the miners enlisted at the beginning of the war in order to defeat the Germans). The losses entailed encouraged the government to decontrol the industry and the owners to cut wages. In April 1921 the miners struck but the Triple Alliance failed to come to their aid (having been enabled to escape their obligations when Lloyd George made a temporary offer to the miners). The miners were defeated by July and their wages were reduced. Perhaps the most crucial factor in this strike had been the failure of the alliance because it showed that unions could not be sure of support and that governments could divide them.

The sequence of the miners' lock-out and the General Strike of 1926 is too well known to need re-telling. The immediate occasion for the threat to reduce miners' wages was the economic disturbance caused by the return to the Gold Standard in 1925,[66] but from most accounts it seems as if the government was spoiling for a fight, felt sure of winning in 1926 and was not concerned to seek any kind of conciliation with the miners.[67] Careful preparations were made for the General Strike by the government, while the Samuel Commission was sitting. The General Council of the T.U.C. was uneasy because in the strike situation initiative passed to local unions. In Durham and Northumberland, after the lock-out of 1926:

> cash wages per shift had been reduced to a far lower level than elsewhere, while the extension of hours combined with the reduction in wages per shift had resulted in a more substantial reduction in wage costs than in any other part of the country...By these means they had been able not only to maintain a greater proportion of overseas trade than other districts, but also to capture a considerable proportion of the coastwise trade of this country.[68]

The figures cited by Garside in his recent book *The Durham Miners, 1919–1960* provide us with an outline of the extent of the miners' relative deprivation after the First World War. In July 1921, 22,000 men were out of work (or almost one-fifth of the membership of the D.M.A.) and by mid-August 60,000 were unemployed; at the end of the month 160 pits lay idle in the county.[69] The miners' wages not only failed to keep abreast of the cost of living, but those in Durham fell behind the rest of the miners: taking the 1914 wage as 100, in 1922 the Durham miners' wages were 146·3 compared with 154·0 for the remainder of the country; in 1929 the indices were 128·2 and 142.4 and in 1938, 156·0 and 173·7.[70]

So desperate was the condition of the Durham, Northumberland and Welsh miners that the Lord Mayor of London launched a national appeal for relief in 1928.[71] In 1931 the institution of the means test added administrative insult to economic injury in the coalfield.[72]

The government and the coal-owners won and in 1927 a Trades Disputes and Trade Union Act was introduced. This Act made the General Strike illegal and introduced 'contracting in' in place of contracting out' for the trade-union political levy, a move which reversed the provision of the 1913 Act (itself reversing the Osborne decision) and weakened Labour Party funds. It would be fair to say that from 1926 onwards Socialism was never again a threat to Labour, nor a real force to be reckoned with in Britain.

THE LIBERAL PARTY

The Liberal Party at the beginning of our period was essentially the Party of Gladstone. Gladstonian Liberalism is usually summed up in the slogan, 'Peace, Retrenchment and Reform'. The elements that made up this slogan have a number of peculiarly ethical aspects which appealed to Non-conformists. The pursuit of peace was based on a 'critical, conscience-searching attitude to foreign and imperial affairs, the willingness to see right triumph over national sentiment. . .idealism, the belief that war was wrong and that in the new world of great inventions and world wide trade civilised nations should not require to settle differences by war'.[73] These attitudes were epitomised in the acceptance of an arbitrated settlement to the 'Alabama' incident, avoidance of engagement in the Franco-Prussian War and, later, conciliation of white South Africans – making friends of enemies – in 1909. In the Anglo-Boer War the Gladstonian spirit was represented by Lloyd George who was a pacifist and by Campbell-Bannerman who courted unpopularity in his denunciation of the British concentration camps.

Retrenchment was based on the notion that private spending was more beneficial than public spending and that men should as far as possible be saved from taxation. Reform was essentially political reform. The Liberals sought to provide better government and to remove disabilities to office-holding. They pursued Irish disestablishment – it being contrary to the Liberal temper for a church to be established in a nation that was mainly of another religion. On social reform, however, the Liberals 'were restrained by their *laissez-faire* doctrines and by their deep aversion to public expenditure'.[74]

The unique mixture of 'ethics and prudence'[75] was embodied in the person of Gladstone of whom McCullum says 'no one could compare in his moral and personal ascendancy'.[76] The Durham miners, through John Wilson, had a peculiarly close relation with Gladstone. In 1893 Gladstone received deputations from the miners in support of the Eight-Hour Bill then before Parliament. Wilson was part of another deputation which included not only spokesmen from the Northumberland and Durham miners, but coal-owners also. This deputation spoke against the Bill to Gladstone and, according to Arnot, Gladstone 'was fairly obviously on the side of Durham and Northumberland'. 'I ought',

Gladstone said, 'perhaps to say that belonging as I do to an old school in politics, my prepossessions. . .are with you, because undoubtedly for the first half or two thirds of my Parliamentary life the disinclination of the most enlightened statesman to interfere with labour. . .was very great indeed, therefore that must be allowed for in anything I say'.[77] Wilson expressed the good wishes of the miners at the end of this meeting.

The 1905 Election returned a Liberal administration, which after many vicissitudes was to remain in power until the First World War – facing the increasing venom of a continually frustrated Conservative Party. The issues that returned them in 1905 speak to the very nature of traditional Liberalism; the Education Bill, temperance, and the employment of Chinese labour in South Africa. Dangerfield neatly summed up the ethical contents of Liberalism: 'For Liberalism, after all, implies rather more than a political creed or an economic philosophy; it is a profoundly conscience-stricken state of mind. It is the final expression of everything which is respectable, God fearing, and frightened.'[78]

During the early years of the century senior Liberals from the days of Gladstone were retiring from the political scene. The Liberal-imperialists were more dominant. Thus in the early years of this century the Liberals were divided into Liberal imperialists and Gladstonian little Englanders.[79] But radicals remained. Morley and Burns were against going to war over Belgium, and Lloyd George would have resigned if Britain had fought over the invasion of France alone.

A new kind of Reformism emerged, seen in Lloyd George's 'People's Budget' of 1909, which represented a sharp break with the policy of retrenchment and which embodied notions of social equity. This 'radicalism' entailed extensive public expenditure contrary to all ideas of retrenchment.

Peace was decreasingly a major feature of Liberal policy: the Hague Conference of 1907 failed and by 1909 the public was blaming the Liberals for not preparing for war because they reduced the Dreadnought programme whilst Tirpitz went ahead with his. Subsequent heavy expenditure on the navy was yet another blow to the idea of retrenchment.

The Liberals were relatively unable to cope with the changes in the economy and in industry that we have already discussed. The Liberal Government also made itself look absurd and then distinctly odious by its treatment of the suffragettes; forcible feeding and cat-and-mouse procedures stand in remarkable contrast to the traditional Liberal belief in the right of the individual to protest against the system that gives him (or her) no legitimate representation.

Above all else, perhaps, the Liberals failed to solve the Irish question. Gladstone had regarded the conciliation of the Irish as a prime task for the Liberal Party. Asquith only showed interest in the problem when he became dependent on Irish nationalist votes at Westminster and in so doing he was accused by the Conservatives of siding with the British enemies. The Conservatives for their part were united, for the first time since 1903, in their support for the Ulster Unionists. The shootings in Bachelor's Walk in 1914 were, in Dangerfield's opinion, an 'obscene little spatter of blood on the Dublin quays [with which] the word *Finis* was written to the great Liberal battles of the nineteenth century'.[80]

The First World War also helped destroy the Liberal Party. It was difficult to wage total war and maintain liberal principles. The Defence of the Realm Act, press censorship, conscription, were all against liberal principles. Wholehearted supporters of the war were virtually Conservatives. The Liberal Party split and never again emerged as a governing Party in the U.K. It may have been that the Liberal Party was by 1914 an uneasy coalition of interests which found occasion to divide in the events of that period. As will be shown below there was very little to hold the party together.

The period of Liberal Government was not, however, entirely a period of disaster and disintegration. It was said earlier that the Liberals adopted policies similar to those of Labour on certain issues. Thus various measures of social reform were set in train that were to contribute to the building of the modern welfare state. The most important were the establishment of labour exchanges (which did not actually solve unemployment as had been hoped) and the National Insurance Act of 1911. They also attempted to reform the 1902 Education Act which had offended Non-conformists and their failure to do so may have contributed to the reform of the Lords who were blocking the attempt. A modest old-age pension was introduced in 1908 and in 1906 an Act to permit local authorities to feed needy schoolchildren was passed. The Liberal Government also reversed the effects of Taff Vale and the Osborne case by legislation.

The fortunes of Non-conformity were closely allied to those of the Liberal Party. Many Non-conformists in the Party were pacifists and anti-war. But 'a war mania gradually gripped the people',[81] and in 1914 the editor of the *British Weekly* came out for conscription, the restriction of enemy aliens and Lloyd George for prime minister. This marked the break between Non-conformist principles and Liberalism.

Another change had also come about in Liberalism. Its high ethical tone had distinctly changed, not just in matters of policy but in the conduct of its leaders. At least it could be said of Campbell-Bannerman that he was 'a man of humanity, principle and courage'.[82] Lloyd George was almost a negation of Gladstonian qualities. His sexual exploits were a public scandal (or joke), and he severely damaged the administration through his involvement in the Marconi scandal. The odour of scandal was hardly dispelled when one beneficiary of the Marconi transaction, Isaacs, shortly afterwards became Lord Chief Justice. Lloyd George roused radical enthusiasm, according to McCallum, by 'sheer class demagogy'[83] a judgement that might well have been shared by disapproving contemporary Non-conformists.

After the war the Liberal Party declined in power. According to A. J. P. Taylor 'the historical Liberal Party committed suicide'[84] on 9 May 1918 when Lloyd George and Asquith came into open parliamentary conflict, dividing the Liberal Party against itself in the Maurice debate, in which Liberals voted either for the prime minister or for the Party leader.[85] The Asquith–Lloyd George conflict within the Party seems to have reduced the effectiveness of the Party in general.[86] The disarray of the Party goes much of the way to explain the disintegration of the Liberal Party in the 1918 Election, there being 136 Liberals and 26 Asquith Liberals returned. The latter joined in opposition with the 57 Labour M.P.s who formed the official opposition.[87]

Social changes were overtaking the Party also. Businessmen and commercial interests were clearly aligned with the Conservative Party, and the landlord–capitalist distinction had disappeared to the point where Liberals could make little or no progress on the basis of the distinction and differences of interests.[88] Liberalism had little to offer at local government level because the local authorities were becoming increasingly the agents of central government policy. There were no more opportunities for the municipal 'socialism' of a Joseph Chamberlain. Who would vote Liberal? It was thought that the 'flappers' would vote Labour as would the young and working class. The Liberal Party, according to Taylor, and as we shall see in more detailed discussion, was ill-suited to becoming a mass party.[89] The Liberals wanted working-class votes, but not working-class participation or control; the Party was linked to the working class by patronage, not participation.

By 1923 a vote for the Liberals would have had the effect of helping the Labour Party to power.[90] The Liberals offered fewer candidates and were short of money.[91] Lloyd George's fund for the Party (mainly raised through the sale of honours) was, in theory, a source of finance, but Lloyd George had personal control of the fund and would only use the money for the Party when it supported free trade, which it did not in 1924. Thus in 1924 the Liberals were only able to contest 122 seats and lost many of them to the Conservatives, and they have never since seemed likely to win power.

The loss of Liberal power and cohesion before the war was, according to Dangerfield, due to the Tories (over House of Lords reform and Ulster), women and the workers. According to Taylor, Liberalism waned because it lacked a strong Party organisation in the country, lacked funds, and above all else because of 'their own disunion'.[92] Internal disunion seems, almost beyond doubt, to have been the main cause of the decline of the Liberal Party, but it may only have been a symptom of the decline of Liberalism. The 'true' causes of the decline of Liberalism may lie outside the party altogether, perhaps in the 1903 Newcastle Conference of the L.R.C. in which the miners accepted the need for a political constitution and when funds were voted for Labour M.P.s. Perhaps the cause lay in the Taff Vale decision which had stiffened the sinews of labour.[93]

An elaboration of Dangerfield's contention that the workers helped bring down the Liberals connects us closely with our main themes. The Minimum Wage Bill of 1912 epitomised Liberal difficulties in developing policies to meet new situations. Dangerfield's words cannot be bettered to describe the events: 'the cautious spirit of the South Wales Miners' Federation had been shamed away, and from now onwards the gospel of the minimum wage was openly preached, not only in Wales, but in every coalfield in Great Britain'.[94]

On 20 February 1912 in the midst of a prolonged industrial crisis, 'The cry for action came swelling up out of South Wales. A general strike was just six days off'.[95] In meeting this crisis the government introduced a Minimum Wage Bill for the miners; as he spoke in the Commons, Asquith wept;[96] 'in the person of Mr. Smillie [Asquith] came face to face with a side of the national life which was altogether beyond his comprehension. Those tears which he shed in the Commons seem more and more like a tragic confession, not merely of personal failure, but of the failure of Liberalism itself'.[97] Asquith's tears did not win the miners. The miners had campaigned for a national minimum wage, 'Five and Two', 5s. per day for men and 2s. for boys.[98] The Act provided for district agreements, with boards to settle the levels of wages, and allowed men to contract out of the terms of the Act. The Labour members in Parliament voted against the Bill. The miners felt that the Act betrayed them.[99]

Few low paid wage-workers were receiving 5s., chairmen of boards were not regarding the average wages of piece-workers in fixing the minimum wage, and some awards entailed 100% work-attendance for the miner to qualify.[100] The principle of district settlement was always seen as an affront to the miners, as it prevented them from negotiating from strength at the national level, and left weak districts without protection. Thus the Liberals did not win back the miners, but further alienated them from the Liberal Party. At the same time they broke with economic principles which were dear to their supporters, for they had taken the unequivocal step of removing one set of wages from the simple operation of the market.

The identity between Liberalism and Non-conformity can no longer be seen to be so obvious or so strong by 1920 as it had been between 1870 and 1900. Of the latter years of the nineteenth century Pelling has said 'Many nonconformists' churches. . .bore an unfortunate resemblance to the Liberal Associations with which they were often closely connected.'[101] There was by 1920 no *prima facie* case for a Methodist to be a Liberal; if he was a radical or reformer he could just as well be a Labour supporter. When we refer to Liberalism in the Durham villages it is essentially to Gladstonian Liberalism, however; a Liberalism of high ethical quality and *laissez-faire* economics. This style of Liberalism survived until the First World War and we will see it expressed locally in attitudes towards education and temperance, and *en passant* towards housing policy, in which public expenditure by local government is rejected, in spite of legislation permitting such expenditure. It was against this Liberalism that Socialists and then the Labour Party struggled; in electoral terms it was a tenacious Liberalism, as Table 1 shows.

In the 1918 Election two out of seven miners' candidates were returned to Parliament for Durham. Galbraith, a miners' leader and the Lib.-Lab. candidate for Spennymoor, was returned also. His constituency did not fall to Labour until 1922. The Barnard Castle constituency went Labour in 1918, was lost by Labour in 1922, regained in the first 1923 Election and lost again in October. Garside noted the surprisingly high Liberal vote in the Durham division as late as 1929.[102] Parts of these three constituencies included parts of our research area.

The Durham division Labour Party was formed in 1918 and in 1919 Durham County Council became the first Labour county council under the chairmanship of Peter Lee. The county council has remained Labour ever since, but without a majority from 1922 to 1925.

We have been describing the national background to events in the villages of the study, with frequent reference to the miners and the Durham miners in particular. In the villages we shall find all that was described at the national level; old Liberal union leaders, friends and colleagues of John Wilson; the younger opponents of these men who set up relatively ephemeral cells in the 'honeycomb of disaffection'; and the unpopular pacifist Socialists who were an embarrassment to the Labour Party. We shall see also that the local miners were

Table 1. *Durham constituencies, 1885–1910*

	% mining vote 1910	1885	1886	1892	1895	1900	1906	1910	1910
N.W. Durham	60+	Lib.	Lib.	Lib.	Lib.	Lib.	Lib.	Lib.	Lib.
Mid-Durham	60+	Lib.-Lab.	Lib.-Lab.	Lib.-Lab.	Lib.-Lab.	Lib.-Lab.	Lib.-Lab.	Lib.-Lab.	Lib.-Lab.[a]
Houghton-le-spring	50+	Lib.-Lab.	C	Lib.	Lib.	Lib.	Lib.	Lib.	Lib.
Chester-le-street	50+	Lib.	Lib.	Lib.	Lib.	Lib.	Lab.	Lab.	Lab.
Bishop Auckland	30+	Lib.	Lib.	Lib.	Lib.	Lib.	Lib.	Lib.[b]	Lib.[c]
S.-E. Durham	30+	Lib.	L.U.	Lib.	L.U.	L.U.	L.U.	Lib.	Lib.
Barnard Castle	30+	Lib.	Lib.	Lib.	Lib.	Lib.	Lab.	Lab.	Lab.
Jarrow	–	–	–	–	–	–	Lib.	Lib.	Lib.[b]
Durham City	10+	C	C	Lib.	Lib.	L.U.	C	U	U
Sunderland { 1	10+	Lib.	Lib.	Lib.	Lib.	C	Lib.	U	Lib.
Sunderland { 2		Lib.	Lib.	Lib.	Lib.	C	Lab.	U	Lab.
South Shields	10+	Lib.	Lib.	Lib.	Lib.	Lib.	Lib.	Lib.	Lib.
Gateshead	10+	Lib.	Lib.	Lib.	Lib.	Lib.	Lib.-Lab.	Lib.	Lib.

Notes. [a] John Wilson's seat.
[b] Lab. bottom of three-cornered contest.
[c] Lab. second of three-cornered contest.
Source. R. Gregory, *The Miners and British Politics, 1906–1914* (O.U.P., 1968), Tables: Appendix B and Appendix to Chapter V.

not converted to Socialism but that the Labour Party won power in the area by compromising with Liberalism, and when they did this the impact of the Socialists declined. We shall see the men striking in 1892 and again in 1912, we shall see them locked out and defeated in 1926. But the central theme will still be the influence of religion on a community and its actions.

RELIGION

While there were quite dramatic changes in the economic and political fields during this period there were also religious changes. The 1851 Census, the evidence of commissions of enquiry into aspects of urban and industrial affairs, and popular surveys at the end of the century all suggested that the great mass of the working class were unchurched. According to Peter Jones the working class was alienated from Christianity because established Christianity buttressed the social order, it taught submission rather than righteous rebellion, future compensation and present charity instead of social justice.[103] Many clergy were supporters of the *status quo* and felt that the poor would always be with them. Others, especially those on the evangelical wing of the Churches, felt, like many of the village Methodists, that, in the words of the 1894 Wesleyan Conference, 'our great work is to save the soul from sin, and if we can accomplish this, all other evils will naturally and necessarily disappear. It is through the individual we must work on society'.[104]

The changes that took place within the Churches are often associated with the rise of Christian Socialism, but it is important to note that whatever the effects of Christian Socialism may have been the actual numbers of Christian Socialists were small. All major denominations and most large cities had a group of Christian Socialists and in Jones' opinion they were drawn from amongst the most talented young Christians and (like other Socialists) they were mainly middle class.[105]

As the above quotation suggests, the charitable and missionary work of the private persons and churches in England was concentrated on the reclamation of the individual from the effects of poverty, intemperance and sin. The change that took place entailed the development of discussion and enquiry into the causes of unemployment, poverty and slums. The timing of this development may be partly connected with the more general questioning of economic and social arrangements associated with the rise of a working-class electorate and a Labour Movement. Nonetheless, it is possible to locate other incentives to question within the Churches. There were certain intellectual blocks to the development of an enquiry into the causes of unemployment and poverty. The main block was the belief in the immutability of economic laws; 'the working classes "might as well try to stop the wind or the tide or to alter day and night" as combine to push up wages' argued an S.P.C.K. pamphlet cited by Inglis.[106] And, of course, 'for the orthodox economy there is, in truth, no social question'.[107] Arnold Toynbee, Alfred Marshall, Henry George, and F. D. Maurice helped to change this situation. Marshall especially made it intellectually respectable to question Liberal economics and to introduce ethical factors into economic discussion. As Inglis observed, it did not much matter whether Marshall was actually read or not, his existence was in itself reassuring for those who wanted to question orthodox economics.[108] Such was the development of the argument about economic relations that at the end of the century 'It now required as much pure faith in dogma to defend the old view as, not long before, it had taken to oppose it.'[109]

T. H. Green, the mentor of the leaders of the C.S.U. (to be discussed below) had introduced into British thought a Hegelian notion of the positive role of the state which contrasted with orthodox *laissez-faire* views. Green's influence during the short period at Oxford, before his early death, was far reaching for he influenced not only Toynbee and others but a whole generation of university-educated men who were to become public servants of a kind quite different from those who served the *laissez-faire* state.

F. D. Maurice inspired many Christian Socialists at the end of the century. Maurice himself was active in the mid-century but the publication of his *Life* and letters in the mid-1880s enabled men to take a renewed interest in his ideas at a time when more general discussions of political and economic affairs were opening up. Maurice and his associates asserted that the Christian Gospel applied to the whole of human society, not to the individual alone. He provided a reasoned, theological basis for challenging the evangelical tradition and for asserting that brotherhood could replace competition in industry and society. Again, as with Marshall, it may not have mattered so much whether one had read Maurice as whether one was encouraged by knowing that it was theologically sound to challenge orthodox political economy.

Christian Socialism was not, however, ideas alone. It did take on institutional forms. Perhaps the two best known were the Guild of St Matthew and the Christian Social Union. The guild was founded in 1877 by Stewart Headlam, a curate in Bethnal Green and a former student of Maurice. The guild was dissolved in 1909 after a period of decline. At its peak in 1895 the guild had 99 clerical members and 265 laymen.[110] The aims of the guild, while never including Socialism specifically, included universal suffrage, abolition of the House of Lords, progressive income tax and land nationalisation. As can be seen from this last point the guild was deeply influenced by the work of Henry George. Headlam was the leading light of the guild, a member of the Fabian Society on the radical wing of the Liberal Party.

The C.S.U. was founded in 1889. Its intellectual leader was Charles Gore. The Union's activities centred on Oxford and London and created a substantial literature of which the most famous work was *Lux Mundi*. Gore and others attempted, in this work, to show that secular knowledge had much to offer to the Christian understanding of the world. Most of the Oxford members were clerics or undergraduates destined for Holy Orders. Branches discussed social and economic reform and attempted to influence local affairs by, for example, producing lists of good and bad employers and suggesting that Christians should not buy goods produced or sold by the latter. The Union was in fact divided between gradualist reformers and those who believed in policies such as nationalisation. The first president of the Union was Bishop Westcott-of Durham whose intervention in the 1893 County Coal Dispute led to a settlement. Between 1889 and 1913, according to Inglis, 16 out of 53 episcopal appointments went to members of the C.S.U.[111] But the Union was even more important than this because it introduced into church debates a new kind of concern with social matters and its arguments and debates bridged the gap between the old social and economic orthodoxies and the newer ways of thought. Many young men, lay and clerical, could also claim to have been influenced by membership of the Union or through reading its publications.

The Wesleyans and the Congregationalists were, as a whole, committed no less deeply than the Church of England to maintaining private property.[112] Within Non-conformity there was a strong evangelical element which was hostile to radical social views. Some elements of this wing found themselves actually 'battling with socialism, in its violent as well as in its more moderate and constitutional form'.[113] This kind of rejection arose not so much from political Conservatism as from a strong belief in the separation of the spiritual and the mundane and in the priority of the spiritual. Although the explicit notion may have been muted this sort of outlook is also tinged with the belief that the poor deserved their poverty and that the well-to-do have probably earned their blessings. In such matters it is difficult to see any difference between middle-class Non-conformist evangelicalism and Anglican evangelicalism. Both were soaked in a 'morbid fear of personal sin'.[114]

The Non-conformists seem to have been under-represented in Christian Socialism. This may in part be due to the difficulties of organising groups within, say, the connexional structure of Methodism (see Glossary). Non-conformists had no easily-made institutional basis from which to operate. Individual names stand out amongst Non-conformists and there were groups of Christian Socialists operating within the established denominations.

The Baptists, according to Jones, were the most conservative and they founded a Non-conformist Anti-Socialist Union in 1909 to 'exterminate socialism from Church and State'.[115] The Unitarians, whilst having a democratic history and a radical intellectual background, including Joseph Priestley, Mary Wollstonecraft and R. W. Emerson, nonetheless included many highly successful businessmen in their ranks. On the whole Unitarians sought respectability. But the Baptists produced John Clifford, and the Unitarians, Philip Wicksteed. Wicksteed, the founder of the London Labour Church, possessed a considerable intellect and was very influential in the Fabians. His own development included a conversion to marginal utility theory from Georgist economics.

The most famous Congregational Socialist was R. J. Campbell, author of *The New Theology*. Campbell was an exponent of Immanentalism: the belief that God was in every man and could be discovered and expressed in every one of one's fellow men. This was plainly a politically most radical doctrine to preach in an unequal society. Campbell was converted to the Labour cause after attacking workers in a sermon in 1904 (this stimulated a considerable correspondence from miners in the *D.C.*). He became minister of the City Temple in London in 1904 and drew crowds of 7,000 to hear him preach. Something of a Campbell cult grew up and he received the sort of adulation later to be given to film stars. He served on the Executive of the Fabian Society from 1908 to 1909 and he created the Progressive League in 1907 and the *Christian Commonwealth* in 1908. For Campbell the task was to overcome the other-worldliness of established Christianity and to commence the job of social reconstruction. He later renounced *The New Theology* and was received back into the church of his birth, the Church of England.

The Congregationalists as a whole took an early interest in social affairs, setting up a fund for the miners in 1893 and asserting the right of humanity over property in economic affairs. Later in the century the Congregational Union took a more subdued interest in social affairs, although individual Congregationalists remained active in politics.

The Quakers also had an active Socialist group, the Socialist Quaker Society. Jones reports what is for us a highly pertinent observation in Quaker Socialism made by Stephen Thorne, the last secretary of the society: 'Thorne sees the inner dynamic of Quaker socialism to be a status conflict between a group of young, unestablished, intellectual radicals of modest means and the great, sturdy Quaker business families, deep-rooted, socially conservative, pious, and rich.'[116] Transposed to a working-class and small shop-keepers' society this describes the situation of the small group of Christian Socialists in our villages.

What then of Methodism? 'Considering its size the Methodist Church produced few Christian Socialists.'[117] This may at first sight seem especially odd given the conventional association between Methodism and working-class movements. But the collectivism of the working classes, expressed in trade unions and the co-operative movement was not a feature of Methodist teaching. The extent to which this can be solely attributed to evangelical concern with the individual is a question which this book explores further. Methodists tried to observe a 'no politics' rule; this did not mean that men should have no political views but that the expression of these views should not create strife in the life of the Church. Throughout the nineteenth century the conferences of all Methodist denominations seem to have been taxed by the problem of political involvement. One problem was that in pursuing political goals the Methodist would have to mix in impure company, he might even become a full-time political worker, or at least be seriously distracted from spiritual discipline and evangelistic activities.[118]

What the no politics rule usually meant was that Conservative or Liberal views could be expressed in sermons or speeches without being identified as 'political', whereas radical or Socialist ideas were seen as political and disruptive. In other words, political dissent, not politics, was excluded from Methodism. The main focus of Methodist political attention was on issues that had a clear ethical aspect; it was this ethical concern which we have seen as linking Methodism and Liberalism so closely. A popular Methodist slogan was that which was morally wrong could not be politically right. This is obviously a sentiment open to widely differing interpretations. On the one hand it could be a basis for opposing political compromises with the brewers, but on the other it could provide a basis for driving Parnell from public office.

There were two important Christian Socialists in Methodism, Hugh Price Hughes and S. E. Keeble. The contrast between them epitomises the range of views that have been called 'Christian Socialist'. Hugh Price Hughes was a compelling preacher and the leader of the so-called 'Forward Movement' in Wesleyan Methodism. He was regarded as a 'fire-brand' and he created controversy within Methodism, especially in the columns of the *Methodist Times* which he founded in 1885 as 'a journal of religious and social movement'. Hughes preached egalitarianism and the elimination of exploitation and degradation in society; he also worked to reduce the middle-class image of Methodism. A man who asserted to middle-class congregations that 'Jesus Christ was essentially a man of the People – a working man' was rather obviously breaking with the tradition of Methodist social comment.[119] But Hughes' concerns remained profoundly ethical, 'How do you expect virtue and morality from people living in one room?' he asked in commenting on the neglect of the London poor.[120] Hughes became president of the Wesleyan conference in 1898; he was never a Socialist in the sense of espousing any kind of Socialist organisation, either religious or secular. Keeble's judgement of Hughes seems sound, he 'had reactionary tendencies, which come out with fearful force at times. But on the whole, he has been the leader of the progressive forces in Methodism and Nonconformity'.[121]

There were, of course, other Methodist Socialists. The Reverend Peter Thompson worked among the London poor and was a founder member of the Anti-Sweating League; D. B. Foster, a Wesleyan preacher, gave up a comfortable life in Leeds to live on a workman's wage and he became secretary of the Leeds L.R.C. in 1902. Foster is of special interest to us because he was associated with the development of the Leeds Brotherhood Church which influenced a few of our village Christian Socialists in the First World War.

But it is S. E. Keeble who enables us to understand the lack of Socialism in men like Hughes. For a while Hughes 'used the vocabulary of the socialist and the policy of the social-mission worker', Keeble rejected the social work and charitable approach and advocated fundamental social change.[122] He split with Hughes because of this difference in approach and he stopped writing for the *Methodist Times.* His own paper, the *Methodist Weekly*, died as a result of its opposition to the Anglo-Boer War. Although Keeble was himself active in practical ways his greatest influence was exercised through his published work; *Christian Daydreams* in 1889 and *The Social Teaching of the Bible* (1909) being especially influential. In these works he displayed a scholarship in the fields of economics and politics that was lacking in many other authors. Keeble was a staunch Labour Party man, but he opposed both Ramsay MacDonald and his electoral 'arrangements' with the Liberals.

What did the Methodist Socialists achieve? They did not convert the Methodist Church to any brand of Socialism. They did force Methodists and the Methodist Church to be more interested in the causes of human degradation and problems of social welfare policy. The advances in these respects were halting and entirely within a Liberal framework. The Churches still accepted a conservative interpretation of Maurice's dictum that it was the Church's mission to be 'the healer of all privations and diseases, the bond of all classes, the instrument for reforming abuses, the admonisher of the rich, the friend of the poor, the asserter of that humanity which Christ bears'.[123] Classes were to be bonded in the Church, not divided. A Congregationalist caricatured this ambiguity in a letter to the *British Weekly*; 'when two countries are at war, is it a friendly act on the part of a neighbouring power to send a vote of sympathy to both sides?'[124] *Christian* Socialism as distinct from Socialism tended to deny that there was a war.

The most important non-Anglican attempt to organise Christian Socialists was the Christian Socialist League which lasted from 1894 to 1898, when it was succeeded by the Christian Social Brotherhood. The leader of the League was John Clifford, a Baptist, who was like many leaders of Christian Socialism a man of considerable intellectual power. The league was a collection of individuals; it set up no journal but provided a list of lecturers who were available to the branches which were set up in London and the provinces. Clifford was a Fabian and the author of two Fabian Tracts. The vice-president of the league was Bruce Wallace who was concerned with the establishment of industrial cooperative and the creation of a 'cooperative commonwealth' to shame capitalism into surrender. He was also involved with J. C. Kenworthy and the Brotherhood Church.

Leading league members were Fabians and not what Jones calls 'full economic Socialists', who would demand fundamental changes in the system of property-holding and the creation of an entirely new and non-competitive social order. League members were active in local affairs like school-board elections. Clifford later organised the passive resistance campaign against the 1902 Education Act. Gore and the C.S.U. opposed Clifford on this issue so Christian Socialists were publicly divided on an important social issue. Some league supporters and members became M.P.s; Percy Alden, for example, and Dr Charles Leak who, as a Liberal, defeated Grayson at Colne Valley in 1910. The league was also internationalist and included pacifists and people interested in the new town movement. It was thus a mixed body of reformers, Liberals and Fabians united in their desire to generate discussion of social questions.[125] Many league members transferred to the Christian Social Brotherhood, which lasted until about 1903; its aims were the same as those of the league and it took over a journal called *Brotherhood*.

The Free Church Socialist League was an entirely Non-conformist Socialist group which arose from a meeting called during the Free Church Council Conference in 1909. The league does not seem to have made a very great impact on the development of Socialism but it is interesting to us because of its membership. Philip Snowden, the Reverend W. Younger and the Reverend J. E. Rattenbury were all Methodists. Younger was a P.M. and an ex-Northumberland miner, and Snowden was a Methodist weaver's son. The purpose of the league in the words of its president, Herbert Dunnico (M.P. for Consett, 1922–31), 'is to take some part in the destruction of the present commercial and industrial system which is based upon greed, lust and unholy rivalry, and the creation of a better system based upon equality, brotherhood and co-operation'.[126] But, he added, the league was mainly 'an ethical and educational rather than a political organisation'.[127]

Philip Snowden, who joined the I.L.P. in 1895, was influenced by Henry George. He had a fine oratorical skill and later became a Labour chancellor of the exchequer and Lord Privy Seal. He wrote a pamphlet *The Christ That Is to Be* in 1905 which typified a major emphasis of the Christian Socialists – the person of Christ.

Not only Clifford and Campbell but our village Christian Socialists, too, concentrated on the personality, the humanity, of Jesus. To them He was the new man, He was what man might be and He was within every man. But men did not live in circumstances which enabled Christ to be expressed in their lives, so the Christian Socialist aimed to change social circumstances to enable men to become more Christ-like. This kind of emphasis also enabled its advocates to avoid more conventional but nonetheless theologically important and difficult questions about the divinity of Christ. The expression 'applied Christianity' was common among Christian Socialists and was often heard in the course of the present research. Christian Socialists believed that there was work to be done in social and economic affairs. An essential part of their message was the idea of the brotherhood of man; this was an important source of their internationalism and pacifism.

We have seen that the Socialism of the Christian Socialists was in many respects an extension of Liberal radicalism. According to the Christian Socialists the state could and should use its power in a positive way. This was an idea which had been developed by T. H. Green and his followers and which was embodied in Fabianism and Lloyd George Liberalism. The techniques of the Christian Socialists were essentially parliamentary and in some cases (Hugh Price Hughes, for example) almost non-political, working through the mission or settlement. There was also a strong element of individual, personal regeneration in the goals of the Christian Socialists.

Christian *Socialism* was a word chosen by its exponents to mean various things, but it never entailed the organisation of a class to overthrow the economic and political system. To this extent *Socialism* is a misnomer.

The Christian Socialists were a minority, active all over the country, whose political impact it is difficult to evaluate except to say that their direct effect was small. The Churches continued much as before, but

61

insofar as they took 'social questions' more seriously they may be said to be responding to Christian Socialist influences. Christian Socialists were prominent in the opposition to the Anglo-Boer War and amongst the pacifists in the First World War. The main efforts of the Christian Socialists seem to have been to convert Christians to Socialism rather than Socialists to Christianity. In direct political terms it was therefore probably the I.L.P. and Fabians who gained most from the Christian Socialists, and this debt to Christian Socialism is still evident in the high moral tone of both the (small) I.L.P. and the Fabian Society.

It would be a mistake to think of the religion or the Churches in this period as organisationally and theologically monolithic structures. New debates were being forced upon the Churches, considerable internal tensions were created by this and the Churches themselves were worried by what they saw as their small and declining grip on the mass of the population.

Perhaps the main failure of Christian Socialism was that it made no great inroads, in any organised way, into the working class. They were less patronising than other members of the middle class; they stressed the dignity of labour and the humanity of the working man. But they never broke the class barrier on any scale, although the same could be said for every other denomination, the Socialists, Marxists, even the agnostics and atheists.

In the North of England the Christian Socialists, the I.L.P. and the Syndicalists were all active. The Reverend J. Stitt Wilson, an American supporter of Eugene V. Debs, had received 50,000 votes as the Socialist candidate for the governorship of California. He addressed mass meetings of 4,000 people in Bradford in 1900 and then during 1907–8 he toured the country, including Glasgow, Halifax, Leeds and South Wales in his itinerary. His campaign was 'intended to be a straight attack upon the capitalist system, as unChristian, unjust and cruel. . .'[128]

The Reverend W. E. Moll arrived in Newcastle in 1893 and soon became identified with radical working-class movements in the area. He also trained four curates who were to become important Christian Socialists in their own right – P. E. T. Widdington, Paul Stacy, Conrad Noel and C. L. Manson.[129] It is difficult to tell directly how important Moll was in the villages. He certainly helped to organise the I.L.P. in the locality and some local Methodists went to hear him preach, from time to time. Moll was not a Non-conformist but a High Church Sacramentalist. He refused to accept the idea that poverty was a result of God's will. He attacked the conventional 'gospel of tea meetings and mission halls', but he believed that the state was a sacred organism which could act in a Christian way for the benefit of the poor. He also believed in disestablishment (which may have compensated for his

Anglicanism amongst his Non-conformist followers). His theological position is summed up in these words to the English Church Union in 1885: 'As a Catholic I believe that the Church is the Body of Christ, filled with this Spirit, bound to do the works which He did on earth. . . As a Catholic I believe that the Church is the Kingdom of Heaven on earth – an organisational society for the promotion of righteousness and freedom and truth among nations.'[130]

Moll, in Jones' opinion, was less of a 'middle class socialist' than many others.[131] He was an egalitarian who helped workers when they were on strike and who opposed the Anglo-Boer War. One can find echoes of his political views in the villages; although his personal influence is debatable, it is most probable that he was well-known by the Christian Socialists there.

With the exceptions already mentioned Methodism does not seem to have been prominent in the production of Christian Socialists. It is the burden of much of our discussion that in order to understand the political effects of Methodism one needs to understand the Methodist–Non-conformist–Liberal linkage in individual and ethical issues. To this extent our study is a microcosmic study of a national phenomenon. Nevertheless there were radicals within Methodism, even though they were a minority. Their main achievement was in spreading the 'social gospel' and thereby drawing attention to issues arising from economic industrial and political developments, rather than issues arising from the shortcoming of individual personalities only. In doing this they tried to make the extension of state intervention in social and economic affairs more acceptable. The P.M. Church became more sympathetic to the Labour cause in the early years of the twentieth century, but there was a tendency to stress industrial reconciliation and compromise, as we shall see, and to avoid any incitements to conflict.[132]

Pickering has suggested that:

> When a church officially, or by implication, identifies itself with a political party which is also supported by the vast majority of its members the inner cohesion of the church becomes all the more strong. This is to be welcomed from the church's point of view just so long as the politico-economic situation remains fairly static. When, however, it is open to rapid change the pursuance of such a policy may mean the extinction of the religious group.[133]

There is, historically, no doubt that Methodism, in all its forms, was closely associated with Liberalism. Shared political outlooks helped to unite the Methodists. But the growth of Labour politics and the adherence of working-class Methodists to the Labour cause might be seen, if Pickering is correct, as a contributory factor in the decline of Methodist influence from the First World War onwards.

2 The Deerness Valley

The Deerness Valley lies a little south of west of Durham City; it extends from two miles to nine miles from the city. Open rolling hills rise 850 feet above sea level from the valley bottom which itself rises from 300 feet at the east to 600 feet in the west. Most of the valley is used for cattle- and sheep-grazing. Three villages lie on the road along the valley; Ushaw Moor, Esh Winning and Waterhouses. Westward from Esh Winning runs the Cornsay Valley, 1¼ miles up which is Cornsay Colliery. Between these two villages is the hamlet of Hamsteels and above Hamsteels, on a bleak fell top, is Quebec, so named because the land upon which the village was built was enclosed in the year of Wolfe's victory at Quebec. Quebec and Hamsteels, though ¼ mile apart, are treated as one village by local residents. The names are used interchangeably and this practice is followed in the present work. Above Esh Winning, in the main valley, are the villages of Waterhouses, Hamilton Row and East Hedleyhope (see map).

The railway from Durham to Waterhouses opened in 1857 and closed in 1963, although passenger services were only provided from the late nineteenth century until 1947. A metalled road from Esh Winning to Waterhouses was built as a local public works project in the 1920s at which time the valley received its first motor-bus service. Durham City was of minor importance to the villages until the building of the road from the villages to the city. Crook, to the south-west, was the source of services and supplies to the villages.

Drift mining commenced in Esh Winning and Waterhouses in the 1850s but there was little house-building in the area until the 1860s. Until then sufficient miners had been able to walk to work from a few local hamlets. The coming of the railway led to the expansion of the pits. The main pits in the valley bottom were developed by Pease and Partners, Cornsay Colliery by Ferens and Love, Quebec–Hamsteels by Johnson and Reay. The Pease pits were 'model villages' offering housing of a high standard for the period; similar developments occurred in the Derbyshire Coalfield.[1]

At Waterhouses the company had built 151 houses by 1874, having

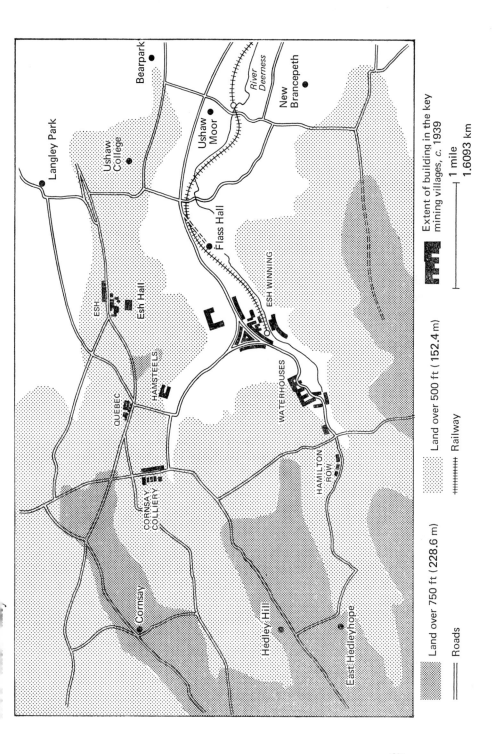

Land over 750 ft (228.6 m)

Roads

Land over 500 ft (152.4 m)

Railway

Extent of building in the key mining villages, *c.* 1939

1 mile

1.6093 km

built a schoolroom ten years previously. A few rows of private houses
were built south of the railway. The village took on its final physical
shape, with school, Miners' Institute, etc., between 1870 and 1890. The
coal winnings were in drifts running into the hillside to the north and
south of the village.

A shaft was sunk in Esh Winning in 1859 and the company built
houses during the 1860s in a square around the pit-head. A further
80 houses and a school were built with the colliery's expansion in the
1890s. In the last three decades of the nineteenth century and the
first of the twentieth there were a series of red-brick private-housing
developments radiating from the market square and to the south of the
village.

Hamsteels Colliery was opened in 1867 and Cornsay in 1869. Hamsteels had a shaft but both collieries were groups of drift mines. The
colliery companies provided housing in both villages. These two
collieries used three-quarters and two-thirds of their coal output respectively for coking. Bricks were produced at Cornsay and Lymington
Terrace (Esh Winning).

The population of the valley grew with the coal and coke trade
from the 1860s onwards and by 1901 over three-quarters of all employed men were working in the industry. The main source of population increase was immigration; from Weardale, Lincolnshire (where
Pease and Partners had a recruiting office), and indirectly from Ireland.
The scope of the migration can be shown by the fact that in June 1860
the Witton Park P.M. anniversary celebration included an afternoon
sermon in Welsh.[2] In 1871 unemployed workers were being encouraged
to move from Deptford, in south-east London, to the Willington pit
and in June 1871 Pease and Partners opened a recruiting office in the
East End of London.[3]

Durham County gained 130,000 persons between 1851 and 1871.
From 1875 to 1887 the labour force remained stable. From 1881 to 1911
there was a net emigration of about 70,000.[4] These population movements in and out of the county take no account of internal migration.
The decline of the lead industry in Weardale, in the west of the county,
provided a labour supply for the coal-mines. Many Weardale and
Teesdale names (Nattress, Vipond, Hewitson, etc.) are to be found in
the Deerness Valley. In fact Durham seems to have experienced a continuous eastward migration; the miners of mid-west Durham have most
recently been migrating to the east-coast pits. Some of the Deerness
Methodists were interviewed on the east coast. Mining villages also
had a high rate of natural increase of population. Irish Catholics seem
to have been especially attracted to Ushaw Moor with its nearby
seminary and Catholic estates belonging to both Ushaw College and

an old Catholic land-owning family. Local workers may have been drawn from agricultural work; most old local families can trace themselves back to rural occupation. Many women today report being 'in service' or 'helping out' on farms. Brinley Thomas has suggested that the 1870s saw a rapid increase in migration from the land in South Wales. The Education Act prevented children from working on the land while non-rural occupations offered adults better wages and shorter hours.[5] *The Victoria County History of Durham* records a drop in agricultural labour from 10,004 in 1851 to 5,049 in 1901.[6] A number of adult men from among the 5,000 lost agricultural workers entered mining.

Populations for the four villages – Esh Winning, Cornsay Colliery, Waterhouses and Quebec–Hamsteels – are not readily calculable. The registrar-general's *Reports of the Census of England and Wales 1871–1961* give data based on administrative areas which include the villages. Quebec–Hamsteels is in the civil parish of Esh; Waterhouses and Esh Winning are in Brandon and Byshottles which also includes the three major villages of Brandon, Sleetburn (New Brancepeth) and Ushaw Moor. Population changes take place within those areas as pits are laid in or opened out, but this may not be distinguishable in a large population or may be compensated for elsewhere in the area. Thus some known pit closures do not affect the census populations. Compounding this problem is the fact of the administration boundaries cutting through the villages – Cornsay and Esh Winning both having boundaries running along their respective main streets.

The most reliable and for us the most relevant indications of village populations can be based on the colliery employment figures. In the first half of this century about three-quarters of all employed men were in the coal trade; latterly the proportion has been falling from one-half.[7] The age structure of the earliest population is of some interest but it cannot be ascertained from published sources. We might sensibly expect to find a high proportion of unmarried migrant men.[8] This expectation is supported by the continual reference to lodgers made by older people recalling the earlier days. Pease and Partners also required their tenants to accept single men as lodgers, as a condition of tenancy.

The Census *Reports* give us the proportion of the population employed in mining and the Home Office *Reports* the numbers actually employed in each pit. Populations estimated in this way are as shown in Table 2.

Thus the population of the whole district was a little over 9,000 at the turn of the century and by the 1920s it had declined to about 7,000. The decline accelerated in the 1930s. During the war, with Cornsay no

Table 2: *Population of the villages, 1895–1951 (totals to nearest 100)*

	1895	1901	1911	1921	1931	1951
Esh Winning	2,090	2,400	3,100	2,500	b	3,400
Waterhouses	1,520	1,900	1,800	1,800	2,200	1,900
Cornsay Colliery	a	2,100	2,200	2,000?	b	b
Quebec–Hamsteels	a	2,700	2,600	1,500	b	b
Total	a	9,100	11,700	7,800	6,100c	6,100c

Notes. a not known; b pit closed; c estimated figure.
(R. Taylor, in 'Implications of Migration for the Durham Coalfield' (Ph.D. thesis, University of Durham, 1966), pp. 42 and 46, has estimated the 1965 population as: Esh Winning 2,979; Waterhouses 1,500.)

longer drawing coal and Esh Wining re-opened, the population probably rose a little to around 6,000. By the late 1960s all pits were closed, only Esh Winning remained as a going concern until 1969, with a population of around 3,000, of whom only a handful were employed in mining. The other villages had probably less than 1,000 inhabitants each.

The dramatic changes that came about in the valley do not seem to have created any conflicts between the original inhabitants and the incomers (but the former were completely outnumbered anyhow). Land-owners like Lord Boyne and Ushaw College received royalties for the coal mined under their land and wayleaves for the coal carried across their land. The Smythes of Flass Hall built terraced houses in Esh Winning which they were able to rent to shopkeepers and minor professionals in the expanding village. Meanwhile farming continued in the valley, and continues today.

If the land-owners had experienced any major clash of interest with the coal-owners they would have been relatively unable to express them, or to organise to pursue their interests, as the coal-owners – as we saw above – spoke for the land-owners, being themselves amongst the largest land-owners in the county (see p. 259, n. 88). The dominance of the mines is shown by the local elections of 1877, when the nominations were as follows: two farmers, three mining engineers, one colliery manager, a colliery-owner, a tradesman and a gentleman.[9] The result was the election of the owner, the manager, three engineers and the gentleman.

RELIGIOUS AFFILIATIONS OF THE POPULATION (see Appendix III)
The data on religious affiliation in the Deerness Valley are incomplete and difficult to interpret. The P.M.s have left the most comprehensive

and useful records. None of the present argument depends on statistical calculations. It can be argued, furthermore, that membership itself is a problematic concept, there being sociologically significantly different ways of 'belonging' to a religious group, that do not coincide with the categories used in record-keeping. Pickering has suggested that beyond the usual categories of membership there are 'irregular' members, those who attend perhaps once a year for festivals. Beyond these again there are men and women who were members or active participants who have lapsed but remain sympathetic and attend the chapels for the community's *rites de passage*.[10] I would also suggest that there are sympathisers who never were active, but whose parents or children were Methodists. Thus whilst it can be said that a local preacher was certainly a Methodist, and a Roman Catholic not a Methodist, there is an indeterminate area of membership and adherence. There is a penumbra of membership which, as will be seen, is drawn into activity at certain times and whose sympathy can be relied upon. It may be that in many subtle ways the Methodist culture is upheld in the penumbral areas as much as in the active centre of chapel life.

Nevertheless it is important to have an overall picture of 'membership' to indicate the support given to religious institutions which were openly influential in the history and biographies of the Deerness Valley.

Various runs of figures for membership, adherence and Sunday school attendance are available. These figures raise problems in interpretation which it is not easy to solve. For example, the difference between a member and an adherent (see Glossary) is only partially recognised by local Methodists and we have no way of telling what (if any) distinction was in use at any time in the records. We do not know how the figures for adherence were arrived at in any case (a list, a count of chapel attenders, and if the latter, was there any double counting?), and there also seems to be a tendency to record the same total as for the previous year, for years on end.

One point emerges clearly. There are fluctuations[11] in Methodist numbers which coincide with local economic circumstances. (Similar features can be seen in the expansion of the Mechanics' Institutes which grew from 1860 onwards.[12]) For example, in 1905 the minister enters in the *Chapel Schedule of the Waterhouse Station* under 'Reasons for decline' the single phrase 'Industrial depression in the valley'. In 1921 in addition to declining numbers the Minister reports 'heavy financial loss due to strike' and in 1923 conditions are reported as difficult. In 1928 the minister reports:

> Not prosperous due to unemployment. This reacts acutely on Finances of Circuit. This also makes for spiritual depression.

Spiritual inspirations are difficult to generate under these conditions [*sic*]. People are leaving for employment elsewhere. We
can not encourage them to remain in these circumstances.

Economic depression does not necessarily stop people being Methodists
but it does make them move away in search of work.

In the 1860s there were a handful of Methodists in the villages,
meeting in private houses and colliery lofts. By 1900 there were over
1,000 P.M.s in the villages. The Primitives, according to the records
and to interviews, always seemed to have outnumbered the Wesleyans
by two to one. By 1911 there seem to have been over 1,800 Methodists
(P.M.s and W.M.s) in the villages. This total was maintained until the
early 1920s. By 1932 the total was a little below 800 and by 1946, 200.
The Sunday schools suffered a more gradual decline, having about 500
regular attenders in the 1890s, falling to about 200 in 1921.

An alternative way of finding how many villagers were Methodists
was adopted in this research. It will be seen in Chapter 5 that this is
perhaps a more relevant way of estimating *communal* membership.
With the aid of electoral registers, discussions on the families who
lived in the colliery rows were held with some of the older women.
Some of the women were able to remember all of the inhabitants in
streets, although not the names of lodgers. From this an estimate
could be made of the people who were *regarded* as Methodists, and
the number of households in which at least one member was so
regarded. The year 1919, which was chosen as 'the year the men came
home from the war', was clearly remembered and fell near the centre
of our period. About 65% of all households had at least one member
who was regarded as belonging to a church, with Roman Catholic and
Church of England having about 10% each, Baptists 4% and no religion
35%. About 40% of all households were regarded as 'Methodist' households. There was some variation between villages; Waterhouses appeared to be the most Methodist, Quebec the least. For Waterhouse
the figure is 43% of households, Esh Winning 38%, Quebec 32%. No
reason for these variations can be found unless Pease and Partners
deliberately favoured Methodists in their recruiting of workers. It
is alleged in the district that this was the company's policy.

Chapel building and closure, like membership figures, seem to
follow the coal-trade. In the whole valley 24 chapels have been built
since 1870: 9 were built between 1870 and 1880 (7 between 1870 and
1875); 5 from 1881 to 1890; 4 from 1896 to 1900. In 1968 11 chapels
were still open (3 out of 9 in the area of this study): 7 closures occurred
between 1920 and 1940 and the remainder from 1955 to 1968. In 1932
the Esh Winning P.M.s and W.M.s united to form one society and in
1935 the present Brandon and Deerness Valley circuit (see Glossary)

was formed. The Esh Winning society gained from the Quebec closures.

The meaning of 'membership' in the Roman Catholic Church and the Church of England is even more difficult to put in simple terms than for Methodism. A baptised person may formally be a member, but not actively so. No Catholic is removed from Church membership unless he formally and publicly renounces his faith. There is a local factor complicating the Catholic figures for the Deerness Valley also. Published figures include the population of Ushaw College seminary and its servants, thus increasing the total Catholic population in a way that makes it almost impossible to discover the proportion of Catholics in the mining population alone. The valley from East Hedleyhope to Ushaw College had a population of about 1,800 Catholics in 1892, rising to 2,600 at the turn of the century and falling to below 1,500 in the 1930s.

The Church of England was the latecomer to the valley. The Waterhouses end of the valley was in Brancepeth parish, the parish church thus being some six miles away, over the hills to the south of the valley. In January 1860 there had been a meeting in Newcastle to discuss the spiritual poverty of the mining districts. This meeting was attended by the bishop of Durham and a number of aristocrats. The meeting, presided over by the Earl Grey, expressed concern at the lack of clergy and the fact that Durham had a new population untouched by the existing clergy and parochial system. In Durham there were 9,000 persons per parish, compared with 5,400 in Manchester. The meeting noted that the existing parishes, which were suitable for agricultural communities, were not suitable for collieries. They noted, too, that the colliery districts were neglected even in comparison with manufacturing areas. The colliers, they asserted, received no ministration, save that of the police.[13] The coal-owners felt that as they paid tithes and royalties to the church commissioners they should not be expected to make large additional donations to meet the needs of the Church in the county.

But no immediate plan of action emerged from this expression of concern save for the establishment of The Durham Diocesan Society for the Employment of Additional Clergy. There was some division in the meeting on whether the church commissioners, who took a lot of money from Durham in the form of coal royalties (about £50,000 a year in 1854), were failing in their duty to promote and finance the Anglican cause in the diocese. An amendment to the Acts relating to

71

the ecclesiastical commissioners passed in August 1860 enabled the diocese to go ahead with a programme of church building and the creation of new parishes. Fifty parishes were created between 1871 and 1881. All were agreed at the 1860 meeting that the church commissioners, the employers, clergy and the laity needed to bring the 'restraints and consolations' of religion to 'those masses earning large wages, [and thus] enabled to indulge their sensualities to any excess'.[14] Perhaps in part due to the delays caused by the debates with the church commissioners, Anglican churches were another fourteen years coming to the valley. St John the Baptist was consecrated in Hamsteels in 1874 and St Paul's Waterhouses in 1879. By these dates the Methodists were firmly established in the valley.

The coal-owners and businessmen of the diocese seemed to have remained reluctant to contribute to the funds of the Church, a factor that will be seen to contrast sharply with the behaviour of the Nonconformist owners towards the chapels. In 1884 Archdeacon Watkins of Durham had to admonish the laity:

> How can Churchmen read their Bibles, and say their prayers, and then spend in luxury, or even save, money won by the brow-sweat and life risk of men who in God's sight are equal to themselves, while these brothers for whom Christ died are practically left without Sacrament, or Minister, or Church?[15]

The only Anglican figures to survive are to be found in ten numbers of the Hamsteels *Parish Magazine* which were found for various dates between 1913 and 1926. The number of communicants at St John's only exceeded 100 in 1915. If we allow for multiple counting of members who communicated more than once a month we would expect the active membership to be less than 100 in that year. Throughout the 1913–26 period communicants averaged about 50. We know, however, that the vicar after the First World War (the Revd E. C. Rust) was not likely to encourage the participation of the miners in the life of his church (see Chapter 8). Thus our figures may under-represent those miners who felt themselves to be Anglicans, but who nonetheless did not attend St John's. But by any method of accounting the Church of England was not numerically strong.

THE OCCUPATIONAL STRUCTURE OF THE POPULATION

The villages were built so that coal could be mined. It is not surprising, therefore, that mining dominated the occupation structures of the villages. The villages of the Deerness Valley were one industry villages throughout their history. The decennial censuses and the registration of births and deaths suggests that nearly 80% of the working population was engaged in mining until the 1920s. 70% of these men were face-workers. By 1930 probably only about 65% were in coal-mining; by 1960, 30% (and many of these were not working in their home pits).[16]

A complete list of shops and shopkeepers in Esh Winning *circa* 1908 was obtained. This showed that 41 shops between them employed 8 workers in addition to the owners and their immediate families: 5 of these 8 workers were accounted for by 2 businesses, another 3 by 3 businesses. In addition to the 41 shops there was a Co-operative store which employed 19 workers. In Waterhouses the store employed about 50 workers. The Co-ops. thus provided a relatively important (because it was the second largest) alternative source of employment – but it was a small source in absolute terms.

THE OCCUPATION OF METHODISTS

Given the very high proportion of miners in the villages it would be reasonable to assume that miners would have been well represented among the Methodists. Nevertheless one cannot assume *a priori* that the Methodists exactly reflect the general occupational structure.

We have no exact record of the occupations of Methodists. Marriage registers do not include all the Methodists in the villages, because they exclude those not marrying and those marrying either in other churches or other villages; nor are all those married in the chapels Methodists. Records which include occupations are limited to legal documents and only record those directly involved in the transaction. Thus our records are of local preachers, trustees, Sunday school teachers and official representatives to such bodies as quarterly meeting and synod – the group usually referred to, sometimes quite loosely, as the leaders (see Glossary). It is possible to gain no more than an impression by reading the available printed and manuscript sources, but this impression is supported by interviews. It appears that in Primitive Methodism miners were under-represented in the leadership. That is to say, the proportion of miners in the Methodist leadership was smaller than their proportion in the whole population. Shopkeepers and Co-op. workers, white-collar workers and officials seem over-represented.[17] The same is true of the Wesleyans, save at Quebec where miners seem to have held all the key positions.

In the late nineteenth century the Waterhouses P.M. Sunday school teachers seem to have been the most 'proletarian' of all the chapel leaders and it was from amongst this group of teachers that a number of important political figures emerged.

One occupational group very much under-represented at all periods is that of the labourers. While railwaymen and craftsmen associated with mining (joiners, bricklayers, etc.) do occasionally appear amongst the leaders of Methodism, unskilled labourers do not. Also, until recently women have not been prominent in leadership positions, although they were very active amongst the membership. It has been suggested that Methodism was a shopkeepers' religion. Pickering certainly found shopkeepers prominent amongst the Non-conformist leadership in his two Yorkshire towns. Probert made similar findings in Cornwall, showing that Methodism failed to draw members from the extremes; namely landed gentry and labourers.[18] The 41 shopkeepers as a whole were not Methodists; 6 were – among whom were one or two leading Methodists – but 11 were Baptists, 6 Roman Catholics, 15 'nothing', 3 not known. The leading Esh Winning Primitive, who died in about 1910, was a draper. In Waterhouses the Co-op. manager was a leading Wesleyan and many of his employees were activists in the chapel also.

What are the implications of the occupation structure of the Methodists? The disproportionate representation of non-miners in the Methodist leadership (if this was actually the case) might be explained, in part, by reference to the following considerations:

men who were independent in their work situation carried this independence into their religious life and became leaders;

officials and white-collar workers were chosen as leaders by the chapels;

men who held positions of trust in the chapels were also trusted with official responsibility and capital.

There appears to be a connection between occupational role and leadership positions in Methodism, and it is fairly clear that the miners who were leaders in Methodism were a 'working-class élite' of piece-rate workers (see Appendix IV). Since the 1920s there have been striking changes in the occupations of the villagers due both to industrial change and social mobility. This is neatly shown by a consideration of 102 Methodists of whom we had sufficient personal details: 75 of their fathers were miners, but of their 35 sons, only 2 were miners.

We are not considering a community against a settled background of relatively unchanging social, economic and political circumstances. To this extent it has not been possible to carry out a study like the traditional anthropological studies of small societies. Nationally and locally changes were taking place that impinged on the day-to-day life of the Methodists and of organised Methodism. Any attempt to establish a 'typical' period or a golden age of the villagers must founder on the simple evidence of continuous social change.

RELIGIOUS CONFLICTS IN THE VILLAGES

The presence of diverse regional and religious groups in the population of the coal-boom villages provided ample opportunity for communal strife. We know from the press, for example, that there was much
anti-Irish feeling in the region at the beginning of our period. Fenian
arms caches were from time to time discovered and occasional ex-
plosions were thought to be 'Fenian outrages'. In 1871 there is evidence
of Fenianism in Newcastle and in Whitton Park, but the nearest such
activities appear to come to the valley is Bishop Auckland, and in the
following year an Orange demonstration in Crook.[19]

The institutionalisation of Anglo–Irish conflict, represented by
Orange demonstrations and Catholic counter-demonstrations does not
seem to have developed in the valley. Nonetheless some of these
antagonisms, expressed so clearly elsewhere in the county, may have
been an element in the drunken brawls that were so common in the
valley. The lack of any research on the history of the Irish in County
Durham constitutes an important gap in the history of the county
which urgently needs filling.

The history of the Irish in the county may prove to be extremely
interesting; on the basis of reading newspapers – without intending to
construct a history of the Irish – the following impressions emerge: Irish
labour was used in the 1840s to build the railways in the county, there
followed a period of unemployment during which a number of Irish
turned to highway robbery, some forming bands of footpads. Irish
robbers seem to have been the terror of the good citizens of Durham
City who had to walk the roads to Shincliffe, Gilesgate and Neville's
Cross. With the sinking of the shafts in mid-Durham (as, for example,
in Esh Winning) new jobs were found for Irishmen, again the heavy
labouring involved in shaft-sinking. When the shafts were sunk the
Irish were employed in labouring and on the coke-ovens in the valley,
according to some aged informants. Only slowly were the Irish able to
gain skilled, piece-rate jobs at the face.

Another unsubstantiated datum from the villages is that the Irish
were segregated in housing 'over the beck' in Esh Winning. As it was
also said that rough elements were 'over the beck' too, we might here
be encountering some confusion between the rough and the Irish –
who might have been equated. No case of anti-Irish activity has been
passed down to the researcher by Methodists or Catholics. The known
cases of conflict, described below, are between the Methodists and the
Catholic Church, not Methodists and Catholics.[20]

Two clear cases of institutional conflict between the Methodists and
the Catholic Church can be recounted. The first comes to us as part of

the folk history of the local Methodists and cannot be checked in any documentary source: Joseph Love wished to build a chapel in Cornsay Colliery, but the land was held by Ushaw College estates, who would not allow a chapel to be built on their land – even within the colliery yard. After much fruitless negotiation Love ceased arguing. One Friday all the Catholics employed in his pit received notice with their pay. The priest went to see Love (or his manager). Love asserted that if the Methodists could not have a chapel, the Catholics could not have jobs. The priest went to Ushaw College to explain the situation and the Methodists received permission to build a chapel and the Catholics were taken on again.

The second account is contained in Patterson's history of Primitive Methodism and is not recalled locally: Joseph Harrison tried to get land for a chapel in Esh Winning in about 1894, but 'many attempts were made to get a site for a chapel, but in vain, as the ground belonged to Roman Catholics'.[21] With the minister (G. W. Moorse), Harrison finally managed to obtain a site. We do not know what persuasions were used in this case, for the land seems to be part of Mr Leadbetter-Smythe's land, and the Smythes are most probably the Catholics referred to. The Smythes had been in the valley since before the Reformation and their house (Flass Hall) had been a refuge for priests in times of persecution. But they clearly made their peace with the Methodists.

Conflict between Methodists and Anglicans does not seem to have been significant at all. The only source of friction in the early part of our period (according to local anecdotes) was over the question of burials, namely whether Non-conformist ministers could bury the dead in churchyards. But in 1879 the vicar of Esh gave a lecture in support of the W.M.s' harmonium fund. Methodist–Anglican conflict was not local, but it certainly had broader dimensions that found expression in the valley. We will see something of this later in the discussion of the campaign against the Education Act of 1902. The Anglican Church, as a national organisation associated in Methodist minds with the brewers and the Tory party, was something against which the Methodists fought with great vigour when it came to the issue.

Why were there so few conflicts apparent in the valley? In the early days of the villages, when Fenianism was an issue, the villages had hardly established themselves in the valley, they were villages of migrants and lodgers brought together in the search for work. It looks as if the various sections of the population were too mixed up in terms of housing and shared associations (pubs and clubs, etc.) to form the kinds of association that are necessary to fight other sections of the population. By the time churches and chapels were built, and separate clubs for Catholics formed, the issue was less salient nationally and regionally. Perhaps also, violent active conflict is a luxury that cannot be enjoyed by men and women who are struggling to establish a life in new territory.

That there was no local conflict between Anglicans and Non-conformists is hardly surprising. The Church of England arrived very much as a dissenting church to evangelise in districts where Methodism was firmly established. Open conflict would have been more likely where Methodism had been attempting to encroach upon established prerogatives of the Church of England. As it was, the Methodists could afford to be tolerant of the Church of England locally, as the Church of England was likely to make little headway among the miners. But as a national organisation with potential control of the education system the Church of England did threaten the Methodists. We do not know how the local Methodists responded to the conflicts within Wesleyan Methodism. Most of the valley Methodists were P.M.s; perhaps they responded with glee at the discomforture of the W.M.s, or they may have been either indifferent or sympathetic. But these events would have shown the consequences of internal conflict.

VILLAGE LIFE

The main body of this work will be concerned primarily with the religious and political life of the villages, and will necessarily give less space to the other aspects of life. The life of the villages was culturally rich and groups of men came together for a very wide range of leisure activities. These included bands, orchestras, gardening, dog-racing, knur and spell (a game played with a stick and a wooden ball), pitch and toss, popular lectures, the Mechanics' Institute (which seemed to grow rapidly in the county around 1860), football, rowing, running and other competitive sports, dinners, picnics and outings of various kinds. The columns of the local papers give an impression throughout the last third of the century of continuous and enthusiastic activity in the villages. Plainly not all activities were well organised, and some activities (like the immensely popular 'spelling bee') were only fashionable for short periods. But villages were not just drab and insanitary settlements of working men who moved only between home, the pit and pub or chapel; the population was able to articulate a whole range of activities of a kind that are perhaps rarely understood by outsiders. Something of the gaiety of life in the villages is captured in literary form in the account of the carnival in Part 3, Chapter 2, of Emile Zola's *Germinal*. The 'picaresque hedonism'[22] of the carnival can still be found on Bank Holidays in the clubs in the valley, although the more serious activities of the Mechanics' Institute are no longer to be found.

3 The social and economic basis of paternalism: the colliery-owners in the Deerness Valley

The collieries of Waterhouses, Esh Winning and Ushaw Moor were part of the industrial empire of the Pease family.[1] The Peases' interests were mainly centred in Tees-side in iron-stone mining, iron and steel, and the North Eastern Railway. The village of Peases West at Crook was a local centre for coal and coke, most of which was supplied to the Peases' own ironworks. Thus the Deerness Valley collieries were part of a closely integrated and economically interdependent set of industries.

The Cornsay Colliery was owned by Ferens and Love. Love had started his working-life as a pit-boy at eight years old; he became a colliery manager, started a grocery and drapery business, and then became a mill-owner, a ship-builder and a ship-owner and finally the part or whole owner of six collieries. He was probably the last coal entrepreneur to rise from the ranks of hewers.

Hamsteels Colliery originally belonged to Johnson and Reay, then to J. B. Johnson, a local Durham City man. Johnson was a small businessman compared with Pease, his enterprises being Hamsteels Colliery and the City Brewery. Johnson died in 1919 and the colliery was purchased by the Saddler brothers in 1921.

Pease and Partners was a family company until 1898 when it became a limited liability company. It thus underwent some reorganisation in the period of the international development of combines and cartels. During the early period, especially under Joseph Whitwell Pease, a tradition of paternalism had developed. The Peases were members of the Society of Friends (Quakers). For the Quakers the callous cash nexus was not the sum of industrial relations. Old Joseph Pease (d. 1872) and his sons believed firstly that the owners and the men worked in partnership in pursuit of common goals, and secondly that the owners had definite responsibilities for their work people. The men in turn they believed, had a responsibility to the owners in allowing the market to operate freely, thus accepting reductions in wages when the price of coal fell, just as they enjoyed increases when the price rose.

The Peases believed that industrial conflict arose from an imperfect understanding of the workings of a market. J. W. Pease M.P., later Sir Joseph Whitwell Pease, Bart., M.P. (1828–1903) advocated education for the working class, so that, *inter alia*, they might better understand the economy and their own interests in it. Like the founders of the Mechanics' Institutes the Peases had mixed motives in promoting education. The entrepreneurial class appreciated the dependence of industry on scientific knowledge. They also wished the newly literate to appreciate improving literature.[2] But education had a social control function also, for it would lay its recipients 'under the restraints which are imposed by enlightened opinion, and which operate so powerfully on the higher and more cultivated classes'.[3] Peel put the issue more bluntly, 'when knowledge was extensively diffused throughout the population of a country, a mob could never acquire any permanent ascendancy'.[4]

Trade unions, according to J. W. Pease, were to act as information networks, to enable men to play the labour market effectively – but they interfered with the operation of the market at great peril. When he visited Esh Winning to see new workings and open the temporary school, Pease said of the trade unions that he

> thought them good in that they pointed out which market gave the best pay for certain work. But when they began to meddle with prices, that were best regulated by the laws of supply and demand, then there was great objection to them. The Master was obliged to give the highest price for labour, according to supply. Men ought to think about this and consider whether Trade Unions were doing them any good at all meddling in the market for labour.

He goes on in the same speech to develop a theme in favour of popular education;

> It was a great advantage to employers when they had educated steady, settled workpeople. It was the comfort of the latter and the prosperity of the former. There was nothing so bad. . .as when a master neglects his duty. . .and afterwards sees there is a feeling of discontent amongst his workmen, which he feels he ought to have prevented years before. Therefore they [Pease and Partners] were constrained to take an immediate interest in these matters.[5]

In other words the masters' neglect led to discontent, while education was one measure that would prevent discontent. Sir Basil Samuelsson, owner of East Hedleyhope Colliery, was also an advocate of education and worked for its extension throughout his career. He was a friend of Mundella and was the first to give evidence to the Royal Commission on Education in 1871.[6] The coal masters seem to have believed this from early on, for after the strike of 1844, Welbourne states, the 'coal-owners became possessed of a new zeal for educational and social improvement'.[7]

Pease again stressed partnership when opening a school at Stanley (Crook).

> He had never admitted, and he hoped he never would admit, that there was any opposing interest between the employer and the employed, at any rate in the coal fields of South Durham [applause]. He might say:
>> 'We have lived and loved together
>> Through many a changing year'
>
> They had had their times of prosperity in which they had rejoiced, and they had had times lately when the workmen's remuneration had been reduced very considerably and when the profits of the coal owners have also been reduced, if not to nothing, to a very low figure. [Pease and Partners] had thrown open their rooms to the Trade Unions, believing and hoping that while the men were looking out for themselves they would look at the position of the employers and the employers also would try while working for themselves to look at the position of the men, so that employer and employed might go hand in hand, not only for the benefit of each other but for the benefit of the community at large.[8]

Arthur Pease spoke at the opening of the Miners' Institute at New Marske, his brother John Whitwell Pease with him. The owners, he said, 'felt that to have a body of intelligent, sober and well-conducted men must ever tend to the prosperity of the works'. In saying that the Unions could meet in the institute he pointed out that 'all recent reductions had been accomplished without a single strike, that was something very remarkable in the progress of the feeling between labour and capital'.[9]

During a strike in 1879 J. W. Pease publicly stated that a complete victory for the owners would be as fatal as complete victory for the men. He believed in arbitration.[10] Partnership, mutual understanding, reasonable settlement, in the context of an unalterable market situation are the main themes of the Peases' view of industrial relations. It could be argued that this was only a gloss on exploitation. The market for coal was interfered with by the owners, both by the formation of cartels and by selling coke to their own subsidiary iron companies at a below market price. A cut in profits bore less heavily on an owner than a cut in the fortnightly wage bore on the pit-man and his family. This would be an oversimplification. While it is true a perfect market was not operating and that pit-men suffered greater hardships than the colliery-owners, it is also true that the views quoted above are entirely consistent with Quaker views. Whatever underlay the Peases' attitude, they presented to the public and the pit-men the attitudes outlined above, and this is important for our analysis.

Economic orthodoxy was embodied in the sliding scale for the miners' wages. But because the price of coal dictated the miners' wages, the owners were able to underbid competitors. The owners were, in fact, in an economically dominant position and they directly controlled both 'the market' and the men's wages.[11] The sliding scale in Durham operated from 1871 to 1878, 1879 to 1881, 1882 to 1883 and 1884 to 1889.

Locally the owners showed concern for their people. In 1871, for example, Pease and Partners distributed coal to the poor of Peases West during a cold winter. In 1879 Ferens gave 5 tons of coal to the poor of Cornsay. Miners' widows were allowed to live in Peases' colliery houses. The term 'their' people is used advisedly. Not only were the villagers Peases' employees, they were their tenants. The colliery houses of Waterhouses and Esh Winning were all provided by Pease and Partners, who stopped rent out of the men's pay. The institutes and the schools were built by the owners also; not only were all these buildings paid for and formally opened by the owners, but built with bricks made from seggar from the local mines. Every brick in the house in which a miner lived was stamped either 'Pease' or 'F & L'.[12] The workers and their families were entirely dependent on the coal-owners and the villages were, in effect, 'company towns'.

The chapels were not company chapels but there was a strong element of company patronage in the foundation and maintenance of chapels. While the coal-owners were believers, they would also have approved of Ure's contention that 'Godliness is great gain' and that, 'animated with a moral population, our factories will flourish in expanding fruitfulness'.[13] But we would misrepresent Pease if we presented him as only under the influence of Ure. Ure scorned the idea of the independent and self-reliant workman and opposed combination. Pease did all he could to encourage independence and self-reliance and he advocated trade unionism, as we have seen. It might be more accurate to characterise Pease as adhering to the beliefs of Samuel Smiles, who, according to Bendix, modified Ure's beliefs in the way we have indicated.[14]

Ferens and Love were both prominent figures in the Methodist New Connexion. Love was a local preacher; he had founded the Durham circuit,[15] and by 1871 he had given over £12,000 for chapels (not all Methodist New Connexion) throughout the country.[16] From time to time Joseph Love would double the sum of money raised through special local efforts by the Methodists; thus in one gesture he demonstrated both his piety and his superior status. In 1874 he gave the Methodist New Connexion £10,000.[17] He was a generous contributor to the funds of local chapels also.[18] Love allowed the Cornsay Methodist New Connexion to use the colliery school, and later he gave them the building; he charged no ground rent, and provided fuel and lighting and the colliery trap for visiting preachers. But he gave the chapel no deed. This caused the Methodists considerable trouble when the colliery was sold, and the new owner (a Catholic) claimed the chapel also.

Welbourne, however, describes a disjunction between Love's religious and business lives. 'There is no doubt that Mr. Love, active Methodist as he was, laid the foundations of the fortune which allowed him to be so lavish in charity by a system of management so callously commercial that it passed unnoticed into absolute robbery.'[19] Love had not only dismissed men for discussing the possibility of forming a union; he had been the prime actor in the breaking of the early miners' union in the dispute over the 'rocking' of tubs in 1863–4.[20] 'Mr. Love's business actions were in sharp contrast to the piety of his private life ...He belonged to a school which had well learned the lesson, to hide from the right hand what its left hand did.'[21] No references can be found locally to this phase of Love's career; it seems unlikely that his past was unknown and had no effect on the miners' attitude towards him. However, whatever the miners knew or thought they probably felt it wiser not to express their opinions too publicly, and perhaps hostility towards Love was in part directed against Curry his manager (see below). The Methodists, in their official statements at least, seem to have forgiven Love. In fact Love's classical 'rags to riches' career was presented by Methodists as a vindication of his piety. Furthermore, he was held up as a model to those with social and economic aspirations; 'From whence did his wealth arise?...It was the result of industry – industry combined with frugality, self-denial, economy; sanctified and regulated by the highest principles of genuine religion.'[22]

Pease and Partners were generous locally. They gave two houses to the Esh Winning P.M.s for conversion to a chapel in 1875, also helping with labour and materials for the conversion.[23] They allowed the W.M.s to meet in a colliery building. They loaned the Baptists the Esh Winning British school.[24] They later donated £25 to the Baptists chapel fund, J. W. Pease also making a personal gift of £22.[25] Arthur Pease laid the foundation stone for the Waterhouses W.M. chapel and Lord Boyne (Brancepeth) gave the land, as he did for the P.M.s also.[26] J. W. Pease contributed to the Crook Methodist New Connexion chapel debt fund in 1871.[27] In 1900 Pease and Partners gave the site and the bricks for building the Ushaw Moor W.M. chapel.[28] Only J. B. Johnson seems to have withheld full support from the Non-conformists. Johnson and Reay had given £100 and a plot for the Quebec P.M. chapel in 1876 and Reay and his son made personal gifts of £52.[29] Johnson does not appear to have given much money, and he insisted on his domestic servants (including the Methodists) attending the Church of England.[30] Ironically J. B. Johnson's house at Saltburn is now a Christian Endeavour conference centre.

Pease and Partners actively encouraged religious and temperance work in the villages. Religion, with education, was seen as a remedy to social disorder as well as being good in itself. In his Stanley speech already cited,[31] J. W. Pease mentioned the prevalence of crime and drink, that there were also more chapels and attenders, more schools and better houses.[32] To encourage religion and temperance, Pease and Partners appointed missionaries and temperance workers to their villages, Thomas Binns and James Dack serving the Deerness group of collieries in succession from the 1870s to Dack's death in 1924. An early letter[33] shows that, in the 1850s at least, the Peases were concerned with the actual doctrines taught by their missionaries as well as the mundane effects of religion. In one Pease and Partners colliery report the manager said that the local labour force was 'religious and industrious'.

Temperance was an active interest of both Pease and Love (clearly Johnson's attitude would be ambiguous). Pease and Partners opposed the licensing of any additional public houses in their colliery villages in the Deerness Valley until 1903. In 1903 they said that the Trust Houses were a responsible enterprise, likely to encourage temperance and 'might mitigate the evils of the club', and so they offered no opposition to the licence application.[34] It is also said by respondents that the managers warned and then sacked habitual drunkards.

Probably the most famous temperance activity of the coal-owners (including Lord Londonderry, the Earl of Durham, the Bearpark Coal Co., Love and Pease) was the attempt to start the British Workmen's Public Houses. These would offer 'all the advantages of drink taverns without the drink'.[35] The Shakespeare British Workman was inaugurated in Durham North Road (near Joseph Love's Bethel Chapel) in March 1874.[36] J. W. Pease also gave his support to the movement for more stringent licensing laws for which the Liberals campaigned in a 'positive mania' after 1872.[37] In 1873 he attempted also to bring certain kinds of gambling under the Vagrancy Act by introducing a Bill to this effect in Parliament.[38]

The Peases' other social concerns need only be listed to fill in the picture of reforming Quaker Liberalism: suppression of slavery, suppression of the opium trade, the abolition of capital punishment (J. W. Pease the leader of the parliamentary campaign), penal reform (the Howard League), the Peace Society (J. W. Pease a vice-president), support for state education and the extension of Sunday schools.[39]

Local causes also received support from Pease and Partners. For the Esh Winning flower show (a county event) Pease and Partners supplied the field, stands, labour and money.[40] The Aged Miners' Homes were opened by Miss Pease. The Esh Winning Miners' Institute (opened 1902 by Pease and Partners) was served by a circulating library run by Pease and Partners.[41] The Waterhouses show, the Crook agricultural show, cricket grounds for Waterhouses and Esh Winning, the Esh Winning colliery band, all received donations from both the company and individual Peases.[42] J. B. Johnson encouraged sport and while he was owner of the colliery Hamsteels fielded a highly successful rugby-football team. It was said the good footballers could always find employment at Hamsteels. The village produced a number of professional footballers.

The owners did not exercise a day-to-day control of the mines or the villages, though both Love and Ferens were to a degree integrated into local society, the former being a local preacher, the latter a Methodist New Connexion circuit steward. To what extent did the managers exercise the same paternalism as the owners? At the personal level it seems impossible that they would have been appointed unless they had some sympathy for the owners' ethos. The fact that the managers all served for quite lengthy periods in the villages indicates that they probably shared much of their outlook, or came to share it. Thomas James retired as under manager at Waterhouses in 1928, having started in management there in 1876 and having become under manager in 1899. Crofton, the manager at Esh Winning, came in 1876 and left about 1920. Ryle (who became Pease and Partners' agent at Crook) lived in Esh Winning probably from at least the 1890s to the 1920s. Curry was manager at Cornsay from 1899 to 1937.

Crofton kept aloof from day-to-day matters in the village; he rode to Esh Winning on a horse, inspected the gardens and insisted on their being properly kept. He was the main supporter of the flower show. Once a year Pease and Partners gave a 'conversazione' in the ballroom flat at Esh Colliery. This large flat at the bottom of the North Drift was made into a 'room' with wall covering and pictures, furniture, carpets and a cradle. A concert or dance was then given for the colliery families,[43] and this event was powerfully symbolic of the total dependence on coal of all present. Crofton was also an ardent supporter of the Church of England (St Stephen's Mission, Esh Winning).[44] He is alleged to have known all the older pit-men by name. Parents taught their children to touch their forelock to Mr Crofton. He was described by one old miner as 'a tough old guy – he believed in keeping miners in their place'.[45]

Ryle was not so remote as Crofton and he played for the Esh Winning cricket team. Bone and Matthews, under managers at Water-houses and Esh Winning respectively, were both active in their local W.M. chapels before the First World War.[46].

Knox, Curry's predecessor, had given tea to the Cornsay chapel choir and the chapel officers. This suggests that he favoured the chapel in some way, but little can be found out about this man, who was no longer manager by 1900.[47] Michael Curry was a member of the Methodist New Connexion and had a reserved pew in the chapel. He was also a J.P. and a councillor on Lanchester Rural District Council.[48] Curry was thought to be a tyrant, being described by an eighty-two-year-old informant as 'the uncrowned king of the area'. He was said to have been a 'bad' manager and a vindictive man. He evicted tenants if one of their sons was seeking work other than at Cornsay Colliery. An eighty-year-old retired miner from Cornsay Colliery recalled Curry sending a man into the pit to tell him to 'be careful' what he said on colliery premises; the miner had been speaking about the Labour Party to a friend while they waited to descend the pit. Few today speak well of Curry, and those who do are Methodists. The non-Methodist octogenarian informant praised the Methodists, Barren and Richardson (see Chapter 6) very highly, so religious prejudice cannot entirely explain his views. He said also that Curry never won a case against Barren on appeal to Newcastle (to the joint committee). Browell, Curry's under manager, was also a member of the Methodist New Connexion and an active leader in the Cornsay society.

Lowden, the manager at Hamsteels, and his son, used to provide musical entertainment for the Methodists in the late 1870s. His predecessor, G. Fletcher, spoke at various W.M. meetings in June 1875 and throughout the late 1870s, and during the 1879 Strike was said to be 'much respected by the men'.[49] The manager from about 1900, Lowden, was chairman of Lanchester Rural District Council and a J.P. (sworn in by John Wilson). He was also Hamsteels church-warden.

The newspapers show that the managers exercised the owners' patronage and themselves patronised many village activities with their active participation or financial donations. They also visited the schools and Sunday schools, sometimes addressing the children.[50] (Andrew Ure the 'leading spokesman'[51] of the entrepreneurs expressed high approval of the Sunday school.[52]) The surviving minute books from the various chapels show that the Methodists frequently sent deputations to the managers for help with repairs, material, labour, donations, etc.

None of this is to say that the managers did not behave as managers. Some of the respondents already cited commented how the managers penalised men who came out-bye (see glossary) early and blacklisted men throughout the county for either drunkenness or their political views. We have been told also that disputes arose through alleged breaches of verbal agreements in the pit and that managers tried to 'blind the men with science'.

Love had set various men on at Cornsay without reference to Curry. These were faithful servants who had worked elsewhere for Love. 'In Mr. Love's pits there was small chance of promotion. All the smaller official positions were filled with friends and relations of the owner.'[53] In any dispute with the management (for example, over the allocation of colliery tenancies) these people could appeal directly to the owners, by-passing the manager. Pease and Partners had made similar appointments at Esh Winning. These men, whilst in one sense undermining the authority of the managers were also useful to management. They tended to be bosses' men during industrial disputes. At Esh Winning in 1926 these men were amongst the leading blacklegs and were members of the N.-P.U. (see Chapter 8). Saddler also had a number of men whom he had engaged personally, sometimes taking their families into domestic service. He used such men, and others specially chosen as 'rate-busters' when opening out new workings, so as to be able to fix a low price for the men. Informants suggest that the 'rate-busters' were stupid rather than calculating. They were thought to be unreliable men and were amongst the first sacked after the 1926 Dispute.[54]

The practice of quite generous patronage by colliery management must not, therefore, lead the observer to view the villages and industrial relations only in terms of cohesive and conflict-free social relations. The managers' attitude to the union leaders in the nineteenth century show that the miners did not pursue 'peace at any price', and that the managers were prepared to use a variety of overt and covert tactics to resist the demands of the men. In 1891, for example, Pease and Partners locked the Esh pit-men out rather than give way to an attempted restriction of output by the union lodge.[55] Given market beliefs the best way of raising wages was by restricting output and raising the price of coal. 'For fifteen years by 1893 the miners' leaders had pinned their faith to this supposed solution.'[56] The managers, like the owners, believed in the efficiency of the market to regulate prices and discipline the men:

> The improved state of the trade, and the consequent increase of wages to the workmen have made them very independent and

bad to deal with. They are worse to deal with now than they have ever been during my course of 30 years experience.[57]

The men have been worse to deal with than ever this year, getting big wages makes them very independent and Pearson the Check-weighman and Miners' Secretary is a very presumptuous man and always trying to interfere with what he has no business. . .I hope we have now seen the maximum of costs, and that we may be able to effect reductions. . .The hewers do not work nearly as hard as they did when wages were lower. . .An effort should be made to get rid of the old inferior men who keep down the average earnings of the hewers, and which cause the owners to have to give higher wages than they would have to do if the inferior men were got rid of.[58]

This latter remark which is devoid of any paternal sentiments is explained by the practice of paying men in relation to average drawings at the pit, a few very poor workers lowered the average substantially and thus the good workers had to be paid for being well above average. Without poor workers the average would go up and the men's wages down.

After the County Strike of 1892 the men returned at a 10% reduction; at Esh Winning the men's conduct was reported as '. . .satisfactory. . . since the strike' in December, and at Waterhouses Crofton could report, 'We have had no trouble with the workmen during the year, they all conducted themselves very well during the twelve weeks of the County Strike.'[59]

The 1892 Strike was conducted with remarkable goodwill in the villages. In the beginning in March the *D.C.* reports: 'The cessation of work has been in a quiet and orderly fashion. There were no outbursts, the interchange of a few friendly words between officials and men being all that was noticeable.'[60] The *D.C.A.* noted that 'The officials continue unmolested in looking after the plant.'[61] The following week, Greener the agent and Crofton the manager gave permission for the men to take coal from the old coal tips, 'which is deemed a privilege' by the men.[62] In April they offered to lead in coal from Stanley Drifts at a nominal price.[63] J. W. Pease spoke out for arbitration – which the other masters were again refusing; the Reverend McPhail gave a 'sermonised address' on 'Capital and labour' and George McLane and Jonathan Stephenson (all Methodists) set about organising a relief committee.

This situation in the valley had to be contrasted with what the owners expected of the Durham miners in general. Troops were moved from York to Newcastle and twenty-five extra policemen were sent to Durham City 'to render assistance in case of need during the strike'.[64]

The distress appears to have been quite serious in the villages of the valley.[65] The colliery-owners contributed to its relief by helping to pay for children's breakfasts.[66] The Waterhouses leadership may, in fact, have been less enthusiastically for the strike than others in the county. The Waterhouses District Executive gave a guarded statement to the *D.C.* on 18 March which included the statement that: 'There is certainly this fact to consider, that should these collieries feel disposed toward a settlement they will be far outnumbered by their brethren in the east.'[67] In April the *D.C.* reported from the Waterhouses area 'The strike continues in a very orderly and quiet manner.'[68]

In 1895 there was '. . .very little trouble' at Esh Winning but at Waterhouses the men were trying to push up the price by restriction of output; they were '. . .very strictly watched that they do not cease work before the proper time each day'. In the following year the men 'are always trying to get advance of hewing price'. This is all normal and expected market behaviour; advances of wages in good times, reductions and unrest in poor trade, each side trying to gain maximum advantage from the market. The manager expects to wait for the market to change before he can 'effect reductions' and presumably resents Pearson interfering with the market. Crofton probably epitomised what he saw as proper management attitudes when in 1895 he reported, on Ushaw Moor Colliery, 'We have not had any trouble during the year with the workmen. They have found out that we are strict and at the same time are prepared to treat the workmen honestly and fairly at all times.'[69]

The fortunes of the coal industry in County Durham were closely related to the iron industry; in fact 70% of Pease and Partners' total output was used for iron-making in 1908.[70] The year 1873 was one of maximum wages, rates rising to 50% above the 1871 level. But by 1879 wages were down 10% on 1871, and emigration from Durham to the colonies increased, as it increased in all periods of economic recession. The year 1880 was another boom one, as a result of the introduction of the Bessemer process in the iron and steel industry. The second sliding scale gave high wages at this time, and was the basis, according to Welbourne, of the leaders' faith in the sliding scale. Wages fell again in 1881, but remained steady until another peak in the early 1890s. Wages again fell and remained at about 10% above the 1879 level until the boom created by the Boer War in 1900. Wages rose to 6% above the 1872 level, declined in 1902, and advanced, but slowly from 1903 onwards. The advance was so slow as to constitute a decline in the living standards of the miners, as was suggested in Chapter 2.

The cost of mining coal in South Durham was rising at the end of the nineteenth century. The easy seams were worked out; in 1907 Pease and Partners reckoned it took 911 men to raise 1,000 tons of coal in a working day, whereas in the previous decade it took only 858.[71] Easier seams were being opened in south Yorkshire, offering severe competition to Durham at a time when the whole coal industry was faced with diminishing profit margins. This situation became especially acute after 1921 and is reflected in the dividends paid by Pease and Partners, which fell to zero in 1927. In the coal industry as a whole labour costs were 71% of production,[72] so that cutting labour costs would be the most effective way of reducing the cost of coal. In times of relative trade depression capital was not available for investment in machinery to raise the productivity of labour. Thus wages had to be cut, according to the owners.

Give and take in the face of the vicissitudes of the market may have been acceptable in the *relatively* prosperous years at the end of the nineteenth century. The 1870s indicate this clearly; in 1871–2 the owners readily concede an increase in wages to the men as the price of coal rises in the market. The men, in turn, from 1879 onwards agree to reductions in the wages as the coal price falls (they do not concede that this should be done unilaterally, only by negotiation). It was the continued insistence that the miners should take a cut in their living standards that led to the erosion of paternalism from the beginning of the twentieth century. Paternalism may bring its own rewards, but it was not cheap in itself; with the decline of profit margins the owners could no longer afford the previous patronage. Yet the owners continued to apply the principle of the 1870s to the 1900s in spite of the greater intensity of trade depression, and insisted that it was only reasonable for the men to take wage cuts. Clearly there was going to be an absolute limit below which the men would not and could not accept cuts. Meanwhile, as we saw in Chapter 2, pressure for a minimum wage, and the eight-hour day was mounting at the beginning of this century. There was plainly going to be a collision.

Pease and Partners also underwent structural changes. They became a limited liability company, answerable to shareholders in 1898, whereas Ferens and Love remained a private company until it closed. They ran into very severe economic difficulties five years later.[73] Within the coal trade more militant attitudes among the men were replacing the older more conciliatory attitudes. A. F. Pease, chairman of Pease and Partners, noted this in 1907, referring to '...some of the younger and keener spirits who think...that they have only to take up a bolder position to substantially raise the relationship between wages and prices'.[74] By 1908 he could comment, however, that 'We have so far

arranged amicably with our men to reduce wages practically in proportion to the scale at which they were put up as prices went up. . .'[75]

The attitude of the Peases may also have lost some of its religious
and ethical rigour. Ure stressed the importance of religion and morality
for owners as well as for workers. Loose-living employers could not
expect their workers to behave in a moral way. Joseph Pease (1799–
1872) embodied Ure's ideal owner in this respect. Joseph Whitwell
Pease lived as a country gentleman and accepted a baronetcy. His son
Joseph Albert was created first Lord Gainford in 1917 and held important government posts (unlike his grandfather Joseph Pease who
had an 'inconspicuous career'[76] in the Commons). Joseph Albert's son,
the last Lord Gainford, was educated at Eton and served in both
World Wars, having ceased to be a Quaker. Faith, the first Baron's
daughter, married into the Beaumont family. The Beaumonts of Allen-
dale made their fortune through the London Lead Company which
mined lead in Weardale. Faith's son is the present Lord Beaumont of
Whitley who was chairman of the Liberal Party from 1967 to 1968.
The grandsons of old Joseph Pease held between them, in the male
line alone, three baronetcies (Hummersknott; Daryngton; and Hutton,
Lowcross and Pinchinthorpe) and a peerage.

Various Peases may appear in this history as the managers and
directors of a public company, but they were becoming part of what
we know as the establishment. The four titles, Eton and the Lovat
Scouts are a far cry from the life of the first Quaker M.P. who affirmed
rather than swear an oath on taking his seat (wearing a brown suit) in
Parliament. We might expect their attitudes to change also.

The hardening managerial attitudes at the beginning of this century
can be seen in 1907 and 1909 when Pease gave warnings of conflicts to
come and showed signs of a hardening of attitude to the unions, as the
unions in turn resisted wage reduction. Pease insisted on arbitration; he
would 'firmly resist' attempts

> to enforce an advance by. . .unconstitutional methods [the strike]
> . . .looking not only at our mere selfish interests as colliery and
> mine owners, but having regard to the general interests of the
> country, we must put our foot down if there is an organised
> attempt on the part of the miners of the country to place them-
> selves in a privileged position. . .and that cost what it may we must
> see the matter through.[77]

In other words, at all costs, the miners must accept wage reductions.
The Durham coal-owners, for their part, were reluctant to effect the
amalgamation through which they could have increased efficiency and
reduced costs.[78]

Nineteenth-century attitudes persisted, however. As late as 1917 A. F.

Pease said to the shareholders, 'every worker should become a capitalist and every capitalist a worker...there must be co-operation between employer and employed...the employer must take trouble to look after the general interests of his workmen and the workman must make it part of his duties to look after the interests of the employer'.[79] These are almost the same words as used by the ex-preacher Pyle, when addressing a strike rally in the valley in 1879, and by J. W. Pease in his Stanley speech.[80]

Nonetheless we are observing at the turn of the century a change in managerial ideology. Bendix[81] developed the idea that at the turn of the eighteenth/nineteenth centuries entrepreneurs moved away from personalised and paternal control of their workers towards more impersonal and calculative control. In this latter circumstances they 'tended to regard the workers as factors of production, whose cost could be calculated'.[82] The Peases and Love seem to have carried paternalistic beliefs into the late nineteenth century, and the change in ideology comes a century later than the change discussed by Bendix. Certainly our quotations indicate that the Pease ownership was passing through a transitional stage of managerial ideology.

From 1921 onwards the company's annual general meeting is repeatedly reminded of the men's responsibility in maintaining profitability. Sir A. F. Pease commented on the *unreasonableness* of the men in 1923, 'I can not understand the great reluctance of the men to work slightly longer hours which would inevitably increase the rate of wages...I can not see why they object so much to working an extra half-hour when they have nothing particular to do with the time.'[83]

The men were developing a different view. The new outlook, promoted by the growing I.L.P., was that men were entitled to a living wage. There seemed to be no end to the sacrifices they were asked to make. They could not accept that their standard of living had to be cut to such an absolutely low level in order to maintain profitability. They were prepared to resist the operation of the market to keep their standard of living up. A political dimension was added to industrial relations that was alien to both owners and traditional unionists in the Deerness Valley. But the course of events in the valley was increasingly out of the local control of both owners and men as the century progressed.

Just as the men attempted to use their political power to resist wage reductions, so the owners were prepared to intervene politically to assert their interests. The outcome of the 1926 Dispute was the reaffirmation of the principle that miners were to have their wages reduced during periods of poor trade. The violence with which this principle was re-established, with police on the streets and poverty in every mining home, destroyed the credibility of the spirit of paternalism of which the principle was very much a part.

The owners were behaving quite logically, given the existence of private enterprise in coal and a market economy. Developments through the century, culminating in 1926, thus occurred with a certain inevitability. The only option open to the miners in this situation was to challenge the adequacy of private enterprise and the market.

We are arguing that Pease and Partners pursued paternalistic policies throughout. They maintained also a consistent political and economic outlook and attitude to trade unionism. It was possible to put these attitudes into practice in a period of relative prosperity, or when there were prospects of trade improvement. Compromise and arbitration, the processes of bargaining, could operate in this situation. The reciprocity implicit in such procedures could be reinforced by patronage in the villages. But when trade declined severely and continuously with no prospect of improvement, the burden of maintaining the relationship became unbearable to the men. They reacted with collective political power; this not only breached the reciprocal relationship but spelt economic disaster to the owners (and liberal economists) – who in turn responded politically and with greater force. Punitive measures after the owners' victory were almost inevitable, and as J. W. Pease had predicted, a complete victory for the masters was a disaster. The management offered no semblance of paternalism in their relations with the villagers after the events of 1926.

4   Village Methodism – I

'Religion' cannot be defined adequately in terms of the single factor of belief; ritual, theology and subjective experiences are all religious phenomena, but none of them alone is religion as a whole. They may be parts of the whole life of the religious man, integrated more or less coherently in his mind or in his actions. Yet such religious phenomena are clearly separable for analytic purposes. Different elements of religion (doctrine, worship, ritual, etc.) are differentially related to what Nadel has called the 'competences' of religion.[1] Doctrines may provide us with explanations of the cosmos, moral values or economic ethics. Worship may function to unite and sustain a congregation as a part or the whole of a wider social order. Ritual may recreate or symbolise the deepest subjective experiences of religion. In attempting to discover the competences or the effects of Methodism in our villages, we will adopt the relatively elementary procedure of Glock and Stark, who designated 'dimensions' of religious commitment.[2]

According to Glock and Stark religion has an *experiential* aspect; the believer may have had a sense of the presence of God, and/or he may have had an experience of conversion. At a certain time, in a particular place, like John Wesley he 'felt his heart strangely warmed'. Secondly, a believer may have more or less knowledge of theology, of the history and doctrine of his church; this we will call the *intellectual* aspect of belief. Thirdly, the believer may accept (or derive from his theology) certain *ideological* notions, concerning work, money, sex, the sabbath, etc. Believers may individually or collectively express their faith through ritual; prayer, singing, recurrent festivals, etc., this is the *ritualistic* aspect of religion. Finally all of these have effects on the believer's life in general and on some aspects more effect than on others. Some will be intended and others unintended, but we will categorise these together as *consequential* aspects of religion.

In studying a concrete historical manifestation of Methodism we face a number of immediate problems. Firstly, we cannot directly examine the mind of the Methodist-in-the-pew by question and answer, nor can we know his subjective religious interpretations of everyday life. It is doubtful whether anyone would, in fact, have such interpretations in the form of a theological commentary on every event around him. Religious interpretations of the world are likely to be partial, not necessarily coherent and, to some extent, inaccessible to the researcher. For the early period (1870–1930) we have to rely almost entirely on written sources; these sources may not be typical (typically written sources do not even survive in working-class communities). It may be that *no* sermon, address, or comment is typical in the sense of average, so too much concern with this problem may be misplaced. For the latter period we can augment written sources with material gathered in interviews with preachers and members of congregations. Contemporary preaching can be reported at first hand although discussion of this is largely omitted from this chapter.

Secondly, traditional Christian belief is not unmixed with what Martin calls 'subterranean theology'.[3] The prevalence of (conventionally) 'superstitious' beliefs about baptism is well established for the mining villages of County Durham. Belief in luck and fate is common among men in hazardous occupations and even those who 'don't really believe in it' might keep the observances 'just in case'. Thus we might find a Methodist holding beliefs incompatible with conventional Christian theology. Such beliefs are unlikely to be recorded as they will not feature in sermons, nor will they be recounted by respondents talking about 'religion'.

Thirdly, we cannot assume *a priori* that the beliefs of Methodists are related to specifically Methodist theological formulations of belief.

Methodism had an early beginning in County Durham and the Northeast. John Wesley preached at Durham to 'a quiet, stupid congregation'[4] in April 1752 and three years later had a fire hose turned on him in Barnard Castle. Wesley's strongest criticisms are directed against the people of Newcastle, 'so much drunkenness, cursing and swearing (even from the mouths of little children) do I never remember to have seen and heard before, in so small a compass of time'.[5] He discovered the appalling conditions of the collieries around Newcastle, and faced some turbulent crowds there.[6] Such occasions were not without their humorous side, as when in 1743 the seats and stage collapsed during the performance of a play against Methodism.[7] Wesley's reception was uneven, however; he developed a special affection for the colliers of Gateshead Fell. These colliers, 'shame the colliers of Kingswood. . .here the house will scarce contain the weekday congregation of a local preacher'.[8]

Many of the W.M.s in Waterhouses and Esh Winning came from

Weardale, bringing their Methodism with them. The chapels in Water-houses seem to have been sponsored by the officials of both main branches of Methodism in Crook. William Burnip, for example, took two years off from his leadership in Crook, whilst residing in Water-houses. He was a key sponsor of the Wesleyan chapel.[9] Wesley had preached in Weardale. Wesleyans in the Deerness Valley sometimes know all the spots at which he was alleged to have spoken in the dale. Wesley found conditions in Weardale much as we found them in Waterhouses in the early days of the societies. He reports in his *Journal* in 1774 that the Weardale activists are young and unmarried (we might assume that they were workers migrating to the lead mines) and that, 'several of these in a little time contracted an inordinate affection for each other, whereby they so grieved the Holy Spirit of God that he in great measure departed from them'.[10]

The descendants of these early Weardale Wesleyans came to the Deerness Valley 100 years later as young men and women and again they contracted inordinate affections for one another. The Methodist society provided an opportunity for young people to meet, and to find marriage partners. Nonetheless this also created a situation in which jealousy could thrive and in which opportunities were available for conduct deemed 'immoral' by the Methodists. In Chapter 5 we shall see how these were the cause of some conflict.

The Methodists brought problems with them but what beliefs did they bring? This is the subject of the present chapter but we should note those aspects of belief that are directly inherited from the traditional beliefs of Methodism. It is our contention that beliefs and practice have peculiarly *local* characteristics, but it is also true that what is localised is *Methodism*. Methodism stresses personal religious experience – it is a 'felt' religion. The doctrine of perfection is uniquely Methodist; it appears as a muted theme amongst our Methodists, not articulated as a doctrine, but expressed in the strivings of the Methodists for a good life. Assurance is an aspect of the felt nature of Methodism, and it is an important theme today in discussing religion with Methodists in the valley. Assurance also expresses itself in the self-assurance and self-confidence of the Methodists in the villages. The nature of this assurance will be illustrated especially clearly in our discussion of the 'respectable Methodists' in Chapter 6. Methodist beliefs have not remained static, we have already suggested that early Methodism was mixed with unorthodox and magical views. Such views would be largely rejected by contemporary valley Methodists. They have been exposed less to the vicissitudes of immigration, social disruption and the onslaught of evangelistic preachers than their predecessors. They have been brought up in the Sunday school and Bible class, perhaps without a clear point of conversion. They have been exposed to years of preaching from the pulpits of sober chapels. This kind of progression from 'visionary and magical aspects of Methodism' to 'restrained Biblicalism and a middle class ethic of individual attainment' has been noted as a feature of an earlier phase of Methodism by Peel.[11]

Perhaps the most important aspect of Methodism found in the villages, belonging to the main stream of Methodist belief and practice, was its fellowship and sense of community. This is the subject of the next chapter. Our study of the villages will underline Peel's judgement that, 'The crucial feature of Methodism was not the politics of its leaders or members but, jointly, its fellowship and its promise of assurance, which had such an appeal, and such an effect on the personality, for men who were undergoing the great anxieties of the Industrial Revolution.'[12] The anxieties with which we will be concerned, however, arise from the foundation of new industrial communities by immigrants and subsequent disruptive changes in the nature of the industry which brought them together.

A 'felt' religion, a main feature of which is a strong sense of community, will not be articulated in clear theological formulae. Simple questioning of Methodists supplies misleading answers; thus 'What are the distinctive features of Methodism?' produces answers like, 'We don't drink', 'We don't believe in gambling'. When pressed, 'But do Methodists have the same religious beliefs as other Christians?', many answered simply 'Yes'. When further pressed 'Even the same as Roman Catholics?' many answered, 'We're all the same.' This is not to say that real differences were not perceived, only that they were not perceived as theological or intellectual differences.

Thus the theology of the average Methodist and adherent is intellectually unsophisticated, confused, unclear, and at times totally unformulated. This may be an illustration of Probert's contention that theology did not develop in Methodism because Methodists hoped to advance by *revival*, rather than rational persuasion.[13] It will perhaps have to be seen in contrast to the more carefully articulated beliefs and ideas (intellectual and ideological) of the local preachers, Sunday school teacher and Bible class leader. It is the ideas of these latter members that have survived to the present day.

The written sources are of three main kinds: sermon notes used by local preachers; addresses given by speakers at special meetings such as rallies or Sunday school teachers' meetings; and lectures and papers written and/or circulated for the Bible and self-improvement classes. Each of these types of material will have been produced for different purposes and different audiences; for example, the self-improvement class would contain non-Methodists whilst the Sunday school teachers would be committed Methodists.

There are two other sources. Diaries and sermon registers give us various combinations of text, title and main points of a sermon. These have the advantage of being dated but do not contain developed arguments. Diaries give the writer's own interpretation of what was said. We also have the private letters and notes of a few individuals and the college essays of a schoolteacher who played a crucial role in one village. This latter source will be discussed in its special context.

What we have described is material likely to provide information on both intellectual and ideological aspects of Methodism, according to our use of Glock and Stark's terminology.

SERMONS

The sermon registers, diaries and sermon notes together give a general indication of the parts of the Bible used in preaching, and the theme of sermons.

An examination of the texts of 435 sermons preached between 1874 and 1923 shows that 290, or two-thirds, were taken from the New Testament, the Gospels of Matthew, Luke and John accounting for over a half of these New Testament texts.[14] Eight books of the Old Testament accounted for over three-quarters of all the Old Testament texts; Psalms and Isaiah constituting a little under half (43%) of all of them. The popular Psalms were 23 (The Lord is My Shepherd) and 84 (How lovely is thy dwelling place, Oh Lord of Hosts).

In the Gospels, John 3 is by far the most popular chapter; its theme is regeneration, conveyed through the story of Nicodemus' visit to Jesus. It is mentioned eleven times as a sermon text. (Any one sermon would be preached at least once in every chapel in the circuit – and repeated in the circuit or elsewhere, by request.) Cited five times or more are the following: Matthew 6, 11, 25; Mark 10; Luke 2, 10, 15. These chapters deal with judgement and salvation, the parables of the talents and the good Samaritan, and the nature of Jesus. Matthew 6 includes the Lord's Prayer and the words of comfort in the Sermon on the Mount. Sermons based on these topics would thus cover the core of Christian teachings on Jesus, on salvation and conduct in the world. From these stories alone, however, we cannot tell *how* the topics were covered.

Of 30 sermons preached in 1968–9, 10 were from the Old Testament, 20 from the New Testament, of which 14 were from the Gospels. None of the 14 broke new ground in as much as they were all based on texts taken from chapters appearing in the 1874–1923 analysis. In terms of simple statistical distribution there seems to have been little shift in the location of texts.

Perhaps this type of analysis tells us very little beyond the stories in the preachers' favourite chapters of the Bible. It may indicate that the main corpus of Christian teaching can be derived from a few chapters of the Bible. Any regular attender at Methodist services or study groups will appreciate the breadth of topics which can be discussed under any text. Nevertheless certain themes are usually developed on particular texts. Not all the subjects preached have survived with their texts, but examples include:

John 3	–	Regeneration; The Incarnation; The Cross (necessary for Salvation)
Matthew 6	–	The Kingdom of God; Success in Life
Matthew 25	–	Man's Moral Probation, Judgement and Punishment
Mark 10	–	The Cross; Eternal Life; Opportunity
Luke 15	–	The Prodigal Son; Salvation, Forgiveness, The New Life, The Christian's Salvation

These are all sermons based on 'well-known' chapters of the Bible which contain either striking stories or parables.

The sermon topics represent a concentration on straightforward biblical exposition. At a glance, it is very 'religious'. We must therefore attempt to reconstruct the substance of the sermons. This we do from incomplete sources; the attempt will be made both chronologically and by themes. It is important to notice and explain any change of substance over time. Four themes present themselves quite plainly. They are salvation, the sacred-secular dichotomy, asceticism (in Weber's sense) and its inner- and other-worldliness, and finally, direct discussions of social and political issues.

One diary records some 40 sermons, 31 of which are preached in 1878, 9 of them in January during a mission at Waterhouses. Another 7 are reported for December, and then after a long gap in the diary, 5 sermons are reported for 1895. On 13 January 1878, the Revd J. D. Thompson, preaching from Matthew 25: 14–30, stressed the necessity of the active use of the talents given to men by God. The faithful servants are 'diligent' and 'active men'.[15] This biblical passage might be seen as the most explicit source of the inner-worldly ascetic spirit. Man is a steward and is required to give an account of his stewardship on the Last Day.

This theme is submerged in the evangelistic preaching of the mission beginning on 21 January. Revd R. Hind[16] begins with four sermons on John 3. His stress is on seeking a change of heart, not an outward change only but a change in inner principles which leads to a new life.[17] A student from the Sunderland Bible Institute preaching on Psalm 19: 40 draws attention to the need for divine mercy.[18] He is followed on subsequent days by Hind who says that whoever believes in Christ's death shall have eternal life through faith; that death, the last enemy of man, is conquered; that salvation delivers us from Hell and that eternal death is the result of unbelief.[19] Two weeks later he preaches on Exodus 24: 18 saying that revelation will not deliver us from 'the present difficulties'; something more is required.[20] Next he preaches on Doubting Thomas. The lessons of the mission are underlined by Revd J. Fenwick who in March reminds the congregation that Christ is their hope for the Glory of Heaven and that those whose names are not in the Book of Life shall be cast into the lake of fire.[21]

Very little analysis is needed to explicate this style of preaching. It offers simple alternatives of life and death, belief and unbelief, a way of salvation through Jesus, and is common to all 'conversionist' sects in their period of evangelical activity.[22] The diary indicates that the style continued at least until the end of the year, when the record ceases. Other records indicate that evangelism of this kind continues into the opening years of this century.[23]

Evangelical preaching stresses the difference between the saved and the unsaved. The related and wider theme of the sacred-secular dichotomy is rather muted. But a sermon in April 1878, points out that Christians, like sheep, are in a small flock; they are defenceless, harmless, clean and useful, they know the voice of the shepherd. In the evening the same preacher preaches of those who are prisoners of sin (preaching to the saved – not the prisoners – in this context).[24] The following week they are told that Heaven is a secure, beautiful and permanent place[25] – by implication more secure, beautiful and permanent than 'the world'. This world is only a stage in human existence; clearly world-acceptance on these terms might be thought to be conditional only.

Seventeen years later the Revd Peter MacPhail draws the sacred-secular distinction very sharply in a sermon on Leviticus 20: 7. The church and the theatre are built of the same bricks and mortar he says, but one is dedicated to God, the other to profanity. He notes the decline of 'personal holiness', that there are not so many holy men as fifty years ago – nor, he says, was there any Higher Criticism. (Here we can see that the discussion of the Higher Criticism makes an early entry in public discussion. The full force was to be felt in 1907 with the publication of R. J. Campbell's *The New Theology*.) He goes on to argue that intellectuality and holiness are antithetical. In the evening he accuses Carlyle of setting the fashion in criticism[26] – a lecturer visiting the district in January had spoken on Carlyle.[27] An undated sermon of 1895, on Galatians 4: 18, also stressed the sacred-secular dichotomy and the diarist's notes finish with the comment that the preacher said Christians should feed the hungry, clothe the naked and 'other secular things'.[28]

This last comment hints at man's call to service in the world, however profane and temporary the world may be. This is the theme of the first sermon cited above, on the talents. In December 1878, the Revd J. Ritson is telling the Waterhouses P.M.s that man is sent into the world for a limited time *for definite work.*[29] The diarist himself has comments to make on this theme, but in another context which we will see below.

Westgarth Adamson was well-known as a local preacher and many of his sermons have survived. None are dated, although a few can be dated by references to contemporary events. He began preaching at the end of the nineteenth century. Being a political militant who had mentioned 'political' topics from the pulpit during or after the First World War, he was not invited to preach in certain chapels.[30] Adamson died in the 1960s. Harvey, the Derbyshire miners' leader, seems to have adopted an approach to preaching that was very similar to Adamson's.[31]

Adamson had no doubts as to the distinction between the sacred and the secular, nor concerning the temporary nature of this life. In a sermon entitled 'Strangers and Pilgrims' he says that we are all strangers *away from our true home,* but pilgrims, *with a purpose.*[32] According to Adamson, example and action are both required of a Christian. In a sermon on 'The Shadows we Cast' he discusses good and evil influences and the example we set the young. He notes parenthetically that pornographers will have much to answer for on Judgement Day. In another sermon, a paean to motherhood, he attacks neglectful mothers, citing nightclubs, dancing, Sabbath-breaking and divorce as activities causing neglect. In 'Serving our Generation' he says that displaying certain qualities of character is in itself a form of service and in a sermon on 'The Value of Ordinary Lives' he points to 'the ministry of your daily toil'. In pursuing their service or their daily toil Christians turn up in unexpected places and are often put in difficult environments, but they can always rise above it – according to the argument of Adamson's sermon on the text 'The Saints (of Caesar's household) Salute You'. The meaning of this is most sharply pointed in another sermon in which Adamson cites the heroism of those who make a sacrificial stand against public opinion or the majority. Religion, he says, has become fashionable, but not Christianity. Jesus says break with the religious traditions.[33]

The stress on Christian activism with the conditionally accepted world is epitomised in an Adamson sermon which is a general plea for practical rather than theoretical Christianity: 'A drop of blood is worth more than a vat of ink', 'Let us not waste our lives in opinions, discussions, etc. . .We must grasp the sword and fight; handle the trowel, etc.'[34]

For Adamson 'handling the trowel' must be taken almost literally. 'If we are to share the mind of Christ we must have a divine discontent with things as they are. We must be unhappy until all the slums are abolished and all back to back hovels removed.'[35] In this sermon (on Jesus weeping over Jerusalem) while speaking of creating a better physical environment Adamson also adds 'Think of the Drinking and Gambling, etc., Sorrow' and 'The church must lead in social reform'.[36] These latter comments leave us unsure whether it is individual reform that should be sought, ultimately.

This ambiguity has been cited as historically central to Methodism by H. Richard Niebuhr (see Chapter 1). Adamson, having made a 'political' point, may have felt it necessary to 'balance' this with a comment about individual sin. The tension between politics and ethics is as clearly seen in his local case as in examples given in Chapter 2. Adamson cast himself, in part, as the Christian heroes cited above, or like Micaiah 'A man not afraid to speak out, even against the king's religious officials. We need such men today in Parliament and the press, etc.'[37]

Adamson's preaching is especially interesting as he was a man who developed his arguments to the limits of acceptability in a Methodist pulpit. Adamson's son said of his father and friends: 'they worked to improve the local area. They suffered for their belief in a God who loved all men. They battled against a capitalist system where the main object was *profit* irrespective of who died and suffered. I hated capitalism from the day I first went down the pit'.[38]

While social matters were mentioned from the pulpit it would seem from the sermon titles and the few notes we have that the sort of 'political' comments quoted from Adamson were fairly rare. Adamson made himself unpopular among Methodists without saying much more than we have quoted here. More typical of social comment would be the temperance sermon preached by John Harrison (a radical Liberal of the previous generation). Harrison actually only mentions drink once: his text in Proverbs 4: 23, 'Keep thy heart with all diligence; for out of it are the issues of life' (*sic*).[39] He says: 'The keeping of the heart, a moral duty injoined on all by God. 1. It is the greatest of all *duties* because it appertains to the concerns of man's highest nature. 2. It is a constant duty dimonding perpetual attention thereoo' (*sic*). Drink, he says, destroys: 'it is one of the powers and influences that the heart must be kept from'.[40]

The figure of Jesus is very prominent in sermons. He is the specific subject of sermons preached by the Revd R. Hind, Taylor and Harrison. Jesus is taken as an example to which man may aspire. In Taylor's words, we may, nourished by the word 'attain to the perfect stature of man in Jesus Christ'.[41] To Harrison, Jesus is an example of, among other things, the perfect man, what humanity can be like.[42] Three points should be noted about this Christological preaching: it ignores any doctrine of the depravity of man; it is the nearest we find to any specific articulation of a doctrine of Perfection. Man is not utterly depraved, nor predestined to salvation or damnation, rather he could and should strive after Christ-like perfection; it is an emphasis which could lead towards a more explicitly Immanentalist position of the kind adopted by Campbell and the Christian Socialists.

A reading of sermon titles only, from registers, suggests that preachers kept themselves very much to the themes of sin and salvation, personal regeneration, problems of the individual and church relating themselves to 'the world', man's call to active service through example and stewardship during his time on earth. But preaching was not totally unaffected by world events: a very sharp illustration of this can be given by comparing the first page of William Foster's sermon register (October–November 1897) with the fourteenth (August 1918–May 1919); the 1897 pages mention five sermons:

> St Matthew 6: 33 ('. . .seek first his kingdom. . .'), subject 'Success in Life';
>
> 1 Chronicles 29: 5, subject 'Consecration';
>
> John 13: 13–14, 'Washing. . .feet';
>
> Acts 5: 4 (Ananias' sin), 'The Enormity of Sin';
>
> Mark 10: 17–31 (the rich young man, etc.), 'Opportunity'.

The 1918 page has seven sermons:

> Matthew 18: 7, 'The World's Woes';
>
> Mark 8: 36 ('. . .what does it profit a man. . .'), 'Profit and Loss';
>
> no text, 'Decision Day';
>
> no text, 'Reconstruction of the Church';
>
> no text, 'A League of Nations';
>
> Hebrews 11: 4 (discourse on faith in Jewish History), 'Faith a Soul Force';
>
> John 8: 32 ('and you will know the truth, and the truth will make you free'), 'Freedom through the Truth'.[43]

The war was plainly influencing the thinking behind Foster's preaching.

We cannot know how effective sermons were in imparting doctrine or ethics. Some preachers were uninspiring, 'putting their nose down' and reading their sermons straight from notes. Even William Foster who seems to have interesting titles is reported to have been one of the most boring preachers in the circuit – this being a comment on style, not content. Recent interviews with older Methodists suggest that to them at least, the most memorable results were conversions through the preaching of a few charismatic preachers (none of whose sermons have survived). Converts gave up drinking and became 'good living men'.[44] Harrison in 'An Account of his life'[45] writes how after receiving his first-class ticket he went with a group of boys to the woods, and some lit their pipes with their tickets. Harrison heard a voice say 'separate'. He ceased to associate with this group, 'the majority went back into the world'. 'I thank God that I obeyed the heavenly voice', he added. Conversion meant not only new personal ethics but some degree of separation from 'the world'. Sermons offered a very this-worldly form of salvation and enjoined hearers to active service in the world. These sermons clearly belong to believers in a type of salvation religion typified by Weber as 'inner-worldly asceticism'.

OTHER ADDRESSES

John Harrison (above) was an active Methodist from 1867 to about 1912. In 1880 when addressing the P.M. Local Preachers' Association on 'Christian Conversation', he extended conversation to mean the whole of life. He stressed the exemplary nature of the Christian life, 'A life correctly lived leads the outsiders to have a better regard and estimate of God. The roads from the manifestos,[46] not merely what a man professes, but from what he has said and done, not merely in his own life and circle but in the reformation of the lives and family circles of others.'[47]

By request Harrison addressed a public meeting in connection with the Sabbath school anniversary on 8 June 1885. He quoted Robert Raikes, with approval, on the functions of the Sunday school; 'The gather[ing] in [of] the young from the world's fair on our Lord's day – to teach them cleanliness, sobriety and virtues: together to read the word of God', as a result of this '. . .young minds are tender, docile and pure, such as good may operate thereon'. Then he discussed the example set by the Sunday school teachers.[48]

Hayson (who recorded the 1878 mission) himself addressed the Sunday school teachers, probably in the late 1880s. He advocated not only virtue, but application: 'some men fail because they do not enter upon their work or business with a determined spirit'. . .'this class of people will never make headway or be successful in anything'. In the face of failure, Hayson said, we must press on; 'we do not labour in vain in the Lord'. Through failure God may be testing our mettle or aiding our spiritual development. Hayson declared that '[that]. . .which ought to characterise all good men. . .[is]. . .determined perseverance'.[49]

Early in 1886 Harrison addressed the Bible class on what is, for us, a vital question: 'The Relation of the Church to the World'. This paper stresses the Church–world dichotomy, but also the Church's mission to the world. He writes of the Church as the light of the world, the yeast in the lump, and of the need to spread godliness.[50] In 1895 Harrison again addressed the Bible class; he read a paper on 'Man's Power and Influence on Earth'. In this paper he criticised 'Voltare', 'Tom Pain' and 'Charles Bradlaw' (*sic*) as being 'wrong at the core' and for having led thousands to 'soul ruin'. In 1897 he addressed the same group on 'National Villages'. He cited various authorities on the state of housing, employment and wages, and his main plea was for a better environment and a more just economy.[51]

We can see from the papers of this one man alone that topics discussed at meetings are not entirely 'religious' and certainly did not stress theological matters. This is not surprising as Bible classes and Sunday school teachers' meetings are not evangelistic events. One is, if not preaching, at least speaking, to the converted. What we see in the papers relating to these meetings is a clear development of the *ideological* aspects of Methodism. But the discussions develop still wider. The diaries of Joe Taylor for 1895 and 1896 demonstrate a great catholicity of discussion at the Methodist Bible class: Garibaldi; Biblical Exposition; Hygiene; Influence of the Bible on the Nation; Womanhood Suffrage; The Independent Labour Party; Capital Punishment – to cite the topics for the first six months of 1895 only.[52]

But Harrison was writing specifically as a Methodist also; his papers include very conventional, and what may have been very unilluminating discourses on biblical topics. Remarkable throughout his work is the range of sources cited; Raikes, Samuel Smiles, Emerson, Newman and others. Nevertheless his work stresses throughout the Church–world dichotomy and the Christian's *duty* of *service* and *example*.

IMPROVEMENT CLASSES

The exact status of the improvement classes is unclear; according to Taylor they are simply improvement classes, but for Harrison they are Bible improvement classes.[53] What is clear is that much general educational activity was going on in Methodist chapels and homes, at the Baptists and in the temperance organisations. There were regular lectures, discussions, and papers were read by members. There were also socials and outings.

Harrison[54] said that '. . .an endeavour to train or cultivate the mind must be made'. In concluding his paper on 'The Mutual Improvement Class' he makes a statement epitomising the self-image of the inner-worldly ascetic. We are getting wisdom and understanding, he says, 'for the sole purpose that we might be a blessing to our fellow men, and an instrument of good in the hands of God'.[55]

Tom Turnbull exhorts his hearers to read good books; behind every book, work of art and melody there is a thinker. Thought is '...the ultimate secret of life, it is its fundamental factor, it lies behind speech, it governs conduct, it creates personality'.[56]

Taylor's *Diaries* can be used to expand the list of topics discussed in the Bible class as such. (We are not treating the Bible class and self-improvement class as entirely distinct from one another in content and purpose.) But the lectures he attended included: 'Evolution and Creation', 'A man's a man for a' that' (chaired by John Wilson, M.P.), 'Women's Work', 'Phrenology' (in the Baptist Chapel), 'Custom Slaves', 'Christian Socialism', 'Coal Dust', 'Jonathan Ireland and the street preacher', 'Sunshine and shade', 'Poets and Poetry' and 'Monopolists or the Multitude, which?'. This list does not include the political and temperance meetings attended by Taylor; nor the weekly Bible class at which he was a regular attender.

The wide variety of practical and theoretical, useful and ephemeral topics discussed is not perhaps, in itself, of the greatest interest. The most striking *consequential* dimension of belief shown by these examples is that men subject themselves to what constitutes a rigorous intellectual discipline; that they did 'endeavour to train or cultivate the mind'. This alone might be sufficient demonstration of the practical outworking of a disciplined, rational, systematic spirit in the daily lives of the Methodists. Harrison's spelling indicates that these men were not great scholars in any formal sense. They had no major public library to hand, a few would have had a rudimentary education at the colliery school, and a few books would have been available in the Miners' Institute and chapels. But their 'distinctive goal always remains the alert, methodical control of one's own pattern of life and behaviour'.[57] They are Weber's inner-worldly ascetics adopting 'planned procedures' for their salvation, deepening their understanding as active instruments of God in the world.

SUNDAY SCHOOLS

The Sunday school lessons are of the very greatest interest; firstly, because they represent the quite deliberate attempt on the part of the older Methodists to impart the main aspects of their faith to the young; secondly, because a higher proportion of the children attended Sunday school than adults attended services. It is said that virtually all non-Catholic children attended Sunday school some time during their childhood, if only for a few weeks. Thus the content of the lessons will consist of the central beliefs and values of Methodism, and this particular mode of transmitting them had a potentially wider scope and greater effect than any other method.

We may examine the Sunday school activities under five headings: the content of the lessons; the practical implications of the lessons as stated by the writer of the lessons; the ethical content of the lessons; the habits and attitudes inculcated in the scholars; the aptitudes learnt in Sunday school.

The content of the lessons

The major part of every week's lesson in the P.M. S.S.J. is biblical exposition. This journal was used from time to time in the district and was read by teachers. It fairly represents typical local teaching even when not actually used. Teachers tended to use local examples drawn from their own experiences to illustrate their lessons. The lessons work systematically through various sections of the Bible. Historical and archaeological background material is provided for the teachers as well as glossaries of difficult words and expressions. The intention seems to be, mainly, to explain the stories as history and then only secondarily to draw conclusions from the stories. When we examine other aspects of the lessons, below, we must always bear in mind that this historical exposition is quantitatively the single most important item in any lesson book. The object of these lessons is, nonetheless, to bring the child to salvation;

> Saved or unsaved is the question which should be uppermost in the mind of every teacher in looking round his class, whilst he resolves, in the strength of God's grace, to do what he can to bring to Christ those entrusted to his care.[58]

> It is the teacher's business to introduce his scholars to Jesus, to direct them in their experiences, testimony and service, as he himself is led by the Holy Spirit. He has of course to deal with heads and habits but his first and highest work is with hearts.[59]

> Appeal to the scholars that the love of the suffering Saviour win their hearts as it won the penitent thief.[60]

The practical implications of the lessons

Christian service is a topic frequently drawn from the Bible story. In commenting on Jesus washing the disciples' feet at the Last Supper the S.S.J. says of *service*: 'What scope there is in human life today for the exercise of this virtue, and what incalculable benefits would its practical observance confer on mankind.'[61] Later in the same lesson the writer refers to 'The dignity of service to others'. In reviewing the work of the second quarter of 1896 the S.S.J. notes;

> The parable of the talents reiterates this lesson of personal accountability to God for the use of the talents we possess. . .The parable of the vine-yard gives increased emphasis to the same fact. The proprietor has a right to expect some adequate return for his outlay. . .On every man there rests a responsibility, irremovable for the use of his privilege and opportunity.[62]

> Our talents vary. . .We can not always command success, but we can deserve it by our zeal and fidelity.[63]

In discussing the death of David, the S.S.J. in 1896 draws the teachers' attention to David's life of service. Later in the same volume it gives a note on 'Christian Service' which entails seeking the lost '. . .in the back alleys and slums as well as the broad avenues and in mansions'.

Service can not be fulfilled merely by going to church. 'Nothing but Christian service of the kind which has self-denial for its cornerstone, and activity for its superstructure, will save the world.'[64] To illustrate the notion of service, stories of Queen Margaret of Scotland were (and still are) often told in the Sunday school.

The theme of service is found in almost every lesson book. On 13 June 1926 there is one reference amongst many to rescue work. Christian service wherever it is carried out, even 'in the back alleys and slums', does not involve a call to political action, but a call to rescue individual sinners.

The ethical content of the lessons

One field in which the Sunday school teachers were urged to advocate state action was in matters of temperance. This is the second most important theme, after the direct exposition of Bible stories.

In March 1906 the Sunday school general secretary comments on the General Election, 'After the wilderness the Promised Land. And we have entered Canaan at last. . .' Education and temperance reform were expected. While prohibition was the ultimate aim, Sunday closing was an interim objective: 'Many a victim is asking to be protected against himself, and, what has so abundantly proved to be good for more than a quarter of a century in Scotland, Ireland, Wales and our self-governing colonies, must surely also be good for England, the loving mother of them all.'[65]

The results of 1905 were partly the outcome of a sustained temperance campaign. In 1896 for example the S.S.J. called for more Temperance meetings and a pledge-signing campaign,[66] and sermons

107

on 26 April and 29 November referred to drink, gambling, vice, bad temper and temperance, respectively. For 27 December there is a temperance address 'Does Drink bring Happiness?' In the 1916 volume of the *Journal* the editor notes that drink and gambling are especially prevalent amongst men called into the army. The *Temperance Notes* for May observe that lighting restrictions are severely inhibiting Band of Hope work and that clubs will win boys to drink if the boys are not firmly grounded in temperance principles. Secondly, they also remark of betting and gambling '...the evil is widespread and persistent. Amongst our soldiers in camp it is dreadfully prevalent.'[67] In fact one might conclude from the *S.S.J.* that the main effect of the war was on temperance work, the threat of Zeppelin raids, for example, being seen as a difficulty in Band of Hope work. The fact that wounded soldiers were not, by regulation, to be served drinks, ought to be used as an example in lessons, said the Notes in the *S.S.J.* of June 1916.

The theme survives all the political turmoil of 1912–14, 1914–18 and 1921–6 and is still alive in 1926; February, May, June bring items on heavy penalties for drunken driving, prohibition, betting and gambling and the Local Option Bill. In May both Hugh Price Hughes and Bishop Westcott are quoted with approval: 'Gambling stands in precisely the same relation to stealing that duelling stands to murder... consent of the victim and chance of being a successful criminal does not in the least degree alter the moral character of the act.'[68] Westcott also typifies gambling as one making a gain from another, with his consent, 'adding nothing to the sum of their commonwealth'.

Comment on temperance, which exercises the *S.S.J.* throughout, becomes remarkably politicised. To return to 1896:

> the traffic in strong drink is a source of wealth to many, and to be engaged in efforts the success of which is intended to diminish that wealth is only likely to stir up strife and hence an active Reformer is often a 'marked man' and made the subject of much persecution...Jesus said 'I come not to send peace on earth, but a sword' and to be one of His warriors to fight His battles is surely the highest distinction conferrable on mortal man – be it ours to fight with courage and success![69]

In June 1906 the following occurs in three pages on temperance:

> No Christian patriot can, on reflection, afford to stand idly by in supine indifference or pharisaic cynicism while the Drink Scourge, which combines in itself the evils of war, famine and pestilence put together, rolls its fiery tide of destruction o'er the land...We are menaced by a colossal and corrupt monopoly calling itself 'the trade' whose capitalised value is estimated at £250m., in direct and daily conflict with the reform and welfare of the people.[70]

In discussing Paul's missionary journeys the writer of the 25 June lesson avers that the authorities' response to the healing of the divining girl was similar to that of the brewers today. Both had vested interests.

Straight economic and political comment is rare outside the temperance context. In 1906 the editor comments:

> There are many Christians who think the minister exceeds his duty in preaching a social gospel; that it does not come within his sphere, for example, to denounce unjust laws or the sweating of labour, or the bad housing of the people or the underfeeding of the children...The pulpit should be concerned with the betterment of the conditions of life in this world as well as concerned with the fitting of human spirits for Heaven...[71]

This might be seen as an example of the growing social concern of the chamber at the turn of the century, but the author then goes on to discuss the two great evils of drink and romanism. These were burning issues relating to the promise of reform of the Licensing Laws and to the 1902 Education Act, both consequent upon the return of the Liberal Government of 1905.

Overtly 'political' comment appears in 1916 and in 1926. In June 1916 an exposition on the Syrian wars includes: 'With wealth and luxury came also selfishness and cruelty, and the rich got too far away from the poor to feel their woes and sympathise with their lot. Social conditions in Israel and Judah became much what they are with us and from similar causes.'[72] Most striking of all is the comment on the parable of the labourers in the vineyard, 'The parable may be regarded as teaching *Payment according to needs rather than results*' (original italics).[73] This lesson also comments that vines were cultivated for 'grape-juice for drinking'.

The ethical message put across in the Sunday school was thus essentially one of personal reform, especially with the respect to drinking and gambling. There are only undeveloped hints that social conditions in general might need changing. Nonetheless there is a clear call to political activity in attempting to use the state in advancing the cause of individual reform in the one area of drink. Socialist comments are remarkable because of their rarity.

The habits and attitudes inculcated

These include meekness, punctuality, exactness and thrift. Jeanie E. Walton in discussing the transformation of a four-year-old convert notes that: 'He became gentle and yielding and full of love, all his old sullen tempers seeming to disappear almost entirely; formerly he was one of the most obstinate and difficult of children.'[74] Patience is stressed in various lessons, for example, 25 October 1896 and June 1896 (à propos David waiting before he could take up his kingship).[75]

Punctuality is insisted on, perhaps as much for convenience as for any moral consideration. *Rules for the Internal Government of the Wesleyan Sunday Schools* (n.d.) suggests a system of rewards for good behaviour, repeating the lesson correctly, and for early attendance. In June 1906 the P.M. Sunday school general secretary's remarks in the *S.S.J.* include praise for and description of a mechanical device to ensure accuracy in recording who was early and late at Sunday school. Diligence and exactness might be said to be clearly associated with punctuality. In the *Lesson for Little Ones* teachers are advised by the *S.S.J.* to 'Illustrate from school-life, and apprenticeship, showing the value of exactness and honest effort.'[76] The need for exactness at work could be well illustrated from mining experience. Doing an honest day's work is reported as a central value to many of the leading Methodists. There is also discussion of cleanliness, good habits, pure thinking, speaking the truth and not yielding to temptation.[77] In 1916 it is noted in a lesson on Paul's missionary journeys that whatever the mind is fed on, so will the character be. Children should avoid books, songs and jests that do harm.[78]

The whole structure of the lessons, thorough and systematic, suggests an expectation of exact, careful, systematic work. This is an expectation of both teachers and scholars, for both of whom examinations are a test of their progress.

Another aspect of this set of attitudes, and one closely associated with the Protestant ethic, is thrift. One good example of this can be given from the 1896 *S.S.J.* in an article entitled 'A Sermon for Children', 'How to make a Penny Grow'.[79] After some discussion of the development of seeds planted in the ground, the sermon proceeds:

> Suppose, now, instead of spending all your pennies, you save some of them and take them to the post office and put them in the bank, you will find at the end of the year, when you come to count up your savings, a magic word written at the bottom: it is the word 'interest'. . .Don't spend all your money on toys and nuts and sweets, but save some part of it. Perhaps you can not put many pennies to grow by multiplication in this way, but the great thing is not the amount you may acquire, but the *formation of habits of thrift and foresight* [italics original].

But:

> Wesley said 'Get all you can, save all you can, give all you can'. We ought not to spend our pennies on selfish gratification, nor even to hoard all for our future use, but we ought to use some of them for the benefit of others. . .One way of doing so is to send

for an African Missionary Box from the General Missionary Secretary (The Reverend J. Smith) and putting your pennies in it to grow into Bibles and Hymn books, and pay for preachers for the little black boys and girls of that *dark* continent [italics original].

The aptitudes learnt in Sunday school

The S.S.J. saw the need to inculcate certain abilities in both teachers and pupils '...it must be taken into account that our teachers are drawn almost entirely from the working classes; that their education has been limited; their present opportunities are few, and the greater part of them are young and inexperienced'.[80] The teachers were encouraged to use a variety of techniques in their work; for the very young there were acrostics for blackboard work at the end of the nineteenth century; by the 1920s work with sand-trays, plants and animals was being recommended. For the older children the bioscope was suggested for 'bringing places to life'; by the Second World War the film strip and films had replaced this. Thus the teachers were expected to be proficient in the use of technical aids to teaching. In the 1960s local Sunday school teachers have commented how they cannot meet all the requirements of the suggested lessons, because of the lack of modern equipment. The preparation of lessons and preparing for examinations was seen as enriching the mind and giving 'a sound basis to character'.[81]

Teachers were encouraged to take stock of their work from time to time so that: 'Nothing is left undone that ingenuity can devise, or enterprise accomplish. These are working principles that are always commended by men of the world, and the lessons are salutary to Sunday school teachers...'[82] Perhaps most obviously, and a factor easily overlooked, teachers were required to prepare lessons and stand in front of classes to give the lessons. Public speaking, the ability to stand up to present an argument, and competence to take charge of a class, were all skills to be cultivated by Sunday school teachers.

The children also were required to speak in public. Every year at the anniversary each child had to 'say his piece' in front of a large congregation of adults. Many of the 'pieces' were meaningless doggerel, some were children's religious poetry but all had to be *learnt, practised* and *spoken in public*. The children also performed plays, presented pageants and group verse-speaking at the anniversaries. These are also activities needing careful preparation by the teachers and rehearsal by the children.

Between meetings of the Sunday school the children were expected to study the lesson and learn a text. They were gradually introduced to the Bible through simple expositions of Bible stories. The aim was to know and understand the Bible; this entailed developing a critical attitude towards it. At no point in the lessons does one find a suggestion that the Bible is literally true, word for word.

The need for some subtlety in reading the Bible is underlined in 1906 in a discussion of the 'Unforgiving Servant'. The exposition does not stress Hell-fire as one might expect, but the fact that 'by his own act he [the servant] shut and bolted mercy's door against himself...'[83] Another example, in 1926, is in an exposition on King David: the S.S.J. points out that one has to understand stories against a background of developing biblical scholarship. Thus the scholars should understand that the story they were studying was written by someone who was hostile to Saul – who thus appeared in a bad light.

Teachers and scholars were also expected to have a wide vocabulary, words such as 'correlative' and 'plethoric' appearing in the lesson notes. In discussing two biblical accounts of one event the lesson notes 'The discrepancy is only apparent' and another says that 'vicarious sacrifice is the law of all being'.

The aims of the Sunday school may be summarised in the words of an article entitled 'The Teacher's Work: What Is It?'.

> The instruction given in the class, like that given from the pulpit, whilst in the first instance it is presented to the mind, is intended to bear practically upon the character and the life...The Sunday school, of all places, is one for developing noble character, forming good habits, and its value in this respect can not be overestimated. There are worse things than learning a catechism and repeating a creed, but a good life is better than either.[84]

The main mode of achieving this good life was through learning spiritual and ethical lessons from systematic study of the Bible.

Very little material has survived from the Deerness Valley Sunday schools. Accounts given suggest that the anniversaries and 'demonstrations' were the highlights of the year. The lessons were based on the kind of material outlined above.

In addition to Harrison's Sunday school address, already cited, three undated addresses given by the Esh Winning P.M. Sunday school superintendent have survived. One is an address on 'The Lure of Strong Drink'. Another is a Christian Endeavour address on 'Review of the Divine Power'. The speaker tells his hearers that God is all powerful, He is a God who has acted in the history of men and who will act in the future. God brings down the mighty. Whatever befalls us in life we must remember that God knows our needs and 'stoops down to help us in our daily toil and care'.

The third address is entitled 'in the School of Christ'. The theme is the analogy between school and life. Life is Christ's school. He is the teacher:

The School of Christ is a very practical establishment. It's very nice to have the theory but theory without the practical is not of much value especially in Christ Service. We know as Miners there are men who are well up in the theory of the Mine but are very little use in the practical...But Christ's teaching is to be applied in conduct and attitude from the earliest lessons...The opportunities of the every day life are all the sphere we need for the practice of His lessons [sic].

This is a very striking example of Methodist teaching. The stress is upon the practical aspects of faith; everyday life in the world of the mine and village is the sphere in which Christianity is practised and Christ is the model of the ideal Christian.

DISCUSSION

Part of our problem is now more clearly stated. The Methodist regards 'the world' as 'other' – he is in it but not of it. He is a stranger and pilgrim, his true home is elsewhere and he is a different sort of man from the unsaved around him. The Methodist does not then seek mystical illumination, he is an active man. For some this entails no more than diligently pursuing his daily work, subjecting it and his whole life to rational norms, minimising contact with the chaotic and unsaved world. This could be the limit of the development of the notion of 'service'.

But we have seen a stronger development of the idea of service, of men being active instruments of the divine, here and now, *in* the world. In other words there is an interpretation of service entailing actual work on and in the fallen institutions of society rather than the diligent and private pursuit of an individual calling alone. Training in the rational and diligent pursuit of service to the world was given in the Sunday school to both scholars and teachers. Three main lines of activity would seem to be relevant to such a view, and they are not mutually exclusive lines: a continuation of evangelistic activity; doing 'the other secular things', 'feeding the hungry', saving the drunkard, helping the gambler's family and in general pursuing individual reform; serving the community as a whole, which could be anything from the practice of good-neighbourliness to serving as a party official or local councillor. These two latter activities in themselves involve very different levels of compromise with worldly political institutions; one can be a 'good neighbour' without admitting the legitimacy or usefulness of political institutions; to accept political office is to accept political institutions as legitimate means for the fulfilment of God's purposes.[85] We might also posit a logical connection between the three

lines of activity. Concern with the sins of the individual leads to a
discussion of the effects of social and physical environment when individual regeneration appears insufficient for the individual's reform.
Environmental and social matters lead to economics and politics and
a discussion of the possibility of social reform on a wide scale. This
is not to say that this is a *necessary* connection, nor the only possible
development. But if Harrison's themes are typical, then this would
appear to be one observable drift of thought and discussion, which has
implications for action.

Political radicalism and then revolutionary politics might be the next
logical stages, but it is important to note that this last stage would be
an activity without the benefit of any of the ideas outlined above to
underpin it. The world may be fallen and alien to the Methodist, one
way or another it should be changed, but its order should not be over-
thrown.

A Methodist may logically progress from neighbour to 'social
worker', to social reformer, to reforming politician, to revolutionary.
Where he stops is a matter for empirical investigation and sociological
explanation.

The very first response listed, piety and diligence, will be the most
relevant in terms of explaining the greatest number of Methodist biographies. But some Methodists, deeply imbued with the 'respectability'
of this position, were forced by events to grapple nonetheless with
dilemmas of political action, of both a reforming and revolutionary
nature.

The crux of the individual reform–social reform dilemma is epitomised in a question-and-answer session at the Waterhouses P.M.
Young People's Institute in 1926. The young people asked 'Was Christ
a socialist, and if so, in what way or ways does his socialism differ or
coincide with that of Karl Marx?' The minister opens his reply, 'The
direct answer to the former part of this question is Yes! Christ was a
socialist, but not in the way in which the term is generally employed
today.' Christ was a Socialist, he continues, because he sought the
transformation of the social order. Christians have seen Jesus

> as assuming that to whatever extent the life of society is affected
> by His life and Teaching, *it must be by influences* emanating from
> *personal centres of activity He Himself has touched*...Christ
> regarded his approach to the mass to be via the individual. He
> contemplated a transformed order of society, but that transformed
> society is to be *affected by personal centres of renewal*. The out-
> ward is to be transformed by the inward.

In response to collectivist ideas the minister asserts the traditional
Methodist belief in personal regeneration.

He makes this point another way! 'it is not my business to criticise the Marxian doctrine. It is rather to point out that it is just this materialistic interpretation of life and history that represents the great point of difference between Marx and Christ'.[86] Man's destiny is not determined by his economic environment, he can rise above it, he can be changed within it; if he has Christian ideals and is a 'centre of renewal' he can change the environment. But individual regeneration must come first.

We shall analyse the consequences of this particular Methodist belief. Beliefs and action themselves change society, or the actor's perception of it, which then has further consequences for the individual and society. We shall be observing the dialectical process outlined by Berger in his *Sacred Canopy*.[87]

COLLECTIVE EXPRESSIONS

Three further points, only, need to be developed briefly at this stage. Firstly, we need to consider the *collective* expression of beliefs amongst Methodists; secondly, to underline the practical importance of the stress on personal experiences as an integral part of the Methodist religious life; thirdly, to assess the thinking of the average Methodist if and insofar as it is different from that of the preachers and leaders we have so far considered.

The two main forms of collective expression of belief within Methodism are the singing of hymns and the offering of prayers at the prayer meeting. These are, in Glock and Stark's terms, ritualistic dimensions of religiosity; we are concerned with the content of that which is expressed ritually and collectively. Singing (and the various anniversaries of which singing formed an important part) has quite important cultural functions. It is mentioned by almost every respondent, Methodist and non-Methodist alike, as an outstanding feature of chapel activity. Every chapel had a choir, some competed successfully in choir competitions at a regional and national level. Thus the Deerness Valley earned the name 'The Singing Valley'.[88]

On Sunday the whole congregation sang, in harmony, with suitable descants by the choir. An attempt was made by the author to establish the most popular hymns at various dates; this proved abortive. The Methodist knew and sang from the whole hymn book. If a visiting preacher chose a hymn used the previous week, the choir-master would use a different tune.

Whilst some hymns are rich in theology and others may be personally significant to individual Methodists, others are theologically meaningless (for example, Newman's 'Lead Kindly Light' (*M.H.B.*, 612) and

Tennyson's 'Crossing the Bar' (*M.H.B.*, 640). The importance of hymn-singing is not in the ideas expressed, but in the act of singing. Singing in harmony entails practice under a choir-master, it requires collective discipline, the cultivation of an 'ear' for music and the development of accurate voice control. The club sing-song, for example, is not marked by disciplined singing or a wide repertoire.

Paradoxically, disciplined singing may at times fulfil some of the functions of alcohol, enabling the miner 'to escape temporarily from the consciousness of the limitations of his way of life'.[89] For the highly self-controlled Methodist it may be the only form of expressive activity available. The tensions and frustrations of daily life can be replaced by a sense of the sublime, a feeling that one is immersed in a collectivity which has a higher destiny. This may include the belief that '...men's circumstances in time may be reversed in eternity';[90] thus the Methodist miner has a foretaste of singing 'with the saints in glory'. But even the expressive behaviour of Methodists is disciplined.

Sacred song, cantatas and solos were popular. These entail even greater skill and training than congregational singing. Such singing enabled individuals to give virtuoso performances, as did the sermon. The entertainment value of such non-congregational singing was high in a community with few leisure facilities. But entertainment does not exhaust the social functions of singing. In *Coal Is Our Life* Ashton Rovers represented Ashton to other villages and the world at large. In our villages the village choirs similarly represented the villages to one another (providing occasions for exchange of visits, especially at the competitive choir festivals and *eisteddfodau*) and to the outside world. Respondents also refer to the joy of singing and to the manner in which it helped to generate religious experience. The look of bliss reported on the choir-master's face as he sat down with eyes closed after the hymn arose from a mixture of spiritual fulfilment and satisfaction in a hymn well sung.

This brief discussion of singing and the suggestion that the singing is at least as important as the song underlines the importance of understanding, or attempting to understand, the *form* of activities and the *mode* of expression of beliefs.

With sermons as well, the form of delivery demanded a degree of discipline in both the preacher and the congregation. It involved a knowledge of the Bible, a willingness to learn, the ability to synthesise or contrast concepts and a critical attitude. Without any consideration of the content of sermons and hymns and sacred songs we could conclude that the Methodist tended to be a highly disciplined, self-controlled person, willing to train his mind in critical thinking and his voice in harmony singing. He engaged and engages in forms of intellectual activity and collective expressions which set him in very sharp contrast to the non-Methodist, who, for example, sings only in the club or pub sing-song. We should, perhaps, be careful not to exaggerate this distinction. Members of other religious groups also had a collective and intellectual life. One group of non-religious miners met on non-pay Fridays in a public house to discuss what a member described as 'philosophical' issues – which included the work of Max Müller. But such would not be the activities of the majority of 'non-religious' miners.

What else may a congregation be doing when it sings hymns? It is more nearly creating the Durkheimian experience of religion than at any other time. The collective singing of hymns, especially with swelling choruses, creates a religious euphoria, induces a sense of external and constraining forces upon the individual. The more the observer becomes participant the more he feels that almost anything might happen when the singing is euphoric. The shared euphoria produces even more fervent singing. An evangelistic service is 'softened up' early on for the evangelical appeal, which may itself be accompanied by 'Last verse again', or 'One more chorus'. This was successful enough for there to be reports of converts leaping over the pews to 'come to the front'. At the end of an ordinary service the congregation collectively assert their solidarity (the little flock) in song, as they prepare to disperse (into 'the world'). Therefore it may matter less what hymns say than what they do to the group and the individual.

Prayer meetings followed the Sunday evening services. These died out after the Second World War and it has not been possible to observe or participate in such meetings. Written records do not exist. From accounts given it seems that the prayer meetings of the 1870s and 1880s matched the evangelical services in their fervour. In the atmosphere of revival and conversion, the singing, preaching and calls to be saved, enormous psychological tensions must have built up within the participants. For some, release would be found in coming forward to be saved. For others, including those known to be saved already, the prayer meeting would have provided an outlet for the tensions. There are no accounts of speaking with tongues as such, but some men are reported to have prayed incomprehensibly or in near-gibberish. This respondents refer to as the 'old ranting style' of prayer meeting. This style can be remembered and respondents say that from the streets you could hear them 'hammering on the pews'. We find little evidence of conversionist meetings of any kind after the earliest years of this century, a finding replicating Pickering's Yorkshire findings.[91] Ranting prayer meetings are recalled from the 1920s, but they were invariably led by men in their seventies. It would seem that the same men led from the early days virtually until the prayer meetings died out. The meetings of the 1920–40 period took a stereotyped form with stylised prayers led by the same people every week. Certain men were expected, and themselves expected, to lead; others were expected to pray at some stage of the meeting, and everyone knew what they were going to say and prompted them if necessary.[92] The congregation were expected to stay for the meeting but it is uncertain how many did stay. The prayer meeting as vital expression of religion was probably a phenomenon confined to the early days of the movement in the villages. The meetings could have become a collective expression of the identity of the chapel élite, but without further evidence it is not possible to draw such a conclusion with certainty. Parenthetically we may note that the prayer meeting was used as an evangelistic technique; Methodists would ask non-members if week-night meetings could be held in their homes.[93]

The class meeting connects collective expressions with personal experience. The class was an 'experience meeting' at which members were expected to be able to give account of their conversion and growth in the Christian life, and to recount experiences. The important point for us is not that the class stressed the importance of personal experience, but they expected members to be able to *give an account* of that experience.[94] The young class member would prepare for his first testimony before a small group of acquaintances. Subsequently he (and the other members) would live from day to day in the consciousness of the need to account for their daily lives, the use of their talents, etc., not only to God on the Last Day, but to the class every week. The class is thus potentially the lynchpin of a disciplined and planned life, lived in a rational accounting spirit. It is precisely at this crucial point of the analysis that our data are most sparse. In fact we have no records of prayer or class meetings at all, save a few very subjective accounts of later meetings in the 1920s.

CONCLUSIONS

However well-argued, the theological content of sermons does not seem to have engraved itself deeply in the minds of the hearers, or certainly not at an intellectual level. Irrespective of the precise content, the simple evangelical preaching with converts coming forward at the end of the service seems to have offered most satisfaction to the Methodist.

> They used to preach the Gospel – but not now, anything that comes into their heads. They used to stick to scriptures, expounding Bible passages, very evangelical. But now you get politics and so on, never hear of any converts.'[95]

Preaching used to be blood and thunder. The pure Gospel; there have been vast changes in the post-war [1939–45] years. We didn't have much Wesleyan theology; too much now, since Union it's been John Wesley at every verse end.[96]

The main significances of being converted, of being a Christian, was for the Methodist what Glock and Stark would call the consequential aspects. It was the pattern of ethical behaviour which defined a man's religion to his neighbours. A pattern of life in which the pivotal ethical issues were drink, gambling, thrift and sabbatarianism. These will be considered in Chapter 6. We may now summarise the discussion so far.

Methodism was an evangelistic religion offering the simple alternatives of eternal life or eternal death. These were plainly represented in this life in the distinction between the upright man and the indebted drunkard.

According to Methodists no man was so depraved as to be beyond salvation. All could, and should, strive for Christlike perfection.

For the average Methodist the faith was simple. He was relatively untheological in his thinking. Religion was something seen essentially in terms of the effects on individual lives.

Thus religion was practical, this-worldly, calling for self-discipline and service, by men and women imbued with a sense of duty and a calling from God.

Orderliness and discipline were maintained and reinforced by the class meeting, and were expressed in the very activities of hearing sermons and singing hymns.

Thus village Methodism conforms to Weber's ideal type, inner-worldly asceticism.

Methodists saw the main social issues as the evils of gambling, drink and debt – personal failings. Therefore they sought indvidual regeneration and beyond this, social reform. Their social analysis was, ultimately, individualistic.

For some Methodists at least a greater understanding of the world was necessary. They subjected themselves to a more rigorous and more intellectual discipline in the Bible and self-improvement class. For these men simple theology was augmented by economics, philosophy, politics, etc., in order to widen their understanding of man, God and society.

These conclusions also indicate the expectations we might reasonably have of Methodist life and behaviour in the villages. In Chapter 6 we shall begin to test these expectations against Methodist biographies, and later against Methodist history.

5 Village Methodism – II: the structure of the Methodist societies in the Deerness Valley

INTRODUCTION

The church–sect dichotomy is probably overworked by sociologists, and the discussion of the dichotomy has generated a literature of its own. It is intended to stand aside from this discussion except insofar as some aspects of it impinge upon our particular analysis.

The differences between a church and a sect involve: differences in beliefs concerning grace and nature, a different theology, Christology and eschatology as well as different ideas concerning the nature of the church itself and different understandings of and responses to 'the world'.[1] No one of these considerations is definitive of a church or a sect. Clusters of ideas have a logical coherence and consistency and they show an 'elective affinity' for one another and particular social structures. It is to the whole group of phenomena that Weber and Troeltsch refer, not to any one aspect of them. Beliefs, especially those shaping attitudes towards the state and towards church membership, have implications for the internal structures of churches and sects.

Richard Niebuhr has suggested that there is a dynamic relation between church and sect.[2] According to him, the sect begins as a movement among the disinherited; the ascetic discipline of the sectarian life leads to prosperity, thus creating economic interests which involve the sect member more deeply in the economic life of the society. Furthermore, and crucially, the sect has to cope with the problem of the second generation. In taking on 'the character of an educational and disciplinary institution, with the purpose of bringing the new generation into conformity with ideals and customs which have come traditional',[3] the sect gives up its demands for religious enthusiasm and the experience of conversion. Routinised admission to the sect often entails the development of a professional ministry, theological colleges and a doctrinal orthodoxy. The sect moves towards a church structure. Thus 'by its very nature the sectarian organisation is valid only for one generation'.[4] The development of an interest in private and corporate material and ideal property leads the sect to compromise with the world. Compromise, Antoni has argued, is the main theme of Troeltsch's *Social Teaching of the Christian Churches.*[5] This 'compromise' also touches fundamentally sociological themes; the relation between beliefs and social structure, the unintended consequences of both adherence to particular beliefs and the creation of certain social institutions.

Wilson contends that Niebuhr was concerned with only one among a number of possible sect types; namely the 'conversionist' sects which seek, through active evangelism, to bring converts into their membership.[6] While readily agreeing that the relation between the sect and 'the world' is the crucial factor for the sect's continuation or change, Wilson demonstrates how *beliefs* determine the church–world relationship in the first place. The conversionist sect needs an organisation adequate to a campaign in 'the world', it needs to make continuous contact with the world, especially when it seeks to absorb newly converted but unsocialised members of worldly society into itself. This is because these sects are 'world conquering': they believe they should try to win the world for God. This raises a set of problems peculiar to conversionist sects. The attempts to solve these problems entail consequences for the sect which may result in a more church-like structure. But the gnostic, adventist and introversionist sects have a quite different 'natural history' from the conversionist sects selected by Niebuhr. Wilson shows that the change towards church structure is by no means universal or inevitable.

The discussion of churches and sects by Troeltsch, Weber, Niebuhr, Wilson and others has been mainly confined to whole religious organisations; churches or sects as national, regional, class or ethnic organisations or movements. Some studies of particular religious groups have attempted to spell out the implications of the particular structure, assuming (but not concentrating on) their position in a church-sect typology, in their particular social contexts. The studies of Amish society and the Moravians by Hostetler and Gillian Gollin in Europe and America are penetrating studies of this kind.[7] On the whole it has nevertheless been assumed that churches and sects are relatively consistent organisations which can be located *as a whole* within a taxonomic and analytical framework of the church–sect dichotomy type.

This assumption is valid if one wishes to study a communitarian religion, or a religious organisation for its own sake. Lenski's statement that '. . .sociologists have regarded [religious groups] as merely one more type of specialised, formal association'[8] is an over-simplification, but he does propose a new application of a familiar dimension to socio-religious groups that helps us overcome this problem of isolating religious groups from a wider social content. Lenski shows that religious groups may be either communal or associational. He demonstrates empirically that communal bonds are strong among Jews and Negro Protestants, while associational links are weak for the former and medium for the latter. In *The Religious Factor* Lenski shows that one may belong to a religious group as one belongs to any other formal association, engaging in a '. . .limited number of highly specialised and relatively impersonal relationships to which the associations give rise . . .'[9] Conversely, one's religious group might be co-terminous with a communal group bonded by marriage, kinship, common upbringing, nationality, language, etc. A communal religious group may be either a sub-community of a wider communal grouping or a small community within a wide association.

There is a probability that religious groups will in fact experience some tension between communal and associational structures and beliefs and display elements of both in their actual structures and beliefs. The two types of bond or social relations can exist simultaneously in the same religious group; for some it may be primarily an association and perhaps secondarily a communal group, while for others the reverse is the case. Lenski is concerned mainly with community and association as objective factors in social structure and their consequences for attitudes, but we note that they could constitute subjective factors also. Communal and associational attitudes might be alternative *orientations* for a religious group, or a religious movement.

These considerations may now be put alongside those of Niebuhr and Wilson. Firstly, in considering the development of a particular sect towards a church-type or in maintaining its sectarian nature, we ought also to consider the implications of its local groups being mainly associations or communities – or in the process of changing between the two. Secondly, we should note the way in which the sect's beliefs affect not only its relations to 'the world' and hence its own social structure (*pace* Wilson) but also how these beliefs directly affect internal social relations and *hence* the sect's relations with the world.

For an example of the first consideration we should note the explanation given for attitudes towards ecumenism: the common professional interests of the clergy and the economies of scale achieved by mergers. Thus, it is argued one can explain why positive ecumenical orientations increase as one moves up a hierarchy. But the converse is also true: the lower down (or further from) a hierarchy one is, the more likely is one's religion to be synonymous with membership of a relatively closed communal group. The 'business-like' mergers seem less relevant from this position. Both these considerations would seem to be important in, for example, explaining the 1969 Methodist voting (at quarterly meetings, synods and conference) on Methodist–Anglican union. The proportion supporting union increased as the voting moved from local to conference level. Thus on a straw vote in the Deerness Valley circuit only two out of a hundred voting voted in favour of union whilst 77% of the assembled ministers and laity voted for union at the Methodist conference. The national percentages were as follows: voting in favour of union, at circuit level 55%; at district level 67%; at conference 77%.

It will be argued below that institutional changes, church-sect and community-association developments, can be independent at different institutional levels. Thus we will argue that Methodism has progressed from a sectarian to church-like structure whilst village Methodism has become more communal and possibly less associational, only formally and lightly linked to the wider association through a few officials. But the two processes do from time to time impinge on one another. For example, the rationalisation of fund-raising expected by the national church conflicts with the pursuit of local activities with a high communal significance: bazaars, jumble sales, concerts and 'special efforts'.

We are not at this stage suggesting a general theory; we can only observe one concrete historical development. Methodism started in the villages as a conversionalist sect (*vis-à-vis* local society). Evangelical activities required the generation of a religious experience, which was generated and renewed collectively. The collective experience became more important to the participants than the evangelism. Endogamy, socialisation, a sharp church-world dichotomy and ethical restraints on crossing the boundary, patterns of cultural activity and the constant stress on collective religious experience were bound to create at least a feeling of isolation from certain major aspects of village life. This was accentuated by the demands made on Methodists who had little time to spare for non-chapel activities. The notion of the Methodist being among 'the saved' further reinforced the sense of being a small religious community. The second generation was brought in through the Sunday school. Some of this second generation were lost through social mobility, itself the result of paternal ascetic discipline and aspirations. Some, lacking the experience of revivalism, found the chapel a congenial club consisting of family friends; others found it religiously or socially irrelevant. The village Methodists resisted, or at least resented, efforts by the Methodist Church nationally to rationalise Church organisation and participate in ecumenical mergers. Village Methodism remained throughout, in theory, a revivalist (conversionist) sect, but with prayer for revival becoming a substitute for revival itself. It still remains apart from the developments in national religious organisations; the ecumenical movement and the discussions of secularisation and 'the death of God' remain the activities of metropolitan Methodists.

The chapels had, in 1969, the formal structure of any (average) Methodist Society. The small numbers of members available for office necessitated plural office-holding and vacant offices. At Esh Winning 22 offices were held by 18 individuals and in the two Waterhouses Societies 12 by 6 and 6 by 4 respectively. Other members had been approached and asked to take office, but (the women particularly) seemed to be unwilling to accept formal responsibility. Many said they were eager to 'help out' with flowers, suppers, cleaning or 'special efforts' but they did not feel competent to hold office. The administrative duties which connected the local society, district and connexion were carried out almost entirely by the senior society steward and the Trust secretary (see Glossary), but in these affairs they were usually assisted by the minister and circuit steward. The office-holders themselves commented on the unwillingness of other members to assume responsibility.

The relative separation of the ordinary Methodist from the administration of his church is matched by ignorance of the general structure of Methodism. In 1968 a decision was taken to close Bourne ex-P.M. chapel (Waterhouses) and to amalgamate the Waterhouses Societies. This decision had not been acted upon by mid-1969, mainly through ignorance of procedures. One trustee, without authority, sought planning permission for change of use of the chapel building. He was told that this would be granted for two years only. The chapel thus became unsaleable. The usual procedure is to sell and leave planning problems to the purchaser. In this case all three prospective buyers would have offered small-scale employment for local people; a circumstance almost certain to attract a more favourable planning decision. The chapel was finally closed in 1971. Discussion in 1968 showed that some trustees and many members believed that they *owned* the chapel rather than holding it in trust for the Connexion. Their parents had raised the money for the building and all had contributed to its upkeep; it seemed only logical to them that the local members should have the right to dispose of the property and the proceeds of any sale. In the course of the meeting to discuss this business some members also asked questions about the leaders' meeting, what it did and who could attend. The names of the leaders are always printed in the *Plan* (see Glossary).

Ignorance of Methodist structures was revealed in the discussion prior to the quarterly meeting which was to vote on Anglican–Methodist union. The meeting at Esh Winning in spring 1969 expressed surprise and dismay when members were told that the decision would not be based on one-Methodist-one-vote. There was an implicit

assumption in the discussion that Methodism as a whole was as democratic as the local society meeting. The system of indirect representation also alarmed many members as they felt that their representatives
might not express the wishes of the membership, a relatively un-
founded fear as the figures for the straw vote suggest. The belief that
the 'high-ups' in Methodism were going to betray the rank and file
at conference by voting for union was expressed explicitly. Therefore
there was a wish for the strongest possible vote against union at the
quarterly meeting as an attempt to constrain conference. When an
attempt was made to clarify the situation at the meeting there was
some verbal conflict over *who* the representatives at quarterly meeting
were. Details of this had been printed in the *Plan* since the formation
of the Society in 1932.

Two notable points arise from a consideration of these two situations.
Firstly, the ignorance about the formal machinery of Methodist
administration was general, as was, secondly, ignorance of the system
of indirect representation which is the very basis of the Methodist
polity, and a major factor in historical conflicts.[10]

In the course of the public discussion of Anglican–Methodist union
a number of Methodists said, in private conversation, that if union
came they would 'go to the Baptists'. This was said without any sense
of changing an historical tradition or altering any beliefs. In the course
of unstructured interviews and three years of regular participant observation no member ever expressed an awareness of any differences of
belief between the Methodists and other churches. About five respondents mentioned the Methodist stress on personal experience as a
feature of the religious life. Many noted ethical and ritualistic
differences, but some respondents said that these were the *only*
characteristics differentiating Methodists, Baptists, Anglicans and
Roman Catholics. Perhaps given the fact that most of the Methodists
were old and had only elementary education it is not surprising that
they had little intellectual grasp of their religion. It is surprising, however, in the light of their exposure to Sunday school teaching and to
preaching. It is remarkable that none showed the slightest knowledge
of historical differences of belief and structure. What is important here
is that theology is not a criterion defining religion for Methodists; behaviour more normally is. Thus Methodists tend to define as Christians,
or good men, all who meet up to Methodist ethical requirements,
irrespective of their formal religious affiliation.

Only 6 out of 77 Methodists, specifically asked, did not come into
Methodism through the Sunday school. The Sunday school is one of
the methods used by a religious group to socialise the younger generation. A sect often substitutes this socialisation for the requirement of

conversion, and only four Methodists claimed to have been converted from a non-religious state. The Deerness Valley Methodists were thus overwhelmingly second generation Methodists (or 'transfers' from other religions). The Sunday schools were more like junior churches than 'schools' in the accepted sense of the word. We find that they formed the main mode of entry to the contemporary chapel.

The language used by Methodists was highly suggestive of their communal orientation to religion. When speaking of the chapel they described how they were 'brought up in it', through the Sunday school, with its anniversaries ('saying my first piece at. . .'), Christian Endeavour, Band of Hope, etc. 'Ten of my family went away from Sunday school [i.e. left the district]. . .*it was Uncle Ernie's Sunday School. . .*' (emphasis added).[11] The older members said how they felt 'at home' in their chapel. Others mentioned ornaments, furnishings and windows, memorials of their family's long connection with and faithful service to the chapel. One middle-aged woman commenting on possible chapel closures said, 'Why close a chapel if it's not in debt and people are happy there? It's a home to some people, they were brought up in it. Closing a chapel is like taking someone's home away. They wouldn't be happy.'[12]

Any visiting preacher could win the approval of the congregation by alluding to his 'warm welcome' and how he enjoyed being back among 'the folk' in the village. 'Methodist folk', 'chapel folk', were highly approved descriptive terms, indicating a Methodist self-image as one of simple, down-to-earth, unassuming and friendly people. The Lord's Prayer was frequently introduced as 'the family prayer' and most of the prayer in the Sunday services was devoted to the village, the old and the sick, and members who could not attend on that day. The preacher used the language of 'community', not the language of 'association'; he referred to folk rather than members. He was expected to stand at the door after the service, to shake the hand of all leaving, to exchange greetings with old friends and welcome newcomers. The most obvious feature of a Sunday service for a newcomer is the warm welcome with which he is received.

The Sunday service, and especially its prayers, are first and foremost directed to the community's spiritual and moral needs. Unpleasant and divisive matters like personal sin are not raised in any individually challenging way. Intercession for the rest of the world is brief and quite lengthy prayers finish with a hasty, '. . .and forgive us all our sins'. This apparent decline of interest in sin may be a result of the loss of the prayer meeting in which sin and forgiveness were major themes, but it is also a mark of the way in which individual and divisive problems have been replaced by family or local issues.

The sense of being a small family or community entails a degree of parochialism. A minister's wife reported extreme difficulty in persuading women to attend meetings in the next village, or even meetings they had not habitually attended previously in their own chapel. An important women's meeting was held in Bearpark when the minister's wife was on holiday. Only two Esh Winning members attended, a mother and a daughter resident in Quebec. The researcher also learns not to ask a society official who is his opposite number in another village. The answer is, 'Oh, that's Waterhouses, I wouldn't know'. This narrowness of orientation was not perceived by the Methodists themselves, for they believed that they maintained not only friendly and warm but *open* relationships. This was clearly illustrated in attitudes to Methodist–Anglican union. The objections to the union scheme most consistently voiced were that the service of reconciliation suggested that Methodist ministers were not as good as Anglican ministers; and that the Church of England had closed communion (voiced mainly in Waterhouses where there is an Anglican church). In Methodism all 'Who love the Lord' were invited to the communion table, in the Anglican Church only confirmed members. Thus the Church of England was seen by Methodists as being a closed group and a group denying the authenticity of the Methodist ministry. These are not theological objections to union, but objections expressed in terms of non-reciprocity.

These orientations described above are more to 'community' than 'association'. In an objective sense the Methodist Society was a community in that it was almost a large extended family. The genealogical tables overleaf show the family trees of Matthew White and Isaac Johnson. We can see from these that they and their children married other Methodists, by and large; White and Johnson lived next door to one another in Waterhouses, and their children played together and were later acquainted with one another's spouses. What these family trees do not show (save in the case of Ann Stephenson) is that White and Johnson had brothers and nephews who were Methodists and their sons had Methodist uncles on both sides of their family. Plainly the families named in these figures were not connected by common membership of a formal organisation alone, nor were they only connected by kinship. More than a half, probably three-quarters, of all the Methodists are related to other Methodists (often Methodists in the same village); many are related to more than one other, and are sometimes related to one person in more than one way. Much anecdotal evidence shows that, for example, choirs tended to be endogamous. From an account given while looking at a 1919 choir photograph it would seem that most of the men in the choir married women from

Family of Matthew White (ages of younger living members are not shown)

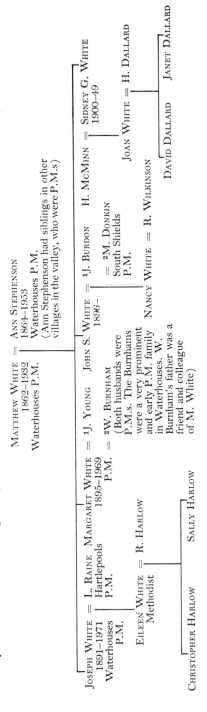

Family of Isaac Johnson (ages of younger living members are not shown)

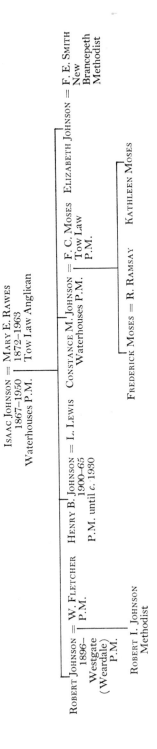

the choir. Methodist parents preferred their children to marry Methodists, and failure to do so was cited as one reason for a falling off in individual church attendance. Parents were not surprised if one spouse attended the other's church; hence changes between societies, between P.M.s and W.M.s or Methodist and Church of England were accepted. Equally acceptable was the idea of one spouse occasionally returning to his or her own chapel.

Intermarriage with Roman Catholics was resisted, sometimes with threats of non-attendance at the wedding. No cases of such a sanction actually being used were recorded. The marriages seemed to be accepted after the event. Resistance was based on rather inchoate dislike of Catholic ethics (as perceived by the Methodists), the alienness of Catholic religious expressions, the power of the priest, and the exclusiveness of the Catholic community, which demands the total commitment of the children of the marriage. These are communally-based objections, not objections based on an explicit understanding of Catholic Church structure and teaching. The objections were rooted in general notions of the sort of people Catholics are and the sort of demands Catholicism makes. The least articulate informants said they had a feeling that such marriages 'wouldn't work' but they would give no reasons – a position often adopted on the proposed marriage of the Methodist and Anglican Churches.

So far we have seen the relatively narrow horizons and communal orientations of the Methodists. They were also detached from the formal structure, business and doctrinal discussions of national Methodism. We have observed also that the Methodists are actually communal groups, strongly linked by kinship ties.

The first response of a Methodist to any general enquiry concerning local Methodism was an enthusiastic account of how there used to be activities in the chapel every night. An interview for 25 August 1966 records the following activities for the two Waterhouses chapels in the first half of this century: Sundays were spent almost entirely in the chapel; services, Sunday school and prayer meetings, and during the week:

	Bourne (P.M.)	Russell Street (W.M.)
Monday	Preaching service	Class meeting
Tuesday	Class Meeting	Preaching service (every other week)
Wednesday	Christian Endeavour	Free
Thursday	Choir practice	Choir practice and friends' own
Friday	Free	Free
Saturday	Special efforts	Special meetings

The Quebec P.M.s had a similar programme:

Monday	Class meeting
Tuesday	Christian Endeavour
Wednesday	Preaching service
Thursday	Band of Hope and choir practice
Friday	Independent Order of Good Templars (temperance)
Saturday	Special efforts

Members of both Waterhouses chapels would attend one another's special efforts. Fridays were free evenings, as the Store (Co-op.) stayed open until 8.00 p.m. on that evening. Today Methodists continually express regret at the passing of 'good times' and say how 'it's a shame' that these social activities no longer take place. The decline – which does not concern us as such here – is ascribed to many causes: materialism, the motor bus, the Durham ice-rink, T.V., etc. No chapels have more than an average of one week-night meeting now.

The chapels were cultural centres in the village; at least, they were non-drinking, non-gambling social centres and almost the only legitimate source of entertainment for the women. The special efforts were usually associated with fund-raising activities. Oriental bazaars, eastern markets, pink suppers (with the hall, food and attendants dressed in pink), concerts, choir recitals, were popular with the villagers and drew good attendances. These activities involved the Methodists in days or weeks of preparation and rehearsal, bringing them together again and again in purposeful and pleasurable activities. Many would be engaged in more than one event; all would attend Sunday services. Thus throughout the week Methodists were continually meeting one another in chapel activities to an extent which precluded non-chapel activities. We observe from the press and individual respondents that very high standards of musical performance were achieved in these chapels indicating not only much rehearsal, but also that musical performances were not only social occasions but a source of non-religious aesthetic pleasure.

Throughout this discussion we have excluded any consideration of work; it is at the place of work and in the associations arising from the work situation that Methodists interact with non-Methodists and take an active part in non-religious organisations. The Methodists had, nevertheless, created a pattern of sociable activities which tended to be exclusive. Methodist activities were, formally, open to all, but few Methodists were themselves active outside their religious community.

Methodist society is discontinuous with the wider community. This is to say that Methodists and non-Methodists tended not to interact in non-work situations except in circumstances where elementary mutual aid was required. Leisure activities were the most sharply segregated. Dennis *et al.* in their study of Ashton, concluded that 'The pursuit of leisure. . .has two principal characteristics. It is vigorous and it is predominantly frivolous.'[13] Leisure pursuits in Ashton embody the principle that 'life must be lived from day to day and whatever surplus income there is over every-day needs should be spent in securing whatever pleasures are possible. In Ashton these pleasures are mainly drinking and gambling.'[14]

Taylor in his work on Durham villages[15] confirmed the short-term hedonistic pattern of gregarious leisure activity and his account of an evening at the club in Craghead exactly describes an evening in the big club in Esh Winning, so the miners' leisure pattern seems to be similar in Yorkshire and Durham. But for the Methodist drinking and gambling are anathema and Methodists were never to be found in the club.

The social segregation of the Methodists in the non-work situation was reinforced by Methodist beliefs. Abhorrence of drink and gambling, their sense of being a saved band of pilgrims in a fallen world, mentally separated them from a wider society, as did the general notions of church and world, sacred and profane, serious and frivolous. The segregation was, in part, mutually acknowledged. Some thought the Methodists stand-offish or snobbish, although we judge this not to have been a very widespread view. It was accepted that one did not swear in front of Methodists (except to provoke or antagonise them) nor expect them to drink or gamble. Malicious gossip against Methodists, on the other hand, often alleged back-door deliveries and secret drinking.

The shared religious experiences of the Methodists underlined their separation from the population at large and linked all the Methodists in a village irrespective of the specialised week-night activities in which they engaged. The Sunday and week-night activities were presided over by a few men who became patriarchs. Large sections of six volumes of interviews are filled with comments on these men; they are remembered as great men, good men to whom one looked up and whom one respected. The lives of these allegedly saintly men, especially anecdotes telling how they commanded the respect of the most profane, constitute the folk history of Methodism: for example, Isaac Hewitson by his very commanding presence broke up the Sunday pitch-and-toss school and Matt White stopping the swearing at his place of work. It is an oral tradition; the memories of these men crowd out more mundane recollections of life in the chapels. These men held unquestioned authority until the 1930s. The consequences of this long period of authority (some fifty years) is discussed elsewhere. Two points are relevant to this discussion. Firstly, long deprivation of authority and lack of experience virtually disqualified the next generation from leadership. Furthermore, the rank and file also were not accustomed to the idea that they might hold responsible positions in the society. Secondly, the type of authority exercised by these men and the response of the ordinary Methodist-in-the-pew to it further reinforced the hierarchical family of the Methodist community. Matt White, Isaac Johnson, Aron Richardson, Isaac Hewitson and Jack Henery were *fathers* of the chapel, who ruled by personal, moral power, not on the basis of any legal–rational authority conferred upon them by an organisation.

Contemporary conflicts within the societies underline further the communal nature of local Methodism. In bureaucratic organisations one might expect to find conflicts over the allocation of capital and other resources and conflict between various officials concerning the status of their office in the organisation.[16] We do not find this in the chapels today. In one village an assistant organist and a society steward fall out every six months and are reconciled by the minister. The cause of this and other conflicts seems to be, in essence, the feeling of individuals or groups that their efforts are not appreciated by others. The deepest split within one society was threatened when the minister paid the cleaner for opening the chapel for a wedding, instead of the caretaker who was away at the time. The caretaker's family were incensed and threatened to leave the chapel; the grievance was partly mollified by the payment of a second fee, and other members pressured the caretaker's family against precipitate action – pointing to the imminent departure of the minister. The basis of conflict seems to be the demand for gratitude and appreciation, and the reaction to slights and insults. 'Family squabbles' more appropriately describe these disputes than terms taken from theories of organisational conflict.

We have a cluster of mutually reinforcing factors which make analysis of the Methodist societies in terms of formal organisations, or associations (in the community–association dichotomy) inappropriate. The societies are relatively small, family-like groups, united by common beliefs, kinship, a shared upbringing, religious, cultural and recreational life, lived under the eye of patriarchal leaders and divided only by personal disputes. The core of this religious community is both objectively and subjectively separated from the wider community by beliefs and the ethical consequences of beliefs. We will show later how this isolation deepened and had significant but unintended consequences.

ASSOCIATION

The local society is part of a nationally organised denomination. Local administration should be conducted in a business-like way. This was especially necessary as the three Methodist Connexions made specific demands of the local societies: the appointment of a full board of trustees, the effective care and maintenance of property, the reduction of debt, contributions to Connexional funds, the provision of returns in respect of finance, numbers and progress of the society as a whole and of Sunday school and temperance work. The Connexions provided loans and insurance facilities, a trained ministry, a central supply of Sunday school material and various journals and magazines, and many other services. Central arrangements largely relieved the local societies of such responsibilities as providing pensions, producing instructional literature, entering the market for loans and insurance, creating committees or negotiating machinery to treat with government, the civil administration and other religious bodies. It is making these provisions for a sect at a national level, Wilson and others have argued, which in part sets off a denominationalising process. But a further consequence is that denominationalising processes are not strongly developed at the local level.

Surviving minute books carefully record decisions, dates are entered and the minutes properly approved and signed. The writing is usually copperplate, written not only with clarity but in an elegant style. Accounts were kept with meticulous care on a simple double-entry system. It is possible to reconstruct the finances of the local societies in great detail, for every penny of income and expenditure is recorded. One schoolteacher reported that as a student in the 1920s he was asked to audit some chapel accounts which he found to be models of good book-keeping. Here we do see the methodical, rational spirit of Methodism; but a spirit expressed, it would seem, by a few men. The trustees and leaders were a relatively small group within the society, some – shopkeepers, for example – recruited to the trustees because of their experience with money. The opportunities for the ordinary Methodist to develop these skills and express them in this way was limited. Nevertheless each group within the chapel (choir, Christian Endeavour, Wesley Guild, etc.) had its committee, and although there was not the same formal obligation to keep records and make returns, some opportunity would be available for a wider group of Methodists to develop basic administrative and clerical skills. Recently a higher proportion of whole societies have had to be involved as trustees and society officers and more women have been drawn into these roles, albeit reluctantly.

What is suggested here is that the attitudes necessary for the maintenance of the economic and administrative structure need not be and are not reflected in orientations to the local religious community itself – beyond perhaps a certain sobriety and orderliness of conduct, a sense of knowing when things are done 'the right way'. The formal requirements of the Connexion are met by the efforts of perhaps only two or three officials and the minister, and official meetings take up little time compared with other activites. Bryan Wilson comments that the minimal administrative requirements of a sect 'may be handled by very rudimentary organisation, or each or any item may entail the establishment in the sect of more elaborate and formalised procedures'.[17] The Methodists in the Deerness Valley seem to have developed an effective but minimal organisation necessary to meet the requirement of the Connexion and the proper conduct of chapel life.

Rational accounting and the ordered conduct of business are demands arising both from the perceived goals of the organisation and its normative demands – we have already seen that Methodism would encourage the diligent pursuit of duties within the society. But 'The sect can not adopt policies and methods with reference to rational or economic criteria alone: its goals are in large part super-terrestrial, and the criteria of success and efficiency employed in the world are inappropriate to it'.[18] We might add that the mundane goals of the sect might also, in large part, be the promotion of communal activities and warm sociability amongst the members. Compartmentalisation of activities and accompanying attitudes is simple – everyone knows (or thinks they know) how the chapel finances should be run, but it would not be relevant to apply business-like or calculating attitudes to the warm fellowship of a week-night meeting. The warm, gregarious activities predominated over business activities. Communal and associational features, both structural and attitudinal, co-existed, but the communal were subjectively more important for the ordinary member.

According to Wilson it is crucially the need to organise, to evangelise and bring in new members which leads to the elaboration of formal structures within a sect.[19] To what extent was this the case in the valley?

The origins of Methodism in the valley are known only through the official histories, it is not at all clear whether the oral history is in fact derived from the written histories or not.[20] Primitive Methodism came to the valley in about 1860 when James Wilson started holding meetings in his house. The next year Crook circuit listed the membership as one. First the colliery hay-loft was borrowed for larger meetings and then the P.M.s alternated with the W.M.s in using the British

134

school for Sunday services. In 1872 the P.M.s built their own chapel. One Primitive arrived in Cornsay in 1869 and found three others already there; they met first in a house, then an empty cottage, then a machine shed and finally the membership, which had by then grown, built the Quebec chapel in 1875. Joseph Harrison moved from Quebec to Esh Winning in 1894 and found twenty members. Through his efforts in overcoming the problem of buying land from Roman Catholics a chapel was built in 1899.

Many of the leaders who are the main subject of the next chapter were products of this heroic age of valley Methodism. In 1880 Matt White, John Stephenson and George McLane were converted and joined John Henery who had been in the society for two or three years. Ralph Hayson, the diarist of the previous chapter, had been a trustee at Waterhouses since 1871, but he eventually moved to Quebec. By 1906 the following, amongst others, had become trustees in line to Hayson: William Burnham (senior), James Fitzpatrick, Isaac Raine and Matt White.

We do not know the exact circumstances of the conversion of many of these men. It is said by some of Matt White that he was converted while drunk, but surviving relatives strongly deny the story. The *D.C.* of 22 October 1880 reported the end of a P.M. mission led by 'Mr. Winter' in which thirty converts had been made. It may be that Matt White was one of these thirty.

It seems as if the small bands of early Methodists were successful in increasing their numbers. Some of the increase may have come from the immigration of Methodists from other areas, as was clearly the case with the Weardale Wesleyans who migrated to the valley. The newspapers suggest that many outside missioners were invited to evangelise the valley; Miss Lee and Miss Peart were two very popular missioners and the Revd James Flanagan of St George's Hall was another, giving popular talks on his work in the East End slums of London.[21] Such missions could be organised by small, *ad hoc* committees, although they needed much supporting activity to provide hospitality, teas and music. The population to be evangelised was not large, and as it was concentrated in small villages, there would have been no need to elaborate extensive administrative machinery to mount missions. The situation in the valley was such that, unlike a national church, Methodism needed no permanent machinery for church extension or 'home missions'.

The Connexion provided services but did not have any day-to-day control over how the local Methodists used them. Suggestions and ideas might be selected, rejected or interpreted locally, providing there was no actual teaching that was contrary to Methodist doctrines. The greatest central demands on local Methodism probably came at the time of the 1907 and 1932 Methodist unions. Although union was intended, among other purposes, to reduce duplication of effort in the country, part of the price paid for the formal union at the national level was the tacit agreement of the Connexion not to press ahead with closures at the local level.[22] The hostile response to the possibility of local closure would have threatened the whole union scheme. In fact expansion made the building of a new Methodist chapel in Esh Winning a necessity in 1932, and the two Waterhouses chapels stood until 1971, each with less than thirty members, despite the formal decision in 1968 to close one and amalgamate the societies. In a declining village rational control would have demanded that one chapel should close, thus reducing expense and pooling resources, but the central organisation did not impose itself locally.

One rationalisation has prevailed. Fund-raising used to depend on special efforts, usually organised by the women, or the choir. The Christian churches in Britain began to appreciate the need, in the 1950s, for a regular, assured and predictable income, and so stewardship schemes were introduced in many churches. In the early 1960s a young minister in the Deerness Valley circuit banned bazaars, sales of work and other similar activities mounted for fund-raising purposes. He thus removed the justification for a whole range of social events from the annual life of the chapels. Respondents said that they missed the old fund-raising activities which provided so much enjoyment in the anticipation, preparation and execution. It is alleged that non-Methodist villagers also missed these occasions and often asked why they were no longer held. The need for the Methodist Church as a national organisation to rationalise its finances has had the unintended and probably unforeseen consequence of destroying a socially significant part of local chapel life. This is probably the clearest illustration we have of the tension between communal and associated tendencies within the religious group.

We have in these villages examples of the 'sect that perpetuates in the present a pattern of social organisation from the past, display[ing] relatively low articulation of distinctively *religious* organisation'.[23] Since such sects, Wilson continues,

> tend to have arisen in rural communities the life patterns of which were not formally organised, they tend to subsume religious organisation in community structure, employing religious sanctions merely as boundary maintaining devices. Religious practice and procedures are continuities of community practice and procedures...the sect boundaries are the community's boundaries, and embrace a congeries of associated families and settlements.

which manifest varying degrees of communal – and thus religious – association. In this case, ethnicity and communal identity are the real determinants of sectarian allegiance and religious solidarity: no formal religious organisation has become necessary [in such a case].[24]

Wilson was discussing the Amish, so we would want to modify his statement by noting that whilst Methodists did not live in segregated settlements, Methodism was still the 'established religion'[25] of the area. Communal identity is the determinant of sectarian allegiance within a religiously heterogeneous society, so boundary maintenance becomes an important function of religion (hence the resistance to intermarriage). Methodism was not coterminous with the *whole* community, but it was sufficiently dominant not to need to develop an elaborate machinery to defend its interests, as it would in a society in which it was a minority with deviant beliefs or practices.[26] Methodism was only deviant insofar as it rejected locally dominant patterns of leisure behaviour. But Methodists did adhere to local ideals of mutuality, they joined unions and helped non-Methodists in time of need. We might even argue that they determined some of the ideals and values of the community, for some of the community's most vital activities derived from the chapel, and many children of non-Methodists were and are still sent to Sunday school.

In sum, local Methodism was not a dissenting or minority religion of the kind Troeltsch and Niebuhr had in mind in their discussion of sect development. Nor was it a religious community as comprehensive as the Amish. It was between these two extremes; the communal aspects of Methodism were expressed in a wide variety of activities, the associational were developed to meet the relatively few formal requirements. As it was a somewhat closed community (confirmed ethically, intellectually and culturally), Methodism could, in the main, only replace its membership from within.

Finally we can illustrate the effects of the progression of the Methodist societies from associations to communities in one very striking way. The early membership would have included many young men who came to the villages to find work in the new pits. One of the few places in which these young men could meet young women suitable for marriage would be in the Methodist societies. These girls were the daughters of the married miners who had migrated with their families. The possibility of meeting girls may have attracted some young men into the chapels – with the kind of results that grieved John Wesley in Weardale.[27] Just such a case seems to have occurred early in the life of the Waterhouses P.M.s. One young person began to behave in a manner that the society regarded as immoral. The society responded unequivocally by resolving 'That J. Bessford be dismissed from the choir for immorality'.[28] The same meeting resolved to dismiss four other members of the choir, for unstated reasons. This is a case of an organisation having rules and applying them without fear or favour. If there were any repercussions among the families involved in this affair, the Methodists did not seem to be influenced by them. They were a group of people who had come together, as relative strangers, to create a new organisation in the village.

In the 1920s a major scandal occured amongst the Methodists. A senior and respected local preacher had a sexual liaison with the young daughter of a Methodist family. What action did the society take when this was discovered? For quite some time nothing happened, everyone seemed embarrassed and no one knew quite what to do. Eventually the preacher left the district. The inaction of the Methodists in something that they would normally judge severely – even in 1970 – needs explaining. The usual answer was that the society lacked the kind of old leaders (men like Isaac Hewitson were cited in this context) who had the authority and the courage to face up to this preacher. Without their initiative no one would grasp the nettle. An alternative explanation could be that the two participants in the scandal were both members of families which had extensive connections within Methodism and the community at large. Any attempt to confront either of them would have implied a reproach to their families as well, members of whom might be friendly with or married into members of the accuser's family. Similarly any decision to use the formal procedures for disciplining an offending Methodist would have entailed even more embarrassment, because of the ritual of debates and resolutions in committees and meetings where friends and relatives of the accused would be present. The simplest way to avoid the issue would have been to classify it as a 'family matter', not appropriate for action or discussion within the society. But plainly it was not resolved in that way, for the Methodists – even today – think that something should have been done. The acute embarrassment caused by the whole affair was clear from the extreme unwillingness to discuss it at all. Some would only refer to it in very oblique terms and all insisted that nothing should be said to anyone else in the valley, in order to prevent accusations of gossip-mongering being laid by the members of the two families. In fact it became too embarrassing to approach the matter directly even though this research was conducted nearly fifty years after the event.

An association of relative strangers is able to operate formally according to tacit social rules. But once the formal relations of the association are tempered by personal connections, the association becomes a community and the more formal codes are replaced by informal, familial relationships.

The importance of communal over associational ties in the societies helps us explain another feature of village Methodism that we have repeatedly stressed, and which will emerge as a very important feature in subsequent chapters. The old leaders from the late nineteenth century dominated Methodism until the 1920s, or until their deaths. The basis of their power in Methodism was not formal office-holding alone, but their position as founders and heads of families in the villages. Positions at the head of large and inter-related families are not positions from which they can be demoted by vote. As in the case of the scandal mentioned above, the formal rules of the association are inappropriate once it has become a community. Thus there were no ways of removing aged officials from office, and to have attempted to do so would have been to create family conflict. Headship of a family 'naturally' fitted the leaders in the chapels to their positions of leadership, and in a sense the older they became (and the more extensive their kinship ties became) the more suited to office they appeared (and perhaps felt). Only hints could be used to persuade men to relinquish their hold on office. Thus one group of Sunday school teachers presented their superintendent with a rocking chair in the hope that he would retire.

The next chapter looks in detail at the men who dominated local Methodism for the whole of their lifetime, from the establishment of Methodism in the 1870s to the acceleration of its decline in the 1920s and 1930s.

6 The respectable Methodists and the old Liberalism

We saw in Chapter 3 that the Deerness Valley grew with the coal-trade. In 1851 the valley was a rural area with a population of 500–600 people. By 1901 the population was 9,100 in these four villages alone. Emigration from and immigration to the villages followed fluctuations in the coal-trade. Rapid growth and changes in a population drawn from a wide area, hard working conditions, and an initial lack of housing and cultural facilities suggest that this early period was likely to have been a period of some social dislocation. We might expect to find conditions similar to those traditionally associated with frontier towns – the relative prosperity and lack of facilities encouraging the rise of drinking and gambling, in turn a cause for violence among a population with many different regional and religious loyalties.

This was the case in the valley in the late nineteenth century. 'Vérité sans peur' writing to the *D.C.* on 22 March 1872, said that Quebec was a blackguard's drunken village, mainly populated by Roman Catholics. A reply on the 29th pointed out that while there was poor housing and no sanitation there were two Sunday schools, an evening school and proposals to establish a reading room and cricket club. Furthermore only 32 out of 125 homes were occupied by Catholics.[1] Fining the Quebec innkeeper for allowing drunkenness, the magistrate said in 1873 that 'Quebec was the most demoralising village in the neighbourhood'[2] (*sic*). From September 1873 to September 1874 the Lanchester Division Police had proceeded against 3,512 offenders as compared with 2,547 and 1,755 in the previous years. There were 1,578 cases of drunkenness, 440 common assault, 49 assaults on police officers and 101 poaching cases.[3] This apparent rise in disorder was not confined to the area containing Quebec. A *D.C.* editorial of 31 March 1875, expresses concern with the rise of drunkenness; it notes the association between this and high wages. The editor also comments on the problem of pit-men's wives drinking and opposes the idea of granting licences to grocers, as being a policy likely to increase female drunkenness.[4] On 24 June the paper reports a temperance speech by Archdeacon Prest. The

140

archdeacon said that the Durham diocese accounted for one-eighth of all the drunkenness in the country; the county headed the list for crime and intemperance (Northumberland was third for intemperance and fifth for crime). There were, he said, 5,000 prisoners in Durham jail last year – of whom 1,954 were women – whose downfall could nearly always be traced to indulgence in intoxicating drink.[5] According to a diocesan report on social conditions in 1909 intemperance, gambling, early marriage and poor housing were serious problems, although the 'Church worked for some improvements through colliery managers and owners'.[6]

Esh Winning was a centre of gambling, as one respondent said, 'Roughs used to come in brakes from Gateshead and Newcastle' to play pitch and toss in the woods behind Lymington Terrace.[7] According to an older respondent the villages of East Hedleyhope and 'Hedley Hill-over-the-hill', a village which had vanished many years before the research began, were known locally as Sodom and Gomorrah. He said that East Hedleyhope (his own village) was a quiet village really but there was drinking and fighting at the weekend.

Drunkenness and fighting on the streets is within living memory. For example: 'The village was very rough. They used to fight with stones in the corner of a handkerchief – swing them. There was gambling and heavy drinking, especially when the pubs were open from 6.00 a.m. to 11.00 p.m.'[8] A retired village doctor said: 'There was more drunkenness in those days [1920s and 1930s]. A high percentage of income was spent on drink. Drunken injuries were more common. . .There wasn't much wife beating, but [it was] mainly by drinkers.'[9] Because of drunkenness and violence, 'Our father used to keep us in the house. One family used to come regularly to our house to sleep when the father was on the rampage. There was a lot of drinking.'[10]

However, the *D.C.* on the miners' gala in June 1872 says that 'the miners (whom we seldom see)' behaved themselves very well. 'The bulk of our mining population is not composed of the ignorant and unruly class of men they [the citizens of Durham] have been wont to regard them.' Nevertheless, drunkenness, fighting and death while drunk appear in the press of the county, and the Deerness Valley until the early part of this century.

Whatever the actual level of drinking and violence was among the miners it loomed large in public discussion at least in the late nineteenth century, and in the Methodist social consciousness throughout our period. Temperance activities were pursued by special organisations, but in the villages temperance work was an integral part of chapel activities. It is not our purpose to discuss this work here. But the very rough social and environmental conditions in which the villagers lived is an important factor in our analysis, for it is against the background of this rough life that we have to understand the Methodist's knowledge of himself as a 'saved' man.

Methodists were, and are, very conscious of the evils of drink: 'pubs were open from the morning until 11.00 p.m. and beer was 3*d.* a pint, no limitations. . .Some men drank all their pay and remained idle from Friday to Tuesday, these men used to get their notice and were black-listed'.[11] Pease and Partners were alleged to have sacked habitual drunkards, a practice of which Andrew Ure would have approved.[12] 'Homes were wrecked through men being drunkards but their lives and homes were brightened by their conversion. Other people could see that this was true. . .Another deadly influence was the Working Men's Club.'[13] The effects of being converted and giving up drinking were plain for all to see in terms of the improved economic status of the convert's family. The worldly consequences of conversion formed a basis of testimony and the proof of the efficacy of religion. Thus a recent convert, harassed by his work mates, was questioned on miracles; did he really believe that Jesus turned water into wine? After floundering in biblical and theological argument the convert asked the men if they remembered his family and the state of his home six months ago; and did they know what it was like now? Well if Jesus could turn beer into clothes for his children, and furniture for his house, would He not be able to turn water into wine? (It is not possible to say whether this is an authentic story, a composite story or a sermon illustration. It is frequently told by the Methodists.)

An evil associated with drink and having similar economic effects was gambling. One respondent recounted how his father at the end of the First World War owed money-lenders a total of £140, debts incurred through gambling. The sons supported the family while the father paid off the debt. During the three years it took to pay the debts the father attended chapel. When the debts were paid he ceased to attend and returned to gambling.[14] George MacLane, a prominent Waterhouses Methodist, in common with many others, allowed no playing cards in his house. A retired coke-worker said he had to leave the Leek club because members were required to sell a book of raffle tickets every year. He offered money instead, but this was unacceptable. The fact that the Church of England countenances gambling ('believe in lotteries') and that members play bingo is frequently quoted as a reason against Anglican–Methodist union.[15] One respondent recounted with horror how the vicar had won money whilst gambling in the Roman Catholic club. The Methodists did not participate in activities associa-

142

ted with drinking and gambling – both were regarded as wasteful and degrading.

The Methodist was thrifty. This thrift took a number of forms. Firstly, many are reported as having 'a few pounds in the Store'[16] as a safeguard against unemployment, illness and other hardships. Secondly, some Methodists saved to set themselves up in business; both James Hammell and Isaac Raine started as labourers, selling from a 'pack' in their spare time. The former eventually owned a hardware and furniture store, the latter purchased a newsagent's shop. Joseph Harrison also built up a very successful drapery and general store. Thirdly, Methodists in the late nineteenth and early twentieth century took an interest in the running of the Co-operative Society. The Co-ops. were seen quite specifically not only as suppliers of unadulterated goods, but as a means to thrift. 'It induced [the working class] to think – taught them to be frugal and careful – encouraged them to be temperate – tended to make them better and wiser men – and enabled them to rise to any position in society they chose.'[17]

Fourthly, Methodist mining families, by making considerable economic sacrifices, were able to keep their children at school or college, even at times of unemployment. One railway signalman had three sons, two of whom went to training college and one to university.[18] This obviously required good domestic management. 'A struggle for us, but you get by somehow, don't you?', commented a Methodist whose son had gone to university.[19]

Collectively the Methodists were men of property. The leading Methodists, as trustees, managed chapels, schoolrooms and manses, paid off debts and raised considerable sums of money for these purposes. This also involved ordinary Methodists in 'sacrificial giving'. So successful were Methodists in handling money that they were sought as advisers on money matters or to act as bankers for friends.[20]

When their savings were exhausted after a period of long unemployment Methodists were reluctant to accept relief. The evidence for this is almost entirely anecdotal; 'We were never allowed to go to the soup kitchen "on principle". Father never took Permanent Relief, though he probably paid for it',[21] was a typical comment from a miner's son. It will be argued below that the Methodists developed a spirit of independence entirely consistent with the refusal of any kind of financial assistance in times of hardship.

Besides being a temperate and thrifty man, the Methodist was a Sabbatarian.[22] Matt White, the most prominent P.M., would not allow his sons to buy newspapers on a Sunday.[23] A respondent remarked how his grandmother had refused to accept a cauliflower from one of her sons, because it had been cut on Sunday. The extent of Sabbatarianism is shown by an expression said to be common amongst the old Methodists in the 1920s: 'Better never born, than Sunday shorn.' The Methodist did not consider it proper to shave on Sunday. Methodists spent most of their Sunday in religious activities, chapel in morning and evening; some devoted the afternoon to teaching in the Sunday school, others travelled the circuit, or further afield, as preachers. The non-Methodist Sunday was a day of rest from heavy labour, when one ate the biggest and best meal of the week, and slept in the afternoon (a good reason for sending the children to Sunday school!). The non-Methodist Sunday makes more sense in terms of the purely physical needs of a working man; but the Methodist subjected himself to a discipline of activity and service because he believed there was more to life than meeting its physical needs.

Thus far we have a picture of the Methodist living a temperate, frugal and disciplined life in contrast to the relatively intemperate, thriftless and violent habits of at least a significant section of the remainder of the population. According to one retired Methodist miner, the distinguishing feature of a Methodist was that he would 'never use bad language or go in a pub'.[24] The Methodist ethos was based on a series of 'Thou shalt not' notions. It was nevertheless a way of life, with practical consequences: more orderly and better furnished homes, adequate clothing for the family, relative economic independence, the collective acquisition of property and, for a few, individual economic prosperity.

Photographs of these Methodists show them wearing dark suits, stiff white collars, pocket watches with chains, bowler hats and bearing themselves with a dignity born of self-assurance and acknowledged respectability. 'Respectable' is still a word in common use today. No sharp distinctions are drawn, but there is almost a 'respectability scale' applied. The word is especially used by Methodists of non-Methodists who meet up to their own approved standards of behaviour. It is, for the Methodists, very much a boundary-defining word.

The leading Methodists (preachers, trustees, circuit officials) were required to exercise their own judgement on matters of finance, property and circuit administration. They also had to select ministers and approve preachers. Matt White, Isaac Johnson and others travelled throughout the region to hear ministers preaching so that an invitation might be given to a man thought suitable for the circuit. We have seen that the chapels received patronage from the coal-owners, but the owners and managers had no say in the choice of ministers. In no sense did the Methodists have 'company parsons' or ministers chosen for their likely compliance with managerial views, as was the case in Gastonia, described by Liston Pope.[25]

Local preachers appeared before an examining board of the circuit, for an oral examination and the 'trial sermon' (a written examination was introduced in the later 1910s). If prospective preachers were not up to the standards of knowledge and preaching ability required, they were failed.[26] We see that within the broad requirements of the Methodist Connexions the local Methodists imposed their own standards on themselves; there was no imposition from outside. These judgements were different from the fairly routinised *election* of an official to an association in which the requirements of the office are relatively obvious and the candidates chosen on simple communal or pragmatic grounds. An example of the exercise of a quite independent initiative is provided by the death of a minister in 1919. Immediately a committee of the quarterly meeting was called; it expressed its sorrow at the minister's death and then proceeded to ask the district to allow the circuit to continue without a minister for the remainder of the quarter so that the widow could enjoy the use of the house and receive the salary due to her late husband.[27] The example may be trivial, but it shows how quick and practical action could be taken by the local leadership, which was accustomed to taking independent decisions.

The sense of being men of independent judgement, under obligation to no man, was something which the Methodists attempted to carry across into their relations with the owners and management of the pits. While the Methodist in his role as trade-union leader may have felt that he could speak to the managers as man to man, it was also true that as a self-made man his views on economic and social matters were unlikely to be revolutionary. From his own experience the Methodist trade unionist believed that it was possible for the lot of the working man to be improved within the given social and economic situation.

The belief in the peaceful advancement of the men's interests by the trade unionists representing the men's interests in discussion with the owners was reciprocated by the owners themselves. Since industrial and political relations are mainly the subject of Chapters 7 and 8, here we only observe that both the union leaders and the owners (in three villages) were Liberals (Pearson, Dove, MacDonald, checkweighmen. White and D. Cheek, lodge chairman and delegate, both councillors, were all active Liberals before 1920. Only D. Cheek was not a Methodist). They believed that differences could be settled amicably on the basis of a 'gentleman's agreement'. A 'gentleman's agreement' implied mutual trust between masters and men, give and take in negotiation and compromise in striking a bargain. A local preacher said he once preached a sermon in the 1930s on the need always to find a middle way between two extremes; he was later told that Matt White, sitting behind him in the choir, was nodding in agreement throughout the sermon. The same preacher, when younger, had been looking at the picture of John Wilson on the Waterhouses' lodge banner; White put his hand on the lad's shoulder and said, '. . .try to be like that man, he was a great man'.[28] John Wilson, as we saw in Chapter 2 had been the local Liberal M.P., a preacher and friend of many of the leading Methodists.[29] He was also a justice of the peace and an honorary doctor of civil law at Durham University. He was latterly referred to as 'Dr Wilson' and was a model of reasonableness, respectability and integrity to Methodist miners. Conversations with Methodists and non-Methodists frequently elicit the comment that the pre-1920 local leadership consciously modelled itself on Wilson. Wilson was not a man to follow what he regarded as 'extremist' policies. Lecturing on 'Christianity and Social and Political Problems' in 1912, Wilson said that problems should be solved man to man, reason to reason; he was against strikes as they damaged trade, and conciliation always brought better conditions than the strike.[30] These are views with which the Methodists in the mining villages would have readily concurred.

Respectability also affected home life. While the Methodists may not have had a monopoly of 'good homes' it is said that Methodists almost invariably had well-kept homes and well-run households. Some of the valley Methodists would have been amongst the large congregation which heard the president of the Wesleyan Methodist conference in Old Elvet (Durham City) in 1900. 'The strength of a nation is its family life, and woman the cornerstone of the whole. . .she was regarded no longer as man's tool and plaything. She was learning to combine two things,' he said, 'strength and modesty'.[31] Young women took very active parts in the life of the chapels, whereas the married women were more confined to the home by the need to feed, bath and wash clothes for one or more working men, and to care for the children. Some married women seem to have been able to attend Sunday evening services only. The women had an immediate interest in the behaviour of their menfolk. A drunken, gambling father meant an ill-clad family, no new furniture and growing debt at the store. It is reported that during missions women had been seen running down the street, still wearing aprons, crying with joy, when hearing of their husband's conversion. Others attended chapel 'to keep their husbands up to the mark'.[32]

We can list the most obvious – and obviously 'respectable' – features of the Methodist home.[33] The house was well furnished, many homes had (and still have) small pipe-organs in the parlour. The family would have 'Sunday best' clothes for chapel and the children would have new clothes for the Sunday school anniversary. The question of the children not attending Sunday school never arose, nor did the question of playing games on Sunday. Sunday entertainment consisted of singing hymns around the organ after the evening service and prayer meeting, and people used to gather in the homes of the Whites, Cheeks and Greeners and others for this.

A discussion of the role of women and family structure in County Durham would be a digression. Nevertheless, it is important to note a factor probably unique to the company villages of Durham. Rent and coal were taken care of by the colliery company, therefore the largest item of household budget was food and clothing, traditionally the mother's responsibility. The women therefore tended to look after the financial side of family affairs. If the father was a heavy drinker, however, the mother was always short of money, and this was plain for all to see: 'If the children came to school in rags you could be pretty sure that the father drank.'[34] The Methodist miner came straight home and 'tipped up' his pay packet to his wife (i.e. they opened it together); she would give him his pocket money and keep the remainder. The working children also handed over their pay, and the father might not even know what they earned.[35] Even in periods of relative prosperity money was never plentiful, so the women had to be good managers and as such they invariably had to struggle. 'My mother used to sit up to two in the morning sewing dresses. We children were always well turned out.'[36] In the course of interviewing all the Methodists, it was noticed that great stress was placed on economic hardship. One woman recounted (with tears in her eyes) how her husband brought home £5 2s. 6d. and that she gave him the half-crown as a fortnight's spending money. Yet these are the same people who could mount anniversaries with the children clad in new clothes, could organise concerts and sales to raise money for a chapel, could build and maintain chapel property and meet the expenses of a circuit.

Methodist domesticity is summarised in a rather glowing account given by a headmaster who came from a Quebec Methodist family. He spoke at length about the cleanliness, thrift and good management of the Methodists:

> The chapel schoolroom floor was kept scrubbed white. [At home] Monday, washing day; Tuesday, tidying up; Thursday, baking day; Friday, cleaning and polishing day – house almost stripped, cleaned from upstairs through to the yard where the quorrels practically shone with brushing (usually brushed Saturday morning). Toilets whitewashed and sanded. Saturday, brasses and clean household gear put down. Sunday, no sewing or darning, some didn't even buy a newspaper. They had tremendous pride and independence.[37]

Finally, at home the Methodist rarely gave outward signs of affection to, or in front of their children. The children of three prominent Methodists specifically said how their fathers were deeply interested in them and were concerned for their futures, and how they felt loved as children. Yet these fathers never made overtly affectionate gestures to them,[38] as compared with non-Methodist fathers who might behave alternately strictly and indulgently. Reserve or restraint is true to the spirit of inner-worldly asceticism.

The spirit of Methodism as here defined can be interpreted, or could actually develop, in unintended or destructive ways. The temperate man can become self-righteous, or the thrifty man can accumulate money for accumulation's sake. The search for compromise can lead to soft settlements in union affairs. The men on good terms with the managers can become the bosses' men. Domestic frugality can be competitive and the desire to be well-turned-out can lead to an invidious 'hat and coat' respectability. One way in which we can gauge the temper of Methodist respectability is by taking the opinions of non-Methodists or outsiders to the villages. No non-Methodists deny that Methodists were 'somebody' in the village and that they commanded respect. 'Anybody who was anybody was a Methodist.'[39] 'People who went to chapel were thought to be "somebody", looked up to and respected. They – especially the local preachers – took a very active part in local affairs – but when they did lead no-one was allowed to challenge their position.' But, 'one thing that the Methodists were not liked for was that they were down on anyone who had a pint of beer; people were very bitter about this'.[40] This bitterness is not, in fact, very evident from other accounts. More typical of comments made in the village was that:

> The Methodists' strict ideas on temperance are a bit far fetched, and some Methodists drink now. This idea was very strong at one time among Methodists in the village, though most of the non-Methodists thought that it was a bit daft. The strong Methodists were real good. A lot of the villagers admired them for sticking to their beliefs. Never any friction between Methodists and non-Methodists over this type of thing.[41]

Club officials confirm this; there was never any trouble over temperance or temperance campaigns (presumably the campaigns of the late nineteenth century were ignored and did not impinge upon the clubs).

A sharper comment was made on attitudes to gambling, 'I was going around selling tickets for a raffle; H. told me off for wasting money.'[42] On thrift and money-raising; 'If he [union leader] looked after No. 2 he had No. 1 in his pocket', 'If he [another Methodist] saw a few lads with 1*d*. or 2*d*. he'd run a tea party to get it off them'.[43] But a Catholic observed, more generously, 'The chapel saved some wasters. Gambling and drinking their pay away – went into chapel, turned around and never drank again.'[44] This last comment was clearly made without any theological approval of Methodism.

While financial matters increasingly occupied the attention of the Methodists from 1920 onwards they may have been overcareful of funds before this. When, for example, in 1906 it was proposed to build a new minister's house, this proposal (at first agreed to and then rescinded) split the quarterly meeting. Subsequently extensive and expensive repairs, decorating and alterations had to be carried out instead on the terraced house which served as a manse. The architect also had to be paid for his unused plan for a new house. We cannot know the full circumstances but it does appear that a good case might have been made for a new building, and that frugality produced at least one case of false economy.

A minister who had lived in Waterhouses as a boy in the 1880s and returned as a minister from 1952–6 stated that 'social climbing was the curse of Methodism'. He pointed out that none of the leading Methodists, and few other Methodists, had sons who went down the pit.[45] This has proved to be so, for none of the Methodists who can be named as leaders or public figures in any of the villages had sons who worked below ground in the mines. In some cases their daughters married miners. Interviews with all the contemporary Methodists showed that over 80% of the men over 60 had worked in the pits, and often spent long periods in unemployment as well. Not one of the younger Methodists had ever worked in the pits. The minister added:

> The children were unconsciously treacherous to the pitmen (but treachery can be very close to noble loyalty) [by which he meant the betrayal of miners as a class may have been an unintended result of doing what parents wanted]. X's sons (X is a terrible snob); one is in administration, another in insurance. . .affected, regard themselves as a cut above the others. . .Getting out of mining was regarded as 'Fruits of the spirit' – this was said from the pulpit. . .The boy who stayed in the pit – even though he may have had to do it to support a widowed mother and family – was a spiritual failure. . .Scholarships, visits to Durham, association with 'better class' people through chapel and its patrons and the Trade Union may have given these people middle-class aspirations.[46]

This is the most extremely critical statement on Methodist ambitions. Another minister put the point less critically: 'miners' families sought something better for their sons than a job down the mine. Wanted to show that they were intelligent. They had a pride of craft, they knew their job to be skilled. But they were declassed by working below – in the eyes of critics. They resented ignorant criticism'.[47] This comment suggests that Methodist miners were concerned with their esteem in the eyes of people outside the mining community itself. This may be connected with stories told by the villagers of national Methodist gatherings or local government conferences, where they had been angered by the surprise of outsiders that they were clean, wore collars and ties, could read and write and did not keep whippets.

It is true that none of White's three sons entered pit work, nor the sons of his three brothers. Aron Richardson's son left and became a minister. We could list all the families that achieved some social mobility, but a simple statement of such facts does not tell us *why* Methodists could rise in the social scale. Among the possible reasons are that:

Methodists' children excelled at school, especially in scholarship examinations. Learning was encouraged at home and examinations were part of Sunday school life, as well as day school;

new opportunities were arising throughout this century for qualified persons in teaching, local government, social services, etc;

parents wanted their sons out of mining because the industry was likely to decline, it was an inherently disagreeable job and they wished to enhance their sons' and their own social status;

the children themselves had status aspirations (derived from school, chapel, Sunday school or home).

Any one or all of these factors could be relevant. The notion of 'calling' and 'service', the idea of stewardship of talents and dedication to selfless work in improving 'the world' enabled Methodists to be upwardly mobile by pursuing useful forms of service. 'Pure' status-seeking may not be compatible with Methodist ethics, but enhanced status is a bonus for service. Moreover the experience of the 1920s and 1930s reduced confidence in the security of employment in coal-mining; whenever opportunities presented themselves it made sense to move out of mining. We have seen that Methodists were especially well motivated and equipped to take advantage of such opportunities. To the picture of the respectable Methodist we add therefore the fact that he probably had sons in 'better' occupations, perhaps a son away at college or university training to be a teacher or doctor.

The political views and industrial activities of the leading Methodists are discussed below. We have already seen that the owners were patrons of the chapels and were certainly sought out by the leaders for small favours (but, we would suggest favours based on gentlemanly understanding – not on condescension).

The owners used to patronise Union leaders; giving them time to go to Durham, etc., and paying them for the shift...in return leaders were meant to take things easy...They did use to go soft, 'sorry boys, couldn't get any more'. Y, for example, was in the Lodge and working with the management.[48]

Y was very thick with the Viewer at Crook. He was one of the very few not to get notice at 65. Immediately after the '26 strike he was put on night shift, only did one shift and he was on day work again.[49]

Z, a leading Methodist and local Councillor, played along with the colliery officials, too much. He would put forward their measures at Council, he became their tool, he was being used and didn't realise it.[50]

Z and Y were allowed to catch the 'bus – this *may* have been because they were friendly with the Viewer'[51] (respondent's emphasis).

The criticism of Z is repeated by all who mention him, and it appears to be substantially justified. Nevertheless Z's most forthright critics admit that personally he was the kindliest man in the village. Other Methodists – not union leaders – also appear to be 'bosses' men'. R. Hayson's relatives recounted how, when the Labour council prevented Colonel Sprott giving Quebec a playing field, Hayson wrote to Sprott (a Tory coal-owner) saying that he (Sprott) was not being treated properly by the men.[52] An elderly preacher said,

the manager was Church of England, stern, but a nice gentleman, he was reasonable...Peases and Joseph Love – social and kind, interested in the affairs of the village. They sought to help any good cause put forward...An honour to have Pease visit the village...We kept the village in good order with our Christian work.[53]

The Methodists' attitudes towards the owners and managers, of respect and helpfulness, are expressed with different degrees of dignity – but they were attitudes likely to attract criticism in due course. As long as the coal-trade remained relatively prosperous, the co-operation could be reciprocated by the management. When reciprocity broke down we might expect to see the Methodist unable to cope with the situation. A seventy-year-old respondent who claimed to have attended as many lodge meetings as he could, but who never took a more active part in union affairs, is representative of the men's attitude to the leaders (and the leaders to the management). 'There was a good understanding between the management and the Union. It helped keep the colliery [Waterhouses] going.'[54] Such comments are common from the older Methodists when they discuss the union leadership.

In summary: the Methodist was a temperate and thrifty man, owning some personal property or sharing in the management of corporate property. He had a 'good home' and a well-turned-out family. He was to be found with his family in chapel on Sundays. He had aspirations for his children, especially his sons, which were very often realised. In a relatively prosperous industry he was on good terms with the management, who in turn respected him. Nevertheless, he maintained independence of thought, judgement and action.

Changes came to the district which made this ideal less appropriate, less practical. A substantial fall in drunkenness and crime made the strictly teetotal position less obviously necessary (the temperance movement had also discredited itself by the 1920s and 30s[55] by campaigning for prohibition). 'Social drinking' was becoming more publicly acceptable. Official attitudes towards the working men's clubs underwent some changes: from 'Resolved':

> That we see with regret the establishment of workmen's clubs in our district, believing that they are a prolific source of physical, moral, mental and spiritual degeneracy. Further we call upon all our Members to have no connection with them either as shareholders, members or employees and that they seek by all legitimate means to counteract the evils of which they are the source,
>
> (Minute 12 of December Quarterly Meeting of Primitive Methodist Circuit 1899, subsequently printed in the *Plan*)

to:

> We recognise that 'Clubs' should have a social and educational value. Since DRINK is made a prominent feature they are a prolific source of evil. OUR MEMBERS are urged to discourage the trade in every way.
>
> (Primitive Methodist Preachers' *Plan*, July–September 1930)

The decline in crimes of violence, on the streets and in the houses made the distinction between rough and respectable less obvious. By the 1920s the villages as a whole were more 'respectable'.

With a levelling off and then decline in employment in the pits, there was less over-crowding in the colliery houses. Middens were replaced by flush toilets. Cholera disappeared. The last smallpox epidemic struck the district in 1926 but it was the only serious epidemic in the twentieth century, whereas there were four outbreaks in the villages between 1871 and 1874 alone. There is no evidence to suggest that these epidemics were followed by religious revivals, as seems to have been the case in South Wales.[56] The environment improved physically and socially. Thus it became less clear what it was a man was 'saved' from when he was converted. In fact an increasing number entered Methodism through the Sunday school and could neither give an account of the moment of their salvation nor understand the full meaning of the testimony of the older men and woman. The vicious circle of drink, gambling, debt, domestic disorder and poor health, broken by the power of religion, was not something that could be easily comprehended by the younger Methodist. Perhaps the best literary (and the most moving) account of the self-respecting miner is to be found in the character of Gwilym in Richard Llewellyn's *How Green Was My Valley*. This novel also illustrates the nature and extent of intergenerational conflict in a situation somewhat similar to the one we are describing. The older men remained in authority virtually until they died, but they upheld an ethic increasingly subjected to outside cultural pressures, as we shall see in Chapter 9.

In the 1920s, and especially after the 1926 lock-out, the thrift-and-independence basis of the old Methodist self-image was subject to the greatest strain. Unemployment and poverty drained what savings the miners had; for example; savings in the Pease and Partners Deposit Scheme fell from £275,000 in 1921 to £10,000 in 1934. All of the present Methodists who had been miners had experienced unemployment for a year or more. One respondent said that her husband had worked only for the first eighteen months of their whole married life. The Waterhouses pit closed for nine months after 1926. Esh Winning was closed from 1930 to 1942. When savings were gone, only the dole remained. To receive the dole one had to be 'genuinely seeking work'. Men who would gladly have taken any job, but who knew that the search would be fruitless, had to give this assurance. A normal practice was for one man to travel the area collecting names of foremen and managers for the other men to report at the Labour Exchange, thus saving hours of pointless, tiring walking. Thus men were reduced to telling untruths in order to receive a bare subsistence. The blow to the Methodist's integrity was severe; no longer able to support his family in the style to which he thought they were entitled, no longer doing 'a fair day's work for a fair day's pay', no longer a practising craftsman respected for the skills he exercised daily. For a man whose word had been his bond, who could be trusted and to whom integrity was everything, the deceits at the Labour Exchange were damaging lies. Ralph Hayson junior tried to resign his membership because he had to be untruthful in order to receive his dole.[57] Whatever outward appearances they might have maintained, there could be no self-deception as to the independence of any mining family in the 1920s and 1930s.

Some refused to accept the dole; for them savings had to be eked out longer and any odd job taken. Mrs Headlam (wife of the Tory M.P.) acted as agent for people in London wishing to employ domestic servants. The bishop of Durham had suggested that unemployed miners should emigrate. Lord Dunglass (later Sir Alec Douglas Home) said that many could be shipped south, as domestic servants. One miner thus was sent a letter offering him a job as an under-gardener in the south; his mother intercepted and burnt the letter, as she did not wish him to take a job which she felt was degrading for a miner.[58] Some who received the dole tried to pay it back, how and if they did this is obscure, but the fact that some contemplated this indicates the pride and independence that were hurt by such circumstances.

A further blow to the Methodists' self-image came with the breakdown of relations with the owners. The owners cut the men's wages without negotiation. Leaders who had preached moderation and condemned the Socialist 'hotheads' found the police on the streets against the men. Men talking, men to men, *might* have agreed that the inexorable forces of the market made cuts in wages inevitable. But victimisation and imprisonment of miners' leaders and violent verbal attacks on the miners cut right across the Methodist leaders' traditional expectations of the management. 'Matt White and Tom Pearson always assumed that management spoke in good faith; they were more sympathetic to management's position...Cheek [see Chapter 7] and the others never believed a word management said.'[59]

The profit margins which for the first twenty years of the century had enabled masters and men to reach a series of 'gentlemen's agreements' were cut to zero (Pease and Partners Ordinary Shares Dividend: 1920 – 18%; 1922 – 5%; 1926 – 0%). There was to be no compromise by the coal-owners, so there was no basis for discussion between master and men locally. Thus the relational basis of the men's trust in their leaders' traditional style of operation disappeared. The basis of the *modus operandi* of the leadership itself, a little economic 'slack' in the system and some give and take between both sides, was gone.

The new attitude of the owners is perhaps best illustrated by two stories from field notes:

> Ask my sister-in-law [recently bereaved], she gave her husband for 52 years and six sons to the pit, and the week he stopped working, they stopped his free coal.[60]

> My grandfather [was] deputy overman [an official] at Waterhouses and worked for the colliery there for 50 years. He felt that he had standing with Pease and Partners. He felt that when he retired they would give him time to look around for a new house to live in. The week he retired, he received his notice to quit. I

shall never forget the stunned look on his face – he just sat there, he couldn't believe it, after all those years.[61]

The days of easy coal winning were over and so were concessions to the men; the family firms were being replaced by public companies, coal itself was failing. The social relations out of which arose the Methodists' image of himself and the basis of his standing in the community, were crumblng.

POLITICAL LEADERSHIP

The Methodist miner was in many ways an independent man; he worked as a skilled and adaptable craftsman at the coal-face, doing a difficult and at times dangerous job in frequently-changing conditions. He purchased his tools at the store, where his wife also purchased food and household goods. The store was the men's own store, the miner could voice an opinion at a meeting or directly participate in its running. He helped to choose the local minister, to examine the local preachers, himself perhaps either teaching at Sunday school or preaching in the circuit. As we have seen above he was also a man of some standing, commanding respect in local society.

The Methodists were especially well represented in the leadership of the Durham miners at county level and locally. Between 1890 and 1920 out of the 26 leading local Methodists whose careers we have been able to reconstruct in detail, 21 held between them 43 trade-union offices; another 21 held 28 posts in political parties, also as councillors and as J.P.s, and approximately 13 held Co-operative Society offices. The overlap and interlocking of roles is obviously considerable. These estimates are based entirely on *named* persons who have been positively identified as Methodists. The names of office-holders cannot always be found for any given time, and some persons named have not been positively identified as Methodists (although it is thought that they were), so these are not included in this estimate. However, it is probable that all of the 26 (except the shopkeepers) served at some time on the Co-op. committee. For considerable periods between 1900 and 1926 all four named officials of the Waterhouses lodge were P.M.s.

Methodists were active in the Liberal and Labour Parties, becoming councillors and J.P.s. We would not therefore expect to find attitudes of deference or total dependence towards the owners and managers of the collieries. There is a sharp contrast between our expectations of the coal-miner and what we know of the Carolinan cotton operatives.[62] We do not need any religious explanation of the differences. In cotton competition was fierce between many small companies, so the workers content with the lowest wages were recruited. The cotton-workers were largely machine-minders, there being no demand for skills which would put workers in a strong bargaining position. Nor does spinning allow for the use of initiative or the development of team work. For much of the earlier part of our period (i.e. up to 1920) coal was a booming industry, so the owners needed labour and could afford to pay *relatively* high wages. The owners collectively agreed prices and found it useful to have a union through which they could communicate with the men. The contrast can thus be explained by economic and technical factors in the case of the Deerness valley, even though Pope showed that in Gastonia religious factors played some part in preventing the rise of trade unions.

The division between management and workers was sharp. The managers lived in big houses apart from the colliery rows. Crofton and other managers sat on the local councils and became magistrates. Love was a national figure in Methodist and free church circles. Ferens was a prominent local Methodist. Joseph Pease was an M.P. and an industrial figure of national importance. Love's son probably 'continued to subscribe on a generous scale to projects at Cornsay' after his father's death,[63] but he did not take much part in local life.

For the Methodists the worker–boss division may not have been the most relevant social division. We have already seen above that a very important distinction for the Methodist was based on the notion of respectability. In Waterhouses, Esh Winning and Cornsay Colliery there were even some owners with whom the Methodist miners could have identified in terms of respectability: the owners were professing Christians; they were advocates of temperance, and patrons of temperance activities; they were liberals, and they were patrons of 'good causes' both locally and nationally.

Lockwood notes that in an 'occupational community', which is something apart from the management and their way of life, 'work-mates are normally leisure time companions, often neighbours and not infrequently kinsmen'.[64] But the Methodists did not share leisure-time activities with their non-Methodist work-mates. Thus for Methodists in these villages any image of society they might have had would include ambiguous continuities and dis-continuities derived from working with men but not sharing their non-work.culture, and being divided from the bosses as workers, but united with them as 'respectable' men.

It would be easy to overstress this religious factor in the social and political relations of the mining community. For example, the owners and workers in some measure also shared a set of assumptions about 'the market' and *laissez-faire*. W. H. Patterson, D.M.A. (and a Methodist), before the Royal Commission on Labour of 1891: *Q. 281.* 'Are you an advocate in any way of the Government being called in to adjust as between capital and labour; and is there any method which you would suggest?' 'So far as I am concerned, I know of no adjustment that would give satisfaction, but of course a question like that I would have to have correct instructions in order to answer.' [65] Another illustration of conventional economic thinking is the relative slowness with which the idea of Aged Miners' Homes was accepted. At one time 'why should we pay for those who haven't saved?' was a common attitude.[66]

The early leaders displayed an implicitly organic, functional view of society. The trade unions were seen as legitimate and necessary, but not for the pursuit of class interests. Unions were seen as representing the interests of the workers who were winning coal in partnership with the masters. Thus at a local strike meeting in 1879, it was said that, '...the men had no interest in damaging the interests of their employers, because the interests of the employers was the interest of the employed, and the men regarded it as their bounden duty to study their employers' interest...'[67]

What had angered the speakers in 1879 was not the reduction in wages as such, but that it had been done unilaterally. The *D.C.* of 16 May hails as a victory for the men the fact that they went back to work at negotiated reductions of between 7% and 9% after a previous series of substantial reductions, when 15% had been demanded by the owners. Although the owners were cutting wages they maintained some degree of reciprocity with the men. In 1879 the manager at East Hedleyhope provided the soup kitchen with a boiler and fuel.[68] The manager at Quebec presided at a Wesleyan lecture (a month before the pit was laid in).[69] It was immediately prior to the 1879 Strike that Ferens gave five tons of coal for the poor at Cornsay.[70] The meeting from which the quotation above is taken was held in a field provided by management.

Pease himself favoured arbitration, saying that he agreed with 'his friend Mr. Burt, M.P.' and William Crawford on the need for arbitration based on a joint committee of masters and men. But he was voted down by the other masters.[71] A letter in the *D.C.* suggested that elsewhere the masters were feeding and paying the police, there had been baton charges at Silksworth Colliery and evictions in other villages. No such aggressive action from the owners had been seen in the valley since Love's attack on the union in Ushaw Moor in 1864.

This situation led the speaker, cited above, in the same speech to say:

Pease wished to submit the matter so far as he was concerned to the principle for which they were contending, but he was prevented from carrying out these wishes by the inexorable law of the masters' association. They won't allow him to 'blackleg', except it be at the enormous cost of £50 a day for six months.[72]

According to two editorial comments in the *D.C.* (throughout this early period the paper is strongly pro-miner; or at least pro-Crawford-style miners) of April 1879 the men accepted the need for reductions in order to reduce labour costs in producing coal; but they wanted the matter settled by arbitration. Better still, according to the men of the Deerness Valley, was a sliding scale, as against 'the old and almost barbarous system of strikes'.[73] In other words the question of wages should, and therefore presumably could, be a purely technical problem, mechanically solved. W. H. Patterson before the Royal Commission: *Q. 90*, '. . .in fact, a sliding scale is a desirable mode of adjusting wages?' 'I think that it is not only desirable but the best.' And in answer to questions on the union's role in reducing strikes (*Q. 347* and *348*) 'We commenced in 1869, and I prevented, during that year, at least 30 or 40 strikes.'

William Crawford at the miners' gala in 1876 said that the union has spent £8,000 on strikes to force arbitration on the owners. Other speakers spoke in favour of moderation and arbitration, 'bad arbitration is better than a good strike'.[74] This type of view persisted as late as the period of unrest in 1912. John Wilson, in one of his monthly circulars stated, 'We shall be none the weaker if we recognise that we can attain our ideals sooner, with less hatred and antagonism, and more reason and compromise.' The strike depends not only on the union's funds, but on public sympathy. 'There are two essentials to make our unions effective for good – discretion and love of conciliation on our part.'[75] Wilson, questioned (*Q. 614*) by Tom Mann on the problem of the owners depressing the price of coal on the sliding scale by selling cheaply to their own iron works, answered 'I am watchful as most can be mind – I like to look around the corner but I like to go with trust.' The miners really only recognised from 1925 onwards the way in which the owners exploited the sliding scale.[76]

The extent of belief in 'the free market' economy and its effects on working-class industrial and political thought and action is, in itself, a substantial subject for a monograph. Market thinking was prevalent throughout the nineteenth century and it was the basis of the Liberal Party's economic policies. Especially in the absence of any other economic theory or political analysis, the laws of supply and demand made sense. It was a neat and coherent body of theory implying that society was an organism based on reciprocal relations. There is no reason to suppose that, insofar as miners thought about this at all, they did not accept this sort of theory. The view is certainly consistent with the Methodists' image of society. (The market enabled men to develop their talents and measure their diligence in economic and social advancement.) 'Depression of trade' was the reason given by owners for putting men out of work, the trade cycle was something objective and external which they could not control. The depression could not be controlled, but the owners did the best they could to relieve local suffering. The owners thus acted 'reasonably' and there were no grounds for conflict. It seems also that Pease and Partners individually were more reasonable than the owners collectively.[77] Severe violence broke out during the 1879 Strike at Esh Winning, Quebec and Waterhouses, but it was directed against *other miners* who accepted the new, un-negotiated and 'unreasonable' agreement that the owners' federation was trying to impose.[78] We would be naive to assume that the owners thought the market was completely free, when they themselves formed cartels and kept the price of coal up. They also sold coal to themselves; Pease and Samuelsson supplied their Middlesborough and Newport iron works with coke from the valley (at a favourably low price). It is difficult to assess the effect of the prevailing economic orthodoxy; the owners may have believed the market was free and yet still restricted it. This was the way in which they exercised the freedom they enjoyed.

It was out of the typical social relations of patronage and paternalism, with liberal economics and liberal politics in the ideological forefront, against a background of relative industrial prosperity, that the Methodist leadership emerged.

Before moving to a consideration of the early leadership (1870–1920) we should note that the Methodist Churches seldom expressed any collective political opinion. Between 1892 and 1932 the P.M. quarterly meeting passed sixteen resolutions for forwarding to the prime minister and local M.P.s. Eight were on temperance, three on gambling, two on the Education Bill and Act (1902–6). Two were on wages and the standard of living (in the 1920s) and one on peace in 1919. They did not feel a responsibility to comment constantly on public affairs, but on nearly three-quarters of the occasions when they did, it was on the questions of drink and gambling. The district meeting observed in May 1911 that the Eight-Hours Bill had upset week-night services. This district meeting also commented that the P.M.s belonged too much to one political party, but that they were social reformers, not politicians.[79] What this really implied was that being a member of the Liberal Party did not count as 'politics', as liberalism was not political. In Waterhouses the Methodists clearly were very much of one party. In 1911 a Waterhouses and district branch of Young Liberals was formed, of which the hon. president was John Wilson. The officers of Young Liberals and committee numbered 22, of whom 18 were P.M.s (and 2 W.M.s). The list included not only the names given below but also the school attendance officer, the headmaster and a clerk (who was to become manager of the Waterhouses Co-op.), all Methodists.[80] The Young Liberals met in the P.M. schoolroom. The earlier Quebec Liberal Association had P.M.s as president and secretary (only 4 officers are recorded).[81]

At the end of the nineteenth and beginning of the twentieth century there were only two major political parties. The reason for the Methodists being Liberal are well-known, but are underlined by a letter from a Sunderland Wesleyan Methodist minister in the *D.C.* of 24 December 1909. He believed that politics should be kept out of the pulpit, but draws the reader's attention to four points:

The Tories were a drink-supported party – 'By the end of the century it [the drink trade] probably *was* contributing heavily to Conservative Party funds and nearly every public house *had* become an unofficial Conservative room for after 1872 a positive mania for licensing reform seized all sections of the Liberal Party',[82] or 'In the public houses, therefore, the Conservatives had a nice little chain of political fortresses, where their cause was loyally upheld by poor men in their cups.'[83]

The Tories were enemies of religious liberty (the writer was presumably thinking of the 1902 Education Act).

'Tariff Reform' meant making the rich richer and poor poorer.

The Tories were against government by and for the people.[84]

In the unopposed bye-election of 1915, on the death of John Wilson, S. Galbraith was Liberal candidate. His nomination papers were signed by 24 Methodists out of 38 nominators. 'Hammel, Harrison, Dack and Matt White were all friends and Liberals and known by John Wilson. Matt was a great follower of John Wilson (who preached at Bourne).'[85] In the 1890s and 1900s the P.M. ministers were active Liberals, the minister at the time of the 1902 Education Act had been a 'passive resister' to the Act and such an active Liberal that he had chaired a Liberal meeting before preaching his first sermon.

The brief biographical notes which follow (see Table 3) are based on newspaper files, interviews, and minutes of societies and quarterly meetings. Accurate dating is not always possible, two or three 'spot dates' are often all we have to guide us. The notes are not exhaustive, and other Methodists are occasionally mentioned in the press, as for example when Pease and Partners temperance missionary (Dack) chairs a Liberal meeting. G. McLane is lodge treasurer and Sunday school superintendent (see Glossary). But these two men are not mentioned as often as those listed. The rule of positive identification is always used; some community leaders are thought to be Methodists, but there is no documentary evidence. Other Methodists are thought to have had important roles in the community and again there may be no written evidence; in neither case is the person cited. Table 3 will thus under-represent the influence of Methodists.

INDUSTRIAL LEADERSHIP

The respectable Methodist leadership was in a position to exercise a substantial influence on industrial relations in the villages. We have already seen that leading Methodists held key posts in the union and in local politics. They were likely to exercise a collective influence also; for example, from 1913 the president, secretary, treasurer and delegate of the Waterhouses lodge of the D.M.A. were all P.M.s. In 1917 at Esh Winning the financial secretary, treasurer, the pit inspectors and at least one committee member were Methodists. We know, therefore, from the positions they occupied that the Methodists were influential.[86] We may project from their general social, economic and political views their likely day-to-day dealing with work-mates and management.

While it remains virtually impossible to reconstruct day-to-day relations at the place of work it is possible from direct accounts, comments passed and impressions gained in the course of research, to build up some picture of the Methodist leaders' behaviour.[87] The interpretations that respondents put upon this behaviour is also indicative of the expectations raised in the minds of observers by the Methodists' actions; for example the more politically active respondents characterise the old leadership as 'peace at any price' men, who believed that half a loaf was better than no bread at all.

Politically the leadership was anti-Socialist. At the meeting at which Matt White and John Henery were elected vice-presidents of the Spennymoor Lib.-Labs., Sammy Galbraith (D.M.A. secretary) spoke against nationalisation. Galbraith spoke thus at a time immediately prior to national discussions within the union of the possibility of extra-parliamentary direct action by the men in favour of nationalisation. Galbraith was 'the last survivor of the old official regime in the Durham Miners' Association'.[88] A disciple of John Wilson, and William Crawford, 'his allegiance brought him into conflict with the new school of Socialist ideas. . .' In 1926 Robert Barren, a life-long Methodist and Liberal who had been checkweighman at Cornsay from 1890–1910 before moving into full-time county politics, often expressed strong disapproval of the General Strike. Furthermore Barren '. . .was a strong critic of the advanced theories in the Labour movement' (Socialism).[89]

Table 3. *The old Liberals*

Name	Occupation	Society	Offices held				
			Lodge	Party	Local govt	Co-op.	Other
Robert Barren, d. 1927; left Cornsay for Durham, 1909	Miners' official	M.N.C. Cornsay and Durham. Sunday school supt.; preacher	Checkweighman; secretary; Sec., Aged Miners' Homes; D.M.A. executive; M.P.R.F. executive	Liberal	Chairman Cornsay parish council; county cttee for Esh	Member Esh Co-op. cttee	Grand president of Oddfellows; active temperance worker; education cttee of D.C.C.
David Cheek, d. 1923	Coal-hewer	Uncertain: did not attend. Sons all P.M.s Quebec	Treasurer 48 years; delegate	Quebec Liberals (committee and speaker)	Quebec council, 1901	–	Citizens' League (anti-Education Bill)
Sam Dove, killed in Cornsay Colliery 1933 or 1934	Hewer and checkweighman	P.M. Esh Winning, probably left or expelled c. 1915. Preacher; trustee; Christian Endeavour national delegate, 1902	Lodge secretary	–	–	Waterhouses Co-op. Cttee, 1903	Club cttee (this was probably the occasion of his withdrawal from Methodism)
J. Fitzpatrick	Small runner	P.M. Waterhouses. Preacher	–	–	Parish council, 1901	Co-op. cttee 1902–[1915]	–

William Foster, left 1920s	Coke-burner (official position)	P.M. Esh Winning. Preacher	—	—	—	Waterhouses delegate to C.W.S.	Sec. Citizens' League; active temperance worker; tried to start League of Nations work in villages; pacifist
J. Hammell, d. 1931	Shopkeeper	P.M. Esh Winning	—	Committee of Esh Winning Young Liberals, 1911	Liberal councillor, 1910; (Poor Law guardian)	—	Chairman of coronation cttee, 1911; ratepayers deputation, 1911; military service tribunal, 1916
Joseph Harrison, d. 1910	Shopkeeper	P.M. Esh Winning. Trustee; circuit steward	—	—	Liberal councillor, 1910; (Poor Law guardian)	—	President of flower show, 1901, 1903, etc.; active against Education Bill 1902–5
John Henery, d. 1930s or 1940s	Deputy	P.M. Water-houses. Trustee	—	Vice-president Spemymoor Lib.-Lab. Assoc.	Liberal councillor, 1905, guardian for 23 yrs; J.P.; chairman U.D.C. 1912–14	Co-op. cttee	Military service tribunal, 1916
Isaac Johnson, d. 1952	Coal-hewer	P.M. Water-houses Sunday school teacher; society and circuit steward; sec. and treasurer of trustees	President and secretary	Liberal	—	Waterhouses Co-op. cttee	—

Table 3 – *continued*

Name	Occupation	Society	Offices held				
			Lodge	Party	Local govt	Co-op.	Other
J. Johnson	Hewer?	P.M.	Treasurer	Young Liberals committee	Parish council, 1901	–	–
Robert Macdonald, last heard of 1926	Hewer	P.M. Quebec. Evangelist preacher; I.O.G.T. member	Sec. M.P.R.F., 1903; checkweighman	Liberal–sec. Quebec Libs., 1903, and then I.L.P.	–	–	Sec. Aged Miners' Homes; active Good Templar
Tom Pearson, d. 1920	Checkweighman	P.M. Waterhouses. Choirmaster	Permanent official; checkweighman; secretary sec. M.P.R.F., 1902	Vice-president Waterhouses Young Liberals, 1911	Councillor, 1904; chairman of U.D.C. Durham (Poor Law guardian)	Co-op. cttee until 1903; chairman of Waterhouses Co-op., 1894	Director of Waterhouses Popular Building Society; sec. flower show, 1903
Aron Richardson, d. Oct. 1986	Hewer	P.M. Quebec. Preacher; S.S. teacher at Waterhouses until 1904	Lodge chairman	Liberal, then Labour	–	–	–
Joseph Stephenson	Hewer?	P.M. Waterhouses. Preacher	–	Liberal	U.D. councillor; county magistrate; guardian	–	–
Matt White, d. 1982	Hewer	P.M. Waterhouses. Trustee; circuit steward; delegate to conference, 1982	Lodge chairman; president, 1915; M.P.R.F. cttee, 1902. Aged Miners' Homes cttee; Lodge sec. for 32 yrs	Vice-pres. Waterhouses Young Libs. Vice-pres. Spennymoor Lib.-Labs., 1919, 1926 Labour	Councillor; guardian; J.P.	Waterhouses committee	Committee work, especially interested in hospital care

Abbreviations. M.P.R.F. – Miners' Permanent Relief Fund; U.D.C. – Urban District Council; D.C.C. – Durham County Council; I.O.G.T. – Independent Order of Good Templars (a temperance organisation); S.S. – Sunday School.

Under the Liberal leadership in Esh Winning and Waterhouses there does appear to have been a more than average reluctance on the part of the men to use the strike weapon in the pursuit of industrial disputes (see Tables 4, 5, 6).

The percentage of lodge members voting for strike action is considerably lower than the national and county average for Esh Winning

Table 4. *1909 National Strike against reduction of Scottish miners' wages*

	For the strike	Against	% for strike
National	518,361	62,980	89
Durham County	25,103	2,786	90
Esh Winning	211	88	70·5[a]
Waterhouses	140	69	67[a]
Hamsteels	365	41	90

Note: [a] Significantly different from county vote at $P > 0.001$.
Source. D.C., 30.7.09.

Table 5. *1912 Minimum Wage Strike ballot*

	For strike action	Against	% for strike
National	445,801	95,919	82·5
Durham	57,490	28,504	66·5
Esh Winning	124	153[a]	44·5
Cornsay	154	68	69

Note: [a] Esh Winning was 1 lodge out of 6 voting against, in a total of 62 lodges.
Source. D.C., 29.1.12. Figures for Waterhouses and Hamsteels not given.

Table 6. *1912 Minimum Wage Strike; ballot to continue strike*

	For continuation	Against	% continue
Durham	48,828	24,511[a]	66·6
Esh Winning	219	325	40
Waterhouses	141	137	50·5[b]
Hamsteels	282	103	73
Cornsay	191	82	70

Notes: [a] There was only a 61·5% poll in the county.
 [b] Significantly different from county vote at $P > 0.001$.
Source. D.C., 5.4.12.

and Waterhouses whilst Hamsteels is at the average level in 1909 and exceeds it in 1912. It is also interesting to note that Esh Winning almost doubles its turn-out to vote on ending the 1912 Strike as compared with voting for the strike in January. (Few figures such as these quoted can be obtained as it was, and still is not, practice to publish separate colliery voting figures. The figures quoted were improperly released to the press.)

At Esh Winning the checkweighman and lodge secretary from the First World War until after the 1926 Dispute, Sam Dove, was addressed by his Christian name by the manager. It is said that he tended to accept what was said by the management when bargaining and that he 'never did his home-work'. The union official who made this latter comment took up a case which the secretary had not pressed and won it for the men. In praising the work of Barren and Richardson at Cornsay one (non-Methodist) ex-miner commented that they 'knew their facts' and 'could talk Curry off his feet'. The ability to stand one's ground in an argument is a highly-prized quality that does not seem to have been lacking among leading Methodists. Interestingly enough Dove was not a leading Methodist, he ceased to be very active in the chapel and eventually became a 'club man'.

In Waterhouses the P.M. leadership was dominant in the lodge and the village from the 1880s. In 1891 and 1892 Tom Pearson was checkweighman during the strikes. In spite of Crofton's allegations of presumptuousness (p. 87) Pearson seems to have been a very moderate leader who brought his men out on strike in a quiet and undramatic manner.

After a brief stoppage at Esh and Waterhouses in 1891 the men agreed to keep the colliery open; 'This may be a certain extent to be attributed largely [*sic*] to the tact and business qualities of the gentlemen who met, amongst whom we may mention the local Secretary, Mr Thomas Pearson, in whom the men have an able representative.'[90] We have already seen that the 1892 Strike was quiet and orderly under Pearson's leadership in Waterhouses (p. 87).[91] Matt White was Pearson's successor. He was allowed certain concessions which the men saw as favour by the management, for example, being allowed to leave the pit early to catch the Durham bus; the greatest favour received by White was that of not having to retire at the age of sixty-five.

When Ryle took over at Pease and Partners as local manager the management committee said that Waterhouses would 'be alright', 'We've always got on well with Matt White' (reported by manager's confidential clerk to a union official). Even after a period of industrial conflict the Methodist leaders still tried to maintain friendly personal relations with the managers; they seemed to feel that personal relations transcended economic conflict. Also, the local colliery managers were of long standing in the locality like the Methodist leadership. When Mr Palmer retired, a collection of over £150 was made; at the presentation three Methodists made speeches. First Matt White on behalf of the Waterhouses workmen: 'Mr. Palmer was a gentleman, ever courteous when they had met him, and he hoped his successor would follow in his footsteps.'[92] Sam Dove spoke on behalf of the Esh Winning miners, and Isaac Findlay for the Ushaw Moor men. Events such as these, perhaps based on genuine affection for a good manager, could not fail to compromise the leaders in the eyes of the men during later events.

In 1926 the police felt that their job was relatively easy in Waterhouses.[93] Matt White discouraged the harassing of blacklegs and maintained the very strictest good order within the lodge. In fulfilling a peace-keeping role Matt White was acting out the role prescribed for the local leadership by the D.M.A., but he was also acting according to his own definition of his role.[94] Few police were stationed in Waterhouses during the dispute (see Chapter 8).

Mutual respect, friendship, or even the exchange of favours does not necessarily mean that either side is failing fully to represent its own interests. The personal reciprocity built up might nonetheless from time to time compromise their official roles. Friendly personal relations between managers and union leaders are more easily maintained in relatively prosperous economic circumstances. The various comments on Pearson indicate that the main area of conflict was over the scope of union intervention, each side having a slightly different idea of where negotiation became interference with the operation of the market.

We have found no evidence to suggest that good personal relations prevented the driving of a hard bargain by either side. The ability to drive such a bargain may have been a part of the basis for mutual respect. But it is quite clear that the good relations were likely to be re-interpreted when the men seemed to be losing their claims. The compromise settlements of the late nineteenth century and early twentieth brought some benefits to the men; when they ceased to do so the men were suspicious of the leaders' relations with the management. However, there seems to be little justification for calling Methodism a 'blackleg religion'.

We conclude therefore that in the economic circumstances of the last quarter of the nineteenth century and in the first few years of this, the Methodist union leadership showed the following characteristics. Firstly, it was deferential in its attitude to the management. Secondly, in this situation the congruence between Methodist Individualism and current economic thinking reinforced a faith in the operation of the market. Industrial relations were seen as a series of compromises within the market context, involving degrees of reciprocity which were re-inforced by the paternalistic outlook and actions of the owners and managers. Thirdly, the union leaders' outlook was essentially personal-istic and traditional; the union leaders, for example, were never able to see themselves as representing one class interest against another in a wholly impersonal economic system – all their traditional relations with the owners and managers militated against this.

Even before the First World War the influence of Labour thinking was being felt at the local level. By 1907 the Durham miners were asking for a living wage and were rejecting the market thinking of the Liberals. It was the politically-conscious younger men who clashed with the older Liberals: 'Matt White's sons and the Bailey boys used to ask questions at political meetings (all parties). Matt called them hot-heads and agitators. He was often distressed by the attitude of the young people in the Union. The older Liberals kept the younger elements in check at Waterhouses.'[95] One of the 'younger element', whom we will consider presently, met the same resistance: 'Matt White was a big Liberal and so was Sam Dove. We started selling *The Herald*; there was much opposition to it, but this was toughest in Esh Winning and Waterhouses. . .Bill Harrison was Liberal, and his friends. They insisted that religion and politics did not mix. But it was *their* politics that was under attack.'[96]

This conflict had consequences for intra-chapel affairs; 'Ben Bailey was left off the (Primitive Methodist) Trustees for being left wing'[97] (an opinion confirmed as fact by one of the then trustees). At Quebec the conflict was more open; 'The time of the service was changed to the morning [this] finished the [I.L.P.] group meeting in chapel. . .the opposition probably thought that religion and politics were separate. Ralph Hayson was in opposition and William Harrison – but not Aron Richardson; he made up his own mind.'[98]

Some of the leading Methodists, especially those in the union, became Labour supporters in the 1920s nonetheless, but even as late as 1927 all the officials of the Esh Winning Liberal Party were Methodists. A retired minister perceptively stated the ethical basis of Methodist Liberalism and typifies the Methodist Liberal for us:

> Liberals in the chapels thought individual life more important than social life. . .they tended to stop at the individual level. Drink was the greatest social evil, so they tackled it. . .But they didn't always look at the social conditions which drove men to drink. . . individualism was a stage in their history – that's why they were free churches.[99]

7 The radicals and the Labour Movement, 1900–1926

The Durham miners were, in Gregory's terms, amongst the 'front-runnners' in the development of the Labour vote in British mining. Given that Methodism was such a strong integrating force in the Liberal establishment at local and regional level, the obvious question is how much Methodism still inhibited the mobilisation of the Labour vote, and the development of class consciousness.

There is the whole class of older Methodists, staunch Liberals, to whom community loyalties were fundamental. The first priority will be to investigate the others who deserted, who they were, where they came from, how radical the switch to Labour affiliation really was, whether they still accommodated their Methodist principles, and if so how.

THE RADICALS

The earliest record of radical non-Liberal political activity is found in Joseph Taylor's diaries for 1895 and 1896. In May 1895 Ed. Cooke read a paper to the Hamsteels Bible class, entitled 'The Independent Labour Party'. In August he read another 'The Defeat of the Liberal Party'. A year later Richard Burleigh, school attendance officer and local preacher (see Glossary) read a paper on 'Christian Socialism'. In November 1896 a visiting preacher spoke on a week-night to the subject 'Monopolists or the Multitudes, Which?' The full membership of this Bible class is unrecorded but among its active members were: John Harrison, Ed. Cooke, and T. Gott. John Harrison was a miner and P.M. local preacher. Cooke, a smallholder, was not a Methodist; people who knew him have variously described him as a Fabian, a non-Christian, a materialist. This latter term was used by an aged informant who attended an improvement class with Cooke. Gott was an active trade unionist and a founder of the Waterhouses Labour Party, but he had no apparent religious affiliation. It seems that Cooke and Gott attended the Bible class for the sake of the discussion.

The main Labour activist at the beginning of this century was a

Roman Catholic, John Holmes; he was also active in the Irish League and trade-union affairs. Holmes spoke in Durham in 1901 of the need for Labour to make small beginnings in local affairs;[1] in May of 1901 Holmes was Labour candidate for the Esh guardians, but he was defeated by the P.M. draper, Joseph Harrison (not related to John Harrison). In the parish Council election he was defeated by the Liberal miner, David Cheek. Holmes was eventually elected and was active on the council into the 1920s.

Radicalism was thus not the monopoly of Methodists in the valley. Holmes plainly was a representative of another religion with a strong associational basis and he belonged to an ethnic group with a radical tradition. Non-religious people too were drawn into the activities of radical groups. Nonetheless when we turn to Cornsay Colliery we find a rather remarkable situation. The Cornsay I.L.P. was formed in 1913. Its main activity and membership was in Quebec; we refer to members as the Quebec radicals. Its core membership was as shown in Table 7.

Table 7. *The Quebec radicals*

Name	Occupation	Religious affiliation	Other
John George Harrison	Schoolteacher	P.M. preacher	Son of John Harrison
Robert and Cuthbert MacDonald	Miners	P.M. evangelists	Bob became check-weighman
Alf, Charlie, Jack and Joe Cheek	Miners	P.M.s	Sons of Cheek
George E. Pritchard	Miner	P.M. preacher	After Lakin, lodge secretary
Joe Taylor	Master's weighman	P.M. preacher	Diarist above
Jimmy Lakin	Miner	P.M. organist	Lodge secretary
Jack Lowden	Miner	P.M.	
George Craddock	Miner	P.M.	
George Gibbon	Miner	Spiritualist	
T. Clough	Miner	W.M. preacher	Esh Winning lodge secretary

The near monopoly of the I.L.P. by the Methodists is confirmed by all informants. The most plausible explanation for this state of affairs would seem to be that the Methodists had a ready-made organisational basis (in this case the Bible class) for forming a political group. The Methodists were prominent amongst the early I.L.P. members in these villages at least because it was in the course of their religious activities

that they discussed political matters, 'converted' one another to new
political ideas and then sought out potential converts. This group's
early activities were mainly the organisation of meetings and dis-
tributing leaflets and newspapers, they are also alleged to have stopped
people on the streets to discuss politics. Mrs Pankhurst, Ben Tillett,
Tom Mann and Jim Larkin ('the Irish agitator') were all brought up to
the village by the group. The group sold the *Clarion*, the *Labour
Leader* and later the *Daily Herald*, around the villages.

J. G. Harrison and George Craddock were first politically active and
continued to be so in the women's suffrage movement. Esther, J.G.'s[2]
sister, a schoolteacher; Connie Ellis, schoolteacher; and Bella Faulkner,
later Mrs J. G. Harrison, were the leading suffragettes. A fourth
woman in the group, Emma Lowes, a schoolteacher, married George
Craddock. Esther and Bella were Methodists and initially non-mili-
tants. Connie was a militant, often a victim of physical violence. All
three were under police surveillance at the beginning of the First
World War.

Thus J.G. gained his early experience of political activity, not in a
Socialist movement but with the suffragettes. J.G. was the intellectual
of the group. Whilst training at Bede College, he read Tolstoy and
developed an interest in pacifism and Socialism. His reading widened
in the next few years (1910–c.1915) to include among other authors:
Thoreau, Emerson, Henry James, F. D. Maurice, Edward Carpenter
and Robert Blatchford. During a period of further study he became
apparently almost obsessed by George Fox's life and writing. At Wood-
brooke College he also became interested in the late eighteenth-
century radical rationalists: William Godwin, Mary Wollstonecraft,
Tom Paine and Shelley. He was also interested in the Diggers and
Utopian movements. The Quebec I.L.P. members, many of whom were
brought up on evangelical Methodism and respectable Liberalism,
must have found the mixture of free-thinking, rationalism, transcenden-
talism, anti-authoritarianism, pacifist Christianity and Christian Socialism bewildering but intellectually challenging. J.G. himself left
Methodism in 1911 after being almost convinced of the truth of
Christian Science; he drifted back into Methodism, next became a
Quaker as a result of the churches' attitude to the First World War, and
then a member of the Brotherhood Church – an anarcho-Christian
pacifist group of Utopians. He died whilst helping to establish a rural
community with the Brotherhood Church.

The fact that he and others were not so firmly integrated into
Methodism as the established members is significant. We would
expect some of the young Methodists to feel themselves marginal to
Methodism because the domination of the older men blocked oppor-

tunities within the chapels for the younger men. But more importantly, we expect political and religious radicals to belong to sectarian kinds of groups and to be more likely to change affiliation in their pursuit of ethical, political or doctrinal purity.

They read, appropriately enough, authors like Maurice, Carpenter and Tolstoy, who represented a peculiarly ethical kind of Socialism. The ideas of Thoreau may also have been in harmony with the individualism and libertarianism that was part of Methodism. If we compare, for example, Thoreau's *Civil Disobedience* with Sorel on the General Strike in *Reflections on Violence* we see the qualitative contrast between a strongly ethical and individualistic political outlook and a radical and violent class consciousness. To this extent we see that Socialism owed something to Methodism, in that Methodism prepared the ground for the acceptance of one kind of Socialism rather than another.

In Quebec J.G. circulated papers on political topics, including his college essays. Respondents agree that although he was a young man among mature miners he impressed and inspired the I.L.P. group with his enthusiasm and his new ideas. A survivor of the group said that they were influenced by both religious and political writers. The group read Blatchford's works; he could remember them discussing *Merrie England*, and reading and discussing the *Clarion* newspaper.

J.G. is worth quoting *in extenso* to illustrate the divergence of his ideas from 'respectable' Methodist Liberalism. In a sermon in 1913 he notes that the converted drunkard may be less generous than in his drinking days. Later in the sermon he says: 'Christians seem to be certain of their own fitness for heaven and their own superiority to the poor people who are supposed to be in poverty because of their wickedness.' He goes on to say that Blatchford's *Not Guilty* had stirred him for the first time, 'to deep pity and sympathy for the tramp, the wastrel or the slum dweller...My early Christian training led me to believe that such people suffered through their own faults'. In some notes of the same period, he writes;

> The historian Myers referring to the early prophets of Israel says: 'These prophets were the first socialists. Theirs was the first passionate plea for the poor, the wretched and the heavy burdened...'

> How much do business methods conform to Christ-likeness?... The unfoldment of good is the true business of man and in this pursuit none can lack God's outstretched arm...The finger posts of duty and expediency seldom point in the same direction. Compromise can never lead to the attainment of the highest ideals.

Citing Mary Wollstonecraft's reply to Burke's *Reflections on the Revo-*

lution in France, J.G. sums up his own attitude to property: 'Security of Property! Behold in a few words, the definition of English Liberty... But softly – it is only the property of the Rich that is secure; the man who lives by the sweat of his brow has no asylum from oppression.'

J.G. said in a letter to 'The Brethren and I.L.P.'ers' in 1916, 'to transform (or transmute) the trade union and labour movement. That is probably my life's work – that and teaching men that Good, Truth and Love are *all* powerful – I want to be convinced, like Keir Hardie, of the reality of spiritual things and the unreality of material things.' Even political success would have its problem for J.G. whose concern remained deeply religious; he feared that Socialist beliefs would make men too materialistic. How will men believe in Christian Science as long as they are physically, materially and spiritually oppressed by the system – 'a nation of Mammon-worshippers?' he asks in 1912. In a fragmentary note J.G. typifies the contemporary political situation, 'big-headed dwarfs as M.P.s, ruling hollow-headed animals'.

We are not suggesting that all the miners in the I.L.P. group were convinced by – or indeed fully comprehended – the full range of J.G.'s ideas. He was a mercurial character with an eclectic mind and an almost manic dedication to a set of widely based and changing ideas. He was also very dogmatic ('Christian theology can only be understood by those who are Christians. The opinion of the non-Christian is worthless for he has no first hand experience.'). Nevertheless for his friends, who valued education and learning, he spoke with authority, and the range and originality of his ideas must have appealed to them. Given that they were nearly all Methodists they would probably have left the group if J.G.'s ideas had given them offence. But they remained in the group. They could not remain uninfluenced by continuous exposure to such radical ideas.

The ideas put forward by J.G. were eclectic but not haphazard.

They contained a systematic and coherent critique of capitalist society, which explained both local economic hardships and international conflict.

He offered a new and optimistic view of man and a vision of a new social order. This vision was put in effective political terms by the I.L.P. nationally.

J.G. questioned the social and economic order in religious and moral terms. This discussion was largely rooted in the Bible and biblical allusion. He provided an intellectual and intelligible bridge from traditional Methodist thinking to a more secular ideology. Religious supporters could thereby adopt more radical political views without a loss of faith. In fact they were offered one language to express their religious and political views.

The significance of these ideas for the traditional Methodists and for our argument should be noted.

They were a conscious identification of the Gospel with the *unredeemed* poor and directly challenged Methodist respectability.

J.G. offered a direct criticism of the capitalist businessman, on Christian ethical grounds.

Compromise was rejected as the best way forward in social, economic and political affairs. In the language of class conflict J.G. said, 'The interests of a coal owner. . .are opposed to those of colliers'.

J.G.'s free and unorthodox biblical exegesis associated him with the *New Theology* of R. J. Campbell and the Higher Criticism. He cited Peake as one of the authors who had influenced him. These new religious ideas had already caused considerable friction within the local chapels. His explicit unorthodoxy reaffirmed for the traditionalists the dangers of abandoning a more fundamentalist position and of adopting a 'social gospel'. It indicated the possibility of further and more dangerous links between religious and political dissent.

Furthermore, the radical ideas contained thinly-veiled promises of social disorder and threats to private property.

In terms of our thesis J.G. was presenting a set of ideas and representing an outlook which was the negation of the principles underlying the social and political gospel of the traditional Methodists. He was plainly making the authentic appeal of the Christian revolutionary to the disinherited. Paradoxically, he also quite explicitly preached perfectionism. Conventional local preachers did not specifically mention this; but when J.G. did he quoted not John Wesley but George Fox.

This last point is crucial to the whole discussion of Methodism and the working class in the Deerness Valley. The Socialists in Quebec owed *nothing* intellectually to Methodism. They communicated in part in the language of the Bible, they discussed their ideas in the Bible class. They certainly preached the Gospel of Socialism with a zeal equal to any Methodist preacher or evangelist (which some of them were). They may have been saved from a life of degradation and been made sensitive to social issues by Methodism. Nevertheless, it remains true that the core of their ideas, the political goals they pursued as Socialists, did not come from Methodism and were antipathetic to Methodist orthodoxy.

The implications of this for social history and the sociology of religion are of some importance. We note that Wearmouth, in commenting on twentieth-century Methodism, assumes that the ideals of Methodist radicals came from Methodism, or were at least of a piece with Methodism. Wearmouth's main thesis is that 'Methodism perhaps made its greatest contribution to the advance of the Labour movement in politics by the provision of suitable and outstanding leadership.'[3] He lists some of the earlier Liberal leaders in his chapter 'Methodism and the Labour Party' and says of them as we saw in Chapter 1, 'These men were not revolutionaries, but God-fearing representatives of the working-class interests. By their integrity and uprightness they demonstrated to the rulers of the land that the country had nothing to fear from the leaders of the working-men.' On the other hand, the Quebec radicals are not the type of Methodists who feature in Wearmouth's analysis, but men belonging to a tradition of Christian radicalism of which the rulers of the land had much to fear. For it is a tradition which includes insurrection as well as pacifism, and a tradition in which the doctrine of the brotherhood of man might be translated into active levelling.

J.G. appears to overshadow the others in the group because he has left copious records of his spiritual and intellectual career. Jack Cheek read Keir Hardie, Ramsay MacDonald, and his father's law book (obviously of great value to a father and son active in union affairs). The MacDonalds were able public speakers and were much concerned with the miners' cause, but they were not 'great readers'. (This informant inherited all Bob's possessions – they included only three or four books.) Nor were the Quebec I.L.P. the first radicals in the district.

Pyle, an ex-preacher, after an early anti-trade union career[4] became a leader in the valley during the industrial dispute of 1879.[5] Holmes took a leading part in the D.M.R.A. at the turn of the century; Wearmouth says of them, '...the rank and file rebelled against their officials and threatened to remove them from office, but wiser counsel prevailed...'[6] Holmes then entered local politics.[7] The D.M.R.A. was the successor to the Durham Miners' Progressive Federation, formed in 1898. Both organisations fought Wilsonism and pressed for the democratisation of the D.M.A. They were part of the national movement for a minimum wage for miners, the eight-hour day and a more militant attitude towards the coal-owners on the part of the union. They were responsible for bringing Socialist speakers to the Durham miners' annual big meeting (gala).[8] J.G.'s father had read a paper on Garibaldi in the Bible class in 1895,[9] and seconded a resolution at the 1879 Strike rally.[10] J.G. said of his father, 'Oh that all fathers were as unorthodox as Bella's and mine, who value reason more than the authority of an inspired book or a clerical coat or a tall hat.'[11] His mother supported the suffragettes and held radical views, if we are to accept the evidence of J.G. in a letter from Burton in 1916; 'The good lady here is very much like my mother...She talks sedition wherever she goes.' David Cheek, for forty-three years treasurer of the Hamsteels lodge, was no 'respectable'

175

Liberal; he gave his notice ten times at the colliery and William House threatened to bring the whole D.M.A. out on strike when Cheek was threatened with eviction.[12] Cooke, the MacDonalds (middle-aged by the First World War) and Joe Taylor may actually have constituted an earlier I.L.P. group.[13]

With a worsening trade situation, local hardship and the threat of war, the socially- and politically-aware miners gathered around a man who had ideas and enthusiasm, who was able to articulate their fears and hopes. Nevertheless, accounts given by members of the group, its friends and critics, all suggest that it was not a one-man enterprise. The Cheeks and the MacDonalds were to a great extent the most active in organising, and in arguing with miners.

The I.L.P. group met at 11.00 a.m. on Sundays in the P.M. Chapel. The P.M.s therefore altered the time of a Sunday meeting in order to exclude the I.L.P. from the use of the chapel. The group then seems to have met in a bell tent in George Craddock's garden. This tent was also used for an I.L.P. summer camp in the Cornsay Valley. The fact that men and women were camping together was another source of offence to the respectable. But the main criticisms voiced were that the group were bringing politics into religion and were splitting the church, at the more personal level it was said that they were hot-heads.

The group never actually achieved a big following in Cornsay and Quebec, although individual members of the group held office in the lodges. The ethical and rather spiritual nature of their Socialism probably gave it a limited appeal, even to those miners who were interested in Socialism as such.[14] Some others were attached to the fringe of the group. One was J. G. Winter, a talented footballer, a miner, P.M., a friend of J. G. Harrison, another was William Cairns, solicitor's clerk, a Methodist local preacher interested in F. D. Maurice and a reader of the *Christian Commonwealth*. George Galley, a rather retiring young local preacher, joined in with the group, mainly to listen, but was seldom very active in the group.

Cairns had been partially alienated from the Methodists. He was a follower of R. J. Cambell's theology, and while making a point in a sermon on the offering of Abraham's son he was interrupted by James Hammell and told, 'Aye hiney if you don't [believe it] you shouldn't be standing there'.[15] J. G. Winter died in Wormwood Scrubs as a conscientious objector in the First World War.

It was probably the association of the I.L.P. in general and the Quebec group in particular with conscientious objection which later alienated potential support. I.L.P. meetings in other parts of the county were broken up during 1917.[16] It had been suggested by miners that conscientious objectors and sympathisers should be sacked and men refuse to work with them.[17] Connie Ellis' husband suffered this treatment at the end of the war, and like J.G., he became a gardener for a while.[18]

The Cornsay I.L.P. represents the most extremely radical response to social and economic conditions in the valley. There was no Communist presence in the district; this would have been an entirely non-religious response. The I.L.P. probably carried the 'religious' response to its limit. Its programme appeared wholly political but was nevertheless based on a moral analysis of society which entailed a mixture of religion and politics. The step beyond this is a purely political analysis based on ideas of class interest alone.

Two approaches to 'the world' are implicit in the division within the Quebec P.M. chapel:

(i) One section very evangelical, drawing a sharp distinction between secular and sacred. Was suspicious of politics, but unconsciously disclosed *Liberal* sympathies. . .

(ii) Another section saw the relevance of Christianity to all aspects of life and implied involvement in politics [i.e. radical politics] to which allegiance was given.

(from a letter to the author from a local preacher born in Quebec)
We will suggest reasons for the second response being so powerful in Quebec, and have already shown that it was the first response that typified the leaders in the other villages.

It was not the I.L.P. alone who were caught up with new political and theological ideas. Aron Richardson and Westgarth Adamson, for example, were radical Methodists who did not join the group.

Richardson had been a preacher from the early 1890s at the latest. He had been described by a number of respondents as an intellectual man and he had an extensive library. He was a coal-hewer and became chairman of the Cornsay lodge. He was a stalwart of the Labour Movement and had a 'rebel temperament'.[19] Richardson believed the I.L.P. group to be agitators and he did not join them, but nevertheless he never opposed them. It seems that while he did not approve of the particular expression of radical views he agreed with many of the basic ideas. Since he was a man of considerable authority, his tacit agreement with the I.L.P. probably carried weight locally.

Westgarth Adamson was a miner and preacher all his life. His preaching was discussed in Chapter 4. His son gave an account of how Westgarth's religious views engaged with politics:

We wanted to bring in the Kingdom of God industrially and socially in five minutes – we were extreme. My father walked the streets for two years – standing up for righteousness. . .some members of the chapel could not understand. They wouldn't speak to Dad – their husbands were officials and the like. . .We couldn't reconcile the Gospel and the social situation. The church didn't rise up. There were external forces on the churches and chapels – they enjoyed the owners' patronage. In the 1920's the Chairman of [a] Methodist Rally was Secretary of the Consett Iron Company. I told them, 'It's only because he gives you a two guinea contribution.'

He [Westgarth] was preaching at Sacriston once. The colliery owner was called Brass [pronounced with short, northern 'a']. Dad preached on Balam and the Ass. 'It takes a lot to stop some asses talking today', he said – Brass was there, and very angry.

He hit out at bad housing in his sermons. There was tremendous opposition to 'politics from the pulpit'. He always preached with urgency – *now* is the day to get it done. . .He was a close friend of Peter Lee.[20]

Adamson expressed his radicalism within the chapel, and later the local Labour Party; his comments were directed towards concrete areas of reform. He offended the respectable Methodists who thought he should not preach politics from the pulpit.

In Cornsay Labour activity centred around Aron Richardson. In Quebec it was difficult to elicit the formal structure of the Labour Party; J.G. and Bob MacDonald died in the early 1920's; Lakin seems to have died or moved away also. Holmes and Cud MacDonald remained active in the village into the 1920s. They both appeared in a delegation to Lanchester guardians to ask for men to be given work. Holmes said that 'if the government could spend millions in killing people they might spend money in keeping them alive'. MacDonald hinted at possible disturbances in the area.[21] Their political vigour seemed unabated. The Cheeks and George Pritchard were active in the lodge and Labour politics. After 1926 Pritchard moved to Blackhall where he became the checkweighman, county councillor and alderman. He became chairman of the fire brigade and education committee. He was nominally a Methodist until he died, but only appeared at chapel for special events. Alf Cheek became a deputy at Cornsay (respondents allege that he 'changed sides'), one brother was killed in the war, another became interested in spiritualism, another became (and still is) a Mormon, the fifth ceased to be active in chapel and lodge.

Prior to 1914–18 the I.L.P. had been a non-respectable body and the Labour cause weak. The activists had been committed Socialists, hostile to the established local leadership, which was Liberal and largely Methodist. After 1918 the Labour Party was sufficiently respectable for non-Socialists to join. Furthermore the rank and file of miners had been swung to the Labour Party. This had been by no means a local Methodist effort, but an effort organised by the Labour Party nationally, by the D.M.A. and many local activists who were not Methodist (not even nominal Methodists). The dates of the deaths of the founding Methodist leaders indicates that generational factors are also important. The older men were being replaced on their death by men with new ideas. For some of these older men the problem of an ideological change did not arise. But if the established local leaders wished to maintain their positions they would have to become Labour. Joining a party to keep in power does not necessitate a change of political ideas. Thus Matt White, for example, was ideologically a Liberal to the end of his days.[22] Similarly, the men who supported Labour in the early 1920s had, as late as 1916, returned a Lib.–Lab. M.P. although not without dispute, Galbraith being more Liberal than Labour.

There was a brief upsurge of radicalism amongst the young people of the Waterhouses P.M.s in the mid 1920s. These were the members of the Young People's Institute whose question on the Socialism of Christ and Marx was cited in Chapter 5.[23] Of the five young men who were known to be very active participants, all left the village, four as schoolteachers, one as a Co-op. employee.

Although the overall economic situation was much the same in all the villages there were factors which made Quebec different from the others and which have thereby presented an important comparison. In Quebec the identification between owners and Methodists was not so complete. J. B. Johnson was acknowledged to be a good employer but he was a brewer, a Tory and an Anglican. *Prima facie* there is reason to suppose that he would not command such Methodist respect as Pease, Ferens and Love. It would be more acceptable to take up a critical attitude towards Johnson in a discussion of local affairs. Here then the power of religion to reduce class antagonism could not operate because religious and ethical beliefs were not shared between potentially conflicting parties.

Social conditions, especially housing, were worse in Quebec than in any of the other villages in the valley, and officially recognised as such.[24] When Esh parish council and Hamsteels lodge sent a deputation to Lanchester rural district council asking for the adoption of Part III of the Housing of the Working Classes Act, their plea was rejected on the grounds that rate-payers should not have to meet the mine-owners' responsibility and that the future of Hamsteels pit was uncertain. The mine-owners and shopkeepers were the main rate-payers. Joseph Harrison and the Esh representative voted against the suggestion.[25] The *D.C.* also suggests that Quebec was an especially bad area for drunkenness and fighting; quite often fighting was between miners with Irish and English names. Thus paternalistic ownership and cooperative union leadership had not aligned themselves in the relative improvement of social conditions.

The vicar of Hamsteels, said to be an eccentric (and a teetotaller), was very contemptuous of the working class and poured scorn and abuse upon them at the time of the General Strike. He also used his parish magazine earlier to attack the miners. For example:

> The saddest event during the past month has been the Welsh Miners' Strike. These men have been enjoying higher wages than almost any other class of workmen. Their average wage has been from £3 to £4 a week and many are earning as much as £5 and £6 a week.
>
> Yet the Welsh miners wanted more, and took advantage of their country's peril to demand higher wages and to go on strike to compel the country to grant their demands.

The question of miners' wages, raised by the Revd E. C. Rust became a matter of controversy in the national press. The I.L.P. group invited a speaker to Quebec to reply to Rust. Rust made much of the fact that the speaker came on a Sunday, thus proving that Socialists were also Sabbath-breakers.[26]

> The Socialists in Wales have shown that they care nothing for their country, that they are ready to endanger the whole of England and the liberties of Europe, in order to enrich one already highly paid class of workmen at the expense of the rest of the community.[27]

> It is a matter of regret, that in spite of every effort on the part of the management, Hamsteels Colliery is laid off. . .It is a direct result of the class warfare which has been so assiduously preached to the working men of late. If by continually demanding more wages and doing less work the men succeed in ruining the masters, they can only succeed in ruining themselves, and the whole of the country.[28]

Rust's activities effectively increased the polarisation of the village and the development of conflict. There may also be a psychological explanation of his apparently very personal hostility to the miners, but nonetheless he was associated with the owners, and Anglicanism was associated with owners in general. So, psychological factors aside this provides a very clear illustration of the way in which religious differences could reinforce economic and political conflict.

It is to be expected that Quebec would be a place where radical views – already spreading throughout the country and the nation – would find ready acceptance. One conclusion is that poor environmental conditions and relational factors (relative social disorganisation, less sympathy between owner and men, more open hostility from the church, differences with the established Liberal–Methodist leadership) produced a leadership more radical than elsewhere in the valley, and this from early on. Interestingly enough Pyle, and twenty years later, Holmes and David Cheek were not Methodists but nonetheless were active in Quebec. While Holmes, for example, represents Hamsteels in the D.M.R.A., Esh Winning and Waterhouses are not reported in the press as being amongst the villages represented at all the D.M.R.A. rallies.

All these factors together made the political situation in Quebec more 'open' than in the other villages. Given this fairly open situation, with no Liberal–Methodist hegemony in 1920, the situation was more suitable for a spontaneous and radical response to the worsening economic situation. There had been an attempt to awaken the Methodist social conscience at the turn of the century as in the example of Hugh Price Hughes and the Forward Movement in Chapter 1. The new Theology and the Higher Criticism were opening up Scriptures afresh to Methodists. The local chapels which had leaders like Harrison and Hammel either remained passive, or actively and successfully resisted the intrusion of new ideas (as in the case of Cairns). Into the Quebec situation came an intellectual, a man with practical ideas for their economic distress, the passive church, and new trends in theology. This man was John George Harrison. J.G. was not entirely a charismatic leader, but acted as a catalyst, in a situation that was ripe for dissent.

These are some of the explanations for the difference between the villages on the valley bottom and Quebec. The group is politically deviant from the pre-1914 norm of Liberalism and therefore needs a special explanation. In fact after 1920, it might have been more accurate to refer to *Waterhouses* as deviant, and needing explanation. One could ask, without the First World War and the rise of the Labour Party as a viable national working-class party, what would have happened to the Quebec radicals?[29] Given continuing economic decline, two possibilities are plausible: it would have continued as one of a possibly increasing number of Socialist cells, perhaps contributing to the rise of a nationwide Socialist movement. The interesting problem is then whether it would have become less overtly religious as it attracted wider support and grappled with more wholly secular issues. Or it could have become a wholly religious movement of a sectarian kind, possibly a millenarial movement. We have indicated that the Cheeks and J.G. were very susceptible to the claims of 'fringe' sects, and thus the group was open to millenarian inspiration.

Two historical events make this an idle historical speculation: the rise of the Labour Party and the economic death of Quebec in 1926. Also Socialism was discredited by its association with the conscientious objectors and the Russian Revolution.[30] Sociologically the speculation is more worthwhile as the Quebec radicals are a classical example of a religio-political protest among the underprivileged, raising important questions in the sociology of religion and political sociology.

THE RISE OF THE LABOUR PARTY

The Revd E. T. Davies in his *Religion in the Industrial Revolution in South Wales* provides us with an interesting and highly relevant comparison with Durham:

> The political wing of Welsh Nonconformity became more and more clamant during and after the 1880's, and their programme became less and less relevant to the problems of an industrial society. . .
>
> The year 1898 may be accepted as a dividing line. For twenty years before that time the miners' Unions were weak. This was the period which, politically, can be called the 'Lib-Lab' period in politics and the 'sliding scale' period in industrial relationships. 'The Rhondda and Aberdare (Miners') Association were specifically devoted to encouraging mutual understanding between employer and workman, and the other district organisation pursued the same policy'. It was the period in which most miners' leaders came from the ranks of Welsh Nonconformity.
>
> 'Political nonconformity and industrial paternalism was still the most important factor in the political structure of the valleys' [But]. . .new voices were heard in the coalfield. Keir Hardie, and not Mabon, became the new symbol. . .The new local leaders . . .were originally chapel men. . .These men were the product of the chapels, their early training left an indelible impression upon them. Socialism and class warfare were the keynotes of the new industrial gospel.
>
> As the Welsh miners developed their own organisation the politics of Welsh nonconformity became more and more irrelevant to them.[31]

The Methodists in Durham were concerned not with disestablishment, as in Wales, but with temperance. Industrially, they were concerned with cordial relations between masters and men. Economically they believed in *laissez-faire* Liberalism. These became increasingly irrelevant to the Durham miner.

The rise of the Labour Party in County Durham is a story which will not be told here. We will only examine the Methodist contribution to the Party's local development. Gregory, in *The Miners and British Politics, 1906–1913*, remarks that while the Lib.-Labs. of 1910 may have been regarded as well to the Left in their younger days, as an entrenched leadership they 'rejected Socialist doctrine and fiercely resented and resisted the concomitant idea of a new and independent working-class party'.[32] Furthermore, according to Gregory, many associated Socialism with the 'eight-hour day' – which the Durham hewers rejected. In accordance with Liberal *laissez-faire* economic thinking they also rejected the notion of the minimum wage when coal was competing in a foreign market.[33] As we saw in Chaper 2 the leaders were anti-socialist; John Wilson was described by Gregory as 'pugnacious and sharp tongued. . .a staunch liberal and a determined opponent of socialism'.[34] Wilson, the M.P. for most of our district, 'Once remarked that he would never vote for a working man who represented working-class interests alone', and, with a touch of unconscious humour added that he did not believe that 'a man should go to Parliament for that and put himself on a level with the landowner and aristocrat'.[35] The M.F.G.B. was the last big union to join the Labour Party but John Wilson and other miners' leaders refused to sign the Party's constitution and the officials remained 'steeped in Liberalism'.[36] (A similar situation, we might note in passing, was to be found in Derbyshire.[37])

By 1914 Wilson was standing as Lib.-Lab. candidate for mid-Durham, without union sponsorship. Arthur Henderson held the Barnard Castle seat for Labour, unsponsored. He had agreed to support the Lib.-Labs. in 1903.[38]

But Socialism and the Labour Movement were growing in the region from the 1890s onwards.

> By 1910 the Durham and Northumberland coalfields had become hotbeds of socialist activity. . .By 1895 there were a number of I.L.P. branches in existence in Durham and within a year or two they were beginning to plague the D.M.A. with resolutions calling for independent representation for Labour in Parliament and an eight hour day in the pits.[39]

Some of these I.L.P. groups were ephemeral. There were few in the Deerness Valley area but Taylor's diaries suggest that there might have been some local groups. The Quebec I.L.P. started by J.G. in 1913 was probably a renewal of a defunct group. The activities of John Holmes, and the local agitation of the D.M.R.A. may both be indications of earlier I.L.P. activity in the district.

By 1905 Socialists were being invited to speak at the miners' big meeting and Wilson was using his monthly circular to counterattack

ideas put across in this way. The I.L.P. *Annual Report* for 1906 notes
that 'the county of Durham especially is in the very van of the movement for Labour and Socialism'.[40] The year 1908–9 marked the break
of the Durham miners with the Liberals.

In the 1910s the Liberals had to start forming election committees
and building a Party machine as when 'officials went over to Labour the
Liberals suddenly found themselves without any electoral machinery at
all'.[41] This explains the formation of Liberal Associations in the Deerness Valley in 1910; it is a mark not of the strength of Liberalism but
its weakness. As the officers of the Liberal Association were overwhelmingly Methodist, we are forced to conclude that leading Methodists
rallied to the Liberal cause when large numbers of miners were moving
towards Labour.

The foundation dates of the local Labour Parties are not known, but
are thought to be soon after the First World War. In Waterhouses, of
the eight earliest founders remembered, four were certainly Methodists,
and one other may have been. Of the ten in Esh Winning, three were
certainly Methodists, two more may have been. None of these Methodists was a leading figure in Methodism, although one was a Wesleyan
Methodist local preacher. Gott, one of the founder members, was not
a Methodist, but as we saw above he had attended the Bible class. The
party started with meetings in members' houses, as had the chapels
sixty-five years before. They eventually acquired Labour halls, two
being ex-Methodist chapels.

The main organiser was Towers, a local schoolteacher, who was not
a Methodist. A Wesleyan Methodist local preacher was an important
activist, becoming a full-time Party organiser after he was 'sacrificed'
in 1926.

The influence of Methodism on the rise of the Labour Party was
mainly negative. Clough, the Wesleyan Methodist local preacher,
Labour Party secretary and election agent, said how he used biblical
texts in political speeches and that he advised speakers to exercise care
in addressing 'Methodistically inclined' audiences.[42] Will Lawther,
when a Labour candidate, according to Clough, was a heavy drinker;
knowing the area 'as Methodist and devotional, in my opinion as Secretary of the Party, something had to change'. According to Clough, Lawther gave up drinking during the campaign. Towers, the schoolmaster,
once made a very violent pro-Labour speech, saying that 'what we need
are sten-guns' to change society. Clough followed with a speech based
on the Sermon on the Mount in a deliberate attempt to win back
Methodists whom he felt would have been offended by the violence of
the first speech. Jones records that a Labour speaker in 1890 was told
'We want no Karl Marx and surplus values and that sort of stuff. Make

it plain and simple. Tha' can put in a long word now and then so as to make them think tha' knows a lot, but keep it simple and then when tha'rt coming t'finishing up, tha' mun put a bit of 'Come to Jesus' in. . .'[43]

In speaking for Turner Samuels, an early Labour candidate and a Jew, Clough pointed out that Christ was a thirty-year-old Jew and that He left His mark on the world. Again, he was making a deliberate appeal to Methodist sensitivities.

In Clough's opinion the major factor in the growth of Labour was the winning over of Liberals, especially lodge officials. This would seem to be an accurate judgement, supported by Gregory's work. Labour would have grown faster and been more influential if the Waterhouses officials had 'come across' sooner. One of the key officials to whom Clough referred was Matt White.

Instead the Labour Party won the rank and file of the D.M.A. to the Party and it was this which in Waterhouses brought Matt White into the Party. Rough handling by the police may have helped the process but Matt was faced with the possibility of losing his local positions if he did not 'take the Labour ticket'. The situation in Esh Winning is not quite so clear as the lodge leadership was weak and vacillating and no point of change from Liberal to Labour can be ascertained. With the defeat of Liberalism at the county level it was inevitable that such men as Aron Richardson should let their support go to Labour while perhaps resisting the claim of Socialism. It has not been possible to unravel developments in Quebec. The I.L.P. group 'finished when the Labour party came into the scene; voluntarily disbanded – it joined in the larger movement rather than keeping on as a single handed group'.[44]

Thus after the war the I.L.P. joined the Labour Party, as it was clearly going to be the working class's Party. The Party's appeal, as a mass appeal, did not need to be to the Quebec radicals, nor to early supporters and sympathisers like Adamson and Richardson but to the men at the valley bottom. The reforming, pro-working-class aspects of the Party made it possible that it would gain power. The Party readily gained support in the valley. Financial support came from the D.M.A. Formal membership on an individual basis was low. There were no street meetings. If the Quebec I.L.P. acted like a Labour sect, the Labour Party acted as the church. It was a merging of unequal forces. The Quebec Socialists and Adamson and Richardson, who joined the Labour Party, were the sort of men who traditionally man the activist wing of the Labour Party, without achieving positions of power or influencing policy.

We are not concerned with the history or sociology of the Labour

Party but these latter points raise two issues of some importance for any study of the Labour Movement.[45] Firstly, what was the effect on the Labour Movement of an influx of local Liberal leaders into the Party machine? The I.L.P. was a small band of devoted volunteers, committed to Socialism, study and debate, inviting distinguished speakers from all over the country to Quebec. They were replaced by a Party machne controlled by the Miners' Union and by 'converted' Liberals, a machine concerned with gaining and keeping power, not with political education and controversy.

Secondly, what was the effect of the Labour Movement seeking *mass* support among Methodists? Current Labour Party opinion in the valley is that all the Methodists vote Labour. This is probably true and the researcher hears many expressions of loyalty to the Party from the Methodists. Nonetheless, a number of Methodists say they would vote Liberal, if there was a candidate. A leading Methodist contested a local election in 1970 (the first election in thirty-years), he stood as an Independent and polled over 1,000 of the 3,000 votes in a contest with Labour. Furthermore Methodist support for Labour is not support for Socialism. Many express deep misgivings about the Welfare State: they allude generally to people who will not work, and to specific persons who live completely without working, and to the fact that they themselves surmounted the problems of economic hardship by their own efforts. Men and women steeped in a religion based on the notion of individual salvation, personal responsibility and self-help do not seem to accept even mildly collectivist ideas very readily.

The Labour Methodist has a real problem for he needs to reconcile two sorts of ideas: firstly, his religious ideas, rooted in 'faith' and the notion of individual salvation; secondly, political ideas based on rational conviction and grounded in the collective solidarity of working men. These ideas are not easily reconciled within Methodism. They are more easily reconciled in a more radical, millenarian tradition, as we have seen with the Quebec I.L.P. The Methodist can possibly compartmentalise his religious and political views under the relatively unexamined assumption that the two sets of ideas are mutually supportive. Some contemporary Methodists adopt this attitude, which is quite tenable in practice as there is no political discussion or activity in the district which raises any difficult question to test this stance.

An alternative is to integrate politics and religion. We have seen that there is no easy fit between Methodist ethical individualism and Labour collectivism. The best example of this attempt at reconciling politics and 'respectable' religion is Westgarth Adamson who was politically and theologically radical. He remained an active preacher and Party worker throughout his life and was a parish councillor. He is our limiting case of the possibility of a radical reconciliation, but he plainly found it an uneasy reconciliation.

Adamson, and men like him, rejected the evangelists who looked for heaven in the skies. This was 'as bad as going to the pub – escapism', according to his son.[46] But this points to a third possibility: that is to drop politics altogether and concentrate on religion. Tom Turnbull and others seemed to have arrived at a wholly pietistic non-political position, which exemplifies this possibility.

Finally, a religious person could drop, or stop thinking about religion (while maintaining some associational contacts perhaps). The three county aldermen from the district were all ex-chapel men, though one continued to attend anniversaries and special events. They became 'communal' rather than 'associational' adherents. They needed to be seen at the communities' important rituals (funerals, Remembrance Day, etc.) in order to be seen as part of the community. But they did not need to think too deeply about religion as such.

Institutionally, Methodism and the Labour Movement were segregated from the beginning. It is in the nature of a mass Party that it should be engaged in activities which Methodists will find objectionable. Firstly, the Party must have its base in a mass following; and the masses in the twentieth century are to be found in the club, not the chapel. Secondly, it must raise funds. Thirdly, it must provide a social life for its members. The second and third functions can both be performed through the activities traditional to mining communities, drinking and gambling. Fourthly, the party claims a universal base for membership which transcends religious divisions. The Party also provides its own pastoral service through councillors and the M.P.s' 'surgeries'. Many immediate problems can be solved by Party officials; housing, social services and questions about education are all within the scope of the local councillor.

Thus the political party takes on a life of its own. Today the Labour Party is very small (perhaps eight paid-up individual members) with an active women's section. Bingo and raffles are both social events and means of raising funds, dances and collections are another means of raising funds for the old people. Old people's outings and treats seem to be the main focus of Labour Party activity. We might note in passing that these activities are very much an extension of the solidarities of the *old* mining community; the Party does not, for example, organise a youth club or any youth activities. Only the one local election mentioned above has been fought in thirty years.

Drinking and gambling are major deterrents to Methodist participation in the life of the Party. The Party is largely a social club and the Methodists have their own social life. However, one fund-raising

187

activity which the Labour Party copied from the chapels was the provision of a beer-tent at the miners' gala (although the Methodists provided tea.) Methodists could be party officials and one of the local M.P.s is a Methodist local preacher, but they are served by the Party, they are not active participants in its daily life. In fact no active Methodist is active in local Labour politics.

What we are describing is the differentiation of political and religious institutions. Each institution now has a separate life of its own; both have social and pastoral functions. Both pursue goals, but on the basis of different belief systems. The process of differentiation began with the rise of Socialism and accelerated with the development of a mass Labour Party. The Labour Party is now theoretically free to organise the people of the valley on a class basis, if it wishes. The chapels meanwhile are free to get on with the task of converting the valley to Christianity untroubled by problems arising from the political responsibilities of its leaders.

We remarked earlier that the chapels were virtually indistinguishable from organised Liberalism. This is only partially true in so far as the union lodge was the key organisation for choosing a parliamentary candidate and bringing out the Liberal vote. It was the overlapping of lodge and chapel leadership which reinforced the position of the Liberals. We have also noted that with the capturing of the union lodges by the Labour Party a Liberal Party machine has to be established.

The Labour Party never seems to have had a large number of individual members. The union lodge was the Party administration, the officers of the lodge were often the officers of the Party also. The radicals thus entirely lacked an institutional base on which to build political power in the Valley. Most miners were members or regarded themselves as members because of the union's affiliation to the Party. Nonetheless with the decline of mining there was a separation of political and trade-union functions of a kind which could be seen in the Labour Movement nationally from much earlier.[47]

Thus we see the Labour Party as a political extension of trade-union activities, and it is not unreasonable to assume that the political consciousness of Labour supporters was an extension of trade-union consciousness. This does not necessarily represent a marked difference from the days of Liberal domination; under both Liberal and Labour leadership trade union and political activities were bargaining activities conducted according to the rules of the market.

The Party pursues this-worldly goals in a realistic manner and it develops a machinery for achieving them. Religious goals can be pursued as a matter of choice, in other institutions. Political radicalism

(Socialism, for example) does not engage with the patrimonial structure of the party; like religion it becomes an alternative to Party politics or an additional interest.

The Liberal Party did not want to be a party of working-class members – it only wanted working-class votes. Therefore the problem of a mass organisation did not arise for the Methodist Liberals because chapel leaders could act as 'brokers' for the Liberal Party. The Methodist leaders willingly played the twin roles of religious and political leaders and in doing this they adopted a position without inconsistencies and arousing no individual conflicts at the level of belief. What we are saying therefore is that empirically, in the historical situation we have described, the only fully consistent positions were those of the traditional Methodist Liberals. Liberalism and respectability 'fit' together. They are congruent with the social expectations we have described as typically existing between owners and the men's leaders in the late nineteenth century. This political outlook based on mutual trust (and a belief in the efficacy of the market) became decreasingly credible in the face of the owners' demands in the twentieth century, as we will see in the next chapter. The rise of a mass Party entailed the ambiguities and personal conflicts described. New leaders emerged from wholly independent working-class organisations. Methodists had to choose the extent of their political involvement. The direct influence of Methodism in politics declined and after the First World War declined further insofar as Methodism was identified with Liberalism.

Nonetheless, any Party seeking mass support in a Liberal stronghold such as the Deerness Valley would have to win over men who still largely believed in arbitration rather than power politics, and others who thought that both private property and the market were good, and the means to general prosperity. Some compromise with Liberalism was necessary. (Such a compromise would have been unacceptable to the Quebec I.L.P. if they alone had made the choice.) The mass movement would also have to be 'respectable' in terms of the social status of its leaders, their acceptability to those in authority and the reasonableness of their policies. After 1918 the Labour Party had sufficiently met these requirements to be able to win a majority of the votes in the valley. It is significant nevertheless that it mattered to Labour men that Matt White 'took the ticket'. As a Liberal he might have split the vote. As a Labour man he enhanced Labour's chance of winning and increasing their respectability. Even if as a Liberal he was sure of crushing defeat, he was still worth winning over to Labour's side.

The Labour Movement had to exist in a culture influenced by Methodist social thought. (In Derbyshire too the Labour Party had to modify its attitudes, 'in the face of a large accession of Lib.–Lab. M.P.s and their supporters'.)[48] It is our contention that the cultural influence and the leadership of the Labour Movement have been more Liberal than Socialist due to their Methodist origin. About a third of the men in the population, or their families, were directly involved with Methodism. Men may have resisted Methodist teaching on drink, they may have believed the Methodist leaders to be politically 'soft'. The men who came into the Labour Party were, nonetheless, men who had been to Sunday school and who believed that labour and capital could work for the common good, even if government intervention was necessary to curb the power of capital. After 1926 they were convinced of the power of the market and the impossibility of a Socialist response to it. The prevalent compromised and non-Socialist attitude was epitomised by the present Labour Party agent, who attended the Sunday school and chapel in his youth, when he said, 'I'm an Englishman first and Labour Party second, because I believe in the royal family'. His religious observances are now confined to the annual Remembrance Service and the miners' service on gala day.[49] But these are speculative propositions supported only by the common-sense observation of the peculiarly Liberal, non-Socialist nature of the Labour Party in County Durham, and by the observation of David Martin and Henry Pelling on the 'striking continuity' between the Labour Party and nineteenth-century liberalism.[50]

8 Methodists in action:
three political case studies

So far we have examined the social characteristics of three groups of the community, the coal-owners, the old Liberal union leadership, and a younger group of radicals. We have also described the background to the situation in which they found themselves. This chapter is a discussion of three series of events, in which Methodists found themselves faced by situations in which they were required to translate their principles into pragmatic terms. The Deerness Valley Methodists were not much involved in day-to-day matters of national politics, but they were directly involved in three issues – or groups of issues. Firstly, the question of the activity of the state and religious liberty; secondly, war and the freedom of the individual conscience; and, thirdly, industrial and class conflict.

We have shown that Methodism is a form of inner-worldly asceticism. So now we discuss the relations of inner-worldly asceticism to the action of the Methodists by giving an account of their response to three situations: the 1902 Education Act and the 1904 Licensing Bill; the First World War – specifically the issue of conscientious objection; and the events of 1926.

1902 TO 1905: THE EDUCATION ACT AND THE LICENSING BILL

The period 1902–5 was one of unprecedented political agitation among Methodists. Two issues dominated the period: temperance and the Education Act of 1902.

The Conservative Government introduced a Licensing Bill in 1902 which tightened the laws against drunkenness. Attempts to reform the licensing laws had been made since 1871; the 1893 attempt had, according to Longmate, helped bring down the Liberal Government.[1] The central issue in 1902–4 was whether publicans, who through no fault of their own lost their licences as the laws were tightened, should be compensated from public funds. In 1904 a Bill was introduced by Balfour which acknowledged the renewal of licences as a right and which made provision for compensation for non-renewal. 'It was the hang-man's whip of the publicans' vote that brought them [the Tories] to the brewers' heel.'[2]

The 1902 legislation was welcomed in Durham where the *D.C.* noted 'cases of persistent drunkenness are very numerous'.[3] The *D.C.* was Liberal and maintained a high level of reporting of temperance activities. A Deerness Valley Temperance and Prohibition Association was active in the valley in the period and it held rallies at which promi-nent speakers like John Wilson were engaged.[4] The Good Templars and Bands of Hope also maintained a high level of activity.[5] In 1903 the Methodists were among those opposing a licence for a new public house in Esh Winning.[6] Pressure seems to have been so effective that at the end of 1903 the Working Men's Clubs conference at Waterhouses discussed, amongst other things, whether they should run candidates for parish and county councils.[7] Understandably, the 1904 Bill was not welcomed by the Methodists.

On 30 May 1902, a public meeting was held to protest at the new Education Act. In July the Waterhouses and District Free Church Council met in Hamsteels to protest. Joseph Harrison was on the plat-form and James Fitzpatrick took the chair in the absence of the Revd R. W. Huddlestone. Various resolutions were passed calling for the complete withdrawal of the Bill.[8]

There seems to have been little action until the levying of the rates began (just as in the mid-1960s there was little discussion of the issue until the Anglican Union vote was actually due). Their disapproval of drink seems to have been overcome temporarily when a meeting was held in the Stag's Head; the meeting was chaired by the W.M. station master and was addressed by the W.M. minister. Objections were raised against the Education Act on the grounds that religious tests might be held for entering training colleges. It was also said that Non-conformists would be barred from many posts unless they were pre-pared to be religious hypocrites. Rate-payers were to be taxed without representation, it was said, for it was not democratic to have four out of six school managers appointed in accordance with schools' 'Trusts'.[9] A similar meeting in the following week included an attack on the Church of England as intolerant, against reform and advocating dear bread during the Corn Law Debates.[10] Anti-Anglican rhetoric reached heights of hyperbole '. . .in catechisms taught in Church schools a ques-tion is asked: "What is sin?" and the answer given is "Attending a Dissenting chapel".'[11]

In August a Citizens' League was formed to oppose the Act; the president, vice-president and secretary were all Methodists (W.M., M.N.C. and P.M. respectively). The league issued a manifesto and the

P.M. minister (Mr Huddlestone) spoke saying that he 'could not voluntarily pay for the dissemination of that which was the direct opposite to what he believed'. (Not elaborated in the press report.) He went on to defend passive resistance to the Act: 'passive resistance to encroachments on conscience was a religious duty, and they would resist these unjust claims upon them in as lawful, constitutional and Christian manner as they possibly could'. It was a Bill 'to strengthen and uphold the bulwarks for the Church of England and to obliterate non-conformity'. Browell, the under manager of Cornsay and a New Connexion Methodist, moved a resolution for passive resistance to paying rates. Aron Richardson seconded this resolution.[12] In October the league organised a meeting at which various M.P.s and county councillors failed to appear to argue their position on the Act. Local councillors did appear. At the end of the meeting D. Cheek seconded the motion 'that we agree to carry out the objects of the League'.[13] In June 1904 Ralph Hayson wrote to the *D.C.* from Quebec, 'I am deeply surprised at the inactivity, the want of agitation, and the want of public meetings in the district of Waterhouses, Esh Winning and Quebec, in relation to the Education Act and the Government's Licensing Bill. . .'[14] Three weeks later the league met again and the last note of the year's campaign came in October with the auctioning of Huddlestone's watch which had been seized in lieu of a rates payment.[15] He alone of the rate-payers (miners were not rate-payers) carried out 'the objective of the League'. The last sign of the campaign was a letter saying that passive resisters were not given a fair hearing at Lanchester Police Court.[16]

We have no means of telling how far the rank and file Methodists were involved in the league, although Methodist leaders were obviously among the leaders of the league. Chapel activities went on much as usual, camp meetings, evangelism, chapel renovations.[17] Some informants, mature men at the time, do not remember anything of the league and its purpose at all.

The turn of 1904–5 was marked by a bitter and public dissension among the P.M.s. The conflict was mainly conducted through the readers' letters columns of the *D.C.* A group of P.M.s had proposed to start a temperance hall in Esh Winning. Huddlestone publicly criticised this. He said there was no guarantee that the hall would not be used for dancing or theatrical companies. He pointed out the danger of trying to rival the Working Men's Clubs and said that the gospel alone was reducing the evils of drink. From this point the dispute developed into a fury of vituperation, personal abuse, accusations of lack of charity, malicious misrepresentation, resignations and disclaimers.[18] The *D.C.*, sensing the entertainment value of these letters, allowed them to run on for nearly ten weeks – with occasional promises of 'more next week', etc.

Among these letters are two which epitomise Methodist ethical and political thinking respectively. Both are written by Huddlestone:

> I stated that amusements which impaired the mental powers, blunted the moral sensibilities, and injured bodily health came under condemnation. Amusements that swallow up the hours sacred to sleep are to be censured.
>
> The midnight dance comes under condemnation...Amusements that arouse and stimulate the lower passions are always to be shunned...The family relation as the ordinances of God lies at the foundation of all human society. Prof. Fairbairn says: 'We must get back to the old staid simplicity of the home. Increased domesticity means the increase of all finer affections'. To help people to value the beauty of the home, to perceive its possibilities of happiness, and to achieve both its discipline and its truest pleasure is of immensely more importance to me than seeking to subordinate God's idea of the family to the social club.[19]

> (Quoting Westcott, Bishop of Durham and a temperance advocate) 'The supremacy of Christianity as the only true remedy goes to the core of all social evils, no less than to all doctrines of God and the single soul.' It approaches the reformation of society through the reformation of the individual.[20]

One striking aspect of this series of events is that the Methodists were so individually committed to a position on the temperance issue that they could let differences of opinion become public disputes. In this way they severely reduced their effectiveness in campaigning against the 1904 Act.

The 1906 Liberal Government was eventually to remove the offending parts of the Acts. The traditional Methodist moderation seems to have gone to the wind in the national response to the Liberal victory:

> After the elections were fairly on the way, and since they have closed, many of my correspondents have jubilantly referred to them. 'Hallelujah', says one, 'Righteousness once more on the throne. Rascals on the gibbet.' 'What a splendid General Election!' exclaims another. 'Prayer and work have done great things for the party of progress'; and so they go on. It is a time to be merry. After the wilderness the Promised Land. And we have entered Canaan at last, in such a goodly majestic fashion; The Amorites, the Jebusites and all the allied forces of Reaction have been scattered and slain. Few of the enemy have escaped the edge of the sword, the wrath of the people. We will rejoice and be glad.[21]

It should be noted that political conflict is described in terms of rascals and the forces of righteousness – not an analysis of the structure of social and economic relations. Furthermore the Methodists, in the moment of triumph, reasserted their belief in the need for social harmony. This harmony should be maintained, if necessary, by the government restraining the rich in the use of their riches:

> The new government and the new Parliament have before them enormous arrears of social reform to make up. . .Nothing worse could happen to our country than the outbreak of class wars between the 'have nots' and the 'haves'. Such wars can only be prevented by the government and Parliament seeing to it that the 'haves' shall not use the power of their millions to grind down the 'have nots' to starvation level. . .and by seeing to it that the 'have nots' who are honest, thrifty and willing to work should have the chance to earn enough. . .[22]

Our data on this period are sparse but three points emerge: whatever the rank and file of Methodism may have thought and done (and from Ralph Hayson's comments, and others, they seem to have done very little), the Methodist leaders became directly and publicly involved in agitation over political issues. Furthermore they stated the duty of the Christian to be to resist oppressive laws; Methodist social principles were reasserted namely, that social reform came through individual reform (with the family as the basis of society) even in discussing temperance, where much pressure was exerted for legislative action, and religious liberty and temperance were both of direct interest to the chapels – they were not 'political' issues in the sense of being wholly worldly.

The Methodists and the Non-conformist coal-owners were united in their opposition to the brewers and to the 1902 Education Act. There was unanimity of ideological interest among the Methodists and neither of the issues touched upon the material interests of the average village Methodist. In respect of the Education Act the Methodists believed they were fighting for survival. They saw it as a Christian duty to resist the state when the state so encroached upon religious liberty. They therefore took action through legitimate channels to bring pressure on the government. In fact they helped change the government. The Non-conformist response to the Act nationally seems to have been a major factor in the defeat of the Conservative Government;

> Non-conformists in every part of the country came forward as Liberal candidates, some confessedly induced to so do by their blazing indignation against the Education Act, but these candidates soon showed themselves to be ardent all-round reformers. . .
> The Free Churches had not been dozing but drilling, and they were now an army fit and eager for the fray. . .[23]

The principle of direct action against the state seems also to have been accepted when the survival of the Methodists was at stake. The main form of action was refusal to pay rates, but this was a form of action open to property-owners only, so we cannot know how popular such action would have been.

On the question of licensing the Methodists believed a great moral issue to be at stake. The brewers, in league with the ruling party (the authors of the Education Act), were using the authority of the state for immoral purposes. The Methodists thus felt themselves to be in opposition to a conspiracy against the public welfare, a conspiracy which would also undo years of work by the Methodists.

Again, political action was confined to legitimate political processes. The re-election of the local Liberal M.P. was a foregone conclusion. The only direct action, therefore, could have been either symbolic protests, or meetings and rallies organised in support of the Liberal candidate. The Methodists were already active in the Liberal Party; the symbolic protests came in passing resolutions on temperance and asking individual members to renew their efforts to extend the membership of local temperance organisations.

There was no need, in either case, to organise direct action (civil disobedience, etc.) until such times as the legitimate means of influencing the state had been tried. There were realistic hopes that the return of the Liberal Party would settle both issues to the satisfaction of the Methodists. This was the case, although there was a long delay in fully reforming the Education Act.

The Methodist attitude to the state is made very clear by these events. The state may and should intervene to protect people from their moral defects, and from the activities of the 'corrupt monopoly'. But when the state actually threatens the religious group it may be resisted, although resistance should take a legitimate form in the first instance.

It should be noted that the Methodists do not imply very wide functions for the state. For example although they advocate prohibition, which would strike at a major capitalist interest, they do not advocate any alteration of the existing property relations. The positive role of the state is confined entirely to the ethical sphere. The Methodists were only concerned with such issues, not politics or economics as such.

THE FIRST WORLD WAR

The Methodist attitude to the war was decided at a national level; it was one of support of a war in a righteous cause.[24] Respondents differ in their manner of reporting local attitudes; one, not a radical, said,

196

'The public were gulled, people swept up in the idea of the rightness of the war – God's war. The lead to war came from the tops of the churches.'[25] Another put it differently, 'Everyone had to do their bit.'[26]

What response might we have expected from the Liberal Methodists? Martin has argued that

> Liberalism is rooted in two major assumptions. The first is that truth and goodness only require correct exposition in order to be accepted. Thus the primary initiative is assigned to ideas and the central problem located in knowledge and education. The second assumption is that the interests of individuals, classes and nations are fundamentally complementary.[27]

Faced with the reality of a war the Liberal found himself in a dilemma which the advocacy of reason and free trade could not solve. One way in which the Liberal Methodists could reconcile themselves to the war was 'by misrepresenting it as a crusade for international righteousness'. More succinctly, given that 'Liberal idealism either crusades for peace or treats war as a crusade'[28] the Liberal had to make the bold shift from the advocacy of peace to advocacy of war – no doubt with all the defensive zeal of the convert. Nationally the war was represented as a crusade by Methodism, and by Non-conformity in general. The certainty of the crusade was perhaps a little clearer at the beginning of the war than at the end.

Local enthusiasm for the war as the 'war mania' spread may be gauged by the high rate of voluntary enlistment. A fifth of all miners volunteered for service at the beginning of the war.[29] 'Some went off thinking, life would be better in the Army, but soon wished they were back down the pit.'[30] There was a high rate of employment in the mines and employers could claim an exemption from military service for their men. Men who had 'signed on' but were not called up could wear special armlets to indicate this. Thus the mustering to the colours of Durham men was enforced neither by law nor economic circumstances. In 1915 the Waterhouses P.M. picnic was addressed by Galbraith and other speakers. Aneurin Williams, M.P., said to the gathering that, 'Every citizen should make it a bond of honour to contribute to the War loan...We should not win if we shirked our part. We should win when every Englishman and Englishwoman realised the absolute necessity for sacrifice. If there was no money, there would be no munitions, and greater sacrifice of life would follow.'[31] Other Methodists were actually on recruiting committees; three out of the five members of the Brandon and Byshottles committee were Methodists, including John Henery and Joseph Stephenson.

In accounting for the exclusion of the Quebec radicals from the use of the chapel a respondent commented, 'some of the older men didn't agree with the group, quite a few of whom were opposed to the war. Older members favoured the war – they thought it was righteous'.[32]

The opposition to the war was, at the time, almost solely confined to the Quebec radicals and their associates. One colleague of the Quebec radicals, who was himself imprisoned, said 'all the Independent Labour Party members were anti-war; John George Harrison probably died from his ill-treatment in prison. . .Lakin, Pritchard, MacDonalds also; Pritchard's brother, J. Pritchard, went to prison as a C.O.'[33] Cairns and J. G. Winter were also among the conscientious objectors.

J. G. Harrison is the only member of the Quebec radicals to leave a written testimony of his pacifism. From the sources already cited it is clear that his grounds would be largely religious. Given the nature of the Quebec group we can assume that some of the others were conscientious objectors on at least a mixture of political and religious grounds. Purely political objections (insofar as motivation can be 'purely' anything in such a situation) seem unlikely because the radicals were all closely associated with Primitive Methodism. They were also, as we have seen, influenced by J.G. J.G. has left copious notes and essays on George Fox, and pacifism; at his tribunal he attributes his pacifism to Tolstoy. In an undated sermon of about 1916, he attacks militarism and jingoism; the enemy, he says, is within – injustice, oppression and fear. He stresses that the messages of the Old Testament prophets were not jingoistic, but directed against rulers and established religion. He quotes Tolstoy and Edward Carpenter; 'the road to peace and the road to righteousness is still the same',[34] he says.

Pacifism was preached from the pulpit and this was a source of further criticism of the radicals.[35] The radicals in turn accused the established Methodists of turning the pulpits into recruiting platforms. J.G. said that being in prison '. . .is better than the pits, it is better than listening to friend Rust or for that matter William Harrison, uttering blasphemies to young children. . .'[36] Rust summarily dismissed J.G. from his teaching job because of his pacifist views, but as a matter of religious principle J.G. refused to take the matter to court. Respondents have suggested, however, that there were few overt attempts to preach war from the pulpits and such attempts were censured and stopped. One attempt to preach war was perhaps regarded as legitimate: in 1916 a memorial service was held at the Baptist chapel, for some local men killed in action, and this sermon dealt with the righteousness of the war, and how men were following the Master's teaching by fighting.[37] The president of the P.M. Conference, speaking in Durham, said that he believed men must fight but he admired men who were prepared to suffer and die for conscience's sake. He thought some tribunals bullied applicants for exemption.

J.G.'s tribunal and appeal dramatically exemplified the dilemma for Methodism. There was a Methodist with unorthodox views, a Socialist, appearing before a tribunal meeting at Lanchester consisting of three members of the Methodist establishment: a national miners' leader, a local shopkeeper and a colliery manager – John Wilson, James Hammel and Michael Curry respectively. J.G. said, 'I can not take the military oath, or surrender my right to judge whether any action would be inconsistent with my desire to serve God. I can best serve my country in its desire for a just and lasting peace by holding out the hand of fellowship to comrade Liebknecht and his friends.' Major Wilkinson commented that:

> the applicant's observations were most disloyal. The claimant denied this, and in answer to questions stated that he applied to be placed on the P.M. preachers' plan, but on account of the Church's attitude to this war as being contrary to Christian teaching, he reluctantly withdrew from the Connexion. . .his opinion had changed since reading Tolstoy, Ralph Waldo Emerson and others. . .Whatever the decision of that tribunal he should adhere to his convictions.
>
> The Chairman said he was sorry the applicant was still acting as a teacher. A member [identified as Hammel. RSM]: 'He is not a suitable person to have charge of children.'[38]

At Durham County Appeals J.G. 'applied for exemption on the ground of conscientious objection, which he said were brought about by reading of Tolstoy. Judge Greenwell: It is a pity you read him. . .Applicant. . .was of the opinion that the nation which took up the principles of Jesus Christ need never be in fear of invasion.'[39]

J.G. was in prison three times, J. G. Winter was imprisoned once (and died almost immediately on admission); the other objector to whom he was handcuffed alleged that he died as a result of being beaten. Jack Pritchard and others whom it has not been possible to identify were also imprisoned. Ironically, J.G.'s physical condition was such that he would almost certainly have been rejected for military service.

The response to conscientious objection at the time was unequivocally hostile. This hostility seems to have moderated itself subsequently for informants made comments varying between, 'The average Methodist was not altogether sympathetic, they felt objectors were letting down the nation. It was a feeling of disappointment rather than animosity',[40] to 'There was a lot of unnecessary punishment of C.O.'s, they believed in peace and they were right (though I disagreed with them then). They were not peace at any price men, but the crowd thought they were dodgers.'[41]

Punitive hostility seems to have prevailed at the time. The miners of East Hetton, Hebburn and Edmondsley called upon the D.M.A. to expel conscientious objectors, for all officials who sympathised to be thrown out, and asked miners not to work with conscientious objectors. The Harrisons had their windows smashed by stones thrown by villagers. J. G. Winter's body was brought back from London for burial in Quebec; only the I.L.P. members attended the funeral. (Village funerals were normally massive demonstrations of solidarity with the deceased and their family – see Chapter 9.) People booed the cortège and stones were thrown at the coffin. Winter was lowered into his grave to the accompaniment of catcalls from a crowd at the cemetery gate and the repeated singing of 'The Red Flag' by his comrades. One of the Quebec radicals understated the case when he said, 'The C.O.'s had a very rough time.'[42]

The war had a disruptive effect on the villages: 125 officials and men in Pease and Partners' employment at Waterhouses joined the army, of whom 22 were killed; at Esh Winning 220 joined and 17 were killed; of the 35 members of Waterhouses P.M.s who went to fight, only one returned to full chapel activities after the war. A plaque in the chapel lists those who served in the war. The issue of conscientious objection and military service further disrupted the community. Men like Hammel were on tribunals, hearing the cases of local men.[43] Thus, for example, John Henery on Brandon Tribunal heard the cases of two Waterhouses and one Esh Winning Methodist early in 1916; the applications were made on non-conscientious grounds and were refused. One such refusal by Henery led to the conscription of a Methodist's son; the son was killed and his father never again attended chapel.[44] We see in this an indication of the possibility of serious and open division even amongst the more traditional Methodists. The conflict between J.G., his friends and relatives and the majority on the other hand was already apparent from before the war, but was heightened by the issues raised by the war. J.G. has, in fact, been partially held responsible for the loss of numbers at Quebec: 'He was a C.O. and a member of the Independent Labour Party. Ruined our chapel; created a lot of disturbances.'[45]

If one consequence of the war and the response to it was dissension and loss of numbers for Methodists, another was the loss of credibility for the Socialists. We have already commented on the breaking up of I.L.P. meetings in the county.[46] Connie Ellis also reported the use of physical violence against anyone speaking for peace – or even a negotiated settlement to the war (such speakers were accused of receiving German gold to save the Kaiser). The peace movement was associated in people's minds with the Socialists, and the I.L.P. members had in fact been predominantly against the war.

'The Wesleyans were anti-socialist right through. Clough and others were not wanted...the anti-socialists always held conscientious objection against these "bolsheviks" too.'[47] 'In building up support for the Labour party the I.L.P. was not much success because of the stigma of objection.'[48] These are two very explicit statements of the fact and there seems also to be general agreement among respondents that this was the case, though the point is more often made obliquely.

The First World War raised the issue not of the survival of Methodism but of individual freedom of conscience. The inner-worldly ascetic may conditionally accept the use of war for just ends. Nonetheless, if the Non-conformist tradition is assumed to be a tradition which defends the rights of individual conscience, why did the Methodists not give support to men who, as a matter of Christian conviction, refused to fight? Martin suggests that: 'the denomination will take note of a divergence and actively acknowledge the right of different members to come to varying conclusions, even though as a body it lends support to the war'.[49] But this does not seem to have been the case in our villages. Why was this? Four reasons may be adduced.

Firstly, the Methodists believed the war to be a just war. Secondly, the attempt to avoid military service caused personal dissension within the village and within Methodism. Two extra points made this worse. There were always some men who sought exemption for reasons other than conscience, treated as shirkers or cowards, and this hostility easily extended to anyone who sought to avoid military service, for whatever reason. And also the Derby scheme involved an invidious system of exemptions and a form of 'creeping conscription'. This was probably intended to create resentments which would make avoidance of military service socially unpleasant. Many Methodists had gone to the war, many families had men away from home fighting. By the time of the tribunal hearings many had lost husband, father and relatives, especially in the bloody battles of 1915. For all those with men serving or dead, the simple question was why should a few avoid their share of fighting the war? Underlying this question also was moral resentment, that a small group of religious men should claim a higher morality and thus implicitly pass judgement on the others.

A third factor also arose from the Derby scheme. At least two of the leading village Methodists were on tribunals, and some of the social conflicts arising from tribunal decisons have already been indicated. The Methodists on the tribunals were representing the state's interest on the right to exemption, and they did not question the right of the state to demand military service; the presence of these Methodists on the tribunals represented a compromise between Methodism and the state. But cases were brought before them by other Methodists in the name of Christianity, who did dispute the right of the state to require them to kill.

Fourthly, within Methodism the dissidents were the followers of R. J. Campbell, and his New Theology. They were also identified with Keir Hardie and Socialism. They thus forfeited all sympathetic consideration by virtue of this association.

Martin's contention that the denomination acknowledges the rights of conscientious objectors does not seem to apply at the local level. The divergence of local expressions of Methodism has become increasingly apparent; it seems to be further verified by the response to conscientious objection. Martin's proposition is not therefore applicable to the kind of community context that we are describing.

Thus the Methodists while officially not completely denying the freedom of conscience of objectors to the war were not committed supporters of that freedom. Despite the rationale of their arguments, the objectors were known as 'trouble-makers' and 'hotheads' and their actions threatened the solidarity of chapel and community. The simplest way to avoid conflict and maintain good relations within the community was to ignore the voice of the minority, for at the local level social harmony was evidently more important than conscience.[50]

THE EVENTS OF 1926

The events of 1902–5 do not appear to have deeply disturbed the relative stability of either Methodism or village society. The First World War period involved the whole population in a collective effort, in shared sorrows and hardships. Families were broken by war and death, but many men came back. Some of the local solidarities were broken by the attitudes taken by the chapels and the conscientious objectors or by the role of Methodist leaders on tribunals. Compared with both these periods, 1926 was a catastrophic year for the valley. There was violent and open conflict on the streets, political passions were aroused and in the conflicts the old paternal order and its concomitant attitudes were finally destroyed; there were large-scale emigrations from the area, and many of the families departing were never to return. The 1920s seem to be the most important social reality for today's Methodists. For many who were then in the prime of their lives, it was a period of almost hopeless unemployment, or under-employment at low wages, or the humiliation of the dole. In a society which values work highly, and with a religion which advocates the full use of human talents, it is not surprising that those experiences should be so memorable to the Methodists.

It is not our purpose to give a full history of the miners' strike in the valley, but only to explain the Methodists' response to the strike and the consequences of their action.

In 1926 the coal-owners were determined to reduce the cost of coal production.[51] In April a meeting was held at Quebec drill hall; Colonel Headlam, Hereward Sadler and Mr and Mrs Hanbury were on the platform, Headlam and Hanbury being Tory M.P.s. The purpose of the meeting was, apparently, to provide an opportunity for Mrs Hanbury to tell horror stories from her visit to Russia. A miner asked Colonel Headlam what he was going to do for the unemployed in the district. Headlam replied that more benefits to the unemployed meant a great tax on labour; the subsidy on coal must go and many pits would close. Nevertheless, said Headlam, he would also try to do what he could and he was investigating particular cases of hardship.[52] Thus were the owners' objectives restated in Quebec; the miners must bear the cost of cheapening the production of coal. Four weeks later the General Strike began. Our main concern is with the much longer miners' lockout which was to last until the first week of December.

The owners' tactics were clear: they had the support of the government, and locally the police acting under the emergency regulations. In County Durham they also had the support at the ideological level of the Established Church. To break the miners' resistance they could encourage men to work, promising favours, promotion, and security in the future; employ officials to produce coal; wait until the men were forced back to work by economic necessity. (The Co-ops. were vital for the union's success. They granted unlimited credit during strikes, which was then paid off by withholding dividend money. The Co-op. was, in effect, the strikers' larder.) To reinforce these three tactics they also needed to reduce the effectiveness of the unions; this could be done by removing the leaders or using legal sanctions against, for example, picketing.

The dispute was not to be won or lost in the valley, but in London. Nonetheless, the union leaders negotiating with the owners and the government needed the backing that could only be provided by a show of resolution, strength and solidarity in the villages.

The men's tactics were therefore to maintain union solidarity and keep the pits idle; to do this they needed to picket the pits and persuade potential workers to stay away from work. In pursuing these policies the miners were peculiarly vulnerable: a picket could be defined as a riotous assembly under the emergency regulations, and the courts were monopolised by owners and managers who would not be sympathetic. But attempts to persuade men not to work could be interpreted as intimidation, and were so interpreted by the bishop of Durham, who in sermons and addresses kept up a continuous verbal attack on the unions.[53] In both picketing and persuading, the leaders of the unions were especially at risk; they could be singled out to face the charges and bear the sentences for riotous assembly and intimidation, and the men would then be deprived of their more experienced leaders.

After the First World War Pease and Partners had employed an official for personnel and welfare duties in the valley. His main task during the strike was to persuade men to return to work. Pease and Partners assured men working that they would receive favourable consideration after the strike.[54] The vicar of Waterhouses asked his congregation to give every assistance to men who were working.[55]

Pease and Partners seem to have been relatively unaggressive in Waterhouses, their main anti-union effort being at Esh Winning where they thought the leadership was weak. Few police were billeted in Waterhouses, and the village remained quiet throughout the strike. The men stood firm under the Liberal and unmilitant leadership of Matt White, and there were only a few blacklegs.

Some fifty policemen meanwhile were billeted in Esh Winning, which became the cockpit of the valley during the strike. Some men worked throughout the strike, but they were escorted to work by the police, and occasionally preceded by the colliery band playing ribald tunes. The villagers lined the streets cat-calling, and meetings were held at the pit as the shift came up at 11.00 a.m. Occasion arose from these activities to prosecute the leaders. Clough, with S. Garr and nineteen others, was charged under Emergency Regulation 21[56] with 'an act likely to cause civil disaffection amongst the civilian population at Esh Winning'. Clough maintains that he prevented men from attacking blacklegs, and that the inspector of police gave evidence to the effect that but for Clough's action there would have been bloodshed in the village. The nineteen received £2 fines, while Clough and the lodge secretary, and Garr the chairman each received a sentence of one month's hard labour. The bench included Basil Saddler (of Saddler Bros., who owned Quebec) as chairman, Curry the manager at Cornsay, and three others, one of whom may have been a colliery manager.[57]

In general the union leadership at Esh Winning seems to have been weak. They were not fully in favour of picketing or bringing sanctions against the blacklegs. Thus up to 150 men worked during the strike. The manager left a rough notebook covering the last part of the strike, listing the workers and the days they worked. The total varies from 58 on 23 October to 72 on 20 November, while in September there were only 250 blacklegs in the whole of County Durham. Between 26 and 27 October the work force was cut from 41 to 10, firm evidence of the success of the activities for which Clough was really imprisoned. Many more worked at the end of the strike: from 17 November at Esh Winning the numbers rose to 70 as men realised they were beaten and would have to return to work at a substantial reduction.[58]

Eighteen of the men working were deputies and not therefore blacklegs in any strict sense of the word. It is clear that men worked by families, as the same surnames appear twice or more often in the lists. This tends to confirm the suggestion that some men worked because they were under pressure from their family and would have been thrown out of their home if they had not worked. Blacklegs seem to have been connected by marriage or patronage – or both – to the managements in many cases. Others seem to have been genuinely lumpen-proletarian, including the rate-busters mentioned in Chapter 3. Of others it was said that 'petticoat government' drove them to work earlier. One Methodist mother with a son at grammar school put sufficient pressure on her husband for him to work (at Waterhouses). Comments tend to be abusive, but informative nonetheless (most informants tried to change the subject when blacklegging was discussed):

They were nearly all members of the N.-P.U. [see p. 208]. P.L. had been a groom at a big house and was recommended to Pease and Partners. He became bosses' groom and odd job man, always looking for a job to ingratiate himself with management, 'Shall I sweep your yard, sir'...The S's, ale-drinkers from Staffordshire, Tories and bosses men. Related by marriage to the H's who all had official positions after the lock-out. Showed weakness to doff their caps to the bosses. Wives no better...B's related to S's, became N.-P.U. E (a Methodist) became Secretary of N.-P.U. A.P. related to management...G.W. driven out of his home to work by his wife wielding a carving knife. She was an official's daughter...T.F. (hewer) became a deputy. G.C. – son of an under-manager, a Wesleyan...J.H. had to drink with the bosses to keep his job. A. and C.G. part-officials...A.C., assistant master's weighman...E.D. a W.M. Society Steward, Assistant Secretary of the N.-P.U.[59]

The whole of this discussion excludes consideration of the last few days of the dispute when union resistance was obviously collapsing nationally and men scrambled for jobs. With this reservation we can say that the Methodists maintained solidary relations with other miners, whatever their personal views may have been on the strike. Among the sixteen hewers and putters regularly working in Esh Winning, only one was a Methodist.

At Quebec there were a few blacklegs throughout the strike, but never more than a lorry-load. They were subjected systematically to the same treatment as the Esh Winning blacklegs. Alf Cheek was charged, like Clough, with causing disaffection; it was said that he threatened a blackleg. Secondly he was charged with 'an act calculated to prevent the proper working of a coal mine' implying that the miners' objective was illegal. This arose from a demonstration and stone-throwing at Old Cornsay landsale pit where men were working. George Pritchard gave evidence on the first charge saying that Cheek used no threats but only attempted to *persuade* the blacklegs not to work. Aron Richardson (now retired) spoke in Cheek's defence on the second charge. Neither spoke to any avail; Cheek received a month's hard labour from the same bench that had sentenced Clough. The evidence as reported in the press (for all the cases mentioned) seems confused and inconclusive.

Jack and Joe Cheek and others were also charged with throwing stones at blacklegs, and with one exception they received twenty-one days' imprisonment. Respondents speak of a degree of arbitrariness in the arrests and sentences. It could have been any of the men's leaders who were picked up by the police. A Labour councillor explained in 1970, 'The smallest gathering was an excuse for a baton charge.' A propos Clough's arrest Westgarth Adamson's daughter said, '. . .it might have been my father, it just depends who was on the streets to be caught. Mother used to keep father in. He was very upset.'[60]

Quebec thus had a very militant leadership. There was 'Great union solidarity throughout the village. Union meetings of 300–400 men were held at the Hamsteels Colliery Inn.'[61] There were disputes between blacklegs and the union, and their representatives were in constant conflict, with argument, abuse and threats of violence on the streets.

The degree to which solidarity was threatened by the strike can be exemplified by two incidents from Quebec: a blackleg slipped when leaving the lorry and fell under the rear wheels. Not one of the men standing around would fetch a stretcher, and when a table-top was brought, none would help lift it. The blackleg died and the inquest recorded accidental death.[62] His widow was one of those at the cemetery gates for Winter's funeral. She claimed compensation for her husband's death from the union. The committee did not want to pay her, but Cud MacDonald took up her case, arguing that blackleg or not, her husband had paid in like the rest of them. MacDonald won and the wife received £600.[63] This should be contrasted with the normally selfless solidarity of miners in an accident situation.[64] The second incident is recounted in the words of an informant: 'He [Saddler] put barbed wire around the village during the '26. And offered incentives

to blacklegs. Police used to bring blacklegs home. My nephew blacklegged; policemen saw my wife on the doorstep and said "one of your
relatives?'" "He was, but he's not now" said my wife.'[65] It is clear that
strike-breaking broke the two closest solidarities of the village, those
of work and kinship.

Some of the men who blacklegged in Quebec are typified in terms
similar to those used of the Esh Winning blacklegs: 'J.L., his wife
threw a bottle at us and hit a policeman; J.G. and F.T...used to carry
crates at the pub to get free beer. People willing to crawl for favours...
the bosses' men, lacking in personality.'[66]

The vicar of Hamsteels heaped abuse and scorn upon the miners
through his parish magazine:

> The T.U.C., in joining with the miners last May to make their
> great attack upon England, said that they did so in order to pre-
> vent the coal owners from degrading the standard of living
> among the miners.
>
> The Trades Union leaders have inflicted a far greater degrada-
> tion in the standards of living upon the miners than ever the
> masters dreamt of. It is pitiful to see the miners and their chil-
> dren, sometimes even their wives grovelling amongst the pit heaps,
> working as hard or harder to pick up a hundredweight of almost
> worthless cinders, as they would do to get a ton of good coal if
> they were working for the masters.[67]

Rust had the support of the bishop and the dean of Durham who were
both firmly on the side of the owners.[68]

At the Hamsteels end of the village there was alleged to have been
a substantial group of 'owners' children', who were 'red hot Tories',
men who, according to a number of informants, 'never thought for
themselves'. Thus at the Taylor pit (Hamsteels) coal was drawn
throughout the dispute, probably by the lorry-load of blacklegs previously mentioned.

The activism in Quebec is not only explained in terms of a radical
union leadership. The leadership was responding to a provocative
management. Saddler on buying the colliery said he would break the
union and have a model colliery.[69] (J. B. Johnson, his predecessor, was
thought to be a 'nice man' and a good employer.[70]) The Saddlers were
not only anti-union, but interfered in day-to-day management and
thus created difficulties for the managers on the spot. They were also
very active in Tory politics, and had the sympathy of Quebec's vicar.

Little information has been forthcoming about Cornsay in this period,
except that coal was drawn throughout – but we do not know to what
extent. Interestingly enough the management in all collieries seemed to
share the miners' contempt for some of the blacklegs, a few of whom

were sacked after the strike according to the manager's notebook at Esh Winning. It seems that a small group of men were *used* by management, but were not thought to be worthy of normal employment. Clough and another militant (one of the nineteen fined) were not taken on again; Clough was evicted from his house and faced eighteen and a half years' unemployment, which he devoted to organising the local Labour Party. Eventually re-elected to the Rural District Council, along with MacDonald he created public works to give men work for the six days when their dole was suspended. (The 1922 Unemployment Insurance Act stipulated that uncovenanted benefit should be paid only in five weekly intervals from April to October 1922, thus a week's benefit was lost every five weeks over a period of thirty weeks.) The other militant, McKenna, became checkweighman at Waterhouses.

During the strike the Methodist union leadership and the rank and file Methodist union members were faced with a quite new situation; the old paternalism was replaced by power politics. The political power was in the very tangible form of the police, backed by emergency legislation. This was one of those relatively rare occasions on which the state realises its ultimate power in the form of violence. There was very little that could be done through *ad hoc* local initiatives. Lacking any experience of class warfare or theories of radical solutions, the Methodists nevertheless remained passively loyal to the unions. The more militant trade unionists saw this as being 'soft'. 'Some Lodge officials were found to be hesitant in 1926; not politically minded, cap-in-hand with colliery management.' 'Blacklegs' names [were] not taken in Waterhouses; nor were they sent to Coventry in Esh Winning.'[71] 'The Methodists couldn't face the music at the end of the General Strike. I had made appeals for the men to stick together'[72] (told by the man handcuffed to J. G. Winter on the way to prison). '[The] great weakness at Esh Winning was X and others. They were slack on pressing claims at the best of times – but during the lock-out of 1926 they never stood their ground on the streets. They were meant to be the men's leaders – but weren't to be seen on the streets. So no wonder the men didn't stand firm.'[73]

Nonetheless there was one other form of radical response open to the miners. This was seen in the right-radicalism of the N.-P.U., i.e. the Miners' Industrial (non-political) Union, most active in Nottinghamshire and Derbyshire.[74] It is difficult to obtain unbiased information on the N.-P.U.; its local centre was Esh Winning, and this was the only village to have a substantial N.-P.U. of some 20–30 men. According to Garside[75] the Durham N.-P.U. had its origin in Esh Winning. It was formed by a group of men who had begun work before the end of the strike and who thus faced deprivation of union benefits from the

D.M.A. The characteristics of its membership were usually given in terms of individual lineage – or character-defects. It consisted of a small group of men, most of whom blacklegged and many of whom were, like the blacklegs, in some way connected to the management. A few were Tory voters, most were ex-Liberals. We have been unable to identify the religious affiliation of the blacklegs who were known not to be Methodists. If they really were the *lumpen* group that their critics say they were, they probably had few associational ties in the villages. A few of them had been active in the union pressing for an 'opting in' rule for the political levy and themselves trying to opt out and persuade others to do so. Once the lodge had 'gone over to Labour' and started levying its members for Party funds there would plainly be a number of ex-Liberals who might resent the automatic levy, and whose resentment might be played upon. The secretary of the N.-P.U., a Methodist, forced the lodge formally to close the union meetings before going to Labour Party business. The group that was to form a branch of 'Spencer's Union' developed among the blacklegs during the General Strike, and the branch died out about two years later.[76] It is possible to sift its policies from vituperative accounts of its activities and membership. It seems to have stood for individual liberty rather than group solidarity, for individual rather than class politics, and against the political involvement of the trade unions. In fact the N.-P.U. view of the trade unions seems to have been very similar to that of J. W. Pease. In effect the N.-P.U. was a highly political organisation, alleged to have been encouraged by the coal-owners in the area, although they could not recognise it formally as the rules of the Owners' Association bound them to recognise only the D.M.A. The N.-P.U. by its very existence caused dissension amongst miners and their families.

The only other Methodist known for certain to have joined the N.-P.U. is said to have joined because he was against the political levy; he is still a Liberal – although if there is no Liberal candidate he says he votes Labour.

It is very significant that Methodists maintained the collective solidarity of men engaged in industrial and class conflict. In a sense, the principles of the N.-P.U. were more consistent with the traditional Liberal Methodist view. 'The Society [Esh Winning Miners' (Non-Political) Society] aimed to establish a means of settling disputes amicably or by independent arbitration without recourse to political activity.'[77] Group solidarity, however, took precedence over theoretical considerations. To have defended Liberal individualistic principles, in the face of the attack by the coal-owners, would have destroyed the miners' resistance and would have divided miner against miner and family against family. The issue was really very simple – an issue of group survival – and the Methodist miners behaved as did all the other men in the same situation.

The pattern of union leadership varied from village to village. The degree of radicalism, measured by industrial militancy (in terms of organising demonstrations and harassing blacklegs), seems to have been in inverse proportion to the number of Methodists in the village population. In Waterhouses there was the quiet and passive solidarity of the old Liberal leadership, and hardly any blacklegging. In Quebec, the very active and militant leadership of the radicals, and some black-legging, leading to violence. In Esh Winning there was a weak Liberal leadership unwilling to take decisive steps to maintain solidarity, and itself challenged by a more radical element. Esh Winning probably experienced more blacklegging than any village in the valley.

It was quite plain that the traditional relations between owners and men were broken. There were evictions after the lock-out and prosecutions during the dispute; instead of men taking coal from the tips by permission of the management, they stole it and were prosecuted. The reciprocal attitudes were also broken; thus when Percy Ryle, the Esh Winning manager, left in 1926, it was the Pease and Partners personnel man, not the union leaders who made the presentation.[78]

Both the old Liberals and the radical Methodists faced a dilemma. It was only at this point that men like Matt White and Isaac Johnson joined the Labour Party. The minister cited in Chapter 6 maintained that 'individualism was the conditioning factor in the Methodist response to 1926'.[79] The minister who was in Waterhouses during the strike reported: 'Some Methodists thought the General Strike was inopportune. They were not against what lay behind it, but the wrong way of going about it. They thought constitutional methods preferable, not strikes and so on. Some Methodists thought that not all the possibilities were exhausted.'[80] This comment, from a man highly sympathetic to the miners, is consistent with and confirmatory of the more moderate attempts at Methodist compromise.

Eventually the Methodist moderation became impractical. The respondent who said, 'The Wesleyans were anti-socialist right through',[81] was suggesting that although their social philosophy was consistent throughout, a series of political incidents from about 1910 onwards culminated in 1926 when Methodists had to decide to which of the two new sides they were to commit themselves. This view is confirmed by this research. We suggested in Chapter 6 that the Methodists thought of social stratification in terms of a 'gradation of respectability' but they were now faced with a simpler confrontation. Methodism could no longer explicitly accommodate both extremes of a village community, yet the response within Methodism continued to be ambiguous.

At one extreme, the superintendent at Crook struck Clough off the preachers' *Plan*, but the other Methodists just separated 'religion' and 'politics', maintained solidarity with their work-mates and went to chapel on Sunday.

Collectively, the Methodists virtually avoided taking sides at all. They gave themselves to work in soup kitchens and other forms of relief work. This was at least quite consistent with ideas of social service.[82] The most common comment on 1926 is that it made little or no difference to the chapels.[83] 'We often wondered which side people took in 1926. But we tried to be Christians and we agreed to differ. 1926 didn't make much difference in the chapel. "Things said" didn't lead to any falling off. At times, chapel cemented things together.'[84] This only underlines the fact that there was sufficient ambiguity in Methodist attitudes for there to be scope to doubt about 'sides'. The political incidents only made slight changes, for instance that 1926 put the chapels in a very difficult financial position at a time when after fifty years or so the buildings were in need of substantial repairs and maintenance. Only one of the minute books of leaders' and trustees' meetings or quarterly meetings in 1926 would give any indication of industrial disputes in progress. As far as these books show, 1926 is absolutely the same as any other year. Ironically, so many men were on the dole that local offices were set up to pay out: the use of Quebec Clowes and Esh Winning Brandon Road Chapels (both P.M.) brought in a rent from the government which became the major source of income.

Practically speaking, however, the whole situation threatened the Methodists' view of economic and industrial relations; open warfare had replaced arbitration. The coal-owners and managers appeared hostile instead of paternal. All the Methodists, save those who were beginning to accept the Labour Party or Socialist analysis of the situation, would have been disturbed and bewildered by developments in the coal industry. Methodists were divided over the strike, some officials, shopkeepers and Conservatives sided with management, and others supported the miners' cause though not their methods.

The under-representation of miners in the leadership is significant in this context. Shopkeepers, officials, railway workers, etc., were threatened by loss of trade and loss of work. The shopkeepers were especially threatened in that strikers received unlimited credit from the Co-op. during the strike. These debts could only be paid off by trading with the Co-op. and accumulating dividend on the resumption of work, thus depriving private shops of trade.

Such divisions of loyalty and opinion also represented potential splits within the chapel, and members were likely to take sides in what proved to be a very bitter struggle.

Thus we can see that the industrial dispute of 1926 threatened the Methodists ideologically, communally and materially. The only local alternatives for action by the Methodists, as Methodists, was to offer verbal support for the miners, or to do nothing. Outright opposition to the other miners would have been unthinkable and would have assured the demise of Methodism.

This was a problem facing a group claiming universal values and with a universal membership basis. The potential conflicts were avoided by Methodism remaining officially 'non-political'. Methodists participated in social work efforts, the relief of individual distress, but did not take sides. There is no evidence that any Methodist changed his economic views during this period. Many, furthermore, disapproved of the strike, feeling that negotiation was the correct solution even when the owners and government were patently unwilling to settle peacefully.

The Methodists were all either dependent on the coal-trade indirectly or directly employed by the mines. The solidary values of work and community were the prime values operative at the time of the strike. Individually Methodists stood by one another and their fellow miners. Methodist union leaders led their local lodges throughout the strike. Methodists were a tiny minority amongs the blacklegs and only two were active, one in the leadership of the right-wing N.-P.U.

A religious explanation of events is therefore not appropriate. The miners faced the owners and the government as miners, not as Catholics, Methodists or Anglicans. The solidarities of the work-place overrode all other loyalties. The actual effects of Methodism on the community in this crisis can only be judged indirectly by the actions of particular Methodists. For while no religious values were specifically at issue in the strike, religion was relevant insofar as it determined the style of leadership. This can clearly be seen by comparing the villages as we have done.

Perhaps the most interesting observation is the quietness of the response at Waterhouses coupled with strong solidarity among the miners, whereas it would seem that attempts to unite the men under a Socialist leadership and appealing to more overtly Socialist principles were divisive, traditional appeals to community values, as embodied in the leadership of Matt White, united the men. This is the best example of the unifying effect of the social and political implications of the Methodist view of the world.

The most salient feature of institutional Methodism was its unwillingness to take sides in the dispute, unlike the Church of England which unequivocally sided with the owners. It sought a compromise solution. This compromise was written into the history of Methodism, in the development of its official view of the world and stress on individual ethics, and locally in its history of good relations with the coal-owners. The compromise is epitomised in a resolution of the Crook W.M.s – 'Crook Circuit Quarterly Meeting: Resolution on Industrial Situation 2nd June 1926':

> This Quarterly Meeting of the Crook Circuit expresses its deep sympathy with the large numbers of our people throughout the Circuit who are being vitally affected by the stoppage in the coal industry. . .the stoppage cannot do other than cause immeasurable suffering and anxiety. We heartily commend all worthy efforts that are being put forward to allay distress.
>
> We would earnestly pray that a speedy and equitable settlement may be secured. We would confirm our conviction that the solution of the problem of the Coal Industry awaits the coming of a new spirit of goodwill, the predominance of the motive of service over the motive of gain; and the recognition of the Christian principle that all members of society, of whatever grade, should justify their comforts and possessions by their service.
>
> In our judgement the way back to prosperity in the Coal Industry was not in longer hours of toil, nor inequitable reductions of wages, but in work better planned and executed, and in more friendly co-operation in controlling the conditions for working and living. It is as the Coal Industry becomes more firmly based upon the principles of the Gospel, and has breathing through it the spirit of Christ that it will function as it ought.

The fact that the potential conflicts within the chapels did not become actual conflicts may be attributed to the community solidarity of Methodism, its universalistic values and its compromise political position. If, in the 1926 situation, the object of Methodism was to survive in the face of potential internal conflict, then it succeeded. But such a compromise was bound to be interpreted as a betrayal by some miners and may in part have contributed to the loss of support for Methodism among the miners.

9　1970 – a postscript

Methodism in the valley seems no longer to be a force with which men have to reckon. From 1930 onwards the numbers of Methodists declined (for an indication of the size of this decline, see Table 13, Appendix III). A 'good' period for Methodism was one in which membership was no more than static. Economic and demographic changes, social and geographical mobility have eroded Methodist members until by 1970 there were only eighty-five households in the four villages that could be called Methodist households. The penumbra of membership was very small.

There are subjective factors which explain why Methodism and the Methodist influence declined. It is possible to detect a vague and scarcely articulated disenchantment with the Methodist record in the First World War. Methodism took an ambiguous stance similar to all other Churches, but the local Methodists actively recruited among the mines and served on tribunals. Then came the disillusionment of the post-war period. Great sacrifices had been called for and made, while the reward for the villagers was continuous hardship and political conflict. Part of the blame for the lack of repayment was therefore directed towards those organisations which had been seen to give active support to the war, like the local Methodist leaders.

The loss of authority by the Methodist leaders after the Strike of 1926 has been discussed. The issues at stake in that dispute were decided at a national level, but the villagers also responded to the attitudes of the local leaders. The Methodist union leadership adopted attitudes which were open to conflicting interpretations and were sufficiently ambiguous in the eyes of some for accusations of disloyalty to the mining community to be made. The conciliatory attitudes of the Methodists were at best seen as non-committal in the industrial conflicts of the 1920s. Thus: 'By 1930 the Methodist leadership of the trade unions was finished; the R.C.'s took over...for example the Esh Winning Lodge is now [1966] a hundred per cent R.C. (twelve elected posts) yet R.C.'s are outnumbered three to one'.[1] 'A lot of the pitmen thought they had been sold – leaders went smooth with the owners. So

214

eventually they chose men with plenty of shout.'[2] We are not describing events unique to the valley, we are recording nation-wide disillusionment in the old Liberal union leadership and the rejection of Wilsonism. A rejection of Wilsonism included a rejection of his Methodism and the Methodist institutional base also. This development had been under way since before the war, and was part of the national trend in the Labour Movement. Conciliatory attitudes were being replaced by a political outlook derived from a wider trade union, as distinct from occupational, consciousness, and a horizontal division by class rather than a vertical division by community. The disparity in attitudes can be seen dramatically in the circumstances of Clough's return from prison. He returned to the village in triumph, he was led in by the colliery band, holding aloft a piece of prison bread and his mailbag needle. Meanwhile, the superintendent of the Crook Wesleyan circuit had struck him off the preachers' *Plan*.

A quite different factor also led to the decline of Methodist influence in the unions. This was the reduction in the numbers of young Methodists going down the pits; so that even had Methodists been acceptable as union leaders they were not available for recruitment to leadership positions. The villages offered very little other than mining occupations, so many young men and women taking white collar and professional jobs had to move away. It is this which the Methodists themselves see as the most important factor in the decline of numbers and influence, and the removal of a young person is accompanied by regretful but sympathetic discussion amongst the Methodists.

Perhaps the single most important factor in the decline of Methodist influence was the closure of the pits. The main opportunity for contact, interchange and community solidarity between Methodists and non-Methodists was the place of work. With the closures, the Methodists were increasingly living in their own social world, and lost the opportunity for evangelism.

We have stressed throughout the significant discontinuities between Methodism and the cultural life of the villages. Meanwhile the chapels provided a wide range of activities which engaged the time and attention of members to the virtual exclusion of all other activities. But why should these exclusive activities have contributed to the decline of Methodism at this late, post-First World War stage? The reason could be that in the inter-war period the village communities were becoming much more socially differentiated than before. By this we mean that specialised agencies were beginning to form for particular social functions rather than a few institutions (like the chapels) performing many. Commercial entertainment was developing in the villages and the nearby towns, and access to this was made available through the provision of a bus service, as well as the trains. Professional entertainers could come to the village and villagers could travel to Newcastle for concerts. Adult education was available through the W.E.A. and the National Council of Labour Colleges, so it was no longer necessary to attend the Bible class for 'a good argument'.[3] But, most importantly, a specialised political Party had developed. The Labour Party was a Party of the working man, it had a branch in some of the villages but mainly organised its vote through the lodge. Prominent Methodists were no longer needed to bring out the vote on election day and the chapels themselves had fewer voters than the clubs. It seems that once the crucial coincidence of chapel, lodge and Liberal Party was broken, the chapels were isolated from an important network of power and influence. From then the entertainment and educational activities of the chapels ceased to service and sustain the network of institutions but rather operated only to sustain the chapels themselves.

In 1926, for example, Esh Winning P.M. choir was described as 'the foremost in local circles' and the columns of the *D.C.A.* suggest a general expansion of traditional musical interests amongst Methodists. But chapel activities were increasingly for chapel folk only. In the 1920s also Methodists were to a degree forced in upon their own affairs by the very great need to raise money to pay off accumulated debts and either to rebuild or repair chapels which had been in continuous use for fifty years. Concerts and similar activities were time-consuming activities which did not require the members to engage with the wider public except in quasi-commercial relations.

The three main areas of public activity in the Methodist chapels now are the Sunday school anniversary, the Sunday service and funerals. Each of these activities entails expressions of communal solidarity in situations where expressions of conflict or contentious issues are not found. The only conflicts in the adult world that can be expressed through the anniversary are status conflicts in which parents are said to vie with one another to have the best-dressed or most successful child. As the Methodists are a small group struggling to survive we would not expect to find expressions of potentially disruptive interest or belief in the Sunday service. Only the best about men is remembered at funerals, and village conflicts are lost in common expressions of grief. Thus the contemporary life of the chapels still underlines the politically neutralising effect of Methodism on the life of its members, and its particularly cohesive influence in the wider community, in the celebration of childhood and in the face of death.

We have suggested that Methodism is an institution in which the members are ageing. Half of the Methodists are over the age of sixty-one, over three-quarters are above the age of fifty (Table 8).

Table 8. *Age and sex of Methodists, 1970 (Esh Winning and Waterhouses residents only)*

Age	Male %	Female %
Under 31	5	6
32–40	3	4
41–50	3	10
51–60	1	16
61–70	10	21
71 and over	8	13
	30	70
	($N = 31$)	($N = 74$)
Total		100%

Nonetheless, one of the largest organisations within the chapel structure is the Sunday school. This shows that Methodism is still able to
draw into its activities members of families who are formally 'outside'
Methodism.

The Sunday school operates under great difficulties due to lack of
teaching personnel and equipment. For many of the older members
the Sunday school anniversary was a highlight of the chapel year. Not
only was the anniversary an entertainment, as Pickering has observed,[4]
but a celebration of the traditional values of the Methodist family and
community. However, the ritual, celebratory, aspects of the anniversary
interfered in the proper conduct of the Sunday school as seen by the
teacher. So the anniversary, in its traditional form, is not universally
observed in Methodism today, being regarded as old-fashioned and
unsuitable to the needs of the pupils. But when the Sunday school was
re-established in Esh Winning in the late 1960s the society members
and the parents insisted on holding an anniversary – against the wishes
of the teachers. The congregation for the 1970 Sunday school anniversary included a number of non-chapel-going families and totalled about
130 adults. In addition there were about 120 children, 70 seated on
staging facing the congregation and the remainder in the body of the
chapel. The anniversary began with the singing of special hymns and
a Bible reading. Then the children began to give recitations, which
were alternated with songs sung in small groups or as solos. The congregation responded to the recitations by laughing at the comic verses,
or at the more self-conscious performers. Tolerance and a sense of
fair play expressed in indulgence for each performer seemed to under-
lie the congregation's response. If a child forgot a line or made a

mistake there was indulgent laughter or smiles. The recitations were
delivered in a mechanical way, suggesting learning by rote, and performances were accompanied by various degrees of finger-twisting,
blushing and shuffling by the performers. One possibly political consequence of the extensive preparations for the anniversary was that
little boys and girls, at very early age, had been taught to stand up to
address a large audience.

It was the entertainment aspect of the anniversary which troubled
the teachers. They did not wish to revive the anniversary, especially as
it interfered with any set course of lessons. A senior official of the
Sunday school observed that the teachers tried to compromise with the
demand for the anniversary by putting on a play:

> But people said, 'That wasn't an Anniversary'. They expect the
> children to twiddle their thumbs and say their pieces. And it
> knocks holes in the Syllabus.
>
> They [the parents] watch the kiddies' clothing rather than
> what they are doing, and the message. . .the girls like the Anniver-
> sary, but the boys do not, they take part reluctantly. Children do
> not like being laughed at. If a child forgets half way through [his
> piece] people think it is funny – that is the bull-ring side of it.[5]

The villagers' expectations of the anniversary are therefore rooted
in tradition and not in the demand for good educational techniques
and sound theological learning. The aniversary is meant to be a joyful
occasion, it is intended to have the atmosphere of a family party as
well as an act of worship. But this has to be expressed in a traditional
form. Thus, whatever the goals of the chapel officials may be they are
constrained by the orientations of the parents and congregation towards
seeing that the children do their pieces in a traditional anniversary, not
towards the formal goals of Methodism or Christian education. The
anniversary is a communal occasion related to traditional expectations
and is, in fact, typical of the contemporary orientation of Methodists
in the valley.

The Sunday service is the main event of the week and is at the centre
of the chapel's life. Here also one can observe the chapels' relative
irrelevance to the wider community. In our observations throughout
four years very little of the old evangelical fervour was seen. The
services were restrained in their religious expressions and there was
little vigorous singing to generate any religious enthusiasm. The
prayers concentrated on the chapel and the people in the village, with
briefer but regular reference to world events. From time to time
prayers included a plea for the spirit of revival to return to the village
and the nation. The plea was made in an unspecific way, with no inti-
mation of how revival might be achieved. Given the age and numbers

of the villagers available for mounting a revival campaign it was perhaps to be expected that the approach was one of leaving the task entirely to the Almighty.

The main criterion of a 'good service' was still the quality of the sermon. As the minister was the preacher heard most regularly, he tended to be judged on the merits of his preaching. The importance of anecdotal and amusing illustrations in giving a good sermon was shown by the case of a recent minister who preached with great simplicity and economy, coming clearly and directly to his point. He was said to be a 'difficult' and 'dry' preacher; but while informants said that he was not very inspiring they admitted that what he said was nonetheless very good.

The Methodists continued to show their faith in reason. The sermon must have an argument and it must assert certain truths for the Methodists. Sermons dealing with ethical matters were well-received. The preacher might assert in general terms that the listeners were sinners but his specific criticisms of people's ethical behaviour might only be directed against outsiders. In other words nothing internally divisive was said. The preachers usually presented their sermons in the form of a reasoned argument, usually making three connected points on the basis of a biblical text. It was difficult to tell the extent to which the hearers appreciated the intellectual force of a sermon because it was never possible to find anyone who could discuss the sermons in detail after the lapse of a few days. At the most people remembered whether it was a good sermon or not; they might remember the text and one or two of the illustrative stories, but not the details of the argument. Sometimes attenders reported that the preacher 'lost me' at a point in the sermon. This at least indicates that sermons were listened to and that hearers attempted to follow the argument.

The task of preaching is mainly undertaken by a dwindling group of local preachers. A preacher visiting from outside the village will always say how happy he is to be among the folk at Esh Winning or Waterhouses, or with the folk, or friends again. In his introductory remarks he will refer to the warm welcome he always receives from the folk and that he looks forward to preaching to them. Thus the preacher upholds the view of the Methodists as a small group of warm-hearted and friendly people. Again, standing at the chapel door after the service the preacher, if he is a local man, or from a nearby village, will ask after sick relatives of members, or express pleasure at hearing of a marriage.

The family nature of the service is heightened by the congregation's own behaviour. Conversations are carried on in the chapel before and after the service, minor items of business are conducted or information passed. But family matters are the main subject of conversation; old age, sickness and death provide staple topics, but also news of returning sons and daughters, or the birth of a grandchild and the exploits of these grandchildren are passed on. Much news seems to be transmitted in the chapel; people find out about other people on Sunday. Plainly this kind of chapel gossip has boundaries which are limited to people with Methodist connections.

What function does the service perform in the life of the Methodists? Attending a service is one of the most important ways of being a Methodist: a Methodist is known by his ethical conduct – being an upright man etc. – but he is most clearly seen to be a Methodist when he goes to and from chapel in his best suit on Sundays. Chapel attendance is thus a simple rite of solidarity, the Methodists collectively asserting to themselves and to the rest of the village who they are. In so doing they gave a Christian witness; the Methodists believe that Sunday is widely misused, but that they show the right use of Sunday.

The service helps define the boundary between Methodists and the 'world', especially where matters of conduct are discussed in the sermon. There is an element of self-assurance in the assertion of the differences between the Methodist and the worldly man. The Methodists do not assert that they are among the elect, nor that the world is damned; but there is a muted suggestion that this could be the case to a greater or lesser extent. The boundary between the Methodists and the 'world' becomes increasingly important as the bridges between them break down. In other words the assertion of separateness is accompanied by a very real lack of opportunities for influencing the rest of the world.

The service may also satisfy individual psychological needs; one of these may be to provide a link with the past. There seem to be minor elements of fantasy in the services which reinforce the lack of this-worldly engagement. The service brings memories crowding in, of families and friends and 'characters' departed, the seats in which they sat, their favourite hymns, the crowds and the 'good times'. This must make the older members sad. Yet they are united in their sadness and their shared memories, the old times seem very close, the communion of saints is expressed in the feeling that the faithful departed are still part of today's life in the chapel. Various memorials to deceased members surround the worshippers as tangible reminders of the past. In the face of adversity and sadness the Methodists assert that God's Will will be done and that He will provide the means to religious revival in His own time. This is an important element in maintaining morale in a situation of relatively rapid social change.

But if this function of the service is correctly interpreted in this way then certain other consequences follow. This form of religous expression only enables the Methodists to survive in the world while not being altogether of the world. It is an expression not only of the essentially communal nature of Methodism (a communality transcending time, we have suggested) but an expression of traditional values which are relevant to a past society. It does not provide the Methodists, and especially the small group of young Methodists, with any intellectual equipment, with any programme of action in the community beyond conventional social work. We might say that Methodism survives apart from the wider community and begins to show what we might simply call pietism. Methodists' religious behaviour is directed not to the world of the 1970s, but to Methodism and its traditional values as expressed in a traditional community.

There is one situation in which Methodism still unites the whole society in a collective religious expression, drawing in the penumbral members and supporters, drawing on the subterranean religious and ethical culture of the valley people. This is the situation in which they come together for the last of a man's *rites de passage*. The chapel comes nearest to being completely filled when there is a funeral. Funerals are very important events in the villages, although many of the traditional rites are no longer observed. Many beyond the immediate family attend a funeral; there are representatives of trade unions, clubs, societies, or temperance organisations, depending on the memberships of the deceased. In the case of a small village, virtually the whole village attends – some taking time off work and attending in their working clothes. A man who died in the mine used to be preceded by the colliery band and the black-draped lodge banner. The funeral is thus a great rite of solidarity and is accompanied by the most potent symbols of working-class solidarity. Many hundreds may still follow a coffin to chapel and graveyard or crematorium.

Such rites mark the death of the 'religious' and the 'non-religious' alike. In death and in the face of death, all become religious. MacIntyre has suggested that even in the modern world we cannot do entirely without the vocabulary of Christianity, because we have no other vocabulary in which to raise certain kinds of questions.[6] Death, and our response to it, is just such a question.

Thus the chapel and Christian beliefs still have meaning for the whole community. The 'meaning' is a mixture of communal response to death and communal sympathy for the bereaved, plus a Christian interpretation of the facts of death and its cosmic meaning. To this extent the villages of the valley have not lost their religion in spite of the empty chapels on Sunday. Nor is Methodism without influence; but it is not the pervasive influence it was before.

Conclusions

The intention of this study was to add to the sociology of religion by analysing one Methodist community in sociological terms. There are two major areas of sociological theory to which it relates directly, and which were mentioned in the Introduction: firstly, the Protestant Ethic thesis and secondly Lenski's distinction between communal and associational types of religious belonging. These are the two sociological debates most relevant to this analysis of the political effects of Methodism.

THE PROTESTANT ETHIC THESIS

Max Weber suggested that Protestantism was necessary both for the rise of an entrepreneurial bourgeoisie and the rationalisation of social and economic relations. The Protestant Ethic provided individual motivation and legitimation for capitalistic enterprise. The Protestant sect provided a group in which the member learnt and practised a rationalistic priest-free ethical discipline. Membership of the sect also assured the Protestant's social and economic credit-worthiness. If these factors are considered together with Protestant theology itself, Protestantism can be seen to have constituted a radical cultural breakthrough leading to a devaluation of traditional social structures and a systematisation and rationalisation of economic affairs.

The present study has examined Protestantism amongst a small elite section of the working class. It has been shown that it is especially important for encouraging a political and economic leadership in the working class. In the form of Methodism, Protestantism provided individual motivation and justification for political and economic enterprise. The Methodist 'class' was a group within which men learnt, and gave account of their practice of a rationalistic, ethical discipline. Membership of the society assured credit-worthiness, but economic credit was less relevant to miners than political trustworthiness, and in fact Methodists were advanced to positions of leadership in working-class political organisations, as the labour historians have observed.

We might say that Methodism performed a liberating function for the late nineteenth- and early twentieth-century working class in our villages which was similar to that performed by Calvinism and Puritanism for the emerging entrepreneurial class in the seventeenth/ eighteenth century. This is especially true at the personal, motivational level, because there was no 'new society' within Methodism, to the image of which the whole society could be brought to conform by the striving of the disciplined Methodist. Methodism was concerned with a new man, not a new society, and offered personal ethics not a political programme. In this particular form Protestantism is more congruent with individualism than with collectivism and class action. Thompson, in drawing our attention to the importance of the desire for personal salvation, seems to have made a point that is valid for Methodism in all historical periods.

Weber also suggested that Protestantism provided a compliant labour force. Andrew Ure was one who believed this to be the case,[1] and it might be argued that the entrepreneurs, among whom Ure was very influential, generally acted on this belief. Protestantism could have been promoted *because* it was believed to provide a compliant labour force. Weber's suggestion seems appropriate, at least for as long as economic conditions appeared to favour the workers' compliance with the employers' demands. But the conclusion would be rash if stated unconditionally, because obviously economic change must be taken into account in considering the formulation of the social and economic views of a religious group. Their behaviour is never determined by theology alone. Economic circumstances became more pressing than basic religious ethics in the later period of overt economic conflict and traditional Methodist ideas were no longer appropriate to the actual social and economic situation.

The miners may have been rendered *relatively* compliant by Methodist views and Methodist leaders, in the earlier period, but Thompson makes the case much too simply. MacIntyre is more accurate, when he says that trade union morality would hold 'that a worker is essentially equal with those with whom he works, that he is also essentially equal with those who claim superiority over him, and that in knowing that he is equal to them he has his chief weapon against them'.[2] This view of equality is intrinsic to the Christian gospel as presented by the Methodists and was plainly an assumption made by the union leaders studied, however deferentially they may have behaved. The union leadership up until the early 1920s consisted largely of 'respectable' Liberal Methodists who felt that they commanded the respect of the owners. The union leaders had an organismic view of society, they believed in reason and reconciliation as a means of settling disputes which were only caused, as they saw it, by temporary imbalances in the market, or misunderstanding. They shared this view with owners and managers, and with regional union leaders who had staked their careers on such a view. One could argue that they were merely justifying what they could not alter, given the relative powerlessness of the miners. The local leaders' outlook was nonetheless coherent with successful conduct of day-to-day relations at the place of work – hard bargaining and 'gentlemen's agreements'. They adhered to MacIntyre's 'secondary virtues' of 'a pragmatic approach to problems, co-operativeness, fair-play, tolerance, a gift for compromise, and fairness'.[3] This outlook became less defensible as economic circumstances changed from 1900 onwards; it was, in fact, the basic pursuit of profit in unfavourable circumstances which opened the gap between miners and employers and culminated in the dispute of 1926. Methodist views in general were still sufficiently 'vertically' or community-orientated for them to be ambivalent towards the strike, which they felt to be an unwise and rash means of achieving a just and desirable end.

The evidence on the actions of the Methodist union leaders is ambiguous. Their 'submission' was not complete and it was perhaps more submission to the logic of a market than directly to a superior class of owners. Furthermore, Hobsbawm has shown quite clearly that the views of the leaders and members of a trade union may differ.[4] We found that this was increasingly true of the miners' unions in the villages in the early twentieth century.

The relation between religious and non-religious ideas and institutions in social history was highlighted by our findings. For example, Methodist social and ethical teaching was found to comply with contemporary liberal *laissez-faire* economic theories and to motivate the Methodists to further social reform. We need to understand how particular economic theories gain currency and the ways in which they both contribute to and result from other ideological beliefs, including religion. In other words, we could develop a fuller understanding of (in this case) the nineteenth century by exploring the sociology of economic theory.

We have also seen the effect of religion in reducing class consciousness and class conflict through the sharing of religious beliefs and institutions by potentially conflicting groups, i.e. vertical integration rather than horizontal division. These Methodists were able to identify themselves ideologically and ethically with the coal-owners, who were themselves successors to the Protestant Ethic of the seventeenth/ eighteenth centuries. This was to some extent paralleled at the national level in the identification of union leadership with Gladstone and Gladstonian Liberalism. In the local situation, the chapels were also economically dependent on the owners. However, the Working Men's Clubs constituted working-class organisations totally independent from the church or the owners, yet do not seem to have produced early leadership in the unions. We probably know less about the role of Working Men's Clubs in the history of the working class than we know about Methodism. A sociological study of this and, another Methodist subject, the importance of temperance in the founding of the Labour Movement, would open up relatively unexplored areas of social and political history.

Weber dismissed the possibility that religion might activate the modern proletariat, and thereby undoubtedly underestimated the ability of the more radical Protestant tradition to generate radical working-class politics. This is because he was concerned with the emergence of a capitalist society and an entrepreneurial class, and believed the Reformation to be a totally spent force, giving the example of Germany at the turn of the century.[5] One of the historically and sociologically most interesting discoveries in the course of this study was the existence of a group of Socialist radicals in one chapel. The intellectual roots of this group lay not in Methodist thought but in seventeenth-century Christian radicalism, eighteenth-century rationalism, Christian Socialism, and Thoreau, Emerson and Tolstoy. The group also showed anarchist tendencies amongst some of its members who had indirect contacts – through the Brotherhood Church – with the Dukhobors. By revealing the exact sources of radicalism among Methodists we have provided one proof of our earlier proposition namely that secular rather than Methodist ideas were the basis of political radicalism in the villages in the late nineteenth and early twentieth centuries.

Nonetheless the radicals began their political careers within Methodism. Their political language was often the language of the Bible. Thus at a relatively simple level we may say that Methodism was conducive to radicalism by providing a language for political protest, giving the religious basis for social and political activity – for those who wished to pursue such activities; heightening social consciousness through study and by providing oratorical and organisational skill.

At the ideological level we can see that Methodism made the radicals receptive to an especially ethical kind of Socialism, the Socialism of F. D. Maurice and Edward Carpenter, and made them not so receptive – it would seem – to Marxism. The Methodist outlook appears to lead men to single out or accentuate the ethical qualities of political beliefs. Thus Methodists adhered to especially ethical kinds of Liberalism and Socialism, in both of which they believed that 'what is morally wrong can not be politically right' (a phrase open to both conservative and radical interpretations).

Another striking feature of the radical outlook was that it was an outlook with wide horizons, embracing the national and international economy, rather than the Durham miners' market interest alone; it could have provided the basis for developing a *class* rather than the narrower trade-union consciousness. Had the radical tradition become dominant in the Labour and trade union movements, their histories would have been very different. But sociologists argue that it is in the nature of the pursuit of political power that such a tradition should not become dominant.

In summary one cannot make simplified statements on the causal effectiveness of beliefs alone. The monolinear theses of Lecky and Halévy emerge from conscientious attempts to organise the mass of data on social change in the most rapid period of industrial development in Britain. The labour historians were trying to explain broad historical movements, and the Methodist historians had the fixed goal of trying to defend Methodism. In arguing their cases all fell prey to over-simplification and made sweeping assertions of the kind which Pope, whom we quoted at the beginning of this book, characterised as: 'Too uncritical and undiscriminating to represent the diverse ways in which religious agencies function' and which fail, 'adequately to allow for the multiplicity and reciprocity of relationships'. The main stream of Methodist thought may have been anti-radical, but familiarising men with the Bible and other religious literature, even in a non-radical context, can mean unintentionally infiltrating radical ideas. Given suitable political situations the radical ideas would find a ready affinity with the radical tradition of the Durham miners which had been suppressed, and passed into legend, by the mid-1860s. It is not enough to look at beliefs and ideas in the abstract. The structures within which religion is institutionalised develop certain organisational skills in men, which can be turned to other uses. Where would early working-class movements have found their leaders without Methodism? One of the major contributions of Methodism was to supply a leadership from the workers, and to determine the nature of that leadership.

COMMUNITY AND ASSOCIATION

Lenski in *The Religious Factor* outlined the differences between communal and associational adherence to religious groups. The importance of this distinction has been elaborated in the present study. We have shown that the Methodist society was a community, in which the ties of kinship and friendly interaction were as important as the nominal demands of membership of a religious association. The ancillary activities of the chapels provided the basis for an intense and warm social life which extended beyond the formal boundaries of the organisation. Involvement in the ancillary activities did not entail a high theological or ideological commitment. Theology was thus relatively unimportant for the average Methodist unless he chose to involve himself in, for example, *The New Theology* and the ensuing debate with the radicals.

The high evaluation of ancillary activities by the participants is a major factor in explaining the chapels' solidarity in the face of the outside world. This factor may have been underestimated in previous studies which have concentrated on belief rather than institutionally-generated constraints. Wherever there were differences of interest amongst chapel members, or whenever potentially divisive issues arose, it was necessary to avoid taking sides in order to preserve the communal life of the chapel.

The importance of this solidarity has been elaborated in our accounts of three series of political events. In the early years of the century the Methodists were all united in opposition to the 1902 Education Act and the drink trade. Their views were also shared by the coal-owners. There was no sense in which these issues, directly bearing upon Methodist ethics, could have divided local Methodism, and so Methodist policy was clear and indisputable.

The First World War created conflicts over conscientious objection and military exemption, and Methodists found themselves judging one another's claims to exemption. The outcome of the judgements and the gossip accompanying the claims alienated a number of families, and was the first sign of division in the community.

In 1926 the Methodists supported the miners passively, but to a degree they were divided. It was possible for the Methodists partially to avoid the conflicts amongst their membership and in the community by engaging in mutual-aid activities on a communal basis rather than acting as a politically-active association. Through social work and mutual aid they were also finding an outlet which enabled them to express social concern in a traditional Methodist form, and thus retreat from potentially volatile issues.

The ability of a group to formulate a clear policy or attitude on any matter which they think important will come to depend on the degree to which the policy issue is potentially divisive of the group internally. Thus the interests of the group *vis-à-vis* the interests of the wider community become crucial. The greater the diversity of economic and status interests there are within a group, the less able will the group be to formulate a policy on economic, social and political issues, at least for as long as it values its communal life more highly than its conscience. The intention to prevent divisive 'political' issues intruding into the life of the Church is also entirely consistent with a view of the Church as an organisation reconciling all interests, in other words, having a universalistic outlook.

Methodism was already declining locally due to economic and demographic factors and its inward-looking solidarity probably made things worse. The Methodists were faced with two possible courses of action, both of which would probably have reduced membership: either to alienate some members by taking a positive stand on an issue, or to make no comment at all on more progressive thinkers. What the Methodists were doing in fact by choosing the second course, was to resist *new* ideas in the twentieth century.

The theology of R. J. Campbell divided preacher against preacher and apparently caused the loss of both members and preachers (although there is no statistical evidence for this). Therefore an attempt was made to reassert the prevailing orthodoxy; this seemed to have been successful because the older men, more traditional thinkers, held power in the chapels. But socialist ideas challenged the whole basis of the established Methodists' world view – and especially the basis of his view of authority and property. The ensuing attempt to keep politics out of the pulpit entailed the assertion of one group's traditional beliefs against the new ideas of another group. This resistance to new ideas by the older men had already been causing conflicts with the younger members from the beginning of the century; the alienation increased as the century progressed. Thus it would seem that, in Kent's words, 'Methodism was both producing men who revolted against the established order and also disowning them, if their activities seemed to imperil the religious society's existence.'[6]

The unintended consequence of the dominance of communal values has been to make the chapels *wholly* communal bodies, with communal benefit taking precedence over every consideration. Thus the chapels have become unable to respond to changing social, economic and religious circumstances. Social changes or the ecumenical movement (for example) were quite irrelevant to the warm social life of the contemporary Methodists, and this was amply borne out by our direct observations of the life of the chapels.

The apparently simple study of Methodism proved, in the event, to be much more difficult than at first expected. The main reason for this was that it was difficult to separate out Methodism as a discrete social phenomenon. Methodism is not theology, nor an organisation, but a way of life, a code of ethics which are often unstated and only implicit in people's behaviour. This is peculiarly problematic when on the surface there are quite obvious characteristics of Methodism, like the familiar chapels and hymn-singing in the valley. The problem is compounded by Methodism co-existing with social and economic philosophies which are also highly ethical, and known to have been penetrated by Non-conformist thought in their development.

Methodism was so much part of a local culture that it is easy to use Methodism as the explanation for every course of events and every aspect of human behaviour. The way to separate out and observe Methodism, or Methodist ethics, most clearly, is to see what persists in religious life when the social background changes. Men and organisations change, as did the Liberal Party from 1870 to 1920. Men and their associations change their labels, as did the villagers in becoming Labour Party supporters. But many of the beliefs held by individuals and expressed by their organisations did not change, or changed very little. This continuity between, for example, the Liberal and Labour Parties is expressed in an ethical tone, in individualism, and this would seem to be one of the important contributions of Methodism to political life.

It has been argued throughout and should be repeated that in understanding the political effects of Methodism one should take into account not only beliefs but the social relations of which those beliefs are a part. It has been necessary to study the relations between miners and coal-owners and the internal relations of the Methodist chapels in order to understand the effects of Methodism.

The objective was not to be concerned with *all* aspects of religious life; some aspects have been ignored or mentioned only *en passant*. We were only concerned with 'those features in the total picture of a religion which have been decisive for the fashioning of a practical way of life'.[7] Most of our attention has been devoted to the political way of life of our villagers.

Until its last appearance at the Miners' gala in July 1969 the Esh Winning lodge banner bore on its reverse side the assertion that 'All Men are Brethren'. Below these words there was a picture of a miner shaking the hand of a tail-coated owner. Above and behind the pair there floats an angel bearing a pink ribbon which bears the legend 'Let Us Work Together'. This legend, which was the basis of the miners' 'practical way of life', cannot be understood without knowing the meaning of Methodism in the lives of the men and women of the Deerness Valley.

APPENDIX I

Research strategy and techniques

STRATEGY

This work has been based on a field study of a fairly intensive kind, a detailed study of a small population in a limited geographical area. The reason for this kind of research was the wish to produce a sociological enquiry which explored the meanings of religion and social and economic relations for the society. For this I needed interactional and highly situational data.

A price has to be paid for the adoption of this strategy. The life of mining villages is not orientated to the production of data for sociologists. Thus the data actually collected may raise issues that are not dealt with in any other literature and it is not possible therefore to gain a ready perspective on their relevance – especially if the issues are not central to this research. For example, the Irish clearly played an important role in the villages, but there is no study of the Irish in County Durham to which the data can be referred. Conversely data that are central to our main themes may not be forthcoming; the obvious example in this case was the lack of hard data on relations at the place of work.

A more eclectic approach would provide a composite sociological picture by taking a sermon from one village, an action from another, the social composition of a chapel in a third village and so on. All these could be brought together to construct a coherent model. This approach might not only produce a spurious coherence, it would vitiate the prime purposes of the reasearch, which was to show the situational relations between beliefs and actions.

The approach to this research also deprives it of important comparative perspectives. Obviously it was an impossibility to compare events in these villages with events in villages that contained fewer Methodist (or Non-conformist) miners. It is an historical fact of some significance that one might have to look beyond the county, or beyond Great Britain, to find a 'non-religious' mining community at the end of the nineteenth century. But only twenty miles away from the villages of the valley there were deep and gassy pits, employing larger numbers of men. These were pits with a long, bitter history of violence and ill-will between ownership and men. Any data from this area were clearly not appropriate to fill gaps in the Deerness Valley data, although they could have been used as control data to test our thesis on the effects of religion in these very different circumstances.

If wide variations are found in the course of the history of just a few villages within County Durham, then how typical of any other mining villages are these of the study? Two indications do make them look not unusual. Firstly, the newspapers for the county in the period concerned give no indication of major variations between villages. Certainly Methodist activities seem to be very much the same from village to village. Secondly, Chapter 2 tried to set the study in a broad historical framework, to show how the chapels, unions and pits tied in with national religious, political and economic developments. One rather curious fact emerged from our study. In treating Methodism we were aware of the major traditions of the denominations; P.M., W.M., and M.N.C. A major presupposition of this research was that there would be significant differences between these traditions as represented in the villages, in terms of membership, chapel polity, style of preaching, social and political outlook. This has not proved to be the case; while in one village it was said that the Wesleyans were a bit staid and snobbish, exactly the same was said of the Primitives in the next village. It is quite possible also that the reported homogeneity of Methodism is a part of the mythology of the village. The villagers have a myth of a 'golden past' in the villages, in which community spirit, homogeneity and mutual support are very important elements. These ideal characteristics are contrasted with the present state of the villages, and the state of the world.

These tentative assertions are not the stuff of which history is made, but until evidence is produced to the contrary we have to assume that the traditional differences are insufficiently represented to be significant. We are therefore deprived of what might have been an important comparative insight in our work. By and large the villages – and their inhabitants: miners, managers and owners – seem to synchronise with national developments in economic and political beliefs and activities.

Having listed the problems raised by this research strategy, one should also state its advantages. Restricting the location of the research required the search for data which might have been overlooked had more accessible data from a wider location been admissible. While it is true that many of the sermons could have been preached in any Methodist chapel at any time, it is better to understand the sermons preached by a particular preacher to a certain group. The ideas in the sermons were congruent with their other beliefs and we can better understand the comunity's behaviour in the light of these beliefs.

Ultimately religion is experienced by men and women according to their worldly situations. At whatever level one may discuss religion, or religion and politics, it is important to know their interpretation of religion. The use of the locality study, in spite of its occasional intrinsic shortcomings, has provided the sociological framework for understanding the meaning that religion had for individuals in their particular situations.

TECHNIQUES

The methods used in the research fall under four broad headings: the study of private and official manuscript and printed sources; the searching of newspapers; interviewing (mainly unstructured); participant observation.

The data needed could not be obtained by the use of any one method on its own; for example, while newspaper accounts gave an adequate chronology of events, interviews were needed to elicit details of the events, and the people concerned. Local interpretations of the events could only be gained from interviews, or, in the case of the late nineteenth century from patchy sources – letters and diaries.

Historical data survive in a random manner. Legal documents are more likely to be preserved than minute books. Only a few members of the working class keep diaries, and only some of their descendants preserve them. Such considerations have made it doubly necessary to cross-check all data wherever possible.

Where complete runs of material were available, i.e. newspapers and Methodist Sunday school books, sampling techniques were used. In searching the newspapers (local weeklies) the first edition of each month was used in order to build up a picture of the routine life of the chapels and villages. If by this method, or from other sources, it was known that important events had taken place (e.g. strikes, elections, etc.) the search was extended to cover every week in all relevant newspapers until the topic was dropped by the press.

Printed Methodist sources were investigated for every ten years, a whole year's material being examined. This reduced the task to manageable proportions and highlighted changes in content and presentation of material by the Methodists. Using the above methods the following investigations have been carried out:

(1) The numbers of Methodists and adherents have been roughly established for the P.M.s and W.M.s. Chapel attendances have been estimated. The occupations of the leading Methodists have been

ascertained. Some estimate has been made of communal and associational membership. Among sources for these data are official Methodist returns, documents relating to trustees, Sunday school registers, minute books, electoral registers and interviews.

(2) The occupational structure of the locality at various dates has been reconstructed through the use of colliery employment records, census material and registration of births and deaths.

(3) Given the problematic question of the nature of beliefs, it has been necessary to study the historical and present beliefs of the Methodists: by reading sermons and notes for sermons, diaries, speeches, etc.; through informal discussions and structured interviews with Methodists; by searching published sources; guides to Sunday school teachers, Methodist magazines, etc.; by participating in the life of the chapels, especially to hear sermons and anniversary addresses.

It has really only become possible to understand Methodist beliefs and undertake the task outlined in (3) by becoming immersed in the culture and history of the villagers. I spent many hours not only in the chapels, but in the homes of Methodists, discussing their beliefs directly, their biographies, the past and contemporary life of the villages. In the light of these discussions the material in (3) had to be re-worked a number of times. Ideally an investigator should keep a field diary recording the developments of his understanding as he learns the nuances of Methodist language – but there is a problem insofar as recording can interfere with understanding. Furthermore changes and understanding develop by a slow accretion of experiences and interpretations of them, not in a way that can be noted at the time.

Important questions of phenomenological method and hermeneutics were raised by these aspects of the study. For example, to what extent was it possible for the investigator adequately to understand and take as given the whole cultural, economic and political life of the villages in the late nineteenth century in order to understand the meaning of, say, becoming a convert to temperance? This problem is not discussed, but for the purposes of the present work it is assumed that one may 'understand' another individual through the spoken or written word. The problem of intersubjectivity is assumed to be surmountable.

(4) One very useful technique used towards the end of the reasearch was to discuss findings with the Methodists, both individually and collectively. This was avoided during the time in which I wished to establish initial rapport.

By talking in homes and giving talks to meetings it was possible to present to the Methodists sociological analyses of the development of Methodism, and its relation to local society. They responded in a thoughtful and lively way to quite abstract discussion. They were willing to confirm certain notions – even those which might be interpreted as personally critical of them. When they understood a point being made they offered evidence in support of it which was better than that offered in the opening talk. They gained new insights *and then* said they were sure the conclusions were right, only they had not seen things 'in that way' before. For example the Methodists always complain that the leadership in the trade unions is 'not what it used to be' (i.e. Methodist); when presented with evidence on the aspirations and social mobility of the Methodists, they saw, and agreed, that the trade unions were bound to lose their Methodist leadership. We were then able to discuss the 'unintended consequences' of actions and beliefs fairly objectively. The meeting at which this was discussed consisted of about forty people, all of whom tried to think of leading Methodists whose sons had gone into pit work – they were unable to do so, confirming the hypotheses of the investigation in a very striking way.

Once the Methodists felt they knew what the research was about, they volunteered information which they regarded as useful; no one seemed offended by comments which I thought might be seen as critical. This seems a legitimate research technique – it points to the desirability of maximum openness between the investigator and his subjects. With such openness (which may not be possible in all research situations) it seems possible to develop techniques of enquiry on the basis of a direct and honest interchange between the sociologist and his subjects – or more strictly, between the participants in a discussion situation. It does not mean that the investigator accepts the story told by his subjects; their response to the presentation of his data is data in itself. A very important observation on Methodists is that they enjoy 'intellectual' discussion in a formal lecture–discussion situation. Another significant fact is that they saw the intellectual enterprise of research as valid and worthwhile. I was never told by a Methodist that I ought to do something more useful than digging up the past of Methodism.

A point of some technical importance arose in asking respondents about historical events. In some cases reports seemed to confirm one another, so I became convinced that I was obtaining valid data. Then it appeared that the *form* of the reporting was also very similar, as well as the content; eventually a common source, in a newspaper or local history was discovered. The key to this was given when one respondent provided great detail on an event which she could not possibly have remembered. People discuss their history and an agreed version emerges, which is so real, so deeply imbedded in the culture, that people may describe events as if they were themselves participants in or eye-witnesses to the history. Investigators concerned with historical data should be prepared for this, and it should not be assumed that there is any absolute truth, something 'which *really* happened' that respondents can recall. It is the interpretations of events that are data; the interpretations may all be similar, or systematically vary between classes. (For example biographical data on a union leader may vary widely – or actually be contradictory – between two groups of 'radical' and 'conservative' workers).

The dramaturgical method

It might be argued that the methods used produced a falsely categorical picture of Methodism. Three dramatic series of events were chosen to illustrate an argument, but the life of the villages and chapels was not all drama. A closer study of the 'normal' life of the villages would have been more relevant to the theme developed. While this criticism is not without substance, the following points need to be set against it:

(1) Data on the normal life of the chapels are not easily recovered. Furthermore, how does the researcher decide which of his respondents' memories are memories of the normal and which of the special? Nonetheless the account of the communal nature of village Methodism, for example, includes some discussion of the routine life of the chapels, and this is very much part of the explanatory framework.

(2) From the beginning there appears to have been quite rapid change in the social and political life of the villages. It is thus very difficult, if not impossible, to say what was normal or average life, because change was in fact continual. Normality is most likely to be defined by the villagers in terms of some sort of golden past, and this in itself can be highly misleading. History is a *social* fact, or a social artifact, interpreted in the light of the present, not necessarily a scientific account of events.

(3) Economic conflict, bargaining and trying to gain an advantage in the market was normal to the mining villages. The events of 1926 were a special case of this, by virtue of a very marked change in the degree of conflict and the sanctions used.

(4) The events that we have described impinge on the main themes of our work, and are used to make sociological points, not to convey the authentic feeling of domestic or pit life in the villages. If we had been studying the family, then other landmarks could have been used to make other points; such data were collected incidentally but not used, because they were not relevant to the thesis.

(5) The 'dramatic' events are especially useful in that they expose the key activists; trade union and political leaders could not avoid action in 1926; men on tribunals could not avoid making decisions in 1916;

Methodist leaders could not stand idly by in 1902. What these men did is, furthermore, public knowledge, and it is public knowledge of men defending some of their most precious ideal and material interests. On this basis alone the dramaturgical method could be justified.

(6) It was not the intention to produce a conventional history of the villages in the sense that this should be the sequential story of the events in the villages from 1870 to 1970. Events were selected according to their relevance to our main themes (see 4 above), and necessarily much was omitted. We have not dwelt on the influence of Catholicism, or the functions of the clubs, nor have we looked at non-religious self-improvement and self-education activities. To some extent this distorts the picture of the villages; our standpoint was the chapels because we were asking questions about religion. Had the standpoint been, as for Dennis *et al.*, the pubs and clubs, the conclusions might have been somewhat different. But although one may contrast, one cannot write from all perspectives at once, and this work is about religion and its effects on local politics and social grouping.

The Methodist community and objections to Anglican union

Towards the end of the research period in the Deerness Valley a short questionaire was conducted among 77 Methodists. The total Methodist membership list was of 130 people in 91 households. Of these people 25 were very well known to me because I had repeatedly visited them and used them as informants on many matters. They had also become my friends. The survey was used to compare the Methodists with whom I was less familiar with the well-known Methodists, in terms of social characteristics and opinions. It is important to note that the 125 Methodists were not *unknown* to me, but only less well known. A total of 28 were not surveyed because of old age, illness or refusal (12 in all) or because they lived outside the four main villages and could not easily be visited in the two weeks set aside for this phase of the research.

Most of the data collected are not relevant to the present work and will not be discussed. One question, however, elicited answers which seem to confirm the contention that Methodist orientations are highly ethical and communal. The question was 'Are you for or against union with the Church of England? Why/Why not?' In answering for or against union respondents gave reasons that can be listed under the following eight headings.

(1) Ethical: Methodists do not drink or gamble, etc., Anglicans do.

(2) Communal: we feel at home in Methodism, we are free and easy, we can talk before the service, etc.

(3) 'Liturgical' (but closely related to (2)): freedom and simplicity of worship in Methodism (in fact Methodist services follow a rigidly conventional form), no elaborate buildings or vestments.

(4) Closed table: Methodists cannot attend Church of England Communion, but they can come to ours.

(5) Theological: Methodists hold certain beliefs that are different from the Church of England.

(6) Organisational: it is a take-over, we will be swallowed up, we are more democratic than the Church of England.

(7) Common sense: silly to duplicate organisations when we both have falling numbers.

(8) There is no difference of any importance between Methodism and other Christian religions.

I divided the respondents into three groups: regular attenders (attending at least once a week), irregular attenders (less than once a week) and non-attenders. The range of views expressed by the regular attenders was similar to views expressed by the members who were not questioned because they and their views were already well-known. The results are as shown in Table 9.

Table 9.　*Methodist attitudes towards Anglican–Methodist union*

		1	2	3	4	5	6	7	8	Don't know	Other	No reason
Regular attenders	(58)	–	–	–	–	–	–	–	–			
For union	(10)	–	3	2	1	1	–	2	–		1	2
Against union	(38)	6	10	15	7	14	8	–	1		2	3
Don't know	(10)	–	–	1	–	–	–	–	–	2	1	2
Irregular attenders	(3)	–	–	–	–	–	–	–	–			
Against union	(1)	–	–	–	–	–	–	–	–			1
Don't know	(2)	1	–	–	–	–	–	–	–	1		
Non-attenders	(16)a	–	–	–	–	–	–	–	–			
For union	(1)	–	–	–	–	–	1	–	–			
Against union	(10)	4	–	4	–	2	1	–	1	1		1
Don't know	(4)	–	–	1	–	–	–	–	2	1		
Totals	(76)a	–	–	–	–	–	–	–	–			
For	(11)	–	3	2	1	1	1	2	–		1	2
Against	(49)	10	10	19	7	16	9	–	2	1	2	5
Don't know	(16)	1	–	–	–	–	–	–	2	4	1	2

Notes: a One no response.
The number of reasons given exceeds the number of respondents because some respondents gave more than one reason.

Thus out of 76 reasons for not supporting union with the Church of England, ethical and communal reasons account for 20. The question of the closed table may also be counted as a communal reason as it entails resentment at lack of reciprocity on the part of the Church of England membership. We might also add the liturgical reasons to our communal grouping, as this seems to represent a preference for the familiar and homely as compared with remote and awesome ritual. By this count, 46 of the 76 responses are accounted for by ethical and communal reasons.

Two other interesting factors are shown up by Table 9: firstly, regular attenders are, when questioned in private, more favourably disposed to union than they indicate in public meetings. Secondly, there is no complete coherence of opinion amongst the Methodists, some are against union, but are unable to say why, and different Methodists give the same kinds of reasons for and against the idea of union.

APPENDIX III

The religious statistics

The figures for Methodist membership and adherence are reported here with very little comment. In introducing these figures only two comments are necessary: firstly, I must reiterate the difficulty of interpreting membership and adherence, because some of the most active Methodists were never formally members of the local society. It is impossible to tell how the totals for adherents were arrived at, or whether an element of multiple counting arises from the method used to arrive at the total for adherence. Secondly, these figures are presented to show the general and long-term trends of support for Methodism and to put on record such statistical data as were collected in the course of research. No detailed interpretation of these figures is possible.

Waterhouses P.M. circuit, members and adherents

Table 10

Year	Members	Adherents	Total
1892	148	500	648
1896	154	500	654
1901	340	1,000	1,340
1906	310	1,140	1,450
1911	305	1,410	1,715
1916	280	1,450	1,730
1921	276	1,450	1,726
1926	263	810	1,073
1931	197	440	637

Waterhouses P.M. circuit, Sunday schools
The returns report the number of children registered; a careful study of the Waterhouses Sunday school register from 1890–1930 suggests that registrations were increasingly in excess of attendance. On the

assumption that this was so for all the villages in the circuit, we apply the 'Waterhouses Ratio' to the registration.

Table 11

Year	Registration	Ratio	Adjusted total
1892	594	0·82	487
1896	703	0·59	415
1901	667	0·55	366
1911	669	0·31	192
1921	652	0·27	176

W.M.s

No early records survive.

Table 12. *Members*

Year	Waterhouses	Esh Winning[a]	Quebec	Total
1911	40	90	25	155
1916	39	81	41	160
1920	40	80	34	174
1932	22	136	15	173

Note: [a] In 1921 there were also 150 'hearers' and in 1931 59 hearers in the mornings and 72 in the evenings.

METHODISM: AMALGAMATION AND AFTER

Table 13. *Memberships*

	1935	1936	1941	1946	1951	1956	1961	1968
Esh Winning (voluntary amalgamation)	131	131	103	116	84	112	133	100
Lymington Tce (ex-P.M.)	10	10	–	–	–	–	–	–
Waterhouses (ex-P.M.)	72	71	52	42	44	41	41	} 52
Waterhouses (ex-W.M.)	22	19	24	25	28	32	30	
Quebec (amalgamated by closures)	46	36	14	13	21	25	27	–
Cornsay Colliery (ex-M.N.C.)	34	29	30	37	37	–	–	–
Total	315	296	223	233	214	210	231	152

OTHER NON-CONFORMISTS

The Baptist membership was drawn from the whole of the valley and membership is given as the number of adults baptised as adults. The earliest indication of attendances is given at the end of 1901 when it was thought that the chapel, seating 200, should be enlarged. In 1918 there were 291 members, in 1932, 187 and in 1961, 298. The Salvation Army was active in the valley in the 1920s, but no records survive. The building used by the Army was accidentally burnt down.

ROMAN CATHOLICS

From 1880 to 1900 the Catholics recommend, on the basis of the 1881 Census, multiplying the number of infant baptisms by 28·5 to arrive at the adult Catholic population. From 1912–14 they make estimates on a different but unstated basis. I have, nevertheless, used the Catholics' own estimates. This therefore includes a substantial number of the young and very young for whom 'membership' has a quite different meaning from both the Church of England and the Methodists (see p. 71).

THE CHURCH OF ENGLAND

Finding reliable membership figures for the Church of England is, according to Highet, 'probably an insoluble problem for the researcher...' (J. Highet, 'Making Sense of Religious Statistics', unpublished, 1966, pp. 13–14). Opinions vary as to the reliability of Easter communicant figures and the electoral roll. The few communion figures available are cited, and the electoral roll figures are as shown in Table 14, recorded from 1931 only.

Table 14. *Church of England: electoral roll*

	1931	1936	1941	1946	1951	1956	1961	1966
Hamsteels	237	369	369	369	369	369	–	190
Waterhouses	330	981	867	867	867	867	–	150

Note: In both cases 1941–56 appear to be cases of recording the same figure as the previous year.

APPENDIX IV

Occupational status, social mobility and the structure of Methodist leadership

THE OCCUPATIONAL STRUCTURE OF THE POPULATION

The villages have been one-industry villages throughout their history; the extent of this is indicated by the registrar general's decennial census figures.

Table 15. *Brandon and Byshottles U.D.: percentage of total occupied men engaged in coal-mines, 1901–51*

1901	1911	1921	1931	1951
76·1	78·2	74·9	63·4	47·6

The category 'engaged in coal-mines' includes many actual occupations and does not distinguish between 'miners' and other workers in the coal industry. An approximate breakdown of the occupational structure is shown by an analysis of the registration of births and deaths carried out for 1910 and 1930 (Table 16). These may be compared with *colliery* household occupancy for 1889 in Esh Winning and Waterhouses, as shown in Table 17.

The results of this analysis suggest that the villages studied had a higher proportion of mine-workers than the urban district. This is a sensible finding, the eastern end of the district including larger villages closer to Durham City. By 1961 mining was a rapidly declining local industry. Taylor, on the basis of his 10% sample, gives the occupational structure for Esh Winning and Waterhouses as shown in Table 18.

Of the 88 miners in both villages in Taylor's sample, 53 worked in their home colliery. Even if we assumed that all the O.A.P.s had been miners, the drop in mining occupations since 1930 would still be very marked. Taylor noted that whilst 50% of the *active* persons in Esh Winning were miners a great variety of occupations (20 in all) are found in the village.

Table 16. *Esh Winning, Cornsay Colliery and Quebec: percentage births and deaths by occupation*[a]

Occupation	1910		1930	
Miner	72·2		55·4	
Mining official	1·7		1·1	
T.U. official	0·7	90·8	–	77·4
Other in mining (incl. coke)	13·7		18·9	
Mining craftsmen	2·5		2·0	
Shopworker	1·0		1·9	
Shopkeeper and services	3·3	5·6	2·0	5·9
White collar, minor professional	1·3		2·0	
Manual unskilled	1·9		6·6	
Manual semi-skilled	0·1	3·4	3·4	13·1
Manual skilled	1·3		2·8	
Self-employed crafts	0·1		0·3	
Other	–		1·8	

Note: [a] Totals 1908–12 and 1928–31, averaged births and deaths by occupation of father or husband for children and women.

Table 17. *Colliery household occupancy, Esh Winning and Waterhouses, 1889*

	No.	%
Miner	270	71
Mining official	32	8
Others in mining (incl. coke workers)	55	14
Mechanics, enginemen, etc.	21	5
Minor professional	5	1
Total	383	100

Source: Manager's Report to Owners, 1889.

In summary it may be said that up until the Second World War at least 70% of the male population were in mining. (Albeit unemployed in mining; for periods Esh Winning closed, from 1932 until 1941, and Waterhouses worked at reduced output. Quebec-Hamsteels closed in 1926.) Of this, 50% to 70% were miners as such. About 1% were mining officials and a further 1% union officials. Between 10% and 20% worked at the pit-head or in the coke yards. An unknown number worked in the large brick and pipeworks at Cornsay Colliery and the smaller Lymington Brick Flat (which closed early in the century). About 4% of the population were involved in keeping or working in shops.

Table 18. *Occupational structure for Esh Winning and Waterhouses, 1961*

Occupation	Waterhouses	E.W.
	%	%
Miner	22·5	31·0
Mining official	3·7	0·9
Driver/conductor	7·5	3·2
Building workers	6·5	3·2
Other	21·5	25·1
Redundant	11·1	3·3
Widows/spinsters	7·3	5·6
O.A.P.s	19·9	27·7

Source: Taylor, *Implication of Migration*, Tables 7 and 9, pp. 43, 47.

INDIVIDUAL MOBILITY

Occupational status

According to accounts given, the miner occupied an élite status in the village. Ambiguities are concealed by such accounts. Being 'a miner' entails passing through a particular occupational cycle. Starting as a pit-lad, perhaps driving the ponies, a young man might graduate to putting after a few years below ground. As a putter he would hope to become a hewer. As a putter or hewer a man would work on piece-work, being paid for his output of coal either as a member of a hewing team or individually as a putter. When too old to hew a man might return to the surface where he would work on the spoil heap, in the lamp cabin, or around the yard as a labourer, until he retired.

The high status ascribed to the hewer is based on the notion that he is doing 'a man's job'; his strength, skill and independence is recognised by managers and 'marrers' alike (see Glossary). His high status is also due to high earning power and high wages. Nonetheless the term 'miner' is used rather indiscriminately of any man who has moved beyond being a pit-lad. The term is also used, especially by women, of any man working in the coal-trade.

The status of a man in the pit-yard is more difficult to ascertain, as is the status of the retired miner. A man who never became or who never tried to become a hewer might occupy a relatively low status. An old or disabled hewer might retain his past reputation as a worker or high wage-earner. Age itself confers some status. A few might enjoy high status through holding an important office in the union lodge. But the ex-hewer would have the same comparatively low earnings as other surface workers.

Within mining status is not based on any one single factor. In such close-knit communities as mining villages it might be more accurate to say that status depends on many factors, including those extrinsic to work. Traditional factors operate in so far as a man's family has been known in the village for more than one generation. Every side of the man is known and rated accordingly. Relevant factors include his position at work, office-holding in the union, recreational or religious organisation, 'respectability', occupation of positions of power or authority in local government, political parties or the judiciary. One can have more or less status and power from any one of these sources and they are probably additive.

Mining villagers are themselves very unclear as to the status hierarchy, probably because it exists not absolutely, but in context. Differences of status are frequently denied although obviously implicit. When asked about the status structure respondents tend to express solidaristic sentiments. They say 'we're all the same' or 'there are no class differences', 'we stick together'. In the face of external threat (or the interview situation) considerations of solidarity are more relevant than status-ascription. The ascription of status is circumstantial, not intrinsic.

Nevertheless it probably remains true to say that the most salient status-conferring factors are class factors, in that they relate to 'specific causal components of life chances, insofar as this component is represented exclusively by economic interest in the possession of. . . opportunities for income' (Gerth and Mills (eds.), *From Max Weber*, p. 181) in a labour market. This seems to be the case in a double sense; the hewer possesses *skills* which give him opportunities in the labour market, and he has a *position* in the productive process which gives him a strong bargaining position *vis-à-vis* the management. Thus class position derived from mining is the basic factor in status, but to this factor can be added the others listed above.

Status and class considerations raise difficulties in locating mining occupations in the whole status spectrum. These arise in part from the miners' own ambivalence towards his work. While mining is a man's job, bringing in good wages, it is also dirty, dangerous and relatively insecure. The shopkeeper is relatively independent, his independence is assured by capital rather than skills, his job is clean and he may receive a high income. The shopkeeper *may* feel that the miner occupies a lower status than himself, but nevertheless he is himself directly dependent on the miners for his income and thus indirectly dependent on the colliery employers also.

According to miners, clerks do easy work. But in the 1930s especially and since the Second World War white-collar jobs offered greater security than mining. Miners value the education which gives access to such occupation but the social mobility entailed threatens the tight-knit community by removing sons and daughters geographically and perhaps making them feel superior.

It is very difficult to proceed from a statement of the occupational structure to a statement about a status system. The idea of a status 'system' with its implication of coherence either for individual or the sociologist is unhelpful. A villager's view of status depends on the *point of view*; it was and is complicated by the ambiguities in rating occupations themselves and occupations *vis-à-vis* others. The sociologists cannot impose a simple scheme upon this.

In our estimation the status hierarchies are as follows:

Methodists' view of occupational status
   (1) white collar and minor professional;
   (2) shopkeeper;
   (3) personal services (*not* domestic service), shopworkers;
   (4) manual skilled: mining official, miners' official;
   (5) miner (respondents' highest occupation in mining considered) – semi-skilled manual;
   (6) unskilled manual, including unskilled in mining (respondents' highest occupation in mining considered);
   (7) unemployed.

Non-Methodists' view of occupational status
   (1) white collar, minor professional;
   (2) shopkeeper;
   (3) all workers involved in mining, including officials;
   (4) skilled manual;
   (5) semi-skilled manual;
   (6) unskilled manual;
   (7) shopworker, personal services;
   (8) unemployed.

These are not the actual rankings given by respondents; the Methodist ranking has been inferred. The non-Methodist ranking, while in the correct direction from the Methodist ranking, deliberately exaggerates the high status of all mining workers and this probably does less than justice to ambiguities.

We now compare the inter-generational mobility of Methodists and non-Methodists on the two scales shown in Tables 19 and 20 (abbreviations used in the table: F – respondent's father; R – respondent; S – respondent's son).

Table 19. *Social mobility, Methodist scale: respondent, father and son*

	Up	Down	Static	N.A./D.K.		Up	Down	Static	N.A./D.K.
Methodist									
F – R	21	19	19	3	R – S	23	5	2	–
Non-Methodist									
F – R	22	13	10	9	R – S	12	9	7	–

No significant differences	Significant at $P = 5$ (almost at $P = 2\cdot5$)

Table 20. *Social mobility, non-Methodist: respondent, father and son*

	Up	Down	Static	N.A./D.K.		Up	Down	Static
Methodist								
F – R	18	13	28	3	R – S	13	15	1
Non-Methodist								
F – R	13	15	17	9	R – S	13	11	4

No significant differences	No significant differences

These tables were constructed by working through a list of the Methodists and entering the occupations of fathers and sons. The non-Methodists were 54 persons drawn at random from the electoral register, from which known Methodists were excluded. Undergraduates as part of their research technique training collected various data from this sample. Only the occupational data were embodied in this research. Like every other attempt to collect statistical data (most of these attempts are not even reported here) we have produced little that is either unambiguous or especially valuable.

The only significant finding is that Methodists' sons have been upwardly mobile according to Methodists' evaluations of social status. This suggests that the evaluation of status by Methodists may in part be based on the experience of the Methodists' sons. This degree of ambiguity is unacceptable and cannot be resolved.

METHODIST LEADERSHIP

Leaders and activists: P.M.s
Local preachers   Of the 1894 list of 19 preachers, 12 have been assigned
an occupation by their surviving contemporaries: 5 were coal-hewers;
3 were mining officials; 2 worked in the coke-yard; 1 was a shopkeeper,
another the school attendance officer; 1 other has been identified as
certainly not a miner. Two of these preachers (including one of the
hewers) later became ministers. Here the researcher tends to be at the
mercy of an informant: in reporting miners they seem to mention the
subject's prime, e.g. a hewer. For non-miners or the socially mobile,
they mention the terminal occupation. Comments on social mobility as
such, were common in the course of interviews.

In 1910, 24 out of 26 have been assigned to their occupations (1 of the
2 remaining is a woman, probably a housewife): 8 were miners and 1
miner's wife, 1 miner's daughter; 2 were officials; 6 shopkeepers and
shop-workers, a farmer, the station master, schoolmaster, attendance
officer, a missionary and clerk make up the remainder of the list. One
of the miners became checkweighman and another an insurance agent.

Of the 1930 list, 6 out of 8 have been identified; 1 was each of the
following – miner, checkweighman, official, greengrocer, shopkeeper,
insurance agent.

Depending on the occupation to which one assigns the unknown we
have the following percentage distribution of miners and officials: 1894,
26–58% miners, 16–50% officials; in 1910, 36–45% miners, about 8%
officials; In 1930 the very small list suggests a fairly evenly mixed
group, excluding non-mining manual occupations.

Sunday school teachers   The only data available are those relating to
Waterhouses from 1890 and 1909 and Cornsay Colliery M.N.C. from
1931 to 1951. Waterhouses lists 18 teachers in 1890; 15 have been
identified, of whom 14 are in the coal-trade (12 miners). The other is
a railway signalman. In 1900 there are 19 names: 14 are of men in the
coal-trade (12 hewers), 3 officials and 2 remain unidentified. In 1909 out
of 15 men listed, 7 are miners, 2 officials. Also in this list are the
station master, missionary, attendance officer, a shopkeeper and insurance agent. Some names appear on two lists, and some on all three,
including the superintendent who was a coal-hewer (and lodge chairman latterly).
The trustees   Trustees are responsible for church property. It has
been suggested that they were often chosen from among businessmen

and would thus not be representative of Methodism as a whole. Furthermore, being a trustee does not necessarily entail any active participation in the life of the chapels. Nevertheless many trustees were active participants and the lists certainly show who the local Methodists regard as suitable for the responsibility of being a trustee. Trustees were not democratically elected; they chose their own membership and replacements.

Quebec, 1874: colliery manager, overman, surveyor, engineer, brickmaker (all officials). *1905*: 8 miners, banksman, salesman, clerk and a farmer. *1908*: 13 miners, deputy, checkweighman, 3 shopkeepers. *1929*: 9 miners, checkweighman, signalman, clerk, salesman, 3 shopkeepers, 2 housewives and an 'agent'. *1937*: 4 miners, 3 shopkeepers, haulier, commercial traveller, 2 retired men, 2 housewives, 2 widows. The fractions of miners are roughly as follows – 1874: nil, 1905: 3/5, 1908: 1/2, 1937: 1/4.

Waterhouses, 1897: 10 miners, small runner, coke-burner, surveyor (i.e. two officials), shopkeeper (3/4 miners). *1906*: 9 miners, 2 officials, 2 other workers in coal-trade, insurance agent, 1 retired man, 2 occupations unknown (1/2 miners). 5 miners, 1 labourer, signalman, 2 teachers, store manager and 2 salesmen, 3 not known (1/3 miners).

Leaders and activists: M.N.C.
Local preachers   The New Connexion was part of the Durham circuit with whom it therefore shared preachers. P.M. and W.M. local preachers also preached regularly at the New Connexion Chapel in Cornsay Colliery. There do not appear to have been more than one or two local New Connexion preachers.

Sunday school teachers   One register survives only, the 1931–51 volume. Two teachers appear throughout the period (one married the other's daughter). Two appear from 1931 to 1941 and 1941 to 1951 respectively. *1931*: 5 teachers were miners, 2 were officials, 1 a brickyard worker, the 3 remaining on the list were a clerk, a butcher and a student respectively (one miner was lodge secretary for a while, the student became the archivist of the Methodist church). *1941*: 3 miners, 1 retired official and a clerk. *1951*: 2 retired officials, a school caretaker, a miner, colliery electrician, a travelling shop-owner and an autobagger operator.

Trustees   No information is available. During the early life of the chapel the building was probably the property of Ferens and Love, on whose colliery ground the building stood. One important factor in the M.N.C. was the prominence of both Ferens and Love in the Connexion. Both held office locally and Love was a national benefactor of the

M.N.C. and other non-conformist churches. No other chapel in the Deerness Valley had such a direct connection with management – a connection reinforced by the manager and an under manager being locally very active in the life of the chapel.

Leaders and activists: W.M.s
Local preachers   The Crook circuit was geographically very extensive, so only those preachers were considered who were resident in the four villages studied. In 1901 there were 10 local preachers: 4 were miners, 1 a coke-worker, 1 was an official, another a blacksmith. The remaining 3 were a signalman, store clerk, and store departmental manager respectively. The clerk became a manager, the blacksmith a senior union official, and one miner became a Methodist minister. In 1911 out of 12 preachers; 3 were miners, 1 a coke-worker. Two officials and a blacksmith complete the list of mining occupations. The remainder were: railway clerk, an insurance agent, a store grocer (became a manager). Two occupations are unknown. One preacher whose occupation is not known became a minister.

In 1920 the list was a follows (total of 12): 4 miners, 2 officials, 1 coke-worker, a council workman, union official, a cashier and a grocer from the store, 1 unknown. One official became a self-employed baker. In 1934 (the year of effective union with the P.M.s) the list was as follows (total of 11); 1 miner, 6 shopkeepers, a store cashier, schoolteacher, signalman and housewife.

Sunday school teachers   No records available.

Trustees   The names of all the trustees have been found; these indicate the wide extent of multiple membership. A Methodist might be a trustee of three or four chapels. Some non-W.M.s were also trustees of W.M. chapels.

Fortunately more interesting lists of the leaders' meetings for all the chapels are available; the leaders are the day-to-day organisers and initiators of chapel activities.

Leaders' meetings
Waterhouses, 1911: 1 miner, small runner, blacksmith, 5 store workers and a railway clerk. *1920*: 1 miner, small runner, electrician, horse-keeper, haulier, 2 store workers, one not known.

Esh Winning, 1911: 6 miners, 1 store worker. *1920*: 8 miners, 2 miners' wives, a roadmender, one not known.

No simple conclusions can be drawn from these Wesleyan data. The management and workers at the Waterhouses store were prominent

both as preachers and chapel leaders. Quebec was throughout dominated by miners. Waterhouses and Quebec are quite sharply contrasted
in their leaders, but Esh Winning seems to change over time, although
the 'not known' categories are of crucial significance in deciding
whether this is a real or apparent change.

Leaders and activists: amalgamated Methodists
Local preachers　After a series of administrative rearrangements leading to the formation of the Brandon and Deerness Valley circuit in 1936
the P.M., W.M., and M.N.C. *Plans* were amalgamated and membership
confined mainly to the valley. The effect of this was to widen the catch-
ment area for the P.M.s, reduce it for the W.M.s and the M.N.C.; at
the same time *local* preachers became a small part of the total preachers
available for the villages. In 1968 the *Plan* was made up as follows: 3
retired miners and one self-employed baker.

Sunday school teachers　By the 1960s the number of school teachers
had fallen dramatically. There were none at Quebec or Cornsay, and
the Sunday schools finished in Waterhouses after a semi-skilled worker
had attempted to keep a small school going at the ex-P.M. chapel,
until 1968. At Esh Winning the superintendent was the local newsagent,
assisted by a retired schoolteacher, a hairdresser and two or three
housewives, plus teenage helpers.

Trustees　Of the 12 Russell Street (ex-W.M.) trustees who lived locally
in 1968, 9 were old-age pensioners; 1 a housewife, 1 a small proprietor
and another a headmistress. With one exception the pensioners were
miners' wives. This pattern of elderly, retired trustees was repeated in
Esh Winning.

Leaders' meeting
　Waterhouses: 2 clerks, 1 music teacher, 1 semi-skilled worker, 2
housewives (ex-P.M.), 1 schoolteacher, 1 retired miner, 2 housewives
(ex-W.M.).
　Esh Winning: Brickworks manager, 5 retired miners, 1 hairdresser,
1 semi-skilled worker, 4 housewives, retired schoolteacher, newsagent.

Other activists
　The P.M. circuit executive in 1916 consisted of the full-time missionary, a shopkeeper and a coke-worker. This executive body seems to
have been short-lived.
　Quebec was not well covered by the records, but an attempt was
made to discover the 'leading lights' of these chapels (to use the res-

252

pondents' term). The occupations were then obtained independently. The period in question is 1908–12, or 'just before the War'. Out of 12 P.M. names given 10 were miners, 1 a coke-worker and the other a shopkeeper. Out of 11 Wesleyan Methodists listed, 4 were miners, 5 officials, 2 Co-op. workers.

The suggestion that shopkeepers tended to be Methodists is not borne out by the evidence. In 1908 the Esh Winning shopkeepers had the religious affiliations shown in Table 21.

Table 21: *Esh Winning shopkeepers' 1908 religious affiliation*

Religion	No.	%
Methodist[a]	6	15
Baptist	11	27
Roman Catholic	6	15
Nothing	15	37
Not known	3	7
Total	41	101

Note. [a] Includes: 4 P.M.s, 1 W.M., 1 Methodist D.K.

In the late 1960s there were only 2 active Methodist shopkeepers, and 1 Methodist who was married to the director of a small chain of shops.

NOTES

INTRODUCTION

1. H. T. Buckle, *History of Civilisation in England* (2 vols, Parker, Son and Brown, 1858 (2nd ed.) and 1861), introduction to vol. II.
2. W. E. H. Lecky, *Rationalism in Europe* (Longmans, Green and Co., 1865), pp. 408–9.
3. Quoted in J. D. Y. Peel, *Herbert Spencer* (Heinemann, 1971), p. 231.
4. See G. Himmelfarb, *Victorian Minds* (Weidenfeld and Nicolson, 1968), pp. 292–9.
5. See, for example, W. J. Townsend (ed.), *A New History of Methodism* (2 vols., Hodder and Stoughton, 1909), vol. I, p. 371.
6. A. Toynbee, *Lectures on the Industrial Revolution of the Eighteenth Century in England* (Longmans, Green and Co., 1896). See, for example, the discussion of the growth of pauperism, pp. 93–105.
7. Ibid., p. 24.
8. Ibid., p. 86.
9. Ibid., pp. 218–19.
10. Ibid., pp. 203–21.
11. Ibid., pp. 148–9.
12. J. Gould and W. L. Kolb, *A Dictionary of the Social Sciences* (Tavistock Publications, 1964), 'Industrial Revolution'.
13. C. Crouch and D. Martin, 'England', in M. S. Archer and S. Giner (eds.), *Contemporary Europe* (Weidenfeld and Nicolson, 1971), especially pp. 268–72.
14. W. E. H. Lecky, *A History of England in the Eighteenth Century* (8 vols., Longmans, Green and Co., 1878–90), vol. II, pp. 637–8.
15. Townsend (ed.), *New History of Methodism*, vol. I, p. 371.
16. Ibid., p. 370.
17. E. Halévy, 'La Naissance du Méthodisme en Angleterre', *La Revue de Paris* (August 1906), pp. 519–39 and 841–67. *Idem, Histoire du Peuple Anglais au XIX⁰ Siècle* (Librairie Hachette et Cie, 1912–). This was translated under the title *History of the English People in the 19th Century*, as follows: *vol. 1 – A History of the English People in 1815*, trans. E. Watkins and D. A. Barker (T. Fisher Unwin, 1924); *England in 1815*, same trans. (Ernest Benn, 1949): *vol. 2 – A History of the English People 1815–1830*, trans. E. Watkins (T. Fisher Unwin, 1926); *The Liberal Awakening 1815–1830*, same trans. (Ernest Benn, 1949): *vol. 3 – A History of the English People 1830–1841*, trans. E. Watkins (T. Fisher Unwin, 1927); *The Triumph of Reform 1830–1841*, same trans. (Ernest Benn, 1950): *vol. 4 – The Age of Peel and Cobden: A History of the English People 1841–1852*, trans. E. Watkins (Ernest Benn, 1947); *Victorian Years 1841–1895*, same trans. (Ernest

Benn, 1951): *vol. 5 – A History of the English People 1895–1905*, trans. E. Watkins (Ernest Benn, 1929); *Imperialism and the Rise of Labour*, same trans. (Ernest Benn, 1951): *vol. 6 – A History of the English People 1905–1915*, trans E. Watkins (Ernest Benn, 1934); *The Rule of Democracy 1905–1914*, books 1 and 2, same trans. (Ernest Benn, 1952). Citation here – Halévy, *History*, trans. Watkins and Barker, vol. 1, *England in 1915*.

18. See my article, 'The Political Effects of Village Methodism', in *A Sociological Yearbook of Religion in Britain*, ed. M. Hill (S.C.M. Press, 1973), pp. 156–82.
19. Halévy, 'La Naissance', p. 524.
20. Ibid., p. 864.
21. Halévy, *History*, trans. Watkins, vol. 4, *Victorian Years 1841–1895*, p. 395.
22. This translation reads ambiguously: the original suggests that a more accurate rendering would be 'the elite of the working class *and* the hard-working and capable bourgeoisie' – 'Un régime de production effectivement anarchique pourrait mettre le royaume en état d'insurrection, si seulement la classe ouvrière trouvait dans la classe moyenne des hommes pour lui donner un idéal, une doctrine, un programme d'action définie. Mais l'élite de la class ouvrière, la bourgeoisie laborieuse, sont, par l'effet du réveil évangélique, animées d'un espirit qui n'a rien de dangereux pour l'ordre établi.'
    The comment in the last sentence is one to be echoed by Wearmouth in his discussion of the nineteenth century: 'These leaders were not revolutionaries. By their integrity and uprightness they demonstrated to the rulers of the land that the country had nothing to fear from the leaders of working men' – R. F. Wearmouth, *The Social and Political Influence of Methodism in the Twentieth Century* (Epworth Press, 1957), p. 245.
23. Halévy, 'La Naissance', p. 539.
24. C. Gillispie, 'The Work of Elie Halévy', *Journal of Modern History*, 22 (1950), 239.
25. Ibid., p. 244.
26. A. MacIntyre, *Secularisation and Moral Change* (C.U.P., 1967), p. 24.
27. Himmelfarb, *Victorian Minds*, pp. 298–9.
28. J. L. and B. Hammond, *The Town Labourer 1760–1832* (2 vols., Guild Books, 1949), vol. II, p. 100.
29. Ibid., pp. 100 and 106.
30. G. Semmel, 'The Halévy Thesis', *Encounter* (July 1971), pp. 52–3.
31. E. Hobsbawm, 'Methodism and the Threat of Revolution in Britain' in his *Labouring Men* (Weidenfeld and Nicolson, 1968), pp. 23–33.
32. Ibid., p. 33.
33. E. P. Thompson, *The Making of the English Working Class* (Penguin Books, 1968).
34. Ibid., p. 390.
35. Ibid., p. 918. See also Thompson's 'Time, Work-Discipline, and Industrial Capitalism', *Past and Present*, no. 38 (December 1967), pp. 56–97.
36. *Making of the English Working Class*, pp. 392–3.
37. Ibid., p. 424.
38. Ibid., p. 433.
39. Ibid., p. 411.
40. Ibid., p. 215.
41. Ibid., p. 416.
42. Ibid., p. 417.

43. R. F. Wearmouth, *Methodism and the Struggle of the Working Classes, 1850–1900* (Edgar Bachus, 1954), p. 125.

44. H. Richard Niebuhr, *The Social Sources of Denominationalism* (Meridian Books, 1957), p. 67.

45. Wearmouth, *Methodism and the Struggle*, p. 146.

46. Ibid., p. 149.

47. Ibid., p. 183.

48. Wearmouth, *The Social and Political Influence*, pp. 111, 127–38, 244–5.

49. Wearmouth, *Methodism and the Struggle*, p. 189.

50. Wearmouth, *The Social and Political Influence*, p. 111.

51. M. Weber, *Economy and Society* (Bedminster Press, 1968), p. 593.

52. D. Lockwood, 'Sources of Variation in Working Class Images of Society', *Sociological Review*, 14, no. 3 (November 1966), 249–67.

53. Ibid., p. 255.

54. N. Dennis, F. Henriques and C. Slaughter, *Coal Is Our Life* (Tavistock Publications, 1969), p. 130.

55. Ibid., p. 142.

56. Ibid., pp. 169–70.

57. See F. Parkin, 'Working Class Conservatives: a Theory of Political Deviance', *British Journal of Sociology*, XVIII, no. 3 (1967), 278–90.

58. R. Moore, 'History, Economics and Religion', in A. Sahay (ed.), *Max Weber and Modern Sociology* (Routledge and Kegan Paul, 1971), pp. 82–96.

59. M. Weber, *The Protestant Ethic and the Spirit of Capitalism* (Unwin University Books, 1965), p. 177.

60. Weber, *Economy and Society*, pp. 541–56.

61. Ibid., p. 543.

62. Ibid., p. 593.

63. Ibid.

64. Ibid., p. 484.

65. Ibid., p. 491.

66. Ibid., p. 486.

67. Ibid., p. 593.

68. Quoted by W. S. F. Pickering, 'The Place of Religion in the Social Structure of Two English Industrial Towns', unpublished Ph.D. thesis (University of London, 1958), p. XII. 32.

69. It is important to note that Pauline functionalism might lend itself to the development of rigid social stratification. A caste system, for example, could be based on the notion of all having immutable functions to perform. An extremely hierarchical structure could develop either from this or from any organismic theory where some talents were thought to be nobler or more sacred than others. We can only note, as an empirical observation, that this is not the case in general in Western Protestantism.

70. Weber, *Economy and Society*, pp. 490–2.

71. D. Martin, 'The Unknown Gods of the English', *The Advancement of Science*, 23, no. 108 (June 1966), 56–60.

72. Pickering, 'The Place of Religion', p. XII. 31.

73. This distinction is derived from F. Tonnies' formulation in *Gemeinschaft und Gesellschaft* (1887), ed. and trans., as *Community and Society*, by C. P. Loomis (Harper Torchbooks, 1957).

74. L. Pope, *Millhands and Preachers* (Yale University Press, 1965).

1: HISTORICAL BACKGROUND

1. W. H. B. Court, *Coal* (H.M.S.O., London, 1951), p. 5.
2. W. H. B. Court, *A Concise Economic History of Britain* (C.U.P., 1954), p. 254.
3. Ibid., pp. 195–6.
4. Ibid., p. 215.
5. Ibid., pp. 231–2.
6. H. Pelling, *Modern Britain, 1885–1955* (Sphere Books, 1969), p. 25; D. Read, *Edwardian England* (Harrap, 1972), pp. 118–19.
7. Read, ibid., p. 120.
8. Ibid.
9. Court, *Coal*, p. 13.
10. Ibid., p. 12.
11. W. R. Garside, *The Durham Miners, 1919–1960* (George Allen and Unwin, 1971), epilogue, pp. 500–9.
12. Ibid., p. 391.
13. H. Clegg, A. Fox and A. F. Thompson, *A History of the British Trade Unions since 1889*; vol. I, *1889–1910* (O.U.P., 1964), p. 96.
14. Ibid., p. 90.
15. F. Bealey, and H. Pelling, *Labour and Politics, 1900–1906* (Macmillan, 1958), p. 58.
16. Clegg *et al.*, *History of the British Trade Unions*, p. 315.
17. Ibid.
18. Bealey and Pelling, *Labour and Politics*, p. 83.
19. H. Pelling, *A Short History of the Labour Party* (Macmillan, 1972), p. 11.
20. Pelling, *Modern Britain*, pp. 15–18.
21. Pelling, *A Short History*, p. 1.
22. Ibid., p. 3.
23. Bealey and Pelling, *Labour and Politics*, pp. 141ff.
24. Pelling, *Modern Britain*, pp. 56–7.
25. Bealey and Pelling, *Labour and Politics*, p. 274.
26. Clegg *et al.*, *History of the British Trade Unions*, p. 99.
27. Ibid., pp. 106–11; R. Page Arnot, *The Miners, 1889–1910: A History of the Miners' Federation of Great Britain* (George Allen and Unwin, 1949), Chapter VIII.
28. E. Welbourne, *The Miners' Unions of Northumberland and Durham* (C.U.P., 1923), Chaps. IV and VI; R. Fynes, *The Miners of Northumberland and Durham* (Thomas Summerbell, Sunderland, 1873), Chaps. IV–VIII, XI–XXIII and XXXIX–XLII; E. W. Evans, *The Miners of South Wales* (University of Wales Press, 1961), Chaps. 3 and 4; J. E. Williams, *The Derbyshire Miners* (George Allen and Unwin, 1962), Chap. III.
29. Evans, *Miners of South Wales*, p. 216.
30. Williams, *Derbyshire Miners*, pp. 303, 376, 416 and Chap. XII; Evans, *Miners of South Wales*, pp. 45, 137–9, 188–9.
31. Williams, *Derbyshire Miners*, p. 276.
32. Arnot, *The Miners*, p. 61.
33. Evans, *Miners of South Wales*, pp. 147–8.
34. Arnot, *The Miners*, p. 223.
35. Williams, *Derbyshire Miners*, p. 338.

36. Evans, *Miners of South Wales,* Chapter XI.
37. Ibid., p. 191.
38. Clegg *et al., History of the British Trade Unions,* p. 242.
39. Ibid., p. 241.
40. Arnot, *The Miners,* p. 370.
41. Court, *Concise Economic History,* p. 286.
42. Clegg *et al., History of the British Trade Unions,* p. 99.
43. Ibid., p. 103.
44. Ibid., p. 240n.
45. Ibid.
46. Arnot, *The Miners,* p. 189.
47. Ibid., p. 323.
48. S. Webb, *The Story of the Durham Miners, 1662–1921* (The Fabian Society, 1921), pp. 83–4. Webb also remarked on the fact that the Durham miners shared the owners' economic outlook (p. 82).
49. Arnot, *The Miners,* p. 190.
50. Personal communication from R. Gregory.
51. W. Kendal, *The Revolutionary Movement in Britain, 1900–1921* (Weidenfeld and Nicolson, 1969), p. 16.
52. R. Page Arnot, *The Miners, Years of Struggle: a History of the Miners' Federation of Great Britain from 1910 onwards* (George Allen and Unwin, 1953), pp. 115–18.
53. I am very grateful to Professor Hugh Clegg for letting me read the early drafts of Chapters I and II of the proposed second volume of his history of the British trade union movement. I have drawn on this unpublished work for this part of the present chapter.
54. G. Dangerfield, *The Strange Death of Liberal England* (Constable and Co. Ltd., 1936), p. 279.
55. Clegg *et al., History of the British Trade Unions,* p. 413.
56. Bealey and Pelling, *Labour and Politics,* p. 10.
57. Ibid., pp. 92–4.
58. Ibid., p. 95.
59. Ibid., p. 197.
60. Ibid., p. 283.
61. Ibid., p. 163.
62. Ibid., p. 219.
63. Pelling, *Modern Britain,* p. 67.
64. Pelling, *A Short History,* pp. 43–4.
65. Pelling, *Modern Britain,* pp. 104–5.
66. Ibid., p. 109.
67. Arnot, *The Miners, Years of Struggle,* Chapter XIII. 2–3; R. Miliband, *Parliamentary Socialism* (Monthly Review Press, 1961), Chapter V. 1–2.
68. J. H. Jones *et al., The Coal Mining Industry* (Pitman, 1939), pp. 46–7.
69. Garside, *Durham Miners,* p. 155.
70. Ibid., pp. 267ff.
71. Ibid., p. 276.
72. Ibid., pp. 279–80.
73. R. B. McCallum, *The Liberal Party from Earl Grey to Asquith* (Gollancz, 1963), p. 69.
74. Ibid., p. 70.
75. Ibid., p. 79.

76. Ibid., p. 122.
77. Arnot, *The Miners*, p. 193.
78. Dangerfield, *Strange Death of Liberal England*, p. 207.
79. Pelling, *Modern Britain*, p. 137.
80. Dangerfield, *Strange Death of Liberal England*, p. 91.
81. C. Cross, *The Liberals in Power, 1905–19* (Barrie and Rockliff with Pall Mall Press, 1963), p. 185.
82. McCallum, *The Liberal Party*, p. 134.
83. Ibid., p. 167. See also A. J. P. Taylor, *English History 1914–1945* (O.U.P., 1965), pp. 105–6.
84. Ibid., p. 105.
85. Pelling, *Modern Britain*, p. 85.
86. Taylor, *English History*, p. 226.
87. Pelling, *Modern Britain*, p. 103.
88. In Durham, for example, colliery-owners farmed land which enabled them to avoid the cost of compensating tenants for mining subsidence. The main farmers (with farms of over 10,000 acres) were the Duke of Cleveland, the Marquis of Londonderry, Viscount Boyne and the Church Commissioners and the first three owned mines and the latter received substantial royalties. Viscount Boyne was an 'inactive Conservative'. *Victoria County History, Durham*, vol. II, p. 362; *D.C.*, 1.11.1872.
89. Taylor, *English History*, Chapter VIII.
90. Ibid., p. 220.
91. Ibid., pp. 324–5.
92. Ibid., p. 334.
93. Bealey and Pelling, *Labour and Politics*, pp. 283–4.
94. Dangerfield, *Strange Death of Liberal England*, p. 237.
95. Ibid., p. 279.
96. Ibid., p. 283.
97. Ibid., p. 287.
98. Arnot, *The Miners, Years of Struggle*, Chapter IV.
99. Ibid., Chapter IV. 4 and IV. 7.
100. Ibid., p. 121.
101. H. Pelling, *The Origins of the Labour Party, 1880–1900* (Macmillan, 1967), p. 136.
102. Garside, *Durham Miners*, p. 338.
103. P. d'A. Jones, *The Christian Socialist Revival, 1877–1914* (Princeton University Press, 1968), p. 72.
104. Ibid., p. 294.
105. Ibid., pp. 5–6, 455.
106. K. S. Inglis, *Churches and the Working Classes in Victorian England* (Routledge and Kegan Paul, 1964), p. 256.
107. Ibid., p. 257.
108. Ibid.
109. Ibid., p. 259.
110. Ibid., p. 274.
111. Ibid., p. 275.
112. Ibid., p. 321.
113. Ibid., p. 305.
114. Jones, *The Christian Socialist Revival*, p. 12.
115. Ibid., p. 392.

116. Ibid., p. 378.
117. Ibid., p. 403
118. See J. Kent, *The Age of Disunity* (Epworth Press, 1966), p. 130 and Chapter 5.
119. Jones, *The Christian Socialist Revival*, p. 407.
120. Ibid.
121. Inglis, *Churches and the Working Classes*, p. 290.
122. Jones, *The Christian Socialist Revival*, p. 408.
123. Inglis, *Churches and the Working Classes*, p. 272.
124. Ibid., p. 320.
125. Jones, *The Christian Socialist Revival*, pp. 345–7.
126. Ibid., p. 351.
127. Ibid., p. 428.
128. Ibid., p. 129.
129. Ibid., p. 124.
130. Ibid., p. 126.
131. Ibid., pp. 122–3, 458.
132. M. Edwards, *Methodism and England* (Epworth Press, 1943), pp. 176ff.
133. Pickering, 'The Place of Religion', p. XIII. 22.

2: THE DEERNESS VALLEY

1. Williams, *Derbyshire Miners*, Chapter XI.
2. *D.C.*, 15.6.60.
3. Ibid., 13.5.71, 30.6.71.
4. B. Thomas, 'The Migration of Labour in the Glamorganshire Coalfield (1861–1911)', in W. E. Minchinton (ed.), *Industrial South Wales 1750–1914* (Frank Cass, 1969), p. 55, n. 46.
5. Ibid., p. 45.
6. P. 367.
7. The percentages based on records of births and deaths for 1910 and 1930 are higher than the census percentages. The effect of this would be to reduce our population totals. See Tables 15–17 in Appendix IV.
8. Thomas, 'The Migration of Labour', pp. 49–50.
9. *D.C.*, 2.11.77.
10. Pickering, 'The Place of Religion', pp. II. 15–II. 21. (For the similar problem of political Party membership see B. Hindess, *The Decline of Working Class Politics* (Paladin, 1971), pp. 57–62.)
11. For earlier examples of fluctuation, see *D.C.*, 10.5.72.
12. T. Kelly, *George Birkbeck* (University of Liverpool Press, 1957), p. 259.
13. *D.C.*, 6.1.60, 13.1.60.
14. Ibid., 13.1.60.
15. *Durham Diocesan Magazine* (1884), p. 116. The whole of Archdeacon Watkin's Charge (pp. 109–20) gives a neat summary of the nineteenth-century history of the Church and Church education in the diocese.
16. See Taylor, 'Implications of Migration', Tables 7 and 9, pp. 43 and 47.
17. Tests of statistical significance are not appropriate given the likely inaccuracies in our estimates of the occupational structure of the population and the small total numbers involved in Methodist leadership. Appendix

IV gives a clear indication of the extent of the non-miner domination of the leadership.

18. J. J. C. Probert, *The Sociology of Cornish Methodism*, Cornish Methodist Historical Association, Occasional Publication, no. 8 (1964), p. 34.
19. *D.C.*, 28.4.71, 6.5.71, 16.8.72.
20. Other aspects of the county unresearched are: the rise of the Labour Party, the social, economic and political effects of the Co-operative Movement and the history of adult education. Each of these gaps will probably be filled in the future, but meanwhile research workers must work in relative darkness, using inferences from work done outside the county, or the patchy local sources within the county.
21. W. M. Patterson, *Northern Primitive Methodism* (E. Dalton, 1909), p. 92.
22. Thompson, *Making of the English Working Class*, p. 918.

3: THE SOCIAL AND ECONOMIC BASIS OF PATERNALISM

1. Garside, *Durham Miners*, pp. 55 and 58.
2. M. Tylecote, *The Mechanics Institutes of Lancashire and Yorkshire before 1851* (Manchester University Press, 1957), Chapter II.
3. J. Austin, quoted in ibid., p. 45.
4. Ibid.; see also Kelly, *George Birkbeck*, pp. 212–16 and 236.
5. *D.C.*, 24.11.71.
6. See also ibid., 29.6.77.
7. Welbourne, *The Miners' Unions*, pp. 79–80.
8. *D.C.*, 15.1.75.
9. Ibid., 10.11.76.
10. Ibid., 2.6.79.
11. Welbourne, *The Miners' Unions*, Chapter XIII.
12. See R. Bendix, *Work and Authority in Industry* (Harper Torchbooks, 1963), pp. 112–13, 210n.
13. A. Ure, *The Philosophy of Manufactures* (1835; Frank Cass, 1967), pp. 416ff. and 428; Bendix, *Work and Authority*, p. 93.
14. Bendix, *Work and Authority*, pp. 109–16.
15. *D.C.*, 27.10.71.
16. Ibid., 3.11.71.
17. Ibid., 26.6.74.
18. See, for examples: *D.C.*, 3.2.71, 21.7.71, 22.9.71, 15.12.71, 7.6.72, 27.9.72, 27.12.72.
19. Welbourne, *The Miners' Unions*, p. 116. See also Fynes, *The Miners of Northumberland and Durham*, Chapter XL.
20. Welbourne, *The Miners' Unions*, pp. 118, 121.
21. Ibid.
22. *D.C.*, 5.3.75.
23. Ibid., 2.4.75.
24. Ibid., 21.12.77.
25. Ibid., 10.5.1901.
26. Ibid., 3.11.71.
27. Ibid., 22.9.71.

28. Ibid., 7.9.1900.
29. Ibid., 24.3.76.
30. Ibid., 1.6.68.
31. Ibid., 15.1.75.
32. Ure, *Philosophy of Manufactures*, pp. 354–5, 408–10.
33. Durham County Record Office: D/40/c52/89.
34. *D.C.*, 20.2.03.
35. Ibid., 24.2.74.
36. Ibid., 13.3.74.
37. N. Longmate, *The Waterdrinkers* (Hamish Hamilton, 1968), p. 232.
38. *D.C.*, 11.4.73.
39. Ibid., 15.4.70, 19.3.75, 7.6.78, 26.6.03.
40. For similar examples from Derbyshire, see Williams, *Derbyshire Miners*, pp. 464ff.
41. Post Office, *Directory for Northumberland and Durham* (1902).
42. *D.C.*, 3.6.70, 1.12.71, 17.11.11.
43. Ibid., 5.4.04.
44. Ibid., 14.2.02.
45. Interviews: 6.7.1966, 15.10.66, 21.7.67, 8.11.68.
46. Ibid., 2.8.68, 5.8.68.
47. *D.C.*, 10.12.75.
48. Ibid., 18.3.04.
49. Ibid, 20.10.76, 15.6.77, 21.3.79, 11.4.79.
50. For example, *D.C.*, 5.9.12.
51. Peel, *Herbert Spencer*, p. 203.
52. Ure, *Philosophy of Manufactures*, pp. 408–10.
53. Welbourne, *The Miners' Unions*, p. 119.
54. Interviews: 2.3.69, 25.7.69, 26.7.69.
55. Welbourne, *The Miners' Unions*, p. 265.
56. Arnot, *The Miners*, p. 223.
57. Manager's *Report* from the Deerness Valley to Pease and Partners for the year ending 31 December 1890 (manager: J. G. Crofton).
58. *Report*, 1891.
59. Ibid., 1892.
60. *D.C.*, 18.3.92.
61. *D.C.A.*, 25.3.92.
62. Ibid., 25.3.92.
63. Ibid., 25.3.92, 8.4.92.
64. Ibid., 1.4.92.
65. Ibid., 22.4.92, 6.5.92, 13.5.92.
66. Ibid., 20.5.92.
67. *D.C.*, 18.3.92.
68. Ibid., 1.4.92, 15.4.92, 22.4.92.
69. *Reports*, 1895, 1896.
70. *Report of Proceedings at the Ordinary General Meeting of Shareholders*, 1908.
71. *Report of Proceedings. . .*, 1907. This section relies heavily on J. Grant's unpublished paper 'The Relation Between Labour and Capital [in Pease and Partners] 1828–1947'.
72. Court, *Coal*, p. 12.
73. *D.C.*, 26.12.02, 29.5.03.

74. *Reports of Proceedings. . .*, 1907.
75. Ibid., 1908.
76. E. Isichei, *Victorian Quakers* (C.U.P., 1971), p. 196.
77. *Reports of Proceedings. . .*, 1907.
78. Garside, *Durham Miners*, pp. 52–4.
79. *Reports of Proceedings. . .*, 1917. See also, Bendix, *Work and Authority*, p. 109.
80. See Chapter 6 and pp. 80 and 157.
81. Bendix, *Work and Authority*, p. 57.
82. Ibid.
83. *Reports of Proceedings. . .*, 1923.

4: VILLAGE METHODISM – I

1. S. F. Nadal, *Nupe Religion* (Routledge and Kegan Paul, 1954), pp. 259–60.
2. C. Y. Glock and R. Stark, *Religion and Society in Tension* (Rand McNally, 1965).
3. Martin, 'The Unknown Gods of the English'.
4. J. Wesley, *Journal*, ed. Nehemiah Cumock (Robert Culley, London, 1909), 29 April 1752.
5. Ibid., 27 May 1742.
6. Ibid., 19 February–7 April 1743.
7. Ibid., 2 November 1743.
8. Ibid., 6 June 1759.
9. *The Crook Circuit Wesleyan Methodist Magazine*, IV, no. 2 (February 1893), (fragments of one edition), 1.
10. Wesley, *Journal*, ed. Cumock, 12 June 1774.
11. Peel, *Herbert Spencer*, p. 40.
12. Ibid., p. 43.
13. Probert, *The Sociology of Cornish Methodism*, p. 47.
14. It has been suggested in a personal communication that the (obviously) neglected Mark deals with problems of disbelief and is thus a 'difficult' Gospel, unlikely to feature in lay preaching of the period.
15. Ralph Hayson (Senior), *Notebook*, entry 13.1.78.
16. J. Ritson's history, *The Romance of Primitive Methodism* (Primitive Methodist Publishing House, 1909), is dedicated to Robert Hind. Hind served in Waterhouses from 1875 to 1878.
17. Hayson, *Notebook*, 21.1.78, 22.1.78.
18. Ibid., 27.1.78.
19. Ibid., 28.1.78 (John 3: 14–15), 29.1.78 (Psalm 68: 18), 30.1.78 (Acts 4: 12).
20. Ibid., 14.2.78.
21. Ibid., 10.3.78 (Colossians 7: 27; Revelations 20: 11–15).
22. B. R. Wilson, *Patterns of Sectarianism* (Heinemann, 1967), Chapter 1.
23. *D.C.*, 3.8.1900, 31.8.00, 6.3.03, 12.6.03. Interviews 14.11.1966, 16.4.67.
24. Hayson, *Notebook*, 14.4.78.
25. Ibid., 21.4.78.
26. Ibid., 31.3.95.
27. J. Taylor, *Diary*, 5.1.95.
28. Hayson, *Notebook*, 1895 n.d., probably 10 March.

29. Ibid., 2.12.78, emphasis added.
30. Interview, August 1968, n.d.
31. Williams, *Derbyshire Miners*, pp. 466–7.
32. W. Adamson, *Papers*, n.d., emphasis added.
33. Ibid., sermons on texts: 1 Samuel 2: 19; Acts 7: 54–60; Ezra 2: 65; Philippians 4: 22; Hebrews 13: 13. None dated.
34. Ibid., n.d.
35. Ibid., n.d.
36. Ibid., n.d.
37. Ibid., sermon on 1 Kings 22: 14, n.d.
38. Interview, 9.8.68, with Adamson's son.
39. Quotations from Harrison are given in his own spelling. Harrison was a child before the days of compulsory primary education.
40. J. Harrison, *Papers*, 'Temperance Sermon', n.d.
41. Taylor, *Diary*, 1895; a sermon written on the fly-leaf of the diary.
42. Harrison, *Papers*, n.d.
43. W. Foster, *Sermon Register, 1897–1954*.
44. Striking vernacular accounts of such conversations are contained in the tape recordings of Thomas Turnbull and Mrs Golightly, in possession of the the author, with second copies deposited at the County Durham Industrial Museum.
45. Harrison, 'An Account of his Life', a few MS. pages among the *Papers*, n.d.
46. This phrase is in the original and makes no sense to a reader. Harrison seems to mean: what is important in a man's life is 'not merely what a man professes, etc.'
47. Harrison, 'Christian Conversation', n.d.
48. Harrison, 'The Sabbath School', n.d.
49. Hayson, *Notebook*, n.d.
50. Harrison, *Papers*.
51. Ibid.
52. Taylor, *Diaries*, 1895, 1896.
53. Ibid.
54. See also Interview, 21.7.67.
55. Harrison, *Papers*.
56. T. Turnbull, *Sermons and Notes*, Sermon on Philippians 4:8, n.d.
57. Weber, *Economy and Society*, p. 544.
58. J. Walton, *Sunday School Teaching: How to Work Successfully* (Wesleyan Methodist Sunday School Union, 1876), p. 12.
59. *S.S.J.* (1896), p. 51.
60. Ibid., p. 226.
61. Ibid., p. 222.
62. Ibid., p. 268.
63. Ibid., p. 269.
64. Ibid. (1906), pp. 248–9 and 282.
65. Ibid., p. 281. Attitudes towards the Empire (and overt racialism) expressed in the *S.S.J.* would provide sufficient material for a separate study.
66. Ibid. (1896), p. 481.
67. Ibid. (1916), p. lv.
68. Ibid. (1926), p. xxiii.
69. Ibid. (1896), p. 238.

70. Ibid. (1906), p. 280.
71. Ibid., p. 286.
72. Ibid. (1916), p. 388.
73. Ibid., Whitsun, unpaginated.
74. Walton, *Sunday School Teaching*, p. 25.
75. S.S.J. (1896), pp. 269 and 277.
76. Ibid. (1906), p. 277.
77. Ibid. (1896), p. 235.
78. Ibid. (1916), p. 349.
79. Ibid. (1896), pp. 232–3.
80. Ibid., p. 259.
81. Ibid., p. 242.
82. Ibid., p. 529.
83. S.S.J. (1906), p. 268.
84. Ibid. (1896), pp. 49–51.
85. See also Weber, *Economy and Society*, Chapter VI. 2, 'Tensions and compromises between ethics and politics'.
86. Document in the possession of the late Reverend J. Patterson Barton. All emphases are Barton's own.
87. P. Berger, *The Sacred Canopy* (Doubleday, 1967).
88. D.C.A., 77.4.44.
89. Dennis *et al.*, *Coal Is Our Life*, p. 183.
90. Ibid., p. 268.
91. Pickering, 'The Place of Religion', p. IV. 42 and 47.
92. Interviews, 17.10.66, 6.12.66.
93. Ibid., 14.11.66.
94. Ibid., 31.8.66.
95. Ibid.
96. Ibid., 25.8.66.

5: VILLAGE METHODISM – II

1. E. Troeltsch, *The Social Teaching of the Christian Churches*, 2 vols. (George Allen and Unwin, 1956), vol. II, pp. 461–3.
2. Niebuhr, *Social Sources of Denominationalism*.
3. Ibid., p. 19.
4. Ibid.
5. See C. Antoni, *From History to Sociology* (Merlin Press, 1962), p. 65.
6. Wilson, *Patterns of Sectarianism*.
7. J. A. Hostetler, *Amish Society* (Johns Hopkins Press, 1970); G. L. Gollin, *Moravians in Two Worlds* (Columbia University Press, 1967).
8. G. Lenski, *The Religious Factor* (Anchor Books, 1963), p. 18.
9. Ibid., p. 19.
10. See R. Currie, *Methodism Divided* (Faber and Faber, 1968).
11. Interview, 22.7.68.
12. Interview, July 1969.
13. Dennis *et al.*, *Coal Is Our Life*, p. 130.
14. Ibid., p. 137.
15. Taylor, 'Implications of Migration', Chapter 1.

16. See, for example, T. Burns and G. M. Stalker, *The Management of Innovation* (Tavistock Publications, 1961), for a discussion of the political and status systems of formal organisations.
17. Wilson, *Patterns of Sectarianism*, p. 15.
18. Ibid., p. 9.
19. Ibid., Chapter I.
20. For example, Patterson's *Northern Primitive Methodism* and the various local jubilee commemorative brochures.
21. *D.C.*, 3.8.1900, 31.8.00.
22. Currie, *Methodism Divided*, pp. 286–9.
23. Wilson, *Patterns of Sectarianism*, p. 12.
24. Ibid.
25. An observation attributed to Bishop Hensley-Henson, bishop of Durham 1920–39.
26. See B. R. Wilson, *Sects and Society* (Heinemann, 1961).
27. *Journal*, 12 June 1774.
28. Waterhouses P.M. Church, Leaders' and Society Meetings, *Minutes, 1863–1885*, minutes of leaders' meeting 18 July 1867.

6: THE RESPECTABLE METHODISTS

1. *D.C.*, 29.3.72. For a description of crowding in village housing, see *D.C.*, 7.6.01. Overcrowding lasted until after the First World War.
2. Ibid., 6.6.73.
3. Ibid., 16.10.64.
4. Ibid., 31.3.76.
5. Ibid., 23.6.76.
6. Ibid., 2.4.09.
7. Interview, 27.8.66.
8. Ibid., 14.8.68.
9. Ibid., 14.9.67.
10. Ibid., 17.3.67.
11. Ibid., 1.9.66, 16.6.67.
12. Ure, *Philsophy of Manufactures*, pp. 354–5.
13. *D.C.*, 14.11.66.
14. See, for example, Interviews 5.8.68 and 8.4.67.
15. Comments made to the author in the course of conducting a small survey by questionnaire in 1969.
16. Interview, 25.7.67.
17. *D.C.*, 25.8.71. See also E. Lloyd, *The Story of Fifty Years of Crook Co-operative Society* (C.W.S. Printing Works, Pelaw-on-Tyne, 1916), Chapter XV. Prominent Waterhouses Methodists appear in this account of the leadership of the Crook Co-op.
18. Interview with the late J. Patterson Barton, 28.1.67.
19. Interview, 5.8.68.
20. Ibid., 16.8.66.
21. Ibid., 25.7.67.
22. See note 15 above.
23. Interview, 14.8.68.

24. Ibid., 1.6.68.
25. Pope, *Millhands and Preachers*.
26. Minutes of various preachers' meetings record examination failures. See for example *Minutes* of Waterhouses Primitive Methodist Circuit, Quarterly Meeting, 1892 – entry for 29.8.11.
27. Ibid., 11.3.19.
28. Interview, 28.7.69.
29. *Interview*, 21.7.67, *D.C.*, 13.1.03. Also a letter in the possession of Mr Stan Harrison, from John Wilson to Mrs Harrison on her husband's death, refers to Harrison as 'my dear friend'.
30. *D.C.*, 27.9.12.
31. Ibid., 30.11.1900.
32. Interview, 16.4.67.
33. Drawing on interviews, conversations, observations, etc.
34. Interview, 6.7.66.
35. Interviews, 29.10.66, 21.7.67, 14.9.67. It has been suggested by some respondents that this kept the children economically incompetent, and was a disadvantage when they married, and when they became chapel officials.
36. Interview, 25.8.66.
37. Ibid., 25.7.67.
38. Ibid., 14.9.67 (retired village doctor).
39. Ibid., n.d.
40. Ibid., 7.7.66.
41. Ibid., 2.1.69.
42. Ibid., 1.9.66.
43. Ibid.
44. Ibid., 22.7.69.
45. Ibid., n.d. July 1969.
46. Ibid.
47. Ibid., 19.12.67.
48. Ibid., 7.7.66.
49. Ibid., 1.9.66.
50. Ibid., 15.10.66.
51. Ibid., 1.9.66.
52. Ibid., 16.4.67.
53. Ibid., 14.11.66.
54. See note 15 above.
55. Longmate, *The Waterdrinkers*, Chapters 23–4.
56. E. T. Davies, *Religion in the Industrial Revolution in South Wales* (University of Wales Press, 1965), pp. 56–8.
57. Interview, 19.8.68.
58. Ibid., 26.7.69.
59. Ibid., 25.7.67.
60. Ibid., 9.8.68.
61. Ibid., 14.8.68.
62. Pope, *Millhands and Preachers*.
63. Personal communication from a friend of J. H. Love.
64. Lockwood, 'Sources of Variation in Working Class Images of Society'.
65. Minutes of Evidence: Group A, Volume 1.
66. Interview, 19.12.67.
67. *D.C.*, 9.5.79.

68. Ibid., 18.5.79.
69. Ibid., 21.3.79.
70. Ibid., 10.1.79.
71. Ibid., 2.5.79.
72. Ibid., 9.5.69.
73. Ibid., 21. 5. 80.
74. Ibid., 7.7.76.
75. Ibid., 4.10.12.
76. Garside, *Durham Miners*, p. 176.
77. *D.C.*, 2.5.79, 9.5.79.
78. Ibid.
79. Ibid., 5.5.11.
80. Ibid., 7.4.11.
81. Ibid., 3.4.03.
82. Longmate, *The Waterdrinkers*, p. 232 (Longmate's emphasis).
83. Dangerfield, *Strange Death of Liberal England*, p. 15.
84. *D.C.*, 23.11. 09.
85. Interview with White's son, 21.7.67.
86. Interviews, 24.7.69, 25.7.69, 26.7.69.
87. *D.C.*, 27.6.19.
88. Wearmouth, *The Social and Political Influence*, p. 128.
89. *D.C.*, 7.7.27.
90. Ibid., 30.1.91.
91. *D.C.A.*, 18.3.92 and Chapter 3.
92. *D.C.*, 14.11.19.
93. See note 15 above.
94. Garside, *Durham Miners*, p. 200.
95. Interview, 21.7.67.
96. Ibid., 19.8.68.
97. Ibid., 15.10.66.
98. Ibid., 27.7.67.
99. Ibid., 19.12.67.

7: THE RADICALS AND THE LABOUR MOVEMENT

1. *D.C.*, 19.4.01.
2. We will refer to J. G. Harrison by his familiar name, used by himself (sometimes signing letters 'Jay Gee') and by his friends.
3. Wearmouth, *The Social and Political Influence*, p. 245.
4. *D.C.*, 18.4.73, 9.5.73, 9.5.79.
5. Ibid., 25.4.79, 2.5.79, 9.5.79.
6. Wearmouth, *The Social and Political Influence*, pp. 112–18.
7. *D.C.*, 16.8.00, 15.3.01, 24.5.01.
8. Welbourne, *The Miners' Unions*, p. 304, and E. Allen, *The D.M.A. 1869–1969* (The Durham Miners' Association, 1969), p. 17.
9. Taylor, *Diary* entry, 29.1.95.
10. *D.C.*, 2.5.79.
11. Letter from Wormwood Scrubs, 21 October 1917.
12. Interview, 19.8.68.

13. Ibid., 1.9.67.
14. Pelling, *Origins of the Labour Party*, p. 151.
15. Interviews, 29.10.66, 2.8.68. See Chapter 1. Campbell's name was specifically associated with Socialism, as well as the new Theology. See, for example, J. R. Gregory in *The Preachers' Magazine*, XVIII (1907), 104–15 and 193–9. Older Methodists report that the New Theology debate severely disrupted the chapels and cost the Methodists a number of preachers.
16. D.C., 5.10.17.
17. Ibid., 22.6.17.
18. Interview, 18.9.67.
19. Ibid., 29.10.66.
20. Ibid., 9.8.68. Peter Lee was a local preacher and union leader. He was a member of the national executive of the M.F.G.B. and first chairman of a Labour county council (Durham, 1920). Peterlee New Town is named after him.
21. D.C., 15.9.21.
22. Interview, 4.10.66.
23. This group submitted questionnaires to the Christian Conference on Politics, Economics and Citizenship on social and economic conditions in the villages, and possible remedies. Unfortunately the questionnaires have been lost.
24. D.C., 7.6.01, 27.12.01. See also Report of County Minister of Health to Lanchester R.D.C., *Minutes* of Lanchester Rural District Council, 4.3.96.
25. D.C., 5.7.01 and *Minutes*, 2.5.01, 30.5.01.
26. St John the Baptist's Church, Hamsteels, *Parish Magazine*, August 1924.
27. Ibid., August 1915.
28. Ibid., August 1924.
29. For a history of the radicals within *national* Methodism, see Edwards, *Methodism and England*, Chapters X and XI.
30. Horror stories were common in the post-1921 period, as was preaching against the 'Bolshevik Menace' (e.g. the Cheeks and George Pritchard). Atrocity stories became part of the stock in trade of Conservative Party speakers, officers returning from service with the White Russians, and the vicar of Hamsteels.
31. Pp. 160–1.
32. Gregory, *Miners and British Politics*, p. 7.
33. Ibid., pp. 64–5.
34. Ibid., p. 69.
35. Ibid., p. 66.
36. Ibid., p. 79.
37. Williams, *Derbyshire Miners*, Chapter XII.
38. Gregory, *Miners and British Politics*, p. 72.
39. Ibid., pp. 67–8.
40. Ibid., p. 69.
41. Ibid., p. 80.
42. Based on a series of conversations with Clough in 1966.
43. Jones, *The Christian Socialist Revival*, p. 353, n. 98.
44. Interview, 29.7.67.
45. There is no full history of the Labour Party in County Durham.
46. Interview, 19.8.68.
47. Pelling, *A Short History*, p. 54.
48. Williams, *Derbyshire Miners*, p. 513.

49. Interview, 26.7.69.
50. David Martin, *Pacifism* (Routledge and Kegan Paul, 1965), pp. 88–9. Pelling, *Origins of the Labour Party*, p. 150.

8: METHODISTS IN ACTION

1. Longmate, *The Waterdrinkers*, p. 242.
2. T. P. Whittaker, cited ibid., p. 247.
3. *D.C.*, 22.8.02.
4. Ibid., 22.8.02.
5. Ibid., 2.5.02, 4.3.04.
6. Ibid., 13.3.03, 20.2.03.
7. Ibid., 13.11.03.
8. Ibid., 11.7.02.
9. Ibid., 3.7.03
10. Ibid., 17.7.03.
11. Ibid., 17.3.05.
12. Ibid., 28.8.03.
13. Ibid., 23.10.03.
14. Ibid., 3.6.04.
15. Ibid., 1.7.04, 21.10.04.
16. Ibid., 17.3.05.
17. Ibid., 8.8.02, 12.6.03, 11.9.03, 4.3.04, 5.8.04, 2.9.04.
18. Ibid., 2.12.04, 9.12.04, 23.12.04, 30.12.04, 6.1.05, 13.1.05, 20.1.05, 3.2.05.
19. Ibid., 3.2.05.
20. Ibid., 30.12.04.
21. *S.S.J.*, March 1906, editorial.
22. *The Primitive Methodist Quarterly Review*, April 1906, p. 325.
23. *S.S.J.*, p. 231.
24. See Edwards, *Methodism and England*, pp. 195–6.
25. Interview, 29.10.66.
26. Ibid., 15.10.66.
27. Martin, *Pacifism*, p. 205.
28. Ibid., pp. 77 and 96.
29. Kendal, *The Revolutionary Movement in Britain*, p. 149.
30. Interview, 15.10.66.
31. *D.C.*, 27.8.15.
32. Interview, 27.7.67.
33. Ibid. (Mid-November 1966).
34. Harrison, *Papers*. Quotation unattributed, but probably Carpenter.
35. Interview, 19.12.67.
36. Harrison, *Letters*, 21.10.17.
37. *D.C.*, 7.12.16.
38. Ibid., 16.3.16.
39. Ibid., 31.3.16.
40. Interview, 19.12.67.
41. Ibid., 14.11.66.
42. Ibid., 9.10.66.
43. Ibid., 19.8.68.

44. Ibid., 15.10.66.
45. Ibid., 19.3.67.
46. See also *D.C.*, 1.11.17 for Mrs Philip Snowden at Stanley, Consett and Gateshead.
47. Interview, 17.10.66. Of the Russian revolution, J.G. had said, in a letter to his wife, dated 14.1.18, 'It is of far more importance than military victory or defeat on the western front.'
48. Interview (mid-November 1966).
49. Martin, *Pacifism*, p. 185.
50. We do not propose to discuss the progress of pacifism in the district. Plainly J.G. adopted the absolutist position, but we do not know how he would have faced the dilemma of preaching 'the good tidings of peace and setting the captives at liberty' (ibid., p. 75). His enthusiasm for the Russian revolution would have raised this issue for him early in the 1920s, had he lived. The pacifism of the I.L.P. was proto-revolutionary and the group was politically very radical as well as pacifist. But Connie Ellis and her husband, for example, at the beginning of the Spanish Civil War, sat up talking all night and in the morning 'We knew we were no longer pacifists'. We cannot say how J.G. would have resolved such an issue.
51. The dispute, precipitated by the owners, clearly had a purely political dimension also. For the owners' and government's preparation for the strike, see Arnot, *The Miners, Years of Struggle*, Chapters XII and XIII.
52. *D.C.*, 2.4.26.
53. See, for example, ibid., 13.8.26, 29.10.26, 11.11.26, 7.1.27.
54. Ibid., 26.11.26.
55. Ibid., 29.11.26.
56. Arnot, *The Miners, Years of Struggle*, p. 422.
57. *D.C.*, 24.10.26.
58. Ibid., 6.7.67.
59. Interview, 30.7.67. 'Part-officials' or 'McGinty' deputies had the responsibilities but not the qualifications of a deputy.
60. Interview, 5.8.66.
61. Ibid., 8.4.67.
62. *D.C.*, 31.12.26.
63. Interview, 1.9.67.
64. Interview, 1.9.67.
65. Interview, 1.9.67.
66. Ibid., 19.8.68.
67. St John the Baptist's Church, Hamsteels, *Parish Magazine*, September 1926.
68. Garside, *Durham Miners*, p. 212.
69. Interviews, 1.9.67, 8.4.67.
70. Ibid., and 19.8.68.
71. Ibid., 9.10.66.
72. Ibid. (mid-November 1966).
73. Ibid., 30.7.67.
74. Williams, *Derbyshire Miners*, Chapter XIX, Sections III and VII.
75. Garside, *Durham Miners*, p. 232.
76. See Arnot, *The Miners, Years of Struggle*, pp. 494–5 and 537.
77. Garside, *Durham Miners*.
78. *D.C.*, 6.7.26.
79. Ibid., 19.12.67.

80. Ibid., 28.1.67.
81. Ibid., 17.10.67.
82. Ibid., 18.11.66.
83. Ibid.
84. Ibid., 5.8.68.

9: 1970 – A POSTSCRIPT

1. The rise to power of the Catholics is a fact that needs explaining. This could be done with a comparative study of Catholicism in the valley. We might suggest a number of possible reasons for the fact. (1) The Catholics were not part of the traditional local establishment and therefore did not lose credibility with that establishment. (2) Irish Catholics were outsiders in the society that grew up in the Durham villages in the late nineteenth century; they were, to some extent a pariah group of workers who first built the railways and then sank the pits but only latterly came to occupy the skilled jobs. This is a situation likely to produce radicals like Johnny Holmes. (3) Catholicism is a more collectivist religion than Methodism, expressing much less individualism than the Methodists and stressing instead the corporate nature of life. (4) With the ending of the Liberal Party the Catholic miners did not lose their political connexions with their fellow workers, as they met them in the clubs. Thus Catholic candidates for office could build up their constituency through the clubs in much the same way as the Methodists had done so through the chapels. (5) Less plausibly, the bishop of Hexham (according to the Methodists) came to the villages and told the Catholics that they had to take over the trade unions.
2. Interview, 7.7.67.
3. Garside, *Durham Miners*, p. 298.
4. 'The Place of Religion', p. XV. 27.
5. Interview with Sunday school superintendent, 1.7.69.
6. *Secularisation and Moral Change*, p. 69.

CONCLUSIONS

1. *The Philosophy of Manufactures*, Book the Third, Chapter III.
2. *Secularisation and Moral Change*, p. 42.
3. Ibid., p. 24.
4. *Labouring Men*, p. 26.
5. Weber, *Economy and Society*, pp. 515–17.
6. *The Age of Disunity*, p. 137.
7. Weber, 'The Protestant Sects and the Spirit of Capitalism' in H. H. Gerth and C. W. Mills (eds.), *From Max Weber* (Routledge and Kegan Paul, 1961), p. 294.

BIBLIOGRAPHY

BOOKS

Allen, E. *The D.M.A. 1869–1969*. The Durham Miners' Association, 1969.

Antoni, C. *From History to Sociology*. Merlin Press, 1962.

Archer, M. S. and Giner, S. (eds.). *Contemporary Europe*. Weidenfeld and Nicolson, 1971.

Arnot, Robert Page. *The Miners: a History of the Miners' Federation of Great Britain 1889–1910*. George Allen and Unwin, 1949.

  The Miners, Years of Struggle: a History of the Miners' Federation of Great Britain from 1910 onwards. George Allen and Unwin, 1953.

  The Miners in Crisis and War: a History of the Miners' Federation of Great Britain from 1930 onwards. George Allen and Unwin, 1961.

Bealey, F. and Pelling, H. *Labour and Politics, 1900–1906*. Macmillan, 1958.

Bendix, R. *Max Weber*. Heinemann, 1960.

  Work and Authority in Industry. Harper Torchbooks, 1963.

Berger, P. *The Sacred Canopy*. Doubleday, 1967.

Berger, P. L. and Luckmann, T. *The Social Construction of Reality*. Allen Lane, the Penguin Press, 1967.

Buckle, H. T. *History of Civilisation in England*. 2 vols., Parker, Son and Bourne, 1858 (2nd ed.) and 1861.

Burns, T. and Stalker, G. M. *The Management of Innovation*. Tavistock Publications, 1961.

Campbell, J. R. *The New Theology*. Mills and Boon, 1907.

Clegg, H., Fox, A. and Thompson, A. F. *A History of the British Trade Unions since 1889*; vol. I, *1889–1910*.

Court, W. H. B. *Coal*. H.M.S.O., London, 1951.

  A Concise Economic History of Britain. C.U.P., 1954.

Cross, C. *The Liberals in Power, 1905–1914*. Barrie and Rockliff with Pall Mall Press, 1963.

Currie, R. *Methodism Divided*. Faber and Faber, 1968.

Dangerfield, G. *The Strange Death of Liberal England*. Constable and Co. Ltd., 1936.

Davies, E. T. *Religion in the Industrial Revolution in South Wales*. University of Wales Press, 1965.

Dennis, N., Henriques, F. and Slaughter, C. *Coal Is Our Life*. Tavistock Publications, 1969.

Edwards, M. *Methodism and England*. Epworth Press, 1943.

Evans, E. W. *The Miners of South Wales*. University of Wales Press, 1961.

Fynes, R. *The Miners of Northumberland and Durham*. Thomas Summerbell, Sunderland, 1873.

Garside, W. R. *The Durham Miners, 1919–1960*. George Allen and Unwin, 1971.

Gerth, H. H. and Mills, C. W. (eds.). *From Max Weber*. Routledge and Kegan Paul, 1961.

Bibliography

Glaser, B. G. and Strauss, A. L. *The Discovery of Grounded Theory*. Weidenfeld and Nicolson, 1968.

Glock, C. Y. and Stark, R. *Religion and Society in Tension*. Rand McNally, 1965.

Goldthorpe, J. H., Lockwood, D., Bechhofer, F. and Platt, J. *The Affluent Worker in the Class Structure*. C.U.P., 1969.

Gollin, G. L. *Moravians in Two Worlds*. Columbia University Press, 1967.

Gould, J. and Kolb, W. L. *A Dictionary of the Social Sciences*. Tavistock Publications, 1964.

Gregory, R. *The Miners and British Politics, 1906–1914*. O.U.P., 1968.

Halévy, E. *Histoire du Peuple Anglais au XIXᵉ Siècle*. Libraire Hachette et Cie, 1912– .

Ibid., translated under the title *History of the English People in the 19th Century* as follows. Vol. 1 – *A History of the English People in 1815*. Trans. E. Watkins and D. A. Barker. T. Fisher Unwin, 1924. *England in 1815*. Same trans. Ernest Benn, 1949. Vol. 2 – *A History of the English People 1815–1830*. Trans. E. Watkins. T. Fisher Unwin, 1926. *The Liberal Awakening 1815–1830*. Same trans. Ernest Benn, 1949. Vol. 3 – *A History of the English People 1830–1841*. Trans. E. Watkins. T. Fisher Unwin, 1927. *The Triumph of Reform 1830–1841*. Same trans. Ernest Benn, 1950. Vol. 4 – *The Age of Peel and Cobden: A History of the English People 1841–1852*. Trans. E. Watkins. Ernest Benn, 1947. *Victorian Years 1841–1895*. Same trans. Ernest Benn, 1951. Vol. 5 – *A History of the English People 1895–1905*. Trans. E. Watkins. Ernest Benn, 1929). *Imperialism and the Rise of Labour*. Same trans. Ernest Benn, 1951. Vol. 6 – *A History of the English People 1905–1915*. Trans. E. Watkins. Ernest Benn, 1934. *The Rule of Democracy 1905–1914*, books 1 and 2. Same trans. Ernest Benn, 1952.

Hammond, J. L. and B. *The Town Labourer 1760–1832*. 2 vols., Guild Books, 1949.

Himmelfarb, G. *Victorian Minds*. Weidenfeld and Nicolson, 1968.

Hindess, B. *The Decline of Working Class Politics*, Paladin, 1971.

Hobsbawm, E. *Primitive Rebels*. Manchester University Press, 1963.
Labouring Men. Weidenfeld and Nicolson, 1968.

Hostetler, J. A. *Amish Society*. John Hopkins Press, 1970.

Hughes, D. Price. *The Life of Hugh Price Hughes*. Hodder and Stoughton, 1904.

Inglis, K. S. *Churches and the Working Classes in Victorian England*. Routledge and Kegan Paul, 1964.

Isichei, E. *Victorian Quakers*. C.U.P., 1971.

Jones, J. H., *et al. The Coal Mining Industry*. Pitman, 1939.

Jones, P. d'A. *The Christian Socialist Revival, 1877–1914*. Princeton University Press, 1968.

Kelly, T. *George Birkbeck*. University of Liverpool Press, 1957.

Kendal, W. *The Revolutionary Movement in Britain, 1900–1921*. Weidenfeld and Nicolson, 1969.

Kent, J. *The Age of Disunity*. Epworth Press, 1966.

Lecky, W. E. H. *Rationalism in Europe*. Longmans, Green and Co., 1865.
A History of England in the Eighteenth Century. 8 vols., Longmans, Green and Co., 1878–90.

Lenski, G. *The Religious Factor*. Anchor Books, 1963.

Llewellyn, R. *How Green Was My Valley*. New English Library, 1972.

Lloyd, E. *The Story of Fifty Years of Crook Co-Operative Society*. C.W.S. Printing Works, Pelaw-on-Tyne, 1916.

Longmate, N. *The Waterdrinkers.* Hamish Hamilton, 1968.

Luckman, T. *The Invisible Religion.* Collier-MacMillan, 1967.

McCallum, R. B. *The Liberal Party from Earl Grey to Asquith.* Gollancz, 1963.

MacIntyre, A. *Secularisation and Moral Change.* C.U.P., 1967.

Martin, D. *Pacifism.* Routledge and Kegan Paul, 1965.

Miliband, R. *Parliamentary Socialism.* Monthly Review Press, 1961.

Nadel, S. F. *Nupe Religion.* Routledge and Kegan Paul, 1954.

Niebuhr, H. Richard. *The Social Sources of Denominationalism.* Meridian Books, 1957.

Parkin, F. *Class Inequality and Political Order.* Paladin, 1972.

Patterson, W. M. *Northern Primitive Methodism.* E. Dalton, 1909.

Peel, J. D. Y. *Herbert Spencer.* Heinemann, 1971.

Pelling, H. *The Origins of the Labour Party, 1880–1900.* Macmillan, 1967.

  The Social Geography of British Elections, 1885–1910. Macmillan, 1967.

  Modern Britain, 1885–1955. Sphere Books, 1969.

  A Short History of the Labour Party. Macmillan, 1972.

Pope, L. *Millhands and Preachers.* Yale University Press, 1965.

Post Office. *Directory for Northumberland and Durham.* 1902.

Probert, J. J. C. *The Sociology of Cornish Methodism.* Cornish Methodist Historical Association, Occasional Publication, no. 8 (1964).

Read, D. *Edwardian England.* Harrap, 1972.

Ritson, J. *The Romance of Primitive Methodism.* Primitive Methodist Publishing House, 1909.

Sorel, G. *Reflections on Violence.* Collier Books, 1967.

Spencer, H. and Finch, E. *The Constitutional Practice and Discipline of the Methodist Church.* The Methodist Publishing House, 1951.

Taylor, A. J. P. *English History 1914–1945.* O.U.P., 1965.

Thompson, E. P. *The Making of the English Working Class.* Penguin Books, 1968.

Thoreau, H. D. *Walden* and *On the Duty of Civil Disobedience.* Collier Books, 1967.

Tonnies, F. *Gemeinschaft und Gesellschaft (1887).* Ed. and trans. as *Community and Society* by C. P. Loomis. Harper Torchbooks, 1957.

Townsend, W. J. (ed.) *A New History of Methodism.* 2 vols., Hodder and Stoughton, 1909.

Toynbee, A. *Lectures on the Industrial Revolution of the Eighteenth Century in England.* Longmans, Green and Co., 1896.

Troeltsch, E. *The Social Teaching of the Christian Churches.* 2 vols., George Allen and Unwin, 1956.

Tylecote, M. *The Mechanics Institutes of Lancashire and Yorkshire before 1851.* Manchester University Press, 1957.

Ure, A. *The Philosophy of Manufactures (1835).* Frank Cass, 1967.

  Victoria County History, Durham, vol. II. Archibald Constable & Co., London, 1907.

Wearmouth, R. F. *Methodism and the Struggle of the Working Classes, 1850–1900.* Edgar Bachus, 1954.

  The Social and Political Influence of Methodism in the Twentieth Century. Epworth Press, 1957.

Webb, S. *The Story of the Durham Miners, 1662–1921.* The Fabian Society, 1921.

Weber, M. *The Protestant Ethic and the Spirit of Capitalism.* Unwin University Books, 1965.

  Economy and Society. Bedminster Press, 1968.

Bibliography

Welbourne, E. *The Miners' Unions of Northumberland and Durham*. C.U.P., 1923.
Wesley, J. *Journal*, ed. Nehemiah Cumock. Robert Culley, London, 1909.
Williams, J. E. *The Derbyshire Miners*. George Allen and Unwin, 1962.
Wilson, B. R. *Sects and Society*. Heinemann, 1961.
  Patterns of Sectarianism. Heinemann, 1967.
Zola, E. *Germinal*. Penguin, 1966.

ARTICLES

Beshers, J. M. and Nishiura, E. N. 'A Theory of Internal Migration Differentials'.
  Social Forces, 39, (1960–1), 214–18.
Gillispie, C. 'The Work of Elie Halévy'. *Journal of Modern History*, 22 (1950),
  239ff.
Goldthorpe, J. H. 'L'image des classes chez les travailleurs manuels aises'. *Revue
  Française de Sociologie*, X (1970), 311–38.
Gollin, G. L. 'The Religious Factor in Social Change; Max Weber and The
  Moravian Paradox'. Paper presented to the World Congress of Sociology,
  Evian, 1956.
Gregory, J. R. Reviews *of The New Theology* [by R. J. Campbell]. *The Preachers'
  Magazine* (1907), pp. 104–15 and 193–9.
Halévy, E. 'La Naissance du Méthodisme en Angleterre'. *La Revue de Paris*
  (August 1906), 519–39 and 841–67.
Highet, J. 'Making Sense of Religious Statistics'. Unpublished paper, 1966.
Lockwood, D. 'Sources of Variation in Working Class Images of Society'.
  Sociological Review, 14, no. 3 (November 1966), 249–67.
Martin, D. 'The Unknown Gods of the English'. *The Advancement of Science*, 23,
  no. 108 (June 1966), 56–60.
Moore, Robert. 'History, Economics and Religion', in A. Sahay (ed.), *Max Weber
  and Modern Sociology*. Routledge and Kegan Paul, 1971.
  'Methodism and Class Conflict'. *Sociological Analysis*, 1, no. 2 (1971), 77–93.
  'Religion as a Source of Variation in Working Class Images of Society', in
  Martin Bulmer (ed.), *Working Papers on Class Imagery*. Routledge and
  Kegan Paul, forthcoming 1974.
  'The Political Effects of Village Methodism', in M. Hill (ed.), *A Sociological
  Yearbook of Religion in Britain*. S.C.M. Press, 1973.
Parkin, F. 'Working Class Conservatives: a Theory of Political Deviance'. *British
  Journal of Sociology*, XVIII, no. 3 (1967), 278–90.
Semmel, G., 'The Halévy Thesis'. *Encounter* (July 1971), pp. 44–55.
Thomas, B. 'The Migration of Labour in the Glamorganshire Coalfield (1861–
  1911)', in W. E. Minchinton, (ed.), *Industrial South Wales 1750–1914*.
  Frank Cass, 1969.

UNPUBLISHED Ph.D. THESES

Pickering, W. S. F. 'The Place of Religion in the Social Structure of Two English
  Industrial Towns'. University of London, 1958.
Taylor, R. 'Implications of Migration for the Durham Coalfield'. University of
  Durham, 1966.

METHODIST SOURCES

GENERAL PUBLISHED SOURCES

The Methodist Hymn Book. Methodist Publishing House, 1933.

The Preachers' Magazine.

The Primitive Methodist Hymnal, with Supplement. Primitive Methodist Publishing House, 1923.

The Primitive Methodist Quarterly Review. London, 1879–1909.

Primitive Methodist Sunday School Journal and Teachers' Magazine. Primitive Methodist Publishing House, 1896, 1906, 1916, 1926.

Walton, J. *Sunday School Teaching: How to Work Successfully*. Wesleyan Methodist Sunday School Union, 1876.

LOCAL MS. SOURCES

Brandon and Deerness Valley circuit (Amalgamated Methodist)
Circuit Schedule Book, 1934–45.
Plan—various.
Quarterly Schedules, 1935–61.
Register of Deeds: probably *c*. 1955.
Register of Deeds, 1961: to replace above which was assumed to be lost.

Cornsay Colliery United Methodist Church
Minutes of Society and Leaders' Meetings, 1924–31.
Minutes of Society and Finance Meetings, 1931–42.
Minutes of Trustees and Leaders' Meetings, 1948–62.
Sunday School Register, 1931–60.
Sunday School Teachers' Meetings, 1929–59.
Trust Account Book, 1948–62.
Trustee Treasurer's Account Book, 1950–62.

Crook W.M. circuit
The Crook Circuit Wesleyan Methodist Magazine fragments of 4, no. 2 (1893).
Plan, 1911–21.

Esh Winning circuit (P.M.) Esh Winning, Brandon Road
Leaders' Meetings, 1928–33.
Minutes of Trustees Meetings, 1907–37.

Quebec Clowes Church
Minutes of Trustees Meeting and Accounts, 1905–66.
Trustee Treasurer's Account Book, 1950–66.

Waterhouses circuit (P.M.)
Minutes of Leaders' and Society Meetings, 1863–85.
Minutes of Quarterly Meetings, 1892–1912.
Minutes of Quarterly Meetings, 1913–34.
Minutes of Trustees Meetings, 1884–1914.
Minutes of Trustees Meetings, 1915–28.
Plan—various.
P.M. Society Book, 18 February 1865—2 December 1886.

Bibliography

P.M. Sunday School Register, 1890–1938.
Quarterly Reports, 1920.
Quarterly Reports, 1921.
Station Reports, 1893–1912.
Station Reports, 1914–19; 1922–32.
Sunday School Teachers' Attendance Register, December 1886—December 1893.
Sunday School Teachers' Attendance Register, December 1900–June 1909.

Waterhouses Wesleyan Chapel.
Minutes of Trustees Meetings, 1876–1925.

OTHER CHURCH MATERIAL

Durham Diocesan Magazine.
Hamsteels, St John the Baptist's Church, *Parish Magazine.*

PEASE AND PARTNERS

Pease and Partners, Esh Colliery, Manager's rough notebooks and rough colliery
diary, June 1926–June 1927.
Pease and Partners, *Managers' Reports from the Deerness Valley.*
Pease and Partners, *Report of Proceedings at the Ordinary General Meeting of
Shareholders.*

OTHER SOURCES

Brandon and Byshottles Urban District Council, *Minutes,* January 1895–April 1937.
D.C., 1860–1960.
D.C.A., 1870–1970.
Lanchester Rural District Council, *Minutes,* 1895–1919.
Lanchester Sanitary Authority, *Minutes,* July 1891.
Royal Commission on Labour, 1891, Minutes of Evidence, Group A. vol. 1.
School Log Books:
  East Hedleyhope Colliery School, 1871–1908.
  East Hedleyhope Council School, 1908–60.
  Cornsay Colliery Infants British School, 1877–1940.
  Cornsay Colliery Junior School, 1876–1944.

PRIVATE PAPERS

Adamson, W. *Papers.*
Barton, J. P. *Prepared Answer to Question asked at Waterhouses Primitive
    Methodist Young Peoples' Institute, 1920.*
Foster, W. *Sermon Register, 1897–1954.*
Harrison, J. *Papers.*
Harrison, J. G. *Papers and Letters.*
Hayson, R. (Senior). *Notebook.*
Taylor, J. *Diary, 1895 and 1896.*
Turnball, T. *Sermons and Notes.*

GLOSSARY

METHODIST

ADHERENT: a person who attends services, or a person who participates in the life of the chapel. Members (q.v.) and adherents do not always observe the difference in their respective statuses.

CIRCUIT: a circuit consists of a group of societies (q.v.) in a geographical area. Ministers are appointed to a circuit and the senior minister is known as the superintendent. A group of circuits constitutes the district, which is presided over by the chairman of the district. (See H. Spencer and E. Finch, *The Constitutional Practice and Discipline of the Methodist Church* (The Methodist Publishing House, 1951), pp. 129–35 and 182–8).

CLASS: the Methodist class is the smallest cell of Methodism. The class ticket was a sign of membership of the society. Classes met weekly under a class leader. Today largely nominal only, none meet in the valley.

CONNEXION: the Methodist Connexion is the whole Methodist Church; it is governed by the annual conference through the officials of the conference. There are various Connexional departments providing central services for the whole Connexion.

LEADERS: the leaders are the members of the leaders' meeting. The constitution of the leaders' meeting varies according to whether it is functioning as a court of discipline, or for other purposes. The widest constitution includes ministers, class leaders, society and poor stewards, Sunday school superintendent, secretaries of various ancillary organisations, local preachers, any circuit officials in the society, and elected representatives. In other words, the leaders are the leaders of the local society, and it is in this sense that the term is used in the present work. (Spencer and Finch, *Constitutional Practice*, pp. 136ff.)

LOCAL PREACHER: a local preacher is a layman qualified to preach by virtue of serving a probationary period ('on trial') and having passed exams based on a prescribed course of study. In the past, and to a certain extent in northern Methodism today, the local preachers are the main preachers, any one chapel having a local preacher take a service more often than a minister.

MEMBER: a member is a person who has been received into membership of the local society, after a period of instruction and a public service of admission. (Today older persons are admitted without the service.) Membership is of the society, not of Methodism in general, it is one of the functions of the circuit to ensure that members are passed from one society to another if they move their home.

PLAN: the circuit *Plan* lists the preaching stations and preachers for the quarter. Each member is expected to possess a *Plan*. It will probably also contain details of society and circuit numbers and officers, etc. When a preacher commences his preaching career he is said to 'come on the *Plan*'.

QUARTERLY MEETING: this meeting governs the circuit (the circuit quarterly meeting). It consists of circuit officials, many of the leaders of the societies and elected representatives. It is responsible for the spiritual and financial oversight of the circuit and appoints the Minister. It sends representatives to synod – the district meeting (see Spencer and Finch, *Constitutional Practice*, pp. 121ff.). There is also a society quarterly meeting: this is another name for the leaders' meeting.

THE SOCIETY: Methodism is made up of societies organised into circuits. The society usually, but not always, has a chapel of its own, it governs its own affairs through the leaders' meeting. All lay Methodists are members of a society and have a right to speak at the society meeting. In the present work *society* is used interchangeably with *chapel* (except when referring to the building); chapel is the more common term locally, it is said that one 'belong t' chapel'.

SUNDAY SCHOOL SUPERINTENDENT: the superintendent is the officer with the oversight of the Sunday school. He is responsible to the leaders' meeting for the conduct of the Sunday school, keeping records and training the teachers. He is usually a teacher himself, a teacher of some seniority. He is a member of the leaders' meeting.

TRUST, TRUSTEES: the trustees are responsible for the upkeep of the physical fabric of chapel, schoolrooms and manse. They have no 'religious' authority but control the use to which their premises are put.

MINING

CAVIL: lots are drawn once a quarter to ensure fair allocation of hard and easy workings. A man's working is his cavil.

KEEKER: the keeker is the official in charge at the pit head.

MARRER: a miner's mate: two marrers are paid as one person for their output, they work as a team in their cavil but on different shifts. Marrers are usually men of roughly equal skill and output. Marrers are chosen by miners themselves, not by the management.

MASTER BURNER: the official in charge of coke ovens.

OFFICIALS: in ascending order of authority: deputy overman (referred to as deputy), overman, undermanager, manager, agent (the agent will be in charge of a group of pits, or an area, for the owners).

OUT-BYE, IN-BYE: a man is said to be 'going in-bye' when he is travelling away from the surface towards the face. Conversely he is going out-bye when moving towards the shaft bottom or the surface. (Drift mines do not have a shaft, so to travel out-bye is to move towards the surface.)

SEGGAR: this is a clay found in the coal. It is used to make refractory bricks. Cornsay Colliery still produces bricks for a Teeside foundry.

SMALL RUNNER: the man who charges coke ovens.

Index

Abraham, William ('Mabon'), S. Wales miners' leader, 37

Adamson, Westgarth, miner, preacher, and radical, 177–8, 186–7; joins Labour Party, 185; in lock-out of 1926, 206; sermons by, 100–1

addresses, by Methodist speakers, 96, 103–4

age, status conferred by, 246

Aged Miners' Homes, 84, 157, 164

agriculture: in Deerness valley, 64, 68; depression of 1870s in, 29; miners drawn from, 67

Alden, Percy, M.P., 60

Amalgamated Society of Engineers, 32

Amalgamated Society of Railway Servants, 32–3

Anglo-Boer war, 33; opposition to, 35, 47, 59, 62, 63

Anti-Sweating League, 59

arbitration between employers and men, 92; Methodist belief in, 189; Pease in favour of, 80, 87, 90, 157; unions' support for, 158

asceticism, inner-worldly, 20–1, 22; of Methodism, 26, 105, 119, 191; reserve and restraint accompanying, 148; as theme of sermons, 98

Asquith, H. H., 49, 50, 51

Bailey, Ben, left out of list of chapel trustees for being left-wing, 168

Band of Hope, 126, 130, 192

baptisms, 'superstitious' beliefs about, 94

Baptists, 57, 125; in Deerness Valley, 70, 74, 82, 242

Barren, Robert, checkweighman at Cornsay Colliery, 85, 161, 166; offices held by, 162

Beaumont family, and London Lead Company, 90

Bell, Richard, L.R.C.-supported M.P. for Derby, 34

Besant, Annie, 22

Bible: higher criticism of, 99, 177, 181; radicals use language of, 225; study of, at Sunday schools, 106, 111–12

Bible classes, 104, 105, 119; discussions at, 169, 170, 174

Binns, Thomas, missionary and temperance worker in Deerness Valley, 83

blacklegs: in Cambrian Combine strike, 42; in lock-out of 1926, 86, 167, 204–205, 206–7, 208, 210

Blatchford, Robert, 171, 172

bond system, D.M.A. negotiates abolition of (1872), 36

Bone, under manager at Waterhouses colliery, 85

Boyne, Lord: coal royalties received by, 68; gives land for chapels, 82

Bradlaugh, Charles, 104

Brancepeth, part of Deerness Valley in parish of, 71

Brandon and Deerness Valley (Methodist) circuit, 70–1

brick-making, in Deerness Valley, 66, 81, 245

British Socialist Party (1911), 35, 44

British Workmen's Public Houses, 83

Brotherhood Church, 171, 225

Browell, under manager at Cornsay Colliery, 85, 193

Burleigh, Richard, school attendance officer and preacher, on Christian Socialism, 169

Burnham, William, chapel trustee at Waterhouses, 135

Burnip, William, Methodist leader in Crook: and founding of Waterhouses chapel, 95

Burns, John, M.P., 48

Burt, Thomas, M.P., 157

bus service, in Deerness Valley, 64, 216

Cairns, solicitor's clerk and preacher, on fringe of I.L.P., 176

Cambrian Combine strike (1910–11), 40, 42

Campbell, R. J., 57, 176, 228; The New Theology by, 99, 174, 202, 227

Campbell-Bannerman, H., 47, 50

capital punishment, campaign for abolition of, 84

Carlyle, Thomas, Methodists on, 99

Carnegie, Andrew, Esh Winning Methodists receive grant for organ from, 12, 29

Carpenter, Edward, J. G. Harrison and, 171, 198, 225
cash nexus, emergence of, 3, 5; Quakers and, 78
census reports, for Deerness Valley, 67–68
chapels (Methodist), in Deerness Valley, 70–1; gifts for building of, 81–2; land for building of, 76, 82, 135; problems arising on closing of, 124, 136; renting of, for payment of unemployment benefit, 211; trustees for, *see* trustees
checkweighmen, 16, 36, 87
Cheek, Alfred (son of D. Cheek), miner, Methodist, member of I.L.P., 170, 178; imprisoned (1926), 206
Cheek, Charlie, Jack, and Joe (sons of D. Cheek), miners, Methodists, members of I.L.P., 170, 178
Cheek, David, hewer, non-Methodist, Liberal, 154, 181; in Citizens' League, 162, 193; offices held by, 145, 162, 170, 175–6
Chinese labour in S. Africa, 35, 48
choirs of Methodist chapels, 115–16, 216; dismissals from, 138
cholera, 152
Christian Endeavour meetings, 126, 129, 130
Christian Science, 171, 173
Christian Social Brotherhood (1898–1903), 60
Christian Social Union, 55, 56, 60
Christian Socialist League (1894–8), 60
Christian Socialists, 54–63, 169
church, development of sect into, 120–3, 133
Church Commissioners, coal royalties paid to, 71, 72
Church of England: in Deerness Valley, 70, 71–2, 83; in Education Act debate, 76, 192; electoral rolls of (1931–66), in Hamsteels and Waterhouses, 72, 242; relations of Methodists with, 76, 77; seen by Methodists as associated with drink trade and Tory party, 76, as associated with colliery owners, 180, as closed group, 127, 237, 238, and as countenancing gambling, 142; supports owners (1926), 203, 204, 207, 212
Citizens' League, opposing 1902 Education Act, 162, 163, 192–3
Clarion Clubs, 35
class conflict: Methodism and, 13, 23–4, 26; Socialism and, 12
class consciousness, 14; as form of deviance in period discussed, 17; Methodism inhibits development of, 26; preceded by trade union consciousness, 18, 43
class meetings of Methodists, 118, 119
Clifford, John, Christian Socialist, 57, 60
Clough, T., miner, preacher, union

lodge secretary, member of I.L.P., 170, 184, 201; in lock-out of 1926, imprisoned, 204, 205, evicted from house and employment, 208, and struck off preachers' list, 211, 215; triumphant return of, to village, 215, and election of, to R.D.C., 208
coal: cost of mining, 89; exports of, 16, 28, 30, 36, 45; free, for miners, 147, 154; gifts of, to poor, 81; 157; miners' strategy of restricting output of, 38, 86, 88; price of, for ironworks, 158, 159; production of, in county Durham (1880–1905), 29; sliding scale system of tying miners' wages to price of, 37, 39, 81, 88, 158; from tips, 87, 210
coal mines: closure of, causes loss of contact between Methodists and non-Methodists, 215; government control of, in war-time, 30–1; nationalisation of, 17, 31, 45, 161; percentage of population employed in (Brandon and Byshottles U.D.), 243; run-down of (1951 onwards), 31
coke ovens, 75, 244
collectivism, not readily accepted by Methodists, 186
colliery managers, 84–6, 156; not involved in choice of Methodist ministers, 144
colliery owners, 78–84, 156, 224; lock-out by (1926), 203, 210; mostly Liberals, 145; as Non-conformists, united with Methodists in opposition to brewers and 1902 Education Act, 195; and Non-Political Union, 209; patrons of Methodist chapels, 150–1, but not involved in choice of ministers, 144
communion service, of Methodists and of Church of England, 127
compromise, industrial, 37, 92, 151, 229; end of, 154; rejected by J. G. Harrison, 174; stressed by Methodists, 63, 145–6, 167
Congregationalists, 56, 57
conscientious objection (First World War), 198–200, 201–2; association of I.L.P. with, 176–7, 182; conflicts within Methodism over, 227
conscription, 49
Conservative Party: and drink trade, 76, 160, 192; and Ireland, 49; and First World War, 49
Conspiracy and Protection of Property Act (1875), 31
conversion: experience of, in Methodism, 23, 93, 96, 103; of drunkards, 142; worldly consequences of, 142
conversionist sects, 120, 121; Methodism begins as, 123
Cooke, Edward, smallholder and I.L.P. member, 169, 176

co-operation, industrial, 60
Co-operative stores in Deerness Valley: credit from (1926), 203, 211; late opening of, on Fridays, 130; manager of, a leading Methodist, 74; Methodists as office-holders in, 155, 162–4; savings in, 143; as sources of employment, 73
Cornsay Colliery (village), owned by Ferens and Love, 64, 66, 78, 81; arrival of Methodists in, 135; in lock-out of 1926, 207; Methodist chapel in, 82, 250; Methodist membership in (1935–68), 241; Methodists in I.L.P. in, 170–7; occupations in, 244; population of, 68; voting for and against strikes by union members in, 165
corporations, industrial: growth of, 29
Craddock, George, miner, Methodist, member of I.L.P., 170, 176; in women's suffrage movement, 171
craftsmen, capitalism and, 3
Crawford, William, Methodist, Durham miners' leader, 12, 37, 157, 158
crimes of violence in Deerness Valley, 140, 141, 179–80; decline in, 152
Crofton, manager at Esh Winning colliery, 84–5, 87, 88, 156, 166
Crook Circuit Methodists: resolution of, on industrial situation (1926), 213
Curry, Michael, manager at Cornsay Colliery, 82, 84, 85, 86; on bench (1926), 204; on Lanchester tribunal (First World War), 199

Dack, James, missionary and temperance worker in Deerness Valley, 83, 160
Deerness Valley, 64–8; history of Methodism, in, 134–6; population of, 66, 67–8, 140; 'the Singing Valley', 115
Deerness Valley Temperance and Prohibition Association, 192
Derbyshire coalfield: housing in, 64; Labour Party in, 189–90; miners' unions in, 37, 183
disestablishment, Welsh concern with, 182
domestic servants, offers to employ miners as, 154
Dove, Sam, hewer and checkweighman, Liberal, 145, 166; and Labour Party, 168; offices held by, 162; speaks at presentation to manager, 167
dramaturgical method of research, 235–236
drink trade: Conservative Party and, 76, 160, 192; issue in 1905 election, 48, 107; Methodist opposition to, 108, 227
drunkenness, in Durham coalfield, 140, 141, 147, 179, 192; fall in, 152
Dublin, strike in, 41, 42
Dukhobors, 225

Dunglass, Lord (Sir Alec Douglas Home), 154
Dunnico, Herbert, M.P., 61
Durham Chronicle (Liberal), reports temperance activities, 192
Durham coalfield: differences between Yorkshire coalfield and, 15–16, 17, 28; export of coal from, 16, 28, 36; miners' unions in, 36, 37; wages and unemployment in, 46; worked from west to east, 31, 66
Durham county: population of, 66, 67; results of elections in constituencies of (1885–1910), 52, 53
Durham County Council, first to be Labour-controlled (1919), 52
Durham Diocesan Society for the Employment of Additional Clergy, 71
Durham Miners' Association (D.M.A.), founded 1869, 36; affiliates to Labour Party, 40; Annual Gala of, 39, 44, 141, 158, 179, 188; breaks with Liberal Party (1908–9), 184, 185; call to expel conscientious objectors from, 200; and compensation for death of blackleg, 206; I.L.P. resolutions to, 183; lodge banners of, 146, 229; Methodist office-holders in, 161, 162–164; Socialists elected to executive committee of, (1898), 39; only union recognised by Owners' Association, 209; voting for and against strikes by members of, compared with national vote, 165
Durham Miners' Progressive Federation, 175
Durham Miners' Reform Association, 175, 181

East Hedleyhope (village), 64, 141, 157; colliery at, 79
ecumenism, 122, 123; irrelevant to social life of chapels, 228; *see also* Methodist-Anglican union
education: advocated by colliery owners, 79–80; Church of England and, 77; sacrifices of Methodist parents to obtain, for their children, 143
Education, Royal Commission on (1871), 79
Education Act (1902): issue in 1905 election, 48, 109; Liberals and L.R.C. stand together on, 35, 49; Methodist opposition to, 159, 227; modifications of (1909), 194; passive resistance to, 60, 160, 192–3
Education Act (1918), 'Geddes axe' and, 45
eight-hour day: campaign for, 16, 17, 40, 47, 89, 175; legislation on, 39, 42, 159; opposed by Durham and Northumberland miners, 38–9, 47–8, 183
elections: general, (1905) 43, 48, 107, 109, (1910) 41, (1918) 50, (1922,

elections: general – *contd.*
1923, 1924), 45; local, in Deerness
Valley (1877), 68; results of general,
in county Durham constituencies
(1885–1910), 52, 53
elective affinity: between clusters of
ideas, 120; between religious and
other ideas, 23, 26
Ellis, Connie, women's suffrage leader,
171, 177, 200
Emerson, R. W., 57; Methodists and,
104, 171, 199, 225
Employers' Parliamentary Council, 32,
43
endogamy, among Methodists, 127, 129
Engineering Employers' Federation, 32
entertainment, commercial, 215–16
equality: assumption of, by Methodists
and trade unionists, 223
Esh Winning (village), owned by Pease
and Partners, 64, 78; Baptists in, 82;
colliery at, 65, 68, 153, 244; housing
in, 66, 68; Irish in, 75; leisure activities in, 84–5, 131, 141; in lock-out of
1891, 86–7; in lock-out of 1926, 204,
208, 210; Methodist chapels in, 82,
135, 136; Methodist membership in
(1935–68), 241; Methodists in D.M.A.
lodge in, 161; Methodists oppose
licence for new public house in, 192;
Non-Political Union in, 208; occupations in, 244; occupations of Methodist leaders in, 251, 252; population
of, 68; proposed temperance hall in,
193; recruits from (and casualties),
First World War, 200; Roman Catholics in union lodge at (1966), 214;
shops in, 73; voting for and against
strikes by union members in, 165, 166
ethics: Gladstone's mixture of prudence
and, 47; of older men, 153; recognition of differences between Methodists and others in, 125, 237, 238; in
Sunday school lessons, 107–11; tension between politics and, 101
evangelical revival (1739), Halévy on,
6–7
Evans, Isaac, S. Wales miners' leader,
37
examinations: for local preachers, 145;
for teachers and scholars at Sunday
schools, 110, 111

Fabian Society, 4, 34; Christian Social-
ists and, 60, 62
Faulker, Bella (Mrs J. G. Harrison),
women's suffrage leader, 171
Fenianism, in county Durham, 75, 76
Fenwick, Revd J., 99
Ferens, colliery owner, Methodist cir-
cuit steward, 84, 251; gives coal for
poor, 157
Ferens and Love, colliery owners at
Cornsay, 64, 89

finances of Methodist societies, 133–4;
effects of 1926 on, 211, 216; fund-
raising activities for, 130; and house
for minister, 149; rationalisation of,
and fund-raising activities, 123, 136
Findley, Isaac, Methodist, speaks for
miners at presentation to manager,
167
First World War: casualties in, 200;
coal mines during, 30; cost of living
during, 29; Labour Party during, 44;
and Liberal Party, 49; Methodist attitude to, 196–7, 214; pacifists in, 62;
sermons during, 102; temperance
work during, 108
Fitzpatrick, James, chapel trustee at
Waterhouses, 135, 192; offices held
by, 162
Flanagan, Revd James, speaker on
work in E. End of London, 135
Fletcher, G., manager at Hamsteels
colliery, 85
Foster, D. B., Methodist and socialist,
59
Foster, William, coke-burner and
preacher: offices held by, 163; sermon
register of, 102
Fox, George, J. G. Harrison and, 171,
174, 198
Free Church Socialist League (1909),
60–1
free trade, debate on, 30, 50
funerals: of conscientious objector, 200;
as expressions of communal solidarity,
69, 216, 221

Gainford, Lord (J. A. Pease), 90
Galbraith, S., Lib.-Lab. M.P. for
Spennymoor, 52, 160, 179, 197;
D.M.A. secretary, 161
Galley, George, preacher, member of
I.L.P. group, 176
gambling: Labour Party and, 187;
Methodist disapproval of, 96, 108,
119, 131, 142; Peases and, 83; resolu-
tions of Methodist quarterly meetings
on, 159; as a serious problem in Deer-
ness Valley (1909), 141
Garr, S., chairman of Esh Winning
Union lodge, imprisoned (1926), 204
'Geddes axe', 45
General Strike (1926), 46, 161, 203, 210
George, Henry, influence of, 55, 56, 61
Gibbon, George, miner, spiritualist,
member of I.L.P., 170
Gladstone, W. E., 47–8, 224
Godwin, William, J. G. Harrison and,
171
gold standard, return to (1925), 46
Good Templars, Independent Order of,
130, 192
Gore, Charles, 56, 60
Gott, T., founder of Waterhouses
Labour Party, 169, 184

Grayson, Victor, M.P., 35, 60
Green, T. H., 55, 61
Greener, agent for colliery owners, 87
Guild of St Matthew (1877–1909), 55

Hague Conference (1907), 48
Hammell, James, labourer and then
  shopkeeper, 143, 160; on military
  service tribunal, 199, 200; offices held
  by, 163
Hamsteels (hamlet), owned by Johnson
  and Reay, 64, 78; Church of St John
  the Baptist at, 72, 242; colliery at,
  65, 180; in lock-out of 1926, 207;
  rugby football team from, 84; voting
  for and against strikes by union members at, 165, 166; *see also* Quebec-
  Hamsteels
Hardie, Keir, M.P. for Merthyr, 34, 40,
  173, 175, 202
Harrison, Esther, women's suffrage
  leader, 171
Harrison, John, miner and preacher,
  101, 169, 175; addresses by 101, 102,
  104–5, 114
Harrison, John George (son of John),
  preacher and I.L.P. member, 170,
  178, 181, 183; authors read by, 171–
  172; imprisoned as pacifist (First
  World War), 198, 199, 200; views of,
  172–4; in women's suffrage move-
  ment, 171
Harrison, Joseph, shopkeeper, Liberal:
  in conflict with Catholic Church over
  land for chapel, 76, 135; offices held
  by, 163, 170; in protest against 1902
  Education Act, 192
Harrison, William, Liberal, 168; J. G.
  Harrison on, 198
Harvey, Derbyshire miners' leader, 37,
  40, 100
Haslam, Derbyshire miners' leader, 37,
  40
Hayson, Ralph, trustee of Waterhouses
  chapel, diary of, 135, 151
Hayson, Ralph, jun., 153; opposes 1902
  Education Act, 193, 195
Headlam, Stewart, 55, 56
Headlam, Mrs, wife of Tory M.P., 154
Henderson, Arthur, Labour M.P. for
  Barnard Castle, 183
Henery, John (Jack), early Methodist,
  132, 135; offices held by, 163; in
  First World War, 197, 200
hewers, high status of, 245, 246
Hewitson, Isaac, leading Methodist, 132,
  138; breaks up Sunday pitch-and-toss
  school, 131
Hind, Revd R., 98, 99, 102
historians, on religion in development
  of modern world, 13–14; Methodist
  (Wearmouth), 3, 11–13, 226; rationalist Liberal (Buckle, Halévy, Lecky,
Weber), 1–2, 5–8, 25, 226; Socialist
  (Hammonds, Hobsbawm, Thompson,
  Webbs), 2–3, 8–11, 13, 25; Toynbee,
  3–4
Holmes, John, Roman Catholic, active
  in Labour Party, Irish League, and
  trade union, 169–70, 178, 183; represents Hamsteels in D.M.A., 181
Home Office reports, give figures for
  numbers employed in mines, 67
House, William, of D.M.A., 176
housing in Deerness Valley, provided by
  colliery owners, 64, 66, 81; evictions
  from (1926), 208, 210; notice to quit,
  on retirement of miner, 154–5; regarded by R.D.C. as mine-owners'
  responsibility, 52, 179
Housing of the Working Classes Act,
  179
Howard League for Penal Reform, 84
Huddlestone: opposes temperance hall,
  193, 194; refuses to pay rates in opposition to 1902 Education Act, 193
Hughes, Hugh Price, 58–9, 61, 108,
  181
hymn-singing by Methodists, 115, 117,
  147

independence, Methodist spirit of, 143,
  145, 152; strain of economic depression on, 153
Independent Labour Party, 34, 43, 91;
  and Christian Socialists, 62; disbanded on growth of Labour Party,
  185; in North of England, 40, 44, 62;
  paper on, read to Methodist Bible
  class, 169; Quebec group of, 168,
  170–7, 183, 198, 225; resolutions of
  branches of, to D.M.A., 183; summer
  camp of, 176; and First World War,
  44
individualism: in Methodist response in
  1926, 210; of Methodists and Liberals,, 167, 168; not easily reconciled
  with collectivism, 186; Protestantism
  and, 223
Industrial Workers of Great Britain
  (1910), 41, 42
Industry and Trade, Royal Commission
  on (1885–6), 29
Ireland, Liberals and, 47, 49
Irish: in Deerness Valley, 66–7, 180,
  230; in county Durham, employed to
  build railways, then unemployed,
  then sink mine shafts, 75
Irish Transport and General Workers'
  Union, 42
iron and steel industry: British, overtaken by Germany and U.S.A., 30;
  coal for, 28; interests of colliery owners in, 78, 80, 88, 158, 159; introduction of Bessemer process in, 88
Isaacs, Lord Chief Justice, 50

Index

Jacques, George, Durham I.L.P. member, 39

James, Thomas, under-manager at Waterhouses colliery, 84

Johnson, Isaac (1867–1950), hewer, leading Methodist, Liberal, 132; 144; family tree of, 128; joins Labour Party, 210; offices held by, 163

Johnson, J., miner, Methodist, Liberal: offices held by, 164

Johnson, J. B., colliery owner, 78, 83, 179, 207

Johnson and Reay, colliery owners at Quebec-Hamsteels, 64, 78, 84; gifts to Methodist chapel from, 83

Joicey, Sir James, Durham colliery owner, 38

Keeble, S. E., 58, 59
Kenworthy, J. C., 60
Kropotkin, Prince, at D.M.A. Gala, 39
Knox, manager at Cornsay Colliery, 85

Labour, Royal Commission on (1891), 157, 158

Labour Colleges, 44, 216

labour exchanges, 49

Labour Party, 33–5, 43; continuity of, with Liberal Party, 12, 190, 229; in Durham county, 40, 52, 182–90; influence of, begins to be felt at local level (1907), 168; Methodists and, 63, 155, 184; Methodists vote for, but would still vote Liberal if candidate available, 186; separation of Methodism from, 187, 216; and Socialism, 19, 35, 43, 44, 52; trade unions and, 44, 45; see also Independent Labour Party

Labour Representation Committee (L.R.C.), 33, 34, 35, 40, 51

labourers, not represented in Methodist leadership, 73–4

Lakin, Jimmy, miner, Methodist, member of I.L.P., 170, 178; in First World War, 198

Lancashire, miners' unions in, 36

landowners, in Deerness Valley, 68

Lansbury, George, 40

Larkin, Jim, 42; in Deerness Valley, 171

Lawther, Will, Labour candidate, 184

leaders of Methodist chapels, 131–2, 139, 153; aged, difficulties of removing from office, 139; women reluctant to act as, 74, 124

Leak, Dr Charles, M.P., 60

Lee, Miss, popular missioner, 135

Lee, Peter, Labour chairman of Durham County Council, 52, 178

Leeds Brotherhood Church, 59

leisure activities, in Deerness Valley, 77, 84, 131; connected with chapels, 130,

215, 227; not shared by Methodists and non-Methodists, 156

Liberal Party, 47–50; colliery owners and trade union leaders as members of, 145; continuity of Labour Party with, 12, 190, 229; decline of, 50–1, 184; Labour government of 1923 dependent on, 45; Methodists in, 155, 162–4, 168; overlapping of union and chapel membership in, reinforces position of, 188, 189; resists Socialist ideas, 40; and social reform, 35, 43, 47, 49; in Waterhouses and district, 159–60; working-class M.P.s of, 33, 34; First World War and, 49

Liberalism: association of Methodism and, 11, 23, 33–4, 58, 63, 159–60; Gladstonian, of high ethical quality and *laissez-faire* economics, 47, 48, 52; Socialism as an extension of, 4

licensing laws, movement for reform of, 83, 109, 160, 191–2

Lincolnshire, migration to Deerness Valley from, 66

Llewellyn, Richard, *How Green was my Valley* by, 153

Lloyd George, D., 45, 46, 47, 48, 49, 50

local government, Methodist officeholders in, 155, 162–4

Local Option Bill (1926), 108

lock-outs by colliery owners: (1891, Esh Winning), 86; (1893, Durham), 16, 36, 39, 56; (1926), 46, 86, 91–2, 167, 202–3, 224, 227

lodgers in Deerness Valley houses, 67, 76

London, migration to Deerness Valley from, 66

London Labour Church, 57

Love, Joseph, hewer, Methodist preacher, becomes colliery owner, 78, 81, 84, 151; colliery appointments made by, 86; in conflict with Catholic Church over land for chapel, 76; gifts to chapels from, 81–2; national figure in Methodism, 156, 251; and trade unions, 82, 157

Lowden, manager at Hamsteels colliery, 85

Lowden, Jack, miner, Methodist, member of I.L.P., 170

Lowes, Emma (Mrs George Craddock), women's suffrage leader, 171

MacDonald, Ramsay, 43, 45, 59, 175

MacDonald, Cuthbert, member of I.L.P., 170, 176, 178; takes up case of widow of blackleg (1926), 206; in First World War, 198

MacDonald, Robert, checkweighman, Methodist, Liberal, 145, 178; member of I.L.P., 170, 175, 176; offices held by, 164; on R.D.C., 208; in First World War, 198

McKenna, checkweighman at Water-houses colliery, militant in 1926, 208

McLane, George, miner, 87, 142; conversion of (1880), 135; offices held by, 160

McPhail, Revd Peter, 87

Mann, Tom, 39, 158; in Deerness Valley, 171

Manson, Revd C. L., Christian Socialist, 62

Marconi scandal, 50

market, economy based on a 'free', 158–9; Liberals and, 23, 52; miners accept, 17, 38, 39, 86, 88, 156–7, 224; miners prepare to resist, 91–2, 154, 168; owners interfere with, 80; 81; Peases see industrial conflict as result of imperfect understanding of, 78–9

Marshall, Alfred, 55

Marx and Marxism, 14, 43, 44, 114–15, 184, 225

Matthews, under manager at Esh Winning colliery, 85

Maurice, F. D., 55, 59, 176, 225; J. G. Harrison and, 171, 172

means test (1931), 46

Mechanics Institutes, 69, 77

Methodism: anti-radical, 12, 186, 201, 210; associational features of, 134, 136, 137; beliefs of, 93–7, 125, 233; and Christian Socialism, 58–60, 63; collective expression of beliefs of, 115–118, 123; communal nature of, 27, 96, 126, 127, 137, 139; conflicts within, 132; as established religion of Deerness Valley, 77, 137; focuses political action on issues with ethical aspect, 58; history of, 5–14; ignorance of structure of, 124–5; individual reform/social reform dilemma in, 113–115; isolating effect of, 130–1, 132; and Labour Party, 12, 187, 216; and Liberalism, 11, 23, 33–4, 58, 63, 159–160; offers personal ethic, not political programme, 21, 26, 223; patriarchs in, 131–2, 139, 153; sociologists on, 4, 14; and the state, 11, 196; unions within (1907, 1932), 136; universalism of, 24; in villages compared with metropolitan, 123, 129

Methodist-Anglican union: answers to questions on, 237–9; attitudes towards, 127, 142; votes on, 122–3, 124–5

Methodist Connexions, 133, 231

Methodist New Connexion, 81, 82, 231; leaders in, 250–1

Methodist Times (1885), 58, 59

Methodist Weekly, 59

Methodists in Deerness Valley: occupations of, 73–4; occupations of leaders of, 249–53; numbers of, 70; numbers

of, now declining, 214–15, and average age advancing, 216–17; *see also* Primitive Methodists, Wesleyan Methodists

migration: into Durham coalfield, 64; out of Durham coalfield, 88, 202

military service tribunals, First World War, 163, 199, 200, 201–2, 214; conflicts within Methodism aroused by, 227

millenarianism, 181, 186

miners, 35–40; of Ashton area, Yorkshire, 15–16; face-workers among, as craftsmen and artisans, 22; Liberal-Non-conformist leadership of (up to First World War), 13, 36; Liberals lose support of, 52; in Methodist leadership, 73, 74; numbers employed as, county Durham (1880, 1905), 29; occupations of fathers of, 74; occupations of sons of, 74, 149–50, 215; percentage of population of Deerness Valley employed as, 72–3; restriction of output by, 38, 86, 88; transfer to Labour Party of (1920s), 169, 178–9; unemployment among, 46, 69–70, 153, 202; widows of, in company houses, 81; in First World War, 45, 197

Miners' Federation of Great Britain (M.F.G.B.), 36, 38–40; and Cambrian Combine Strike, 42; last big union to affiliate to Labour Party, 35, 40, 183

Miners' Institutes, 66, 84

Minimum Wage Bill (1912), 51; *for minimum wage, see under* wages

ministers of Methodist chapels, provided by the Connexions, 133; as active Liberals, 160; travel by trustees to hear preaching by, 144

missionaries, appointed by Pease and Partners, 83

Moll, Revd W. E., Christian Socialist, Newcastle, 62–3

Morgan, David, S. Wales miners' leader, 37

Morley, John, 48

musical performances, by chapel members, 116, 130; *see also* choirs

mysticism, other-worldly and inner-worldly, 20

National Free Labour Association (strike-breakers), 32, 33, 42

National Council of Labour Colleges, 216

National Insurance Act (1911), 49

navy, Liberals and, 48

negotiation, of miners with owners: machinery for, in Durham coalfield, 39, 89

Noel, Revd Conrad, Christian socialist, 62

Non-conformist Anti-Socialist Union (1909), 57
Non-conformists: and Christian Socialism, 56–7; and Liberal Party, 49, 52
Non-Political Union (1926), 205, 208–9
Northumberland: miners' unions in, work with Durham unions, 36, 37, 38; unofficial strikes in, 39; wages and unemployment in, 46

occupations in Deerness Valley, 66, 67, 72–3, 243–5; of Methodist leaders, 249–53; of Methodists, 73–4; relative status of, 245–7
old age pensions, 49
Orange demonstrations, in county Durham, 75
Osborne judgement, on political levy by trade unions, 41, 47, 49
Owners' Association, bound to recognise only D.M.A., 209

pacifism, 52, 198; of Christian Socialists, 61, 62
Paine, Tom, 104, 171
Palmer, manager: speeches and presentation at retirement of, 167
Pankhurst, Mrs, in Deerness Valley, 171
parishes: creation of new, in county Durham, 72
parochialism, of Methodists, 127
paternalism of colliery owners, 78, 84, 92, 151, 168; erosion of, 89; final destruction of (1926), 92, 202, 208
patience, inculcated in Sunday schools, 110
Patterson, W. H., to Royal Commission on Labour (1891), 157, 158
peace, retrenchment, and reform: slogan of Gladstonian Liberals, 47
Peace Society, 84
Peake, author influencing J. G. Harrison, 174
Pearson, Tom, checkweighman, Liberal, 145, 154, 166, 167; offices held by, 164
Peart, Miss, popular missioner, 135
Pease, Arthur, 80, 82
Pease, Sir A. F., 89–90, 91
Pease, John Whitwell, 80
Pease, Joseph (1799–1872), colliery owner, M.P., and leading industrialist, 78, 90, 156
Pease, Joseph Albert (Lord Gainford), 90
Pease, Joseph Whitwell (1828–1903), 78, 83, 84, 90; contributes to Baptists and Methodists, 82; in favour of arbitration, 87, 92, 157; stresses partnership, 79–80; and unions, 79, 80, 81, 209
Pease and Partners, colliery owners in Deerness Valley, 64; appointments in collieries made directly by, 86; be-

come limited liability company (1898), 78; dividends paid by, 89, 154; gifts of coal by, 81; habitual drunkards sacked by, 142; ironworks of, 78, 159; lock-out by (1891), 86; in lock-out of 1926, 153, 154–5, 159; missionaries and temperance workers appointed by, 83; paternalism of, 78, 89, 92, 151; personnel and welfare officer employed by, 204; recruiting offices of, Lincolnshire and London, 66; said to favour Methodists in recruiting, 70
Peases West (hamlet), 78, 81
Peel, Sir Robert, on education, 79
perfection, Methodist doctrine of, 95, 102; preached by J. G. Harrison, 174
Pickard, Ben, Methodist, Liberal, secretary of Yorkshire miners' union, 16; chairman of M.F.G.B., 17
picketing, by miners in 1926, 203–4
pietism, of present-day Methodism, 221
playing cards, Methodists and, 142
police: during lock-out in 1926, 167, 204; during strike in 1892, 87–8
political levy, by trade unions, 41, 46–7, 209
political organisations: Methodist avoidance of, 58; vocation for work in, 21–22
politics: and drink trade, 108; separation of religion from, 211; tension between ethics and, 101
Pontefract, troops called to (1893), 16
population of Deerness Valley, 66, 67–8; occupational structure of, 72–4, 243–245; Roman Catholics in, 71
prayer meetings of Methodists, 117–18, 126
preachers, Methodist local, 219; examination and trial sermon required from, 145; occupations of, 249, 251, 252
Prest, Archdeacon, temperance speech by, 140–1
prices, retail (1896–1913, 1920), 29
Priestley, Joseph, 57
Primitive Methodists (P.M.s), in Deerness Valley, 68, 70, 82, 231; miners under-represented in leadership of, 73, 74; number of (Waterhouses, 1892–1931), 240; office holders of, 162–4; resolutions passed by quarterly meetings of (1892–1932), 159
Pritchard, George E., miner, Methodist preacher, member of I.L.P., 170; checkweighman, county councillor, 178; in lock-out of 1926, 206; in First World War, 198
Pritchard, J. (brother of George), in prison as conscientious objector, 198, 199
profits, of colliery owners, 154
Progressive League (1907), 57
Protestant Ethic, 2, 19–20, 222–6

public houses, in Deerness Valley, 83
public works, set in hand by R.D.C. for unemployed during suspension of benefit, 208
publicans, compensation for non-renewal of licences of, 191–2
punctuality, inculcated in Sunday schools, 110
puritanism, Halévy on, 5, 7
Pyle, preacher, non-Methodist, leader in 1879 strike, 175, 181

Quakers, 57–8; Pease family as, 78, 81
Quebec (Quebec-Hamsteels) (village), owned by Johnson and Reay, 64; attitude to owners in, 179; drunkenness in (1870), 140; economic death of (1926), 182, 244; I.L.P. in, 168, 170–177, 183, 198, 225; in lock-out of 1926, 206–7, 210; Methodist chapel in, 83, 135; Methodist membership in (1935–68), 241; Methodists in, 70; miners as Methodist leaders in, 73; occupations in, 244; occupations of leading Methodists in, 250, 252, 253; population of, 68; social conditions in, 179–80; in First World War, 200
Quebec Liberal Association, 160

Raikes, Ribert, 103, 104
railway, in Deerness Valley, 64
Raine, Isaac, chapel trustee in Waterhouses, 135, 143
'rate-busters', 86
Rattenbury, Revd J. E., Methodist member of Free Church Socialist League, 60
Reay, colliery owner: gifts to Methodists from, 83; *see also* Johnson and Reay
recruiting committees, First World War: Methodists on, 197
Redistribution Act (1884), 32
Reform Act (1884), 32
religion: cultural influence of, 25; different aspects of, 93; interpretation of experience of, 232; separation of politics and, 211
religious affiliations, of population in Deerness Valley, 68–72
religious conflicts, in Deerness Valley, 75–7
religious groups, associational and communal, 27, 121–2, 187, 226–9; associational features of Methodism, 134, 136, 137; communal nature of Methodism, 27, 96, 126, 127, 129, 137, 139; tension between communal and associational tendencies, 136
respectability, concept of, 146, 148, 156; challenge to, 174; Labour Party and, 189; Liberalism and, 189; social stratification in terms of gradation of, 144, 210

revolution: religion in avoidance of, in Britain, 2, 5
Richardson, Aron, hewer, Methodist, Liberal, 85, 132, 166, 168; in lock-out of 1926, 206; offices held by, 164; opposes 1902 Education Act, 193; radical, but not in I.L.P. group, 177, 178 (joins Labour Party, 185); son of, leaves mine to become minister, 150
Ritson, Revd J., 100
ritual of Methodists, 115–18, 237, 238; recognition of differences between Methodists and others in, 125
road, built in Deerness Valley, 64
Roman Catholics in Deerness Valley, 66, 70, 71, 74, 140; attitudes of Methodists towards, 129; and land for chapels, 76, 135; on Methodists, 149; in trade unions (1966), 214
Rosebery, Lord, negotiates settlement of 1893 coal strike, 39
Royal Commissions: Education (1871), 79; Industry and Trade (1885–6), 29; Labour (1891), 157, 158
royalties on coal, 68, 71
Russian Revolution, 182
Rust, Revd E. C., Vicar of St John's, Hamsteels: and J. G. Harrison, 198; in lock-out of 1926, 180, 207
Ryle, agent for Pease and Partners, 84, 85, 166; presentation on leaving of (1926), 210

Sabbatarianism of Methodists, 119, 143–144, 147
sacred-secular dichotomy: in approach to 'the world', 56, 119, 177; in sermons, 98, 99, 100, 104
Saddler, Basil, on bench (1926), 204
Saddler brothers, buy Hamsteels Colliery (1921), 78, 207; appointments in colliery made by, 86; in lock-out of 1926, 206
St John the Baptist Church, Hamsteels, 72; electoral roll of (1931–66), 242
St Paul's Church, Waterhouses, 72; electoral roll of (1931–62), 242
St Stephen's Mission, Esh Winning, 84
salvation, 9, 21, 119, 223; as theme of sermons, 98, and of Sunday school teaching, 106
Salvation Army, in Deerness Valley, 242
Samuel Commission, 46
Samuels, Turner, Labour candidate, 185
Samuelsson, Sir Basil, colliery owner, advocates education, 79–80
Sankey Commission, 30, 45
schools: colliery managers at, 85; at Cornsay Colliery, 82; at Esh Winning, 66, 79, 82; at Waterhouses, 65; *see also* Sunday schools
Scotland, miners' unions in, 36, 38
seamen, strikes of, 41, 42

Second World War, coal mines during, 30–1
sect: development of, into church, 120–123, 133
sedition, early association of Methodism with, 8
self-assurance, aspect of Methodism, 95, 96
self-discipline of Methodists, 116, 119, 144
self-improvement classes of Methodists, 96, 104–5, 119
sermons, of Methodist preachers, 96, 97–103, 116, 118–19, 219, 231–2; trial, from local preachers, 145
service: enhanced status as bonus for, 150; as theme of Sunday school lessons, 106–7, 113
services in Methodist chapels, 126, 216, 218–21
Shelley, P. B., J. G. Harrison and, 171
shopkeepers: in Esh Winning (1908), 73; in lock-out of 1926, 211; religious affiliations of, 74, 253; status of, 246–247
sliding scale, tying miners' wages to price of coal, 37, 39, 81, 88, 158
smallpox, 152
Smiles, Samuel, 4, 81, 104
Smillie, Robert, 51
Smythe family of Flass Hall, Catholics, 67, 76; build houses in Esh Winning, 68
Snowden, Philip, 60
social class: development of consciousness of, 17, 18, 19, 43; development inhibited by Methodism, 26; religion in context of, 4; in status, 246; working-class views of, 14–15, 18
social mobility, 24, 248; sometimes a result of Methodism, 123, 149, 150; and trade union leadership, 234
social and political issues, Methodists and, 63, 98, 101, 104, 109, 114
social reform: Liberal Party and, 35, 43, 47, 49; Methodists and, 224
social status, 245–7
Socialism: definitions of, 4, 19; form of deviance in period discussed, 17, 19; First World War and attitude to, 200–1, 202; Labour Party and, 19, 35, 43, 44, 52; Methodism and, 12, 174, 186, 225, 228; miners and, 39–40; rise of, 34; see also Christian Socialism, Independent Labour Party.
Socialist Democratic Federation, 34
Socialist Quaker Society, 57
socialists: among London unemployed (1880s), 32; in Labour Party, 43–4; and miners, 39, 40
sociologists: and church-sect dichotomy, 120–3; and religion in development of modern world, 1–2, 4–5, 14–19
solidarity: Methodist services as rites of,

220; Methodist funerals as rites of, 69, 216, 221; more relevant than status, 246
soup kitchens, 143, 157, 211
South Wales coalfield: miners' unions in, 36, 37, 38; wages and unemployment in, 46
Sprott, Col., Tory colliery owner, 151
Stacy, Revd Paul, Christian Socialist, 62
standard of living: rising (1850–86), 28; falling (1899–1913), 29, 88
state, the: Christian Socialists and, 61; Hegelian view of, 55; Methodist attitude to, 11, 22, 196; Toynbee on functions of, 4
Stephenson, John, conversion of (1880), 135
Stephenson, Jonathan, Methodist, 87
Stephenson, Joseph, miner and Methodist: offices held by, 164; in First World War, 197
strikes, 40–2; see also General Strike
strikes of miners, 36, 158; (1844), 80; (1879), 80, 157, 159, 175; (1887: Northumberland), 39; (1892: Durham), 11, 36, 39, 54, 87–8, 166; (1910–11: Cambrian Combine), 40, 42; (1910: Durham), 41; (1912), 41, 54, 165, 166; (1921), 46; percentage of union members voting for and against (1909, 1912), 165, 166; see also lock-outs
suffragettes, 48
Sunday schools, Methodist, 105–6, 147; attendances at, 70, 240–1; anniversaries of, 103, 111, 126, 146, 216, 217–18; children of non-Methodists at, 137, 144; closing of (1960s), 252; colliery managers at, 85; entry to Methodism mainly through, 125–6, 153; habits and attitudes inculcated at, 109–13; lessons at, 106–9; teachers at, 73, 111, 249, 250
Sunderland Bible Institute, 99
swearing, Methodist disapproval of, 131, 144
Syndicalists, 41, 42–3, 44; in North of England, 62

Taff Vale decision, on picketing by unions, 32–3, 34, 40, 49, 51
Tariff Reform, 35, 45, 160
Taylor, Joseph, master's weighman, Methodist preacher, member of I.L.P., 102, 170, 176; diaries of, 104, 105, 169
temperance: as feature of Methodism, 96, 119, 131, 141–2, 148, 182; Labour Party and, 187, 225; movement for prohibition (1920s and 1930s), 152; Pease and Partners and, 83; resolutions of Methodist quarterly meetings on, 159; sermons on, 101, 140–1; in

Sunday school lessons, 107–9; *see also* drink trade
temperance workers, appointed by Pease and Partners, 83
theology: of church and sect, 120; of Methodism, 96, 237; not a criterion defining religion for Methodists, 125; subterranean, 94
Thompson, Revd J. D., 98
Thompson, Revd Peter, Methodist and Socialist, 59
Thoreau, H. D., J. G. Harrison and, 171, 172, 225
Thorne, Stephen, secretary of Quaker Socialist Society, 57
Thorne, Will, 32
thrift, Methodist virtue, 119, 143, 149; inculcated in Sunday schools, 110
Tillett, Ben, in Deerness Valley, 171
Tolstoy, J. G. Harrison and, 171, 172, 198, 199, 225
Towers, schoolteacher and organiser of Labour Party branches, 184
Toynbee, Arnold, 55
trade cycle, 159
Trade Union Act (1871), 31
Trade Union Act Amendment Act (1876), 31
trade union consciousness, 14, 18, 43
trade unions, 4, 31–3; in choosing of parliamentary candidate and bringing out vote, 188; colliery owners and, 79, 80, 81, 82, 209; co-operation between management and, 151, 157, 167, 223; and Labour Party, 44, 45; leadership of, 20, 145, 210, 214, 224, 234; Methodists in, 13, 145, 155–68; political levy by, 41, 46–7, 209; vocation for work in, 21; *see also* Durham Miners' Association
Trades Disputes Act (1906), 35
Trades Disputes and Trade Union Act (1927), 46–7
Trades Union Congress, 32, 42; and General Strike, 46; parliamentary committee of, 38
Triple Alliance (of miners, railwaymen, and transport workers), 41, 44, 46
Trust Houses, 83
trustees for Methodist property, 143; occupations of, 250, 251, 252
Turnbull, Tom: address by, 105; pietistic non-political position of, 187

unemployment of miners, in 1920s and 1930s, 46, 153, 202; reflection of, in reports of Methodist chapels, 69–70
Unemployment Insurance Act (1922): benefit under, 153–4; benefit suspended 1 week in 5 under, 208
Unitarians, 57
Ushaw College, Roman Catholic seminary, 66; coal royalties received by,
68; and land for Methodist chapel, 76, 135; in population figures, 71
Ushaw Moor (village), owned by Pease and Partners, 64, 78; Irish at, 66; Methodist chapel at, 83
Utilitarians, 4

vocation or calling, 21, 22
Voltaire, 104

wages, 28, 88; pressure for minimum, 16, 17, 37, 39, 40, 51, 89, 175
wages of miners: as percentage of cost of mining coal, 89; relatively high until 1920, 156, then relatively low, 46; sliding scale for, in some areas, 37, 39, 81, 88, 158
Wales: migration to Deerness Valley from, 66; political development in, 182; *see also* South Wales coalfield
Wallace, Bruce, Christian Socialist, 60
Waterhouses (village), owned by Pease and Partners, 64, 78; Church of St Paul at, 72, 242; colliery at, 88, 153, 244; in lock-out of 1926, 204, 210, 212; Methodist chapels in, 82, 124, 136; Methodist membership in, 240, 241; Methodist Sunday school in, 73, 240–1; Methodist weekly activities in, 129–30; Methodists in, 70; Methodists in union lodge in, 161; occupations of Methodist leaders in, 250, 251; population of, 68; recruits from (and casualties), First World War, 200; in strike of 1892, 87, 88; voting for and against strikes by union members in, 165, 166; Young People's (Methodist) Institute in (1926), 114, 179
Watkins, Archdeacon (Durham), 72
Weardale: London Lead Co. in, 90; migrants to Deerness Valley from, 66; migrants often Methodists, 94–5, 135; Wesley in, 95, 137
welfare state: Liberal contributions to, 49; Methodist misgivings about, 186
Wesley, John, in county Durham, 94, 95, 137
Wesleyan Conference (1894): 'our great work is to save the soul from sin', 54
Wesleyan Methodists (W.M.s), in Deerness Valley, 70, 82, 231; miners under-represented in leadership of (except at Quebec), 73; numbers of (1911–32), 241; occupations of leaders of, 251–2; unite with Primitive Methodists at Esh Winning (1932), 70
Westcott, Brooke, Bishop of Durham, 56, 108
White, Matthew (1862–1932), hewer, leading Methodist, Liberal, 132, 135, 144; approves mutual trust of owners and miners, 145–6, 154; conversion of (1880), 135; family tree of, 128; ideologically Liberal, 168, 179, but

White, Matthew – *contd.*
joins Labour Party, 185, 189, 210; in lock-out of 1926, 167; offices held by, 145, 160, 164, 166; Sabbatarian, 143; sons of, not miners, 150; speaks at presentation to manager, 167; stops swearing at work, 131
Wicksteed, Philip, 57
Widdington, Revd P. E. T., Christian Socialist, 62
Williams, Aneurin, M.P., at Waterhouses Methodist picnic, 197
Wilson, Revd J. Stitt, American socialist, 62
Wilson, James, early Methodist in Deerness Valley, 134
Wilson, John, Methodist, leader of D.M.A., Liberal M.P. for mid-Durham, 12, 37, 146; in Deerness Valley, 105, 160; and Gladstone, 47; on military service tribunal, 199; opposes eight-hour day, 38; opposes Socialism, 183; stands for compromise between owners and miners, 39, 158; speaks at temperance rallies, 192; his views come to be rejected, 215
Winter, J. G., miner, Methodist, attached to fringe of I.LP.: dies as conscientious objector, 199; funeral of, 200, 206

Wollstonecraft, Mary, 57; J. G. Harrison and, 171, 172
women: active in Methodist membership, but not leadership, 74, 124; chapel activities only source of entertainment for, 130; drunkenness among (1870s), 140, 141; in Methodist homes, 146, 147; recently drawn into roles of society officers, 133
women's suffrage movement, 171, 175
work discipline, Methodism as a source of, 9, 20
Workers' Educational Association, 216
working-class leaders: from Methodism, 9, 12, 13, 222, 226; from Protestantism, 3
Working Men's Clubs, 225; consider running candidates for parish and county councils, 192; dangerous for Methodists to try to rival, 193; drinking at, 142; Methodist opposition to, 152

Yorkshire coalfield: competes with Durham coalfield, 89; differences between Durham and, 15–16, 19, 28
Younger, Revd W., Methodist member of Free Church Socialist League, 60

'Zinoviev letter', 45
Zola, Emile, *Germinal* by, 77